Islam in History

Other books by Bernard Lewis

The Origins of Ismāʿīlism
British Contributions to Arabic Studies
A Handbook of Diplomatic and Political Arabic
Land of Enchanters: Egyptian Short Stories From the Earliest Times to the Present Day (ed.)
The Arabs in History
Notes and Documents from the Turkish Archives
The Emergence of Modern Turkey
The Kingly Crown
Historians of the Middle East (co-ed.)
Istanbul and the Civilisation of the Ottoman Empire
The Middle East and the West
The Assassins; A Radical Sect in Islam
The Cambridge History of Islam (co-ed.)
The Encyclopaedia of Islam (co-ed.)
Race and Color in Islam

Islam in History:

Ideas, Men and Events in the Middle East

by BERNARD LEWIS

Alcove Press

First Published in 1973 by
Alcove Press Limited
59 St Martin's Lane London WC2N 4JS

Printed in Great Britain
by Watmoughs Limited
Bradford and London

ISBN: 0 85657 007 9

For Brian

in mutual acceptance

Acknowledgements

I am grateful to the publishers and editors for permission to reprint the following:

The Study of Islam *(Encounter)*; Some English Travellers in the East *(Middle Eastern Studies)*; The Decolonization of History *(Times Literary Supplement)*; On Writing the Modern History of the Middle East *(Middle East Forum & Middle Eastern Studies)*; On Nationalism and Revolution *(The Spectator)*; Sources for the Economic History of the Middle East *(Studies in the Economic History of the Middle East:* Oxford University Press); The Muslim Discovery of Europe *(Bulletin of the School of Oriental and African Studies)*; The Use by Muslim Historians of Non-Muslim Sources *(Historians of the Middle East:* Oxford University Press); The Cult of Spain and the Turkish Romantics *(Études d'orientalisme dédiées à la mémoire de Lévi-Provençal:* G. P. Maisonneuve and Larose); The Pro-Islamic Jews *(Judaism)*; Semites and Anti-Semites *(Survey)*; An Ode Against the Jews *(Salo W. Baron Jubilee Volume:* American Academy for Jewish Research); The Sultan, the King and the Jewish Doctor *(Eretz-Israel)*; The Mongols, the Turks and the Muslim Polity *(Transactions of the Royal Historical Society)*; Ottoman Observers of Ottoman Decline *(Islamic Studies)*; The Significance of Heresy in Islam *(Studia Islamica)*; The Revolutions in Early Islam *(Studia Islamica)*; Islamic Concepts of Revolution *(Revolution in the Middle East:* George Allen and Unwin); The Idea of Freedom in Modern Islamic Political Thought *(Encyclopaedia of Islam)*; On Modern Arabic Political Terms (Comité pro Homenaje F. M. Pareja); Islam and Development: the Revaluation of Values *(Social Aspects of Economic Development:* Economic and Social Studies Conference Board).

My special thanks are due to Miss Bryan Healing and Mrs Alice Watson for their hawk-eyed and dove-mannered editing of my text, to Mrs V. E. Irvine for preparing the index, and to Mr R. M. Burrell for reading and correcting a set of proofs.

Contents

I

THE WESTERN APPROACHES

1. *The Study of Islam*

During the 19th century the forms, language, and to some extent even the structures of public life in the Muslim countries were given a Western and therefore a secular appearance. In those countries which were under European domination, the process was slow, cautious, and incomplete; in those where Muslim rulers retained political independence, they were able to impose Westernizing reforms with greater ruthlessness and fewer fears or inhibitions. By nationalizing the *waqf* revenues and introducing modern—*i.e.* Western-style—law and education, they simultaneously deprived the ulema both of their financial independence and of a large part of their functions and influence, and reduced them in effect to a branch of the bureaucracy. The men of the faith now became servants and spokesmen of the state, who successively justified reform, reaction, liberalism and socialism, from the same texts and by the same methods of exegesis.

The state itself, struggling for survival in a world dominated by the European powers, adopted European forms and procedures, and drew increasingly, in the recruitment and promotion of its personnel, on those whose education and aptitudes enabled them to meet the needs of this situation—that is to say, on the minority who knew a Western language, had at least a tincture of Western education, and had therefore acquired some Western habits of behavior and perhaps of thought. From this time onwards, identity is defined and loyalty claimed on national rather than communal lines; criticism and aspiration are formulated in secular, not religious terms. New books replace the sacred and classical texts as the pabulum of the literate and governing élite; journalists, lawyers and professors take over from the ulema; not theology, but politics provides the basis of argument and the form of expression.

The exponents of Islam have always been of two very different kinds, sometimes in conflict, usually interacting. On the one hand there were the ulema, the upholders of orthodoxy and authority, of dogma and of law; on the other the dervishes and their equivalents, preserving a tradition—or rather many local traditions—of popular religion and religiosity. Both groups have a habit of submission to political authority: the ulema of active support, the dervishes of passive if critical acquiescence—though the latter were often treated with mistrust by governments, because of the powerful pent-up emotions and energies which they could control or release.

The Westernizing reforms affected both groups adversely. The ulema, already to some extent associated with political power, now became completely subservient to it, and lost touch with the people. The dervishes, together with the masses to whom they belonged, were separated by a widening gulf from the Westernized political and intellectual élites, who no longer shared the same universe of discourse or even wore the same clothes as the un-Westernized majority. Ulema and dervishes alike were out of touch with the modern world, against which the new élites were struggling, and which at the same time they were striving to join.

In this new world, theology was seen as old-fashioned and irrelevant; dervish mysticism as a shameful and dangerous superstition. The only hope of salvation was economic, social, and above all political reform, conceived and, as it were, applied in accordance with a succession of imported European ideologies.

In the last hundred years Europe and, later, North America have seen the Islamic world through a distorting glass of European and, later, North American categories and terminologies. Muslims, for reasons of fashion, prestige, or perhaps even conviction, frequently describe the affairs of their countries in these Western terms. Western observers—journalists, politicians, scholars—gratefully accept these terms, for their own convenience and that of their readers. This has led to the curious but widespread belief that the authentic and significant forces in the Muslim world can be adequately denoted and classified by such parochial Western terms as nationalist and socialist, progressive and revolutionary—even, the ultimate absurdity, right-wing and left-wing. The results are about as informative as an account of a cricket match written by a baseball correspondent.

From time to time some incident, perhaps trivial in itself, allows a glimpse of the hard realities under the verbiage. On 25 April 1967 the Syrian army magazine *Jaysh al-Sha'b* (The People's Army) published an article by one Second Lieutenant Ibrāhīm Khalāṣ, entitled "The Means of Creating a New Arab Man". The only way to build Arab society and civilization, the author argued, was to create

> a new Arab socialist man, who believes that God, religions, feudalism, capital, and all the values which prevailed in the pre-existing society were no more than mummies in the museums of history.... There is only one value: absolute faith in the new man of destiny ... who relies only on himself and on his own contribution to humanity ... because he knows that his inescapable end is death and nothing beyond death ... no heaven and no hell.... We have no need of men who kneel and beg for grace and pity....

This was the first time that such sentiments had appeared in print in any of the revolutionary Arab states.

The result was electrifying. The Syrian population seemed thoroughly cowed, and had already passively acquiesced in a whole series of radical political and economic changes. The suppression of free speech, the control of movement, the confiscation of property all passed without incident—but an attack on God and religion in an officially sponsored publication revealed the limits of acquiescence, the final values for which a Muslim people was willing to stand up and resist.

In the face of mounting tension and hostility, the government beat a retreat. On 5 May the author of the article and the editors of the journal were arrested. The following day the semi-official newspaper *al-Thawra* (The Revolution) proclaimed its respect for religion, and shortly afterwards it was announced that the article was planted by the C.I.A., and the resistance concerted with "the Americans, the English, the Jordanians, the Saudis, the Zionists, and Selīm Ḥāṭūm (a Druze opponent of the régime)." The troubles continued, and on 11 May the author and editors were sentenced by a military court to life imprisonment. Thereafter the problem was appositely overshadowed by a new crisis between Syria and Israel, which in due course led to the Six Day War.

There have been other occasions too—the passionate outburst of prayer and anathema after the Mosul massacres of March 1959,[1] the immediate response to the fire in the al-Aqṣā mosque in August 1969, the recurrent clashes in India and Indonesia—which suggest that Islam is still the most powerful rallying-cry, and that it is for Islam, more than for any other cause, that men are still willing to kill and be killed—provided of course that they are convinced that Islam, as they understand it, is really under attack, and not merely exploited, as so often, for political ends.

This is the crux. The response to the al-Aqṣā affair illustrates perfectly both the power and the limitations of Islam as a political factor. The anger of the Muslim masses at what they at first saw as a threat to the faith was strong and real—but the attempt to use that anger for political ends failed utterly. One reason for this failure was the patent insincerity of the attempt. The revolutionary Arab leaders made no secret of their desire to subordinate Islamic to Arab purposes; the conservative potentates were visibly more concerned about the oil in Alaska than about the fire in al-Aqṣā. Another reason no doubt was the gradual realization of the basic triviality of the incident—especially when contrasted with the unambiguous communal carnage in India at the same time.

Islam can no longer be harnessed, yet it remains a force—even when it ceases to command belief. As W. Cantwell Smith remarked of modernist Muslim intellectuals—they revere "Islam in history along with, or even instead of, God. . ."[2]

It is curious that only two Muslim states, Turkey and Tunisia, have legally abolished polygamy. Neither would rank as "progressive" by the currently fashionable definition of the term—though both would qualify in an earlier, more conventionally liberal meaning of progress. The same cannot be said of the revolutionary states, which are intellectually and socially far more conservative, and have in recent years become more, not less, self-consciously Islamic, both in their deference to their own religion, and in their treatment of others. The lesson of April 1967 was well learnt. During the last three years, more mosques have been built in Syria than in the previous thirty, while a Christian Arab writer describes the feelings of the growing number of Christian emigrants in these terms:

> Christians [they say] have no future in a country which is becoming all the time more socialist and totalitarian. Their children are indoctrinated in the schools, where the syllabus is devoted more and more to Islam and their faith is in danger. Debarred increasingly from public office and from nationalised societies [sic], robbed of the property of their parents and unable to engage in profitable business in a society where almost everything is under state control, how can they survive?[3]

Even when Muslims cease to believe in Islam, they may retain Islamic habits and attitudes. Thus, among Muslim Marxists, there are both ulema and dervishes, defending the creed and proclaiming the (revolutionary) holy war against the (imperialist) infidel. At the moment, the ulema of Marxism incline towards Moscow, the dervishes towards Peking or Havana. *"There is no God and Mao is His Prophet!"* Even when the faith dies, loyalty survives. Even when loyalty fades, the old identity, and with it a complex of old attitudes and desires, remains, as the only reality under the superficial, artificial covering of new values and ideologies. For those who would understand the ways of Muslim peoples, some study of Islam, both formal and popular, is a necessity. It is important to observe Islam; and indeed Christendom, the closest neighbor and greatest rival of Islam, has been observing it for a long time.

It has not generally been the habit, in the past, for civilizations and religions to attempt a sympathetic study of their neighbors and rivals. Civilization meant our civilization, and the rest were barbarians. Religion meant our religion, and the rest were infidels. Occasionally an author like Herodotus in ancient Greece or Rashīd al-Dīn in medieval Persia was moved by curiosity or other causes to attempt the study of remote peoples and alien cultures. They remained exceptions and found few if any imitators. The first civilization known to history which seriously undertook the study of others not in order to conquer or convert them but merely in order to know about them, is that of Western Europe. Its example has now spread to other parts of the world.

The observation of Islam from Christendom has been going on for many centuries. Though often marred by prejudice and interest, it has nevertheless produced an understanding which is far deeper, knowledge far more extensive and more accurate, than the corresponding and simultaneous observation of Christendom from Islam.

To medieval Europe, Islam was the great adversary, and its study was required for good practical reasons. One was polemic—to understand the rival faith in order to refute and destroy it. Another was to learn. There were men in Europe who, though good Christians, recognized that the Muslims in Spain and the East knew more than they did of science, medicine and philosophy. They were anxious to learn from them, and some even learnt Arabic for this purpose.

Religious polemic against Islam was frequent in the Middle Ages, especially during the struggles in Spain and in the Levant, and many tracts were written, either to protect Christians from Muslim blandishments, or to convert Muslims to Christianity. This literature died out when the one task was seen as unnecessary, the other as impossible. There was a brief revival during the period of the great Ottoman conquests, but broadly speaking, after the end of the Middle Ages, Islam was no longer regarded in Christian Europe as a serious intellectual rival. This is the more notable, in that this attitude continued even at the time when the great challenge of Ottoman military power constituted a major threat to Europe, and Ottoman social policies offered a dangerous attraction to European peasants.

Anti-Islamic polemic continued in a desultory sort of way in missionary and theological circles, but is of no great importance except in so far as it affects and distorts the growth of scholarship in the West. To a remarkable extent theology has remained the starting point of those who undertake the academic study of oriental civilizations and religions. Though most—not all—are free from the prejudices and purposes of earlier days, these studies have not yet been entirely emancipated from their theological origins. The prejudices of the medieval schoolmen may still at times be detected lurking behind the serrated footnotes of the academic apparatus.

Broadly speaking, however, Western theologians, even missionaries, working on Islam no longer have it as their purpose—at least as their direct purpose—to convert Muslims to Christianity. Their approach to Islam has rather been in the spirit of the Dutch poet and scholar Willem Bilderdijk (1756–1831), who argued that "Mohammedans must be brought to Christ through the Koran", by showing them that "Mohammed was a Christian at heart . . . a tool in the hands of a benevolent Providence, and pioneer of salvation to Pagans and Manicheans."[4] Similar views were expressed by the English missionary Charles Forster, who in his *Mahometanism Unveiled* (1829) saw Islam as a "half-way house"—a "middle term" between Christianity and paganism. "It is only by fairly acknowledging what they have," says Forster, "that we can hope to make them sensible of what they have not."[5] With the direct attack now generally abandoned as impracticable if not unnecessary, missionary interest takes other forms—sometimes in the guise of ecumenism, sometimes clothed in the desire to join forces against a common enemy, variously defined.

The earlier type of study of Islam for purposes of polemic and refutation reappears in the 20th century only in one place—in the Soviet Union. In the early days after the Revolution, Russian scholarship on the Islamic lands was dominated by the need to refute and undermine Islamic and nationalist movements in the Muslim territories of the former Russian Empire, and to destroy Islam in order to prepare and facilitate the conversion of the Muslim peoples of the Union to communism. The anti-Islamic literature produced in Moscow in the 1920s and early '30s in many ways closely resembles that emanating from the monasteries of medieval Western Europe. Their interpretation of Islam, based on *a priori* theoretical principles and directed to practical purposes, belongs to the literature of religious polemic rather than of scholarship. Much Marxist writing on Islam is similarly determined, though that which is produced outside the Soviet Union usually shows greater intellectual sophistication and less obvious polemic aims. In Muslim countries, no doubt for tactical reasons, Marxists often adopt, *mutatis mutandis*, a sort of Bilderdijk approach, presenting Muḥammad as a socialist at heart, a tool in the hands of the inexorable laws of history, and a potential pioneer of communism to Muslims. This approach has so far won little support, except among the official ideologues of the régimes.

Apart from the work of a few scholarly broad-church Western Marxists, the literature of polemic, whether Marxist or Christian, shows little sign of intellectual curiosity or detachment—a quality which was indeed regarded by the one as a sin, by the other as an ideological error.

In the West, the polemicist was succeeded by a new figure, who came to be known by the odd term "orientalist". This word designates, with extreme vagueness, the object of the scholar's studies, but gives no indication of his method or purpose. Usually, his disciplines were theology and philology, his motive scientific curiosity—though the opportunities to indulge his curiosity were often the result of political and economic needs.

The new phase began with the Renaissance, amid a uniquely favorable combination of circumstances. The classical revival and the voyages of exploration both contributed greatly to the growth of orientalist scholarship. The old authors, and especially Herodotus, provided the model for the study of remote and alien peoples; the new scholarship furnished the philological method that was required for such studies; the expansion of Europe provided at once the scope, the need, and the material.

While Europe was expanding at both ends, across the steppes and the oceans, Islam, now represented by the Ottoman Empire, was advancing through the Balkans towards Vienna. For a while, Turkey seemed to offer a major threat to the survival of Christian civilization—but at the same time her vast territories offered a great opportunity for European commercial enterprise. Both as enemy and as market, she was an important field of study.

Finally, the Reformation and Counter-Reformation injected a new religious concern into European affairs. Protestants and especially Unitarians showed for a while an interest in Islam—in this faith which, by its hostility to polytheism and images, seemed to offer some affinities with the Protestant challenge to Catholicism. Added to this was the tempting possibility of a Turkish alliance against the Catholic powers. Though all this came to nothing, it nevertheless left some effects on the growth of European scholarship.

European writing on Islam from the 16th century onwards is of two main kinds, with two very different approaches.

1. The first of these is what one might call the scholarly, dominated by theology and philology, concerned primarily with the scriptures and with the classics of Islam. The Qur'ān and the ancient Arabian literature were studied in the same way and by the same techniques as the Bible and the classics of Greece and Rome had been studied in Europe. The greatest attention was devoted to Arabic, somewhat less to Persian. Characteristically, hardly any attention at all was given to Turkish which, though it was the major language of the Muslim world at that time, had the disadvantage of being a living language and therefore, like English, French and German, unworthy of serious scholarly attention.

2. A second group of writings was practical, concerned with the news from Turkey and, to a lesser extent, other Muslim countries. Many books were produced on the subject of the Turkish Empire, its resources, its population, its military strength, and of course, among other things, its religion, including the different forms of worship, of organization, and of belief which existed among the peoples of that Empire. This literature is based in the main on direct observation, and is intended to satisfy the need for accurate practical information about this dangerous yet interesting neighbor of Christendom. It may be noted that this neighbor was still seen primarily in religious rather than national terms, and that even such ethnic names as "Turk" and "Moor" were commonly used in a

religious sense, as synonyms for Muslim. Eastern Christians were not normally called by either name, while a European who adopted Islam was said to have "turned Turk".

During the 19th century European scholarship on Islam received a tremendous new impetus. Several new developments contributed to this great growth. One of these was the application to Islamic studies of the critical historical method which was being developed by European and especially German scholars for the study of Greek, Roman, and European history. The use of these methods for the study of the early history of Islam, the life of the Prophet, the foundation of the Caliphate, the great Arab conquests and the like, carried these studies a major step forward and formed the basis for most subsequent writing, in the Islamic world as well as in Europe.

A second important development was the emancipation of the European Jews, and the consequent entry of Jewish scholars into the European Universities. From the first, Jewish scholars made a major contribution to the development of Arabic and Islamic studies—a contribution which still continues to the present day, as far as politically-minded administrators and benefactors permit. Like their Christian colleagues, most of them had a theological background, transferring from the rabbinical schools and seminaries where they had studied Hebrew and Talmud, to the study of Arabic and of Islam. They differed however in several important respects from their Christian colleagues. The Jewish scholar, unlike many of his Christian colleagues, had no missionary ambitions, no nostalgia for the Crusades, no concern with the Eastern question. He was free from the inherited fears, prejudices, and inhibitions that had often marred Christian scholarship.

On the contrary, in two important respects he was favorably inclined to the object of his studies. One of these was practical and real. Hebrew and Arabic are cognate languages; Judaism and Islam are sister religions, with many important resemblances between them. A Jew, particularly a learned Jew, had a head start over his Christian colleagues in the study of Islam, and an immediacy of understanding which they could not easily attain.

There was in addition a further reason for Jewish sympathy with Islam. This was the period when old-fashioned religious anti-Judaism in Christendom was giving way to the new racially expressed anti-Semitism, and the Jew was being attacked no longer as an unbeliever (a charge unworthy of the enlightened 19th century) but as a racial inferior, an Asian alien in Europe. Rejected as an Oriental intruder, he turned to other, more powerful orientals for support, rather as some American blacks look to Africa and even Asia at the present time, with about as much justification in either case. Though this affinity was largely imaginary and entirely unreciprocated, it was nevertheless an important factor in arousing Jewish sympathy for Islam and interest in Islamic studies. Jewish scholars were among the first who attempted to present Islam to European readers as the Muslims themselves see it, and to stress, to recognize and indeed sometimes romanticize the merits and achievements of Muslim civilization in its great days.[6]

The major development of the 19th century which affected the growth of Oriental studies was of course the rise of Imperialism and the consolidation of European power over the greater part of the Muslim world. The main countries concerned were Britain, ruling India and, later, parts of the Middle East and of Africa; France, in North and, later, Western and Central Africa; Holland, which came to dominate the greater part of Muslim South-east Asia; and Russia, which conquered the Muslim peoples of the Volga, the Crimea, the Caucasus, and the old Muslim Kingdoms of Central Asia. These were the four major imperial powers which divided the world of Islam between them. In addition, Germany and Austria developed a semi-colonial relationship with the Ottoman Empire; and later Italy, for a brief but important interval, ruled over parts of North and East Africa.

The charge is often brought, by orientals against orientalists, that they are the servants of imperialism, and that their work is designed to serve the needs of the administrator, the trader, the diplomat, the agent and the missionary. The charge is not entirely without foundation, and finds added support in the occasional appearances of the orientalist in person in one or other of these roles. In the only surviving European empire ruling over Islamic lands, that of Russia, scholarship is unmistakably—indeed avowedly—harnessed to the policies and purposes of the state.

Yet, as an assessment of the motives that impelled Western man, even till now almost alone among mankind, to undertake the study of alien civilizations, this charge is ludicrously inadequate. Empire and commerce may have provided the stimulus and also the opportunity to undertake such studies; they did not, in free societies, direct them. The missionary and the colonial expert have, on the whole, played only a minor part in the development of Islamic scholarship in the West, and their work, with very few exceptions, has won scant respect and enjoyed little influence among scholars. The major advances were the work of men whose driving force was the desire to know and to understand, and whose methods were those of critical scholarship. Most of them were university teachers, independent of, and sometimes opposed to, the great imperial and commercial interests.

The first of the social sciences to give attention to Islam was history. Practical men wrote or sponsored histories of Ottoman Turkey, the last surviving Muslim great power; scholars examined the origins and early history of the Islamic faith and community. The former produced work which is now of interest only in so far as it is contemporary and first-hand; the latter laid the foundations of a great—and continuing—scholarly tradition.

It has been said that the history of the Arabs has been written in the West chiefly by historians who know no Arabic and by Arabists who know no history. If we add Persian, Turkish, and some other languages to the formula, it may be extended to cover the history of Islam as a whole. Even now it must be admitted, at whatever cost in professional self-esteem, that academic standards in Middle Eastern studies are recognizably lower than in other, more frequented disciplines. Nevertheless there has been progress; and during the past century-and-a-half a series of scholars who were both historians and orientalists have added substantially to our understanding of the history of Islam—and not only to our understanding, but also to that of the Muslims themselves.

Even when writing of the past, historians are the captives of their own times—in their materials and their methods, their concepts and their concerns. Historians of classical Islam could not but be influenced by the contemporary Islam which they saw, and particularly therefore by that part of the Islamic world to which circumstances, personal or national, gave them access. British, French, Russian, or German Islamicists therefore tended to see Islam in an Indian, North African, Central Asian, or late Ottoman guise. The historian is also guided, in the questions he asks and the answers he finds, by the preoccupations of his own time and milieu. Edward Pococke, the first great English Arabist, working at Oxford during the Civil War, hinted at parallels, in the Caliphate of al-Ma'mūn, to the clash of forces and doctrines that he saw around him; 19th-century European scholars discerned currents of liberalism and nationalism in the religious and sectarian struggles of early Islam; 20th-century scholars, looking in the mirror of history, found economic change and social conflict—and turned to the new techniques and concepts of the social scientists for help in understanding them.

The first European observers to make significant generalizations about Islamic society were—not surprisingly—travelers. Certainly the most influential of these was François Bernier (1620–1688), a French physician and natural historian who spent twelve years in India and shorter periods in Syria and Egypt. As well as describing Islamic society, Bernier tried to analyze the causes of its relative poverty and backwardness in the arts, sciences, and agriculture. He found the explanation in the lack of private landed property and the seizure of the land by the ruler, which led, directly or indirectly, to a stagnant society and a despotic régime.[7] Bernier's ideas influenced many later writers, notably Montesquieu; they were also adopted by Karl Marx, and thus place him with Adam Smith and the English Utilitarians among the ancestors of the Marxist doctrine of the "Asiatic mode of production".

Another philosophical Frenchman, the famous Volney (1757–1820), spent three years in Egypt and Syria. Unlike so many travelers, he tells us nothing of his own journeys and adventures. Instead, he describes, systematically and in detail, the condition of the countries which he visited, and examines the causes of what he describes. It is a somber picture that he paints—of poverty and fear, ignorance and backwardness, tyranny, brigandage and insecurity, and a general listlessness broken only by sudden fits of pointless violence. Volney rejects the theory, current in his day, that these evils are due to climate and its effect on character. The true cause, he argues, lies in social institutions—in government and religion, the despotic misrule of the one sustained by the quietist teaching of the other. Volney, writing again after the French Revolution, was optimistic, believing that what despotism had marred, liberty could mend. Social backwardness was a temporary setback on the march of progress, which change and reform would overcome.[8]

Half a century later Adolphus Slade (1804–1877), a British naval officer who was in Turkey during the great reforms of Sultan Mahmud II and his successors, took a different view. His books have not received the attention they deserve—partly no doubt because of their form as old-fashioned personal narratives, perhaps more because their findings clashed with the liberal orthodoxy of the time. Unlike most European observers, Slade was convinced neither of the iniquities of the old régime, nor of the advantages of the new. A critical but sympathetic observer, he was aware of the defects of the old order, yet found much in it to admire; while seeing the need for some change he condemns the indiscriminate haste with which it was enforced, and shows how liberal reform, by disrupting a traditional society, may lead to a loss of liberty. The old nobility, however ineffectual, had generosity, honor, and a certain grace; the new nobility, thrown up by the reforms, was greedy, violent and corrupt. "The old nobility, profuse and open-handed, lived on their estates: their ovens were never cool; their pilaf cauldrons never empty. The State was the estate of the new nobility."[9] These judgments, with others of similar prescience, range Slade with Burke and Tocqueville as a conservative prophet of radical doom.

These—two French philosophers and an English sailor—are but three, among the best, of the many travelers who returned from the East to enlighten their compatriots about Islam. Their writings helped, even more than those of the historians, to form and shape the image of Islam and Islamic civilization, as reflected in Western thought and scholarship.

From the 18th century onwards most of the great political and social thinkers have something to say about the nearest neighbor of Christendom. In France, Montesquieu and Voltaire spoke of ideas and institutions; in Germany, Herder and Hegel discussed the deeper philosophical implications; in England, Burke considered the legal and political character of Muslim government as it affected the case of Warren Hastings, while Adam Smith, Richard Jones, and the elder and younger Mill commented on the economic and social structures of the Muslim Empires. At some distance after these came Spengler, Toynbee, and other exponents of metahistory, as it is now called, though catahistory might be a better designation for their endeavors.

In this connection one other group of writings may be mentioned in passing, though it has only minor relevance to the subject under discussion. In the literature of self-doubt and self-chastisement[10] which has become an essential part of the Western tradition, the Muslim—like other non-Westerners—is often used as a sort of lay figure, or rather a ventriloquist's dummy, with an assigned part to speak in a purely Western dialogue. All this has nothing to do with either Islam or scholarship, and contributes about as much to our understanding of Islam as *Gulliver's Travels* or the *Lettres Persanes* to our knowledge of cartography or Persia—and far less to our edification.

Several of the founders of modern social science had something to say about Islam. For Auguste Comte, Islam, like Christianity, was medieval and superseded, and was doomed to make way for the new religion of scientific positivism; he followed the Ottoman reforms with sympathetic interest, and had some impact on the Young Turks of the next generation, whose slogan "Union and Progress" was an adaptation of

Comte's "Order and Progress". Max Weber died before he could add Islam to the other religions which he examined in detail, but his works contain numerous indications of his thinking on Islam, much influenced by the writings of Julius Wellhausen. Karl Marx, like other Victorians, saw the Ottoman Empire chiefly in terms of the Eastern Question, and the Arabs not at all. He did, however, devote some attention to India and South-east Asia, and sketched the theory of the Asiatic mode of production, which was subsequently developed by others.

Not surprisingly, given the inadequate and inaccurate information available to them, the contribution of the sociological founding fathers to the understanding of Islam was of limited value—though some of them, notably Comte, Durkheim, and the otherwise unremarkable Gustave Le Bon and Edmond Demolins, had a considerable influence on Muslim writers. Of greater significance was the stimulus which they gave to the orientalists, to elaborate, or, more often, to refute their specific assertions, and—more important—to use their concepts and methods in new lines of inquiry. Since the beginning of this century a number of Islamicists have followed this path. Prince Caetani, a disciple of Comte, brought a positivistic analysis to bear on the career of the Prophet and the beginnings of Islam. Carl Heinrich Becker, a friend of Weber and Troeltsch, tried to prove that Islam was not by nature hostile to economic progress, and that Islamic civilization, Hellenistic in origin, belonged with Christendom and not with the true Asia. Other social theorists—such as Pareto, Le Play, Breysig, Durkheim—have had their disciples among the orientalists, as have also more recent scholars, notably Robert Redfield of Chicago.

One case is of special interest—that of Karl Marx. Marxist analysis of Islam has been, broadly, of three types. One of these is the doctrine of the Asiatic mode of production. Briefly sketched by Marx and Engels, in modest recognition that their system of categories, derived from European history, might not be of universal validity, it was taken up by some later Marxist scholastics who, by combining passages or even single sentences, written at different times, some of them in letters, drafts, and newspaper articles, were able to construct a coherent system of revealed thought. Most discussion of the Asiatic mode of production has been concerned with China, some with India; the Islamic world has received little attention. Recently, however, the current revival of interest in this branch of Marxism has spread to Turkey, where a few young economists have tried to detect the Asiatic mode of production in the Ottoman Empire.[11]

The Asiatic mode of production, in which there is no private ownership of land and consequently no class war, only a simple opposition between the terrorized mass of the population and the all-encompassing state bureaucracy, is one of Marx's most accurate insights—not as history, but as prophecy. For some reason Stalin disliked the theory of the Asiatic mode of production, and had virtually banned it by 1938.

Since then, Soviet scholarship has had to fit the history of Islam into the authorized sequence of the ancient (*i.e.* slave), feudal, and bourgeois modes of production. There has been much argument on how precisely this is to be done. A good example of this literature, by the late Professor E. A. Belyaev, has recently become available in English.[12]

Covering the period from the fifth to the tenth centuries, it presents what one might call a moderate Soviet Russian orthodox interpretation of the mission of Muḥammad and the rise of Islam, with a characteristic mixture of loyalties, concepts, and purposes. The Slavs make a brief appearance as those to whom "the working masses" of the Byzantine Empire looked "as their allies and deliverers". The endless sufferings, untiring energy, and "productive activity of the toiling masses" are duly contrasted with the perfidy, cruelty, and general villainy of their royal, feudal and religious exploiters. Special stress is laid on the horrors of Arab conquest and rule in Central Asia, in much the same way as French historians of an earlier generation used to dwell on the devastation which the Arab raiders had wrought in North Africa—and no doubt for the same reasons.

Not the least interesting parts of Belyaev's book are the surveys of previous scholarly work at the beginning of each chapter. These deal with both Western and Soviet scholarship (modern Arab and other Muslim scholarship is contemptuously dismissed as worthless or at best secondary). Only two Arab authors, Bandali Juzi and Emil Tuma, both Marxists, receive special mention. By a curious coincidence both are Orthodox Christians. Among Western historians of the Arabs, he considers Clément Huart and Philip Hitti the best, and also speaks very highly of the Belgian Jesuit scholar Henri Lammens. Among Soviet scholars, the prime concern was how to fit Islamic history into the given, predetermined framework. Belyaev rejects the "merchant-capitalistic" theory of Islamic origins, as "clearly at variance with the fundamental tenets of Marxism-Leninism", and also condemns the widely accepted "early feudal" interpretation, on the lesser charge that it does not accord with the evidence. The attempts by Morozov, Klimovitch and Tolstov to prove that Muḥammad never existed are similarly rejected. In Belyaev's view, the motive force of Islam came from the slave-owning mercantile bourgeoisie of Mecca and Medina, which arose within a decaying primitive-communal society. The Qur'ān, which he considers to have been concocted after the death of Muḥammad, expresses the new ideology, justifying "inequality in property, slavery and development of exchanges." "A slave-holding Allah is described as a typical merchant, reflecting all the features of the trading community of Mecca." Only after the conquest, and under the Caliphate, did an early feudal order replace slave production. The main purpose of the early Caliphate was "to ensure by armed might the economic subservience of the laboring majority to the wealthy minority."

On the economic and social history of the early Caliphate, Belyaev makes a number of interesting and sometimes stimulating suggestions—not of course offered as such, but rather laid down with a certitude unknown to Western scholarship since the Reformation.

The purpose of this and many other writings of the same kind is basically polemical; to refute, rather than to explain, Islamic beliefs, and to discredit any view of the Islamic past which might nurture Muslim pride and encourage oppposition to

Soviet rule in Muslim lands. Similar purposes, at an earlier date, inspired some British, French, and Dutch colonial historians—though these never enjoyed the right to silence those who disagreed with them. More recently there have been attempts at a less crudely propagandist Marxist study of Islam, by scholars like I. P. Petrushevsky in Russia and Maxime Rodinson in France, notably in the latter's *Islam et capitalisme* (1966). M. Rodinson declares his unorthodoxy, and disclaims what he variously calls vulgar Marxism, demi-Marxism, pseudo-Marxism, pragmatist Marxism, philosophic Marxism, and institutional Marxism. He even complains of the imprecision of Marx's use of "feudal", and considers the term inappropriate to medieval Islamic society. Nevertheless, he remains a practicing Marxist, and devotes much effort to intra-Marxist disputation and to problems of the correct disposition of Islamic social and economic history in Marxist terms.

Many besides Marxists share the two underlying assumptions—first, that there is some universal pattern or sequence of economic and social development, and second, that a model or norm of this development can be constructed from Western experience, which combines the advantages of being the best studied, and our own. Both assumptions are questionable.

For some time the contribution of social science to the study of Islam consisted of the *obiter dicta*—mostly ill-informed—of the great generalists, and the responses or reactions of orientalists—mostly philologists and historians—who read their works. The next stage came when scholars trained in a social science discipline began to deal directly and at first hand with Islamic problems, and undertake field work in Islamic countries. This happened in several stages.

Imperial administration naturally gave special importance to ethnography, the relevance of which will be clear to all readers of Rudyard Kipling's *Kim* and of *Sovietskaya Etnografiya*. In the British, Russian, French, and Dutch Empires useful ethnographic surveys and monographs were produced, dealing with tribal and local customs, with local saint worship, with religious brotherhoods and much else. Most of this was purely descriptive—the only theoretical consideration, if indeed such it may be called, being the needs of the Imperial administration.

In time this kind of descriptive ethnography gave way to anthropological studies, of which a considerable number have by now been published. Usually, these are studies in detail—a village in Turkey, a tribe in Arabia, a sect in North Africa, and the like. Until very recently they were carried out for the most part by techniques evolved for use in the study of primitive and non-literate societies.

Anthropologists working in Islamic countries have usually fought shy of generalizations about Islam. At one time they refused, almost as a matter of principle, to take cognizance of literary evidence or even of scholarship based on such evidence. Latterly, they have become aware of the rewards—and hazards—of literary and historical studies, and have usually preferred to renounce the one and thus avoid the other.

Sociologists found greater difficulty than anthropologists in persuading themselves that the literary evidence of a literate society was irrelevant to their inquiries. For a long time they warily left the sociology of Islam to the orientalist, who, trusting in his philological sword and buckler to strike true and guard him from error, tackled sociology and history, theology and literature with equal readiness and often, alas, with equal competence.

A new phase began when social scientists, while remaining primarily concerned with their discipline, acquired sufficient linguistic and historical knowledge to become acceptable regional specialists—acceptable, that is, to those whose criteria were linguistic and historical. These are still very few, and usually owe their rare combination of skills to personal circumstances—to the accidental opportunities of birth, war, and employment.

Professor Clifford Geertz's *Islam Observed* (1968)[13] is thus a work of courage as well as distinction. An anthropologist with field experience in both Morocco and Java, he has had the interesting idea of studying and comparing the development and condition of Islam in these two countries, at opposite ends of the Islamic world. At first sight, this might seem a strange approach. What, one might ask, could a Muslim observer learn of Christianity by comparing the practice of the faith in, say, California and Ethiopia?

There are two answers to this question. The first is that an informed, perceptive, and rigorous Muslim observer might indeed learn a great deal about the nature of the Christian religion from such an inquiry, especially if he could speak and read both English and Amharic. The second, which is more immediately to the point, is that Islam has not yet undergone the differentiation which has overtaken Christianity in the last few centuries. Islam, not only chronologically, is in its 14th not its 20th century; it has still to experience the processes of reform and secularization which have transformed and divided the once-united Christian world. In modern times, Islamic identity has been reinforced by a new shared experience—the penetration, domination and (in most areas) the departure of European colonialists.

It is obvious that there is much that the social scientist can contribute to the study of Islam, and that there are many things, in early as well as modern times, which he alone, with the special skills of his profession, is able to study and explain. Social scientists, or historians using social science concepts, have already made distinctive and important contributions to the study of Islam, and it may well be that these transplants will in time produce a flowering comparable with those of European oriental scholarship following the Renaissance, the Reformation, and the philological golden age in the 19th century.

Before that can happen, however, there are certain difficulties that must be overcome. It may be noticed that among modern scholars using the sociological approach, the most successful are those who have also served a philological apprenticeship. For the others there remains the problem of how to understand a society for which the principal written sources of study are locked in a strange script, requiring the mastery of a difficult language to read them, and the intimate study of a civilization to interpret them. Most of the solutions propounded to the problem rest on one or both of two dubious assumptions: that it is possible for the social scientist to acquire within a short time a "working knowledge" of an oriental language which will be sufficient for his purpose, and that the use of translators and informants is an adequate substitute for direct personal access to the evidence.

Some branches of Islamic civilization, such as art and architecture, can be studied without much reference to texts. But the greater part is beset with pitfalls for the unwary student who would venture into the field without adequate study of the language in which his sources are written and in which the people whose lives and endeavors he is examining think, write, and speak. Most modern techniques of field research in the social sciences relate to one of two situations: either the researcher is dealing with a sector of his own civilization, whose historical and cultural pattern is known to him as part of his own education and upbringing, or else he is dealing with a primitive society, where historical and literary evidence can be disregarded because it does not exist. What has not yet been adequately faced is the problem of field research in a literate, historical society other than that of the field-researcher himself. This, it seems to me, is the basic problem which must be solved before Western social science can make a really effective and autonomous contribution to the better understanding of Islam.

2. *Some English Travelers in the East*

Travelers who describe the countries and peoples of the Middle East have always attracted a wide readership. For the general reader they supply, so he believes, the superior knowledge and consequent superior wisdom of the man (or woman) who has Been There and Met Them and Knows. This belief even now miraculously survives the daily and weekly fatuities of special correspondents. For "experts" of various kinds, who wish to specialize on the Middle East without actually having to learn a Middle Eastern language, they offer the comforting appearance of inside information—a primary source for the historian, a field report for the social scientist, a first-hand informant for the political analyst.

There has been a long series of travelers from Europe to the East; pilgrims and crusaders in the Middle Ages, followed, with the growing sophistication of Christendom, by diplomats and spies, tourists and traders, renegades and missionaries, soldiers and politicians, artists, scholars and *littérateurs,* and some, in modern times, who manage to combine several or even all of these functions.

In our own day the traveler is enjoying a new popularity, in a new role. Some of the earlier functions of travel literature are now variously discharged by the monograph, the guide-book, the hand-out, and other works of reference; some by the cinema and television. The travel writer has however retained some of these functions; in addition he has found a new purpose, in part usurping the roles previously played by the novelist, the essayist, even the publicist and the historian. In turn discursive, reflective and informative, he brings comfort to a wide circle of readers, including, as in the past, those who fear the cost and hardship of travel, reinforced by those who shun the rigors of scholarship.

Interest in the records of past and recent travel is reflected in the growing learned literature devoted to the subject—bibliographies, surveys and monographs, dealing with the travelers by period and by language, by the countries from which they came and to which they went, and even by the libraries in which their books are to be found.[1] Travel, it is said, broadens the mind. Travel books certainly lengthen the bibliography, and travelers' tales have a not unimportant place in history, at least in that part of it which is concerned with the formation and projection of images. Such influence may extend from the past to the future, as politicians making decisions are swayed by memories and reports of journeys abroad, their own and other men's.

But what are these memories and reports really worth, either as a source of information on the past, or a guide to conduct in the future? Some two hundred years ago the great orientalist Sir William Jones surveyed and deplored the state of European knowledge concerning the Ottoman Empire and, remarked:

> It has generally happened, that the persons who have resided among the TURKS, and who, from their skill in the EASTERN dialects, have best been qualified to present us with an exact account of that nation, were either confined to a low sphere of life, or engaged in views of interest, and but little addicted to polite letters or philosophy; while they, who, from their exalted stations and refined taste for literature, have had both the opportunity and inclination of penetrating into the secrets of TURKISH policy, were totally ignorant of the language used at Constantinople, and consequently were destitute of the sole means by which they might learn, with any degree of certainty, the sentiments and prejudices of so singular a people. . . . As to the generality of interpreters, we cannot expect from men of their condition any depth of reasoning, or acuteness of observation; if mere words are all they profess, mere words must be all they can pretend to know.[2]

Sir William's judgment may seem harsh, but of the great majority of previous and subsequent travelers it is lamentably just. Even those whose professional duty it was to observe and report—the diplomats and journalists—are rarely better and sometimes worse than the more casual visitors. For the historian of, let us say, Turkey or Egypt, press reports and diplomatic despatches are an essential source of information on foreign activities and international relations—on the evolution of opinions, attitudes, and even, it may be, policies in the home country. But for the history of internal affairs, even at the personal and political level, they are only rarely and accidentally of value. The reports of such travelers on the countries in which they worked, the people among whom they lived, the forces and stresses of society, culture and government, are usually trivial and frequently wrong, and the information they provide is insignificant compared with that which is available from indigenous sources—literary, documentary, even journalistic. Turning to more recent times, who can fail to remember—or be reminded of—the pathetic series of eminent dupes who had the honor of calling on Herr Hitler, and returned to assure us of his essential moderation and peaceful intentions? It is customary nowadays to divide politicians into hawks and doves. An ornithology of travel might well classify these birds of passage into gulls and parrots.

The major disability of the travelers, of which their writings show the clearest evidence and the dimmest awareness, is ignorance. It is of many kinds—diffident and confident, simple and complex, ductile and rigid, elemental and compounded with prejudice, arrogance, and, latterly, guilt. The point was well made by Dr Johnson: "Books of travel will be good in proportion to what a man has previously in his mind. . . . As the Spanish proverb says: 'He, who would bring home the wealth of the Indies, must carry the wealth of the Indies with him.' So it is in travelling; a man must carry knowledge with him, if he would bring home knowledge." (Conversation of 17 April 1778.) For visitors to lands of alien culture, the first essential is that to which Sir William Jones drew attention—knowledge of the language, "the sole means by which they might learn, with any degree of certainty, the sentiments and prejudices" of the people among whom they travel and about whom they write. Admittedly, knowledge of the language is no longer as important now as it was in Sir William's day, when it was unheard of for native Muslims to learn a Western language and associate with Westerners, and when even written translations were few, scarce and for the most part inaccurate. But even now, the student of, say, Turkish or Arab affairs who has no Turkish or Arabic is at a crippling disadvantage. He has no access to the history and culture of these peoples save at second hand—that is, through materials selected and processed by other men for other purposes. He is similarly cut off from the vernacular press, and can use it, if at all, only through digests, summaries and translations, which are sometimes tendentious, often defective, and always inadequate. In his personal contacts he is limited to those who have mastered a Western language, and by this very fact are untypical and unrepresentative of their countrymen. In their conversations with the traveler, they will probably be untypical even of themselves, for no man talking with an inquiring foreigner in a foreign language, in the Middle East or anywhere else, will reveal himself in quite the same way as he would in the natural intimacy of his mother-tongue.

This means that the traveler is limited, in collecting information, to what is conveyed to him by members of a minority group. In earlier times, this meant members of a religious minority, usually Christians, occasionally Jews. Today this is no longer true, and there are many Muslims who have received a Western or Westernized education and can communicate freely with Westerners. It is now generally understood—though it was not at the time—that the Christian informants of Western travelers in the Ottoman Empire conveyed a sectional and therefore somewhat distorted view. It is not sufficiently realized that the informants of modern visitors to the Middle East, though nominally adherents of the majority religion and members of the majority nation, may also form a minority—cultural, social, political—which is in many ways more alienated and more untypical than were the Greek dragomans and Armenian merchants of the Ottoman Empire. The situation is not improved when the traveler and his informant are, respectively, the guest and spokesman of an autocratic régime.

The specialized guidance of their local informants was not the only kind of distortion to which the travelers were subject. Though unencumbered with any previous knowledge, the traveler might nevertheless carry other impedimenta, in the form of preconceptions, prejudices, purposes, and a variety of psychological and ideological baggage. For many, travel was a quest—a pilgrimage to the Holy Land or Hellas or The Thousand and One Nights; a search for the benighted heathen, the exotic oriental, or the noble savage; an inspection of the achievements of Empire or the evils of imperialism; a visit to the heirs, custodians or destroyers of ancient glories. Travelers' needs, if not previously known, were soon discovered; interest and courtesy combined to gratify their desires. There were few who did not return from their travels with their beliefs confirmed and their prejudices agreeably titillated.

There are of course exceptions, some of them outstanding. From time to time a traveler manages to achieve and communicate some new insight, and thus to illuminate a patch of reality for his own and future generations. He may be a journalist or a diplomat, a soldier, sailor or gentleman of leisure—even, it may yet be, a politician returning from a tryst in some presidential palace. The literature of Middle Eastern travel cannot as yet claim a Tocqueville or a Madame de Staël. It does however include the writings of Niebuhr, Volney, Burckhardt, Lane, Burton, Doughty,[3] and some few others of comparable stature.

One of the most remarkable was Lady Mary Wortley Montagu, *née* Pierrepoint, who followed her husband to Istanbul, where he was ambassador, in February 1717, stayed there until July 1718, and recorded her impressions in a number of letters.[4] She had several advantages. As a woman she could enter freely into the harem, and penetrate the exotic mysteries that had tantalized and preoccupied so many less fortunate males; as an ambassadress, she could enjoy the social opportunities without the political limitations of her husband's office. In addition, she had the advantage, perhaps even rarer, of being intelligent, cultivated and perceptive.

Historically too Lady Mary went to Turkey at a fortunate moment. The overwhelming religious certitude, which for centuries had caused Christian Europeans to despise Islam as something irretrievably false, hostile and inferior, had begun to falter; the new European mood of self-questioning, which in time and for some grew to self-doubt and self-hate, had hardly begun to work. Galland's translation of *The Thousand and One Nights,* the fountainhead of the new romantic cult of the East, had only just appeared. Lady Mary was between myths—the old one of the Muslim as barbarous infidel, the new ones of the oriental as the embodiment of mystery and romance, and, later, as the paragon of virtue, wisdom and wronged innocence. For her, Turkey was a country and the Turks were people to be respected, studied, and as far as possible understood, through the medium of their own language and culture, and in reference to their own standards and values.

Lady Mary was keenly aware of the limitations of mere travel as a source of knowledge. "'Tis certain," she says in a letter dated 1 April 1717, "we have but very imperfect relations of the manners and Religion of these people, this part of the world being seldom visited but by merchants who mind little but their own Affairs, or Travellers who make too short a stay to be able to report any thing exactly of their own knowledge. The Turks are too proud to converse familiarly with merchants etc., who can only pick up some confused informations which are generally false, and they can give no better an account of the ways here than a French refugee lodging in a Garret in Greek street could write of the Court of England."[5] She returns to the subject, and in a letter dated 17 June 1717 admonishes a correspondent: "Your whole letter is full of mistakes from one end to t'other. I see you have taken your Ideas of Turkey from that worthy author Dumont, who has writ with equal ignorance and confidence. 'Tis a particular pleasure to me here to read the voyages to the Levant, which are generally so far removed from Truth and so full of Absurditys I am very well diverted with 'em. They never fail giving you an Account of the Women, which 'tis certain they never saw, and talking very wisely of the Genius of the Men, into whose Company they are never admitted, and very often describe Mosques, which they dare not peep into. . . ."[6] On 10 April 1718 she writes, in a letter addressed to Lady Bristol: "Since my Last I have stay'd quietly at

Constantinople, a City that I ought in Conscience to give you Ladyship a right Notion of, Since I know You can have none but what is Partial and mistaken from the writings of Travellers. 'Tis certain there are many people that pass years here in Pera without having ever seen it, and yet they all pretend to describe it."[7]

Lady Mary spent just over a year in Turkey, during which time she had a baby. She also managed to learn some Turkish, and was able to write to Alexander Pope about Turkish poetry. She met and conversed with a number of Turkish ladies, in their homes, and was even able to charm some Turkish gentlemen into discussing religion, literature and public affairs with her. She is at her best in describing Turkish home life—food, clothing, interior decoration and amenities, the family and staff, social and domestic usage and entertainment, which she describes with accuracy, sympathy and wit. Her observations are not however limited to such matters. Through her female informants she knew—and understood—a good deal about the life of the Palace and the great houses; on her journeys from the border to Edirne and Istanbul she saw something of Turkish provincial government and rural life, and has sharp comments to make on both. She describes the role of the ulema in Ottoman government and society, and the dance of the whirling dervishes; the merits and wiles of Turkish wives and the ferocity of the Janissaries; the interiors and congregations of both mosques and baths. Her last letter from Istanbul ends with an eloquent if somewhat wayward defense of what she conceives to be the Turkish way of life:

> Thus you see, Sir, these people are not so unpolish'd as we represent them. Tis true their magnificence is of a different taste from ours, and perhaps of a better. I am allmost of opinion they have a right notion of Life; while they consume it in Music, Gardens, Wine, and delicate eating, while we are tormenting our brains with some Scheme of Politics or studying some Science to which we can never attain, or if we do, cannot perswade people to set that value upon it we do our selves. . . . I allow you to laugh at me for the sensual declaration that I had rather be a rich Effendi with all his ignorance, than Sir Isaac Newton with all his knowledge.[8]

Lady Mary was no doubt being playful, but the cloud no larger than a woman's pen was already discernible in the sky.

Lady Mary enjoyed one distinction very rare among travelers—that of being translated into the language of the people among whom she traveled. It is a remarkable indication of the poverty of travel literature on the countries of the Middle East, that even in an age of massive translation and manic self-absorption in these countries, so few travel writers were thought to be worth the trouble of translation. One was Lady Mary Wortley Montagu;[9] another was Adolphus Slade, a British naval officer who first went to Turkey in 1829. He traveled extensively during the 1830s, and published two books, the first in 1832, the second in 1837.[10] In 1849 he was lent to the Turkish Navy, and remained there as adviser—Mushavir Pasha—for the next seventeen years. In 1867 he published an account of the Crimean War.[11]

Slade seems to have had some influence in Turkey, partly no doubt through his personal role as naval adviser, partly through his books. According to the economist Nassau W. Senior, who was in Turkey in 1857–8, Ahmed Vefik Pasha read and admired Slade's writings, which he praised for their "fidelity" and considered to be among the "best works on Turkey".[12] One of Slade's favorite themes, the role of the Janissaries as a "Chamber of Deputies" embodying the will and defending the rights of the nation, is taken up and developed by no less a writer than Namik Kemal. This is probably not due to coincidence.[13] His book on the Crimean War was published in Turkish translation in 1943, his first book of travels in 1945.

In the West, Slade has been unjustly neglected; his books have never been reprinted, and are rarely even cited by modern scholars. One reason for this may be the form in which they are cast. His major works are travel books—stories of personal experience and adventures which, though very well told, are of limited interest to the modern reader. Yet, interspersed with the narrative, there are passages of comment and analysis—political, social, cultural—which are profoundly interesting, and reveal Slade as one of the few Western travelers in the Middle East whose works can be compared with the classics of Western travel.

Another possible reason for his neglect may be found in the nature of his insights. Slade's travels in Turkey were carried out during the period of the great reforms of Mahmud II and his successors, and much of what he has to say is concerned with these reforms. His approach however is strikingly different from that of most other European observers of his day. He does not share the common assumptions of the time, that the old order is irredeemably bad, that the only way of improvement is liberalizing reform, and that such reform is necessarily conducive to greater happiness, prosperity, and freedom. On the contrary, he finds much that is good and admirable in the old order, and notes that the effects of the reforms have often been less happiness, less prosperity, and even—perhaps especially—less freedom. Though Slade was conservative, and at times perhaps reactionary in his views, he was not opposed to reform as such. What he criticizes is rapid, violent and indiscriminate reform, which destroys the good as well as (or sometimes instead of) the bad parts of the old order, and installs new and more efficient iniquities in their place. He is not unaware of the evils of traditional society and government, nor unwilling to mend them; but he is also deeply conscious of the virtues of the old order, which he describes with sympathy and knowledge, yet entirely without romanticism.

Part of his judgment was personal—respect and liking for Turks of the old school, and mistrust of the manners and motives of their successors. Of Pertev Pasha, Slade remarks that he was "commonly styled the last of the Turks—of the Turks who were loyal without flattery, hospitable without ostentation, self-respectful without arrogance, and who with the vices possessed the virtues of a dominant race."[14] The new élite was quite different. "The men who had floated to the surface on the wreck of the orthodox Turkish party were in general needy, unillustrated by descent. They had to acquire wealth to gain influence and make partisans, in default of which they would be mere bubbles on a troubled sea. Each enriching himself had to wink at his colleague's infirmity, and partisans could only be retained on like conditions. The old nobility, profuse and open-handed, lived on their estates: their ovens were never cool; their pilaf cauldrons never empty. The State was the estate of the new nobility."[15] Slade may be biassed in his affection for the old aristocracy and gentry, but his final comment on the "new nobility" shows devastating accuracy and prescience.

Slade's defense of the old order must have shocked many of his readers, extending as it did to some of the legendary evils ascribed to "Turkish tyranny". He defends the Sultans, the Janissaries, and the ulema; he has much to say in praise, as well as in blame, of old-style Turkish practice and government, and even of their treatment of the Greeks and other Christians, whose lot was in many respects better than under some Christian rulers. Slade protests repeatedly against the self-righteousness and superficiality shown by Western critics of Turkey and Islam. "Slavery sounds revolting to an English ear; change the name, where is the country in which it does not exist? The labourer is chained to his plough, the mechanic to his loom, the pauper to the workhouse."[16] Nor is the parallel limited to economic slavery. After describing the proceedings of a purchaser in the slave-market, Slade drily adds: "The waltz allows nearly as much liberty before hundreds of eyes."[17] He can even see some merit in public executions:

> Orientals are moved to reflection through the medium of their senses. The sight of one brigand hung on the theatre of his exploits has more effect than the report of a hundred brigands wasting away in chains in the bagnio. Whatever may be advanced against public executions, it will be admitted that punishment without example has the taint of vengeance—a reproach sure to be levelled in time against the cloistral imprisonment of the 19th century; the horrors of which cannot be imagined, nor conveyed even faintly to the imagination by the pen of a Sterne or a Dickens. Public execution is the only guarantee for the mass that criminals of a certain quality do suffer death, and in times of social excitement, that criminals of another stamp are becomingly dealt by.[18]

Once again Slade's judgments have not lost their relevance, even in modern times. Modernity takes different forms. In some countries public executions are abolished; in others they are televised.

Despite his aristocratic conservatism and his mistrust of the new men, Slade is not unsympathetic to the reforms. His judgment of the working of the Rescript of the Rose Bower of 1839 is much more favorable than those of the impatient liberals: "This famous proclamation, conceived in a spirit of clemency and tolerance, inaugurated a new era for Turkey. The direct power of death by decapitation was taken from scores of vizirs; the indirect power of death by vexation, from hundreds of inferior station. Oriental ductility was severely tested. An ensanguined nation was ordered to be gentle, and the order was obeyed. Pashas used to rule with the sabre were required to rule by exhortation. Mudirs and agas, wont to admonish rayas with the stick, were enjoined to be civil to them. The exhaustion of the nation, after twenty years of unparalleled suffering, favoured the experiment; anything for quiet was the universal aspiration. The Ottomans, with the instincts of a dominant race, adapted themselves to altered circumstances; they leant upon their prestige, and it did not fail them."[19]

Slade's severest strictures are reserved for the autocratic reforming rulers, and above all for Sultan Mahmud II, whom he accuses of "the entire subversion of the liberties of his subjects".[20] Realizing that the use of this expression in relation to Turkey would startle his Western readers, Slade explains his meaning. Though the autocracy of the Sultan was nominally supreme, the people in effect possessed three great checks against tyrany. These were the *derebeys,* a hereditary nobility, whose domains "were oases in the desert";[21] the *ayan,* a provincial and urban magistracy; and the ulema, the "Mussulman hierarchy . . . a most powerful body, its existence, founded on religion, being cemented by the respect of the nation. It is the peerage of Turkey, sole intermedium now existing between tyranny and slavery. . . ."[22]

In his policy of centralization, Mahmud set to work to destroy or undermine all three. Slade does not object to his restraining the great pashas governing the provinces—"men who usually sprang from insignificance, owing their elevation to baseness, supporting it by tyranny—sycophants in the capital, tyrants in the provinces. . . ."[23] These men were an unmitigated evil, and had Mahmud contented himself with replacing them by "men of integrity, if such could be found, he would have given a solid proof of an enlarged understanding".[24]

It was however, his appetite, not his understanding, that was enlarged. The *derebeys* "had two crimes in the eyes of Mahmoud II: they held their property from their ancestors, and they had riches. To alter the tenure of the former, the destination of the latter, was his object. The *derebeys*—unlike the seraglio dependents, brought up to distrust their own shadows—had no causes for suspicion, and therefore became easy dupes of the grossest treachery. The unbending spirits were removed to another world, the flexible were despoiled of their wealth."[25] In the same way he set to work to abrogate or enfeeble the intermediate powers of the *ayan* and the ulema, and thus reinforce his own autocracy.

Slade views these changes with misgiving, and is impatient with Western observers who hope for their success:

> It is strange that many Franks in Turkey hope that Sultan Mahmoud may succeed in overturning the ulema, as he has done the Janizzaries. They appear to think that no permanent reformation can take place while one of the ancient institutions exist. Who, when the machine is entirely disorganized, is to remodel it,—when every element of discontent is loosened, is to allay them,—when the fabric of centuries is violently shaken, is to consolidate it?[26]

Who indeed.

Mahmud was unfortunate in his choice of example.

> He took Mehemet Ali for his guide, and the rule of Mehemet Ali was to extort money from every source, by any means; to render himself sole proprietor of Egypt. An enlarged view of things, joined to unparalleled cruelty and duplicity, with a perfect knowledge of the evil ways of mankind in the East, gained during the various phazes of his life, (he has been a cavedgi, a tobacco merchant, a chavass, a klephte, a bim bashi, a pasha), enabled him to succeed. Excepting cruelty, Mahmoud had none of these advantages; truth never found the way to his ear, and he always saw with others' eyes—the natural consequences of his station. He thought that the other owed his success entirely to having overturned existing institutions, and he flattered himself, when he should have accomplished the same, to be able to rule Turkey and to till it.[27]

Slade's judgments of the results are worth quoting *in extenso:*

Travellers are apt to laud Mehemet Ali: but let them consider the condition of his subjects—let them recollect, what they must have seen, the multitudes labouring naked in the cotton and rice grounds, goaded on by overseers, the numbers perishing on the banks of the canal, or in the towns,—the only bar between life and death, of those who survive a few years, black bread and the water of the Nile, their only enjoyment—shared with animals, as transitorily and as soullessly—multiplying their wretched species,—they will not wish his doctrines to be extended to Turkey. If the attributes of civilization,—armies, fleets, canals, roads, palaces,—can only be obtained by similar means, humanity would decline them. . . .

Civilization, forced, is as inimical to a people's happiness as is a constitution abruptly presented. That deprives them of their liberties; this of their judgment: the shackles of the former are felt, before the corresponding silken bands are fitted to disguise the iron; the condescension of the latter is abused before its beauty is respected: the one sharpens the sword of state; the other puts clubs in the hands of the mob. For the former hypothesis look at Russia; for the latter observe France.

When a nation, comparatively barbarous, copies the finished experience of a highly civilized state, without going through the intermediate stages of advancement, the few are strengthened against the many, the powerful armed against the weak. The sovereign, who before found his power (despotic in name) circumscribed, because with all the will, he had not the real art of oppressing, by the aid of science finds himself a giant—his mace exchanged for a sword. In scanning over the riches of civilization, spread out before him for acceptance, he contemptuously rejects those calculated to benefit his people, and chooses the modern scientific governing machine, result of ages of experiments, with its patent screws for extracting blood and treasure,—conscription and taxation. He hires foreign engineers to work it, and waits the promised result—absolute power. His subjects, who before had a thousand modes of avoiding his tyranny, have not now a loop-hole to escape by: the operations of the uncorroding engine meet them at every turn, and, to increase their despair, its movement accelerates with use, and winds closer their chains. A people thus taken by surprise, and thrown off their guard, will be centuries before they acquire sufficient knowledge—every beam of which is carefully hid from them by the clouds of despotism—to compare their situation with that of their neighbours—(who, although ruled by the same means, have advantages to counterbalance its weight)—to assert human rights, and to dare to say "we are men". In the mean time, they are dispersed or collected, or worked, as cattle; suffered to perish of disease, or starve, as things of no import; compelled to march like puppets from zone to zone, for the caprice of one man—to slaughter and be slaughtered for his pleasure; and if any one, using his reason, pronounce such proceedings against the eternal fitness of things, he is denounced as revolutionary, an enemy of order, little short of mad, and unfit to live. Such are the fruits which civilization, so called, has produced in one country. Newspapers act as oil to the engine, are, under such auspices, the direst enemies of freedom and rational reform, simply because they dare only espouse one side of a question, the side which suits the powers that are. Even supposing, which is not probable, the editors to have any thing dearer at heart than their own profits, they dare not expose corruption in the heads of departments, and therefore, as a juste milieu is seldom the part of a newspaper, they applaud their measures, however tyrannical, the more particularly if they receive money for so doing. It is a long time in any state before the press acquires sufficient respectability, as well as independence, to expose abuses; until that time it only serves to abet them . . . the establishment of gazettes in Turkey, though exceedingly captivating in sound, quite refreshing to the ears of liberals, a harbinger of freedom, is in fact very anti-liberal, a corruption promoter, an aegis for the greatly wicked.

It is curious to observe the similarity of advantages which are enjoyed by nations in opposite spheres of knowledge, and separated by perfectly distinct manners and religion. Hitherto the Osmanley has enjoyed by custom some of the dearest privileges of freemen, for which Christian nations have so long struggled. He paid nothing to the government beyond a moderate landtax, although liable, it is true, to extortions, which might be classed with assessed taxes. He paid no tithes, the vacouf [*waqf*] sufficing for the maintenance of the ministers of Islamism. He travelled where he pleased without passports; no custom-house officer intruded his eyes and dirty fingers among his baggage; no police watched his motions, or listened for his words. His house was sacred. His sons were never taken from his side to be soldiers, unless war called them. His views of ambition were not restricted by the barriers of birth and wealth; from the lowest origin he might aspire without presumption to the rank of pasha; if he could read, to that of grand vizir; and this consciousness, instilled and supported, by numberless precedents, ennobled his mind, and enabled him to enter on the duties of high office without embarrassment. Is not this the advantage so prized by free nations? Did not the exclusion of the people from posts of honour tend to the French revolution? For this freedom, this capability of realizing the wildest wishes, what equivalent does the sultan offer? It may be said none.[28]

An interesting contrast with Slade's writings is provided by a far more famous book, Sir Charles Eliot's *Turkey in Europe*. Originally published under the pseudonym Odysseus in 1900, it was re-issued with additional material in 1908, and reprinted from the second edition in 1965.[29] The two authors have much in common. Both were active public servants—Slade a naval officer, Eliot a diplomat and, later, a university administrator. Both were superb writers—shrewd and accurate in their observation, clear, forceful and often witty in their exposition. Both were helped by a knowledge of Turkish and a sympathy for the Turks; yet both were sustained by a confidence in their own civilization which, to the modern Western reader accustomed to liberal self-abasement, may look rather like arrogance. They had standards, by which they were prepared to judge their own as well as other peoples, and other peoples as well as their own. Eliot in particular often expresses judgments, and clothes them in language, which to contemporary taste may seem offensive and even cruel. Much more than Slade, he views the East from a position of amused and comfortable superiority. His disapproval looks like disdain; even his sympathy smacks of condescension. This attitude, and the prejudices that go with it, will no doubt delight some readers, and shock, offend or irritate many others. But even these may appreciate his robust frankness, his freedom from the anxious and piacular humbug of much modern Western writing on the non-Western world.

Eliot's Turkey is different from Slade's. The reformers and, so it seemed, the reforms were dead and buried; Abdülhamid II, the arch-reactionary, was master. Liberal circles had given up all hope of the Turks, and had espoused the cause of the subject peoples of the Turkish Empire; even conservatives were weakening in their traditional support for Turkish integrity, as the sultan on the one hand oppressed his subjects, on the other drew nearer to Germany. Eliot's sympathy for the Turks is much less pronounced than Slade's—but it is no less out of accord with the prevailing attitudes of his time. Still more discordant was his disenchanted view of the Christian subjects of the Turks—their characters and their aspirations.

There is another important difference between the two travelers. Eliot was an intellectual—a brilliant linguist who mastered more than a score of languages, a learned and imaginative scholar who later in life wrote standard works on Hinduism and Buddhism. While Slade's books are rambling, discursive and personal, Eliot's *Turkey in Europe* is organized and analytical, combining direct knowledge with immense philological, historical, and even theological erudition. No other author has dealt as clearly and effectively with the different peoples, faiths and institutions that made up the Ottoman Empire at the end of the 19th century.

He has his blind spots. A keen observer of the present and a learned student of the past, his scholarship is literary and linguistic rather than historical. Thus, he is capable of writing: "We must draw a distinction between the history of the Turks and the history of their Christian subjects. The former is a purely military record. Modern writers are unwilling to regard history as a mere catalogue of reigns and battles, and pay more attention to the various movements, political, religious, intellectual, social, and commercial which the life of each nation presents. This is very just in the case of nearly all nations; but the peculiarity of the Turks is at once apparent when we observe that their history is almost exclusively a catalogue of names and battles."[30] Despite Eliot's knowledge and intelligence, it does not seem to have occurred to him that the "peculiarity" he describes is one of historiography, not of history—a deficiency not of the Turks but of the books he had read about them. The same historical impercipience is shown in his insistence that despite all the reforms there had been no real change, that "without Janissaries, and without Phanariots, it [the Ottoman Empire] is still, in the first decade of the twentieth century very much what it was in the first decade of the nineteenth."[31] Slade, though without scholarly pretensions, would not have made such mistakes, and indeed shows a keen awareness of social, economic and cultural change. In the same spirit Eliot lays great stress on the eternal "nomadism" of the Turks, who after centuries of occupation, according to him, are still strangers in Europe—pastoral marauders who have used the country but contributed nothing to it, and who have never really adapted themselves to urban or sedentary living. The point is made, with a characteristic blend of shrewdness and prejudice, in this description of the Yildiz Palace secretariat: "I have seen a number of secretaries and officials working in a room decked with red plush and the ordinary furniture of European palaces. Some were sitting curled up in armchairs, with their inkpots poised perilously on the arms, the idea of having a writing-table never having come into their heads. Some were squatting on the floor, eating with their fingers off broad dishes placed on a low table. One was taking a siesta in a corner. Nothing could have more vividly suggested the idea of a party of tent-dwellers who had suddenly occupied a European house, and did not quite know how to use it."[32] It seems a strange comment on an Empire which had cherished and maintained such monuments of the past as Santa Sophia, and had added greatly to them.

Despite such lapses, Eliot has many insights to offer, especially in his thumb-nail sketches of persons and situations. Some of his dicta may still be of interest even to the contemporary student—of other places if not of Turkey. "When one reads European reports on the condition of the Turkish provinces, or reflects on the wonderful things one has seen with one's own eyes, one is inclined to think that the system cannot go on. It is annually proved that the machinery of government is collapsing; that there is no money and no food; that no one can pay any taxes, and that everybody must starve. Yet it all goes on next year eskisi gibi—'the same old way'. They that had been skinned are skinned again, and they that were starving are starving still, but not dead. . . . It may safely be affirmed that if any European Power were to undertake to finance Turkey, the whole place would be bankrupt in a week, and need years of recuperation. But political economy seems to be one of those things which must be accepted or rejected as a whole. Partial and blundering acceptance means collapse, but if, like the Sublime Porte, you reject it in toto, if you discard such conceptions as the National Debt, and pay no regard to the theory of wages, the theory of demand and supply, and all other theories what ever, it seems to make no difference."[33] There may still be a few places in the world where Eliot's economic wisdom is relevant. There are many more where students and practitioners of politics would do well to heed another of his warnings:

Before I proceed any further I had better emphasize a distinction which has probably already dawned upon the reader—that between the real and the paper government of Turkey. If one takes as a basis the laws, statistics, and budgets as printed, it is easy to prove that the Ottoman Empire is in a state of unexampled prosperity. Life and property are secure; perfect liberty and toleration are enjoyed by all; taxation is light, balances large, trade flourishing. Those who had not an extensive personal acquaintance with Turkey may regard such accounts with suspicion and think them highly coloured, but they find it difficult to realize that all this official literature is absolute fiction, and for practical purposes unworthy of a moment's attention. Once in Russia, which is in many ways an Eastern country, I missed a steamer on the Neva owing to its having left a certain pier half-an-hour before the time advertised. I tried to appeal to the pier-keeper's sense of justice by pointing to the time-table displayed in his office, but he would not see the point of my argument, and merely replied, "You should never pay attention to what is printed." You never should, at any rate in Turkey. No reform is clamoured for which does not already figure in the statute-book; no complaint is made which cannot be disproved by statistics. This is partly due to the Oriental idea of literature. Just as no one would use the language of everyday life in the most trifling letter, so everyday facts are felt to be inappropriate to literary composition. You cannot write a letter without describing yourself as a slave and ascribing all virtues to your correspondent. Similarly you cannot write a history without describing the Sultan as ever-victorious, and you cannot write of his country without describing it as well defended and prosperous. The natural divorce between literature and facts is so complete that the Oriental attaches little more importance to striking statistics or to declarations of the Imperial clemency than he does to epistolatory compliments. He feels that it would be rude and bad style to say anything else.[34]

3. *The Decolonization of History*

When the colonialists finally packed and departed from the countries they had ruled, their former subjects faced a new task. The present was saved, the future preserved from the colonialist grasp. There remained the task of liberating the past. The decolonization of history, as it was called, attracted considerable attention and energy in the new states of Asia and Africa. The line of argument was much the same in most of them, and ran something like this. Ever since the advent of European rule, the writing of history had been controlled by colonialist historians and their native disciples. These historians had a purpose: to justify the establishment and facilitate the maintenance of colonial domination. This they did by blackening the pre-colonial era, which they depicted as an age of barbarism and backwardness, and whitewashing the colonial régime, which they presented as an instrument of enlightenment and progress. This kind of history, which was taught to both the rulers and the ruled, served the double purpose of demoralizing the latter and nerving the former for the sometimes disagreeable duties which they had to perform. A further aim was to divide the subject peoples by inventing fictitious national entities.

If, as was believed, this was a correct assessment of the historiography inherited from the colonial régimes, it was obviously unsuited to the schools and universities of the newly independent states. A new historiography was needed, which would rescue the forgotten—or rather the deliberately hidden—glories of the national past and set right the record of colonialism. In this way the citizens of the new states would attain the pride and self-confidence that come from the consciousness of one's national heritage, and would abandon the unjustified and undignified deference which they had previously shown to their European mentors.

The first of the subject peoples to react in this way against imperialist historiography were those of the Russian Empire. The fall of Tsardom, the new revolutionary iconoclasm, and the temporary relaxation of imperial control brought a great wave of new historical thinking, in which Russian orientalists, in sympathy with the subject peoples, played no small part. National and religious leaders who had resisted Russian expansion were rediscovered and celebrated, and the remoter glories of the Turkish, Tatar, Iranian and Islamic past studied and acclaimed. The Muslim peoples of Asiatic Russia were recovering their common identity—were learning that they were not an ethnic dust of broken tribes inevitably attracted to Great Russia but the scattered remnants of a great civilization.

This trend, strong in the 1920s, was slowed down in the 1930s and decisively reversed in the late 1940s—sometimes with some personal inconvenience to the scholars concerned. Two points were now firmly established; first that the Russian conquest of Asia, even under the Tsars, was "objectively" progressive, and resistance to it therefore "objectively" reactionary; second, that the Uzbeks, Kirgiz, etc., were separate and distinct peoples whose national identity had in the past been suppressed by Tatar, Iranian and Islamic tyrannies, and must not now be obscured by pan-Turkish, pan-Iranian or pan-Islamic propaganda. Those who held otherwise were variously accused of chauvinism, racialism, clericalism, feudal idealism and bourgeois objectivism. Particularly condemned was the racialist or clericalist idealization of the pre-Russian past.

Though the decolonization of history was halted and reversed in the Soviet Union, it was taken up with enthusiasm in other countries, notably in India, Egypt, and North Africa. Begun while the British and French colonialists were still in power, it has continued apace since their departure, and a considerable body of decolonized historiography, ranging from accurate scholarship to unbridled fantasy, has appeared. By a fortunate coincidence, Marxist scientific analysis, while condemning pan-Turkism and pan-Iranism, allows pan-Arabism; it also denies to the British in India or the French in North Africa the enlightened and progressive role played by Tsarist Russia in Central Asia and Trans-Caucasia.

M. Lacoste is a French Marxist, whose aim is to assist the people of North Africa in the liberation of their past.* The issue, he points out, is not an academic one, nor a mere intellectual exercise: it is directly relevant to the problems of under-development, which are the main concern of the Third World. Under-development is the result of colonial misrule—on this M. Lacoste has no doubts and uses no half-tones. It is therefore necessary to make a critical examination of the misdeeds of the colonialists, and also of those factors in pre-colonial society which delayed or prevented economic, social or political development, and thus allowed the colonialists to enter. The great Arab historian Ibn Khaldūn is of particular value for this second purpose.

One of the gravest misdeeds of the French in North Africa, according to M. Lacoste, was the creation of a mythical version of North African history, which has no basis in historical reality. The word myth should not mislead us into thinking in terms of spontaneous generation and development:

> This myth is not the fruit of chance. It was consciously forged, and inculcated in the framework of colonialist ideology. This judgment, which may at first sight seem excessive and partisan, is only in conformity with the historic reality.

The content of the myth is the basic antagonism of nomads and sedentary peoples, of Arabs and Berbers. The method of the myth-makers is to portray the Arabs as destructive invaders, from whose yoke the Berbers were finally liberated by the coming of the French. The purposes of the myth were to divide Arab from Berber in order to rule both; to undermine any sense of nationality or patriotism which might arise among them; to prove the impossibility of any separate political existence for North Africa; to demonstrate the social, economic

* *Ibn Khaldoun: naissance de l'histoire passé au tiers-monde.* By Yves Lacoste. (Paris, 1968)

and cultural backwardness bequeathed by the invaders; and, by these means, to justify and preserve the "civilizing mission of France". To sustain his argument, M. Lacoste quotes passages from such French writers on North Africa as E. F. Gautier *("un des plus brillants idéologues de la colonisation")* and Louis Bertrand *("chantre officiel du Gouvernement Général de l'Algérie")*.

The parallels between the French interpretation of North African history described by M. Lacoste and the Russian view of Central Asian history imposed during the past twenty years are obvious and striking: the French Berber policy and the Russian policy of local nationalities; the French disparagement of Arabism and the Russian rejection of both the Iranian and the Tatar heritages; the insistence of both on their own "civilizing" or "objectively progressive" role. There are of course two important differences: one is that M. Lacoste, in refuting the views of Gautier and Bertrand, is able to draw on a solid body of critical French scholarship; the other is that the French no longer rule North Africa.

M. Lacoste, though a believer in comparative studies, attempts no such comparison. Instead, he is concerned to rescue Ibn Khaldūn from the malice of colonialist historians, who have fraudulently *("frauduleusement")* distorted his writings for their own nefarious ends. Ibn Khaldūn's famous description of the enduring devastation brought to North Africa by the Beduin migrations in the 11th century has indeed been extensively used by Gautier and other French writers; together with other passages on the characteristics of the Arab nomads, it led an Egyptian philosopher (Ahmad Fu'ād al-Ahwānī, *Al-Qawmiyya al-'arabiyya,* Cairo 1960, page 98) to remark that the orientalists had only accepted Ibn Khaldūn because of his attacks on Arabism; it also led, for a while, to the banning of Ibn Khaldūn's works in the Republic of Iraq. M. Lacoste is at some pains to show that the events described by Ibn Khaldūn never happened, and that in fact Ibn Khaldūn never described them.

Part of the book is devoted to finding alternative explanations of the factors exploited by colonialist historians, part to presenting and interpreting Ibn Khaldūn in a new light. There have been many studies of Ibn Khaldūn in which disciples of Durkheim, Breysig, etc., have explained him as a precursor of Durkheim, Breysig, etc. He has even been presented (though not by a disciple) as a kind of Ur-Toynbee. M. Lacoste does not commit the error of making Ibn Khaldūn a Marxist: yet, by a sort of materialist election of grace, he admits him to Marxist salvation. Philosophically, M. Lacoste admits, he was no nationalist. On the contrary, he was religious, and at times subject to "mystical obscurantism". He was unable to define his essential ideas with precision, because the conceptual equipment of the time was too undeveloped and "objective realities" insufficiently differentiated. Yet, M. Lacoste believes, he came very near to historical materialism. To study Ibn Khaldūn with modern (*videlicet* Marxist) concepts thus involves no distortion or anachronism. It is the only way to discover and define his real meaning, which he himself could not define for lack of conceptual tools. Ibn Khaldūn's views are incomplete, but not obsolete, according to M. Lacoste, and it is the task of the modern scholar to carry through the analysis which Ibn Khaldūn, apparently without realizing what he was doing, began in the 14th century.

M. Lacoste's approach to Islamic history is somewhat idiosyncratic. He believes that the 14th century was the most brilliant in the history of medieval Egypt; that Ibn Hawqal was an historian; that the Fatimid Empire represented the revolt of a group of mountain tribes. Some of his arguments bring much-needed corrections to established errors—as for example in describing the Hilali migration as a deportation and invitation rather than an invasion; others, in the absence of documentary as distinct from theoretical evidence, fail to carry conviction. The last part of the book is devoted to establishing the place of Ibn Khaldūn in the development of scientific historical thought and method, and his relevance as an analyst of under-development to the present-day problems of the Third World.

For the reader who would like to know what Ibn Khaldūn himself actually said, the new volume edited by Mr N. J.

Dawood* provides an excellent introduction. Mr. Dawood has already shown his skill as a translator of the Qur'ān and of the *Thousand and One Nights*—two of the three Arabic books known by name in the West. He now turns his attention to the third, the *Prolegomena* of Ibn Khaldūn. Using as his base the monumental three-volume translation by Professor Rosenthal of Yale, he has, by skilful abridgment and deft but unobtrusive editing, produced an attractive and manageable volume, which should make the essential ideas of Ibn Khaldūn accessible to a wide circle of readers.

* *The Muqaddima: An Introduction to History.* Edited and abridged by N. J. Dawood. Translated by Franz Rosenthal. (London, 1968)

4. On Writing the Modern History of the Middle East

The classical Western form of orientalism is an offshoot of the main tradition of European academic scholarship, which has grown up in the great universities of Europe since the Middle Ages. Orientalist studies—that is, studies of oriental civilizations by Western scholars—are a part of that tradition, and have their roots deep in European history and culture. Their origins were in the sister disciplines of classics and theology, which for so long dominated the European universities. Through centuries of study of Latin, Greek, and Hebrew texts, and of Christian and Jewish belief and doctrine, the scholars of Europe perfected a philological and philosophical method and discipline which became, in their skillful hands, a precise and effective instrument of study and research. The achievement of the first great European orientalists was to take this instrument, fashioned for another purpose, and apply it to the study of Arabic and Islam. The labors of subsequent generations of orientalists have consisted largely of wielding this instrument, and making such minor modifications to it as seemed necessary.

In the early 19th century the new European school of scientific history also found its disciples among the orientalists. The studies of Ranke and Niebuhr on European and Roman history inspired a number of orientalists to try and apply their methods to the study of Islam. The first pioneer was Gustav Weil (1808–1889), who in his biography of the Prophet and his history of the Caliphs made the first attempt to treat these topics in accordance with the methods and objectives of critical historical scholarship. Since then others have followed him, and Western orientalists have been able to make a profoundly significant contribution to the understanding of medieval Arab history—a contribution of incalculable importance to the historical self-awareness, at the present day, of the Arabs themselves.

It is, however, almost exclusively with the *medieval* history of the Arabs that the orientalists have concerned themselves. For one thing, it is in medieval history, based on chronicles and inscriptions, that the method of philological, textual scholarship is most effective—and it is in the use of this method that the orientalist is at his best and happiest. For another, it was the ancient and medieval periods that were intrinsically more interesting to these scholars. As long as Islam was an independent and distinctive civilization, it was a subject worthy of classical studies. In the periods of decline and change—particularly of change in the direction of a greater resemblance to themselves—it ceased to attract them. As Arabic literature became more European in its forms and themes, it became less interesting to European orientalists, who were drawn precisely by what was distinctive and unfamiliar in the classical Arab past. The modern Arabs were of no more interest to the old-style orientalist than were the modern inhabitants of Greece and Italy to the old-style Hellenist or Latinist.

In recent years some orientalists have begun to interest themselves in modern history, and have produced work of value, particularly since the opening of the great Turkish archives has at last made possible the serious historical study of the Ottoman period. They are still, however, very few. On the history of the Middle East in modern times—that is, since the rise of European influence—the orientalists have little to say, and have left the field to writers of another kind.

For some time now there has been a growing Western interest in the modern Middle East, and this has stimulated the production of a very large number of books, of varying purpose and value. Some are the work of European and American writers; others are written by authors of Middle Eastern nationality, of whom there are increasing numbers able to write in a Western language and for a Western reading public.

Many of these books, though purporting to be works of history, are in fact nothing of the kind, but are exercises in quite different professions. One group may be best described as journalism. The honest and conscientious journalist follows an honourable profession, with a useful, indeed an essential function in the modern world. It may often happen that the journalist, with the special methods and insights of his craft, achieves a truer and deeper understanding of contemporary events than the historian, and produces material of great value to present-day and future historians. Nevertheless he is not writing history. Reportage and news comment between hard covers are still journalism, and belong fundamentally with the daily or weekly newspaper and periodical, rather than with the monograph of the critical historian.

The advocate too follows an honorable calling, at least when his character is clear and undisguised. Advocacy is not confined to courts of law. The writer who sets forth a version of events designed to convince an invisible judge and jury of the rightness of his client's cause is also an advocate, whether his client be a party, a nation, a class, a church, or a continent. From the clash of argument truth may emerge; but the advocate is not primarily concerned with arriving at the truth. That is the business of the judge and jury. The advocate's task is to state the best possible case for his client, and leave his opponents to state their own. His writings, like those of the journalist, may be invaluable source-material for the historian. They are not history.

Propaganda has been defined as the art of persuading other people of what one does not believe oneself. The word has a respectable ancestry, having originally been used by the faithful of the propagation of their own religious faith. But in our own day, like so much else, it has gone through a process of devaluation, and only the most cynical will accept it as a definition of their own activities. Basically, the propagandist, as the word is used nowadays, is not concerned with the truth of what he preaches. He considers that it will benefit the cause or interests which he serves if certain people believe certain things; he therefore tries by all the means in his power to convince them of these things. Whether these things are true or false is irrelevant both to his purpose and to his chances of achieving it. It is hardly necessary to assert the distinction between propaganda and history; it is often however difficult to demonstrate it to the propagandist's victims.

To journalism, advocacy, and propaganda we may add a fourth category of non-historical writings on history, which for want of a better name we may call mythology. The ancient peoples expressed their religious beliefs and scientific principles —the two were much the same—in the form of myths; modern nations express their guiding and sustaining assumptions in the form of national historiographic myths, absorbed in childhood from home and school, and held through life without doubt or question. A depressingly large proportion of the so-called history in our school manuals is no more than mythology—deeply-held beliefs which gratify and solace those who hold them, but which have little or no foundation in fact. In some countries the advance of historical research has been able to penetrate from the learned quarterlies into the school textbooks, and to give people a more balanced and objective view of their national past and present. In other countries national history is still a twilight world of myth and fantasy, in which all virtue is with the patriots and all evil comes from foreigners (in certain situations this myth may be inverted, but the principle is the same). This is neither an adult nor a dignified posture; nor is it one from which one can conveniently step forward.

Of the vast literature published in recent years on the modern history of the Middle East, a large part, perhaps the greater part, belongs to one or other of these categories, and cannot properly be classed as historical writing at all. Such works are written from the standpoint and in the interest of one or another party to Middle Eastern conflicts, and they offer only precarious guidance to the student of history.

If however we set aside the many books written to serve political or commercial purposes or to relieve personal tensions, there still remains a sizable body of work produced by professional scholars on the modern history of the Middle East. Some of it has been written by orientalists, but not much. In the main they have neglected this subject and have left it to the colonial (and anti-colonial) historian and to a variety of specialists in economics, politics and international relations.

Between the modernist and the orientalist there has been remarkably little cooperation. While it would probably be an exaggeration to say that the twain never meet, one might not unfairly remark that they pass one another with cold and perfunctory greeting, sometimes even with averted eyes. Modern historians and political scientists anxious to work on the Third Republic or the Third Reich are not required to begin their studies with the *Chanson de Roland* or the *Nibelungenlied*, nor would such studies, however illuminating, be regarded as a sufficient disciplinary training. They are however expected to know French and German. While most would agree that the time has come to emancipate oriental history from philological domination, it is by now clear that we cannot afford to emancipate this study from all philological discipline.

The 19th century has fared badly at the hands of historians of the Middle East. The Orientalists have, in the main, shown little interest in a period so near to our own, when the qualities which first attracted them to study Islamic society are attenuated and contaminated by contact with our own Western civilization and thus lose their attraction. The modernists have done useful work, but have usually been ignorant of the languages of the Middle East, and therefore limited to sources in European languages. They have thus been debarred from access to the material with which alone they could weave their narratives of external political and economic action into the texture of the internal history of the region—even, it might be said, from an adequate treatment of the political and economic events which are their primary concern. History moves at many levels, and it is only the surface movements of events which can be seen from the outside. It is generally conceded that the study of modern France requires some knowledge of the French language and of French writings. Why should the Arabs, Persians, Turks or Israelis be different? It is true that their languages are more difficult, but that is not really an adequate answer.

There has long been a kind of diplomatic convention in the West that the Turks took no active part in the political struggle over Turkey, and that there are no Turkish sources for its history—with parallel conventions for other countries of the Middle East. It is noteworthy, for example, that, leaving aside the archives, the great mass even of published Turkish documents and memoirs has passed almost unnoticed in the vast literature on the Eastern Question. The result has been a view of history in which the Middle East was no more than a stage, with the Ottoman Empire as backdrop, where European actors performed the main roles in the drama. Other writers *(quorum pars minima fui)* have erred in the opposite direction. Reacting against the exclusively Western approach of the historians of the Eastern Question, they have concentrated so heavily on oriental sources as to neglect not only the evidence of European documentation but also the effects of European action—without which, ultimately, the history of the Middle East in the 19th and 20th centuries is not intelligible.

The emergence of a new generation of historians of Middle Eastern origin, trained in the methods and devoted to the standards of modern critical scholarship, might have been expected to carry these studies an important step forward. The results, for 19th-century history, have so far been rather disappointing. Most of these historians have been attracted by the times of ancient glory and current revival in the histories of their peoples, and have turned away from a period which, in the main and in their eyes, was one of weakness and degradation.

There have, however, been some—recently increasing in number—who have taken the 19th century as their field. Much could be expected of these. Able to use both Eastern and Western sources, trained as historians and familiar with the language, culture, traditions and attitudes of their own countries, they might have achieved that synthesis which in the West had eluded both the historian and the orientalist.

In the main it has eluded them too. There have, of course, been distinguished exceptions—obvious names will come to mind—but they are few, and most of them have concentrated on the early and late parts of the century.

A good deal of recent work has been devoted to the history of ideas—some of it using the arts of the taxidermist rather than of the historian. This is a comparatively new field of interest for historians of the modern Middle East. Some of these writings have been works of scholarship, throwing light into hitherto obscure corners of intellectual and indeed general history; others have been affected by a variety of polemic or apologetic purposes—to provide a past for some current ideological nostrum, to project an attractive image, or to assuage wounded pride. Indeed, of late the study of the politically sensitive 19th century has in a larger sense been menaced by new ideologies, which regard the past as another region to be "liberated" by assault, and scholarship as another industry ripe for nationalization.

What is still lacking is good solid research on 19th-century history, conducted by the tried and tested methods of critical historical scholarship, using both Western and Middle Eastern sources, and not governed by the desire to prove the virtue or villainy of persons, parties, classes, sects or nations. There are such works, produced both in the Middle East and elsewhere, but their numbers are still lamentably few.

The student of modern history therefore has a difficult task. Without any really authoritative works to guide him, he must pick his way warily between imperialist, nationalist and latterly ideological prejudice and propaganda, and listen for the thin voice of truth almost drowned by the rolling of logs and the grinding of axes.

The question may be asked at this point whether there really is any possibility, in the Middle East or for that matter in any other area, of writing modern history in a scholarly, detached, and objective way. Where passion and interest are so strongly involved, where so much relevant information is withheld from the historian by official secrecy, is it possible for him to write history at all?

I believe that in spite of these very real difficulties, it is still possible to treat the modern history of the Middle East in a way that deserves the name of historical scholarship, provided that certain conditions are fulfilled. Of these I shall mention what seem to me the most important.

First, the historian must possess a scholarly knowledge of his subject. That is to say, in addition to the professional skills of the historian, he must be acquainted with the history, language, and culture of the people of whom he writes.

In other fields to state this is to state the obvious, but unfortunately in Middle Eastern studies the point still needs to be emphasized. Professional advancement, success and reputation in this area are compatible with a degree of ignorance and incompetence which would not be tolerated in other more developed fields of study. This has led to low standards of entry, performance and promotion in academic institutions, and to the acceptance and acclamation as authorities, even as "standard works", of books of breathtaking superficiality and inaccuracy. Unfortunately such books really are "standard works" in the sense that they are cited, recommended and even read by many people, in many places, for long periods.

The Middle Eastern historian, to achieve reasonable professional competence, must know the language of the people with whom he is concerned well enough to read their books and newspapers in the original and preferably also to converse with them in their own idiom. The use of translations and digests is legitimate for certain limited purposes, but cannot replace this knowledge as a basis for serious historical study.

Second, the historian must strive to achieve as great a degree of objectivity as possible. This too is a truism which still needs emphasis in relation to the Middle East. This is an area in which there are violent disputes and one in particular which arouses strong emotions and stirs deep-seated prejudices and loyalties. It is also an area in which powerful material interests are involved. There are many who support one side or another in Middle Eastern conflicts because they have a material interest in doing so. This may be political, e.g. the pursuit of votes in domestic elections, or commercial, e.g. the pursuit of concessions or other commercial advantages in Middle Eastern countries. The elected politician responding to the wishes of his electors, the corporation employee advancing the interests of his stockholders, the public relations consultant diligently burnishing the image of his current or prospective client are all no doubt ennobling spectacles. None of them is a safe guide to the study of history—yet all of them try to penetrate the places where history is written and taught.

In the course of his inquiries the historian of the Middle East will have to review a great deal of evidence, some of which he will dismiss as irrelevant or untrue. The great danger is that he may use two standards of judgment, one for items favorable to his thesis, his loyalties, or his prejudices, the other for items that are not favorable. The scholarly historian must try, as far as he can, to select, evaluate, and interpret his sources according to objective and constant criteria, and not according to the results at which he would prefer to arrive. No man can be entirely detached from the events of the time in which he lives; no scholar can become sufficiently interested in a subject to write about it without developing opinions and perhaps sentiments. The scholar, however, will not give way to his prejudices. He will recognize them, control them, allow for them, and by a process of intellectual self-discipline reduce their working to a minimum. There is an old Eastern proverb which runs: "Me and my tribe against the world; me and my clan against my tribe; me and my brothers against my clan; me, against my brothers!" The historian too is a man in a social context, and will identify himself with different loyalty-groups in different circumstances. Thus, a Maronite Christian historian in Lebanon might, with equal sincerity, identify himself with the Arabs against the West, with the Levant against Egypt, with Lebanon against Syria, with the Christians against the Muslims, with the Maronites against the other Christians, with his clan against the rest. These loyalties may well influence his choice of subject of research; they should not influence his treatment of it. If, in the course of his researches, he finds that the group with which he identifies himself is always right, and those other groups with which it is in conflict are always wrong, then he would be well advised to question his conclusions, and to reexamine the hypotheses on the basis of which he selected and interpreted his evidence; for it is not in the nature of human communities to be always right.

Finally, the historian must be fair and honest in the way he presents his story. That is not to say that he must confine himself to a bare recital of definitely established facts. At many stages in his work the historian must formulate hypotheses and make judgments. The important thing is that he should do so consciously and explicitly, reviewing the evidence for and against his conclusions, examining the various possible interpretations, and stating explicitly what his decision is, and how and why he reached it.

A single example from recent history may serve to illustrate these points—the rebuff offered to King Saud, during his visit to the United States in 1957, by Mayor Wagner of New York. Much has been written about this incident by journalists, advocates, propagandists, and mythologists—little if anything by historians. Let us imagine two propagandists, one a Zionist and the other an Arab nationalist; dealing with the same group of known facts, each will try to present them in a form creditable to his own side and discreditable to that of his opponent. Their presentations might run something like this.

The Arab nationalist could begin by attributing the Mayor's action to political vote-grabbing, and point out how many Jews there are in New York. The Zionist would probably make no allusion to this aspect at all. If forced to admit that the presence of a large Jewish electorate had some bearing on the Mayor's action, he would argue that there is nothing wrong in a democratically elected officer acting in accordance with the wishes of his electors, and might claim the Catholic electors as being equally opposed to a king who, he would point out, had outlawed the celebration of Mass by Americans resident in Arabia. He would of course lay great stress on the reasons given by the Mayor himself for his action—distaste for a ruler who practices slavery and religious discrimination in his country. The Arab nationalist would dismiss this as an excuse for pandering to the Jewish voters, and might indicate nearer objects for the Mayor's moral indignation. He would avoid any discussion of slavery and religious discrimination in Saudi Arabia. In certain circumstances he might deny that they exist.

The Arab nationalist would accuse the Mayor of putting party before country, and of sacrificing the national interests of the United States—for which he would profess great concern—for the sake of an advantage in New York City politics. The Zionist would play down this point, and could argue that what are called the national interests of the United States are in fact the commercial interests of some oil companies. The argument could then continue with a discussion on the comparative merits of profits from Arabs and votes from Jews—which are more democratic, which are more sordid, which are more beneficial, and to whom? In conclusion, the Mayor, in acting as he did, could be either

1. A sordid and irresponsible city politician, sacrificing the national interests of his country and insulting an honored guest in order to grab votes by pandering to a selfish sectional interest in the city—or
2. A man of principle, who would not bow down before the sordid commercial interests of an oil company, and refused to dishonor the great and free city of which he is the elected leader by welcoming a monarch whose hands are stained with slavery and persecution.

The same canvas, the same palette—and two quite different pictures. But what kind of picture will the historian paint? Probably, he will paint neither the one nor the other, but a composition containing elements of both. He is not precluded from forming and expressing a judgment on the motives of Mayor Wagner's action—indeed, it is his duty to do so. Where he differs from the controversialist is that in what he writes he will review all the evidence, and not just the part that supports his opinion; all the possible interpretations, and not just the one he adopts. Most important of all, he will, to the best of his ability, form his opinion by a dispassionate study of the facts, and not in response to the call of blood or faith or the wishes of a paymaster. And when he has formed his opinion, he will state it clearly and give his reasons for it.

What he should not do is present an artificial selection of evidence, chosen to support his own view, and tacitly suppress the rest; he should not convey his assumptions and his judgments by implication, suggestion, or innuendo, nor by the use of emotionally charged language. For if he does these things he may be writing controversy—without the candor of the avowed controversialist; or journalism—without the professional competence of the journalist. He is not writing history.

5. *On Nationalism and Revolution*

In our permissive age we pride ourselves on a freedom of speech in which all the restrictions on discussion and criticism have disappeared. In fact, however, our freedom is not as great as we would like to believe. It is true that religion and sex are now deprived of the protection which they once enjoyed and have become so free that blasphemy and obscenity have lost their force, and those who seek outrage must find or invent new outlets. On the other hand the great political and social myths of our time still enjoy a surprising measure of protection. These are the beliefs which guide and inspire what may be called the liberal establishment. To deny them, even to question them, can involve risks to status, career, and even, in some academic circles, to personal safety. One of the most important myths of our time is the demiurgic struggle between imperialism and nationalism, ending in the triumph of the latter, a struggle which is never completed but always in need of ritual re-enactment.

It is therefore with a sense of shock that one finds Professor Kedourie, in his long and brilliant introduction to his collection of texts on nationalism,* adopting an attitude of what might be called ideological agnosticism. Professor Kedourie does not believe in the primacy of economic causes; he is not convinced of the diabolic origin of imperialism, and he even harbors doubts about the virgin birth of Afro-Asian nationalist movements.

Professor Kedourie begins his discussion with an analysis of imperialism, the evil to which nationalism is said to have been a reaction. After briefly reviewing the earlier history and usage

* *Nationalism in Asia and Africa.* Edited by Elie Kedourie. (London, 1971)

of the term he examines the economic definition of imperialism given by J. A. Hobson and later elaborated and made famous by Lenin. Since then their definition of imperialism—the subjugation and exploitation of colonial peoples for the benefit of investors and, behind them, of financiers in the metropolis—has been generally accepted, even by many whose political philosophies and purposes are very remote from those of Lenin or Hobson. Professor Kedourie questions the commonly accepted axiom, and succeeds with surprisingly little difficulty in demonstrating its falsity. European activities in Africa and Asia were in origin primarily commercial; their subsequent development into imperial domination owed little to economic and financial interests. Professor Kedourie sees imperialism as basically a political force, determined by political, military, and sometimes cultural factors. Political domination and economic exploitation both existed, but the causal connection between them is the product of what Professor Kedourie calls "ideological and mystificatory" arguments.

Just as imperialism was not primarily an economic domination, so nationalism was not primarily an economic revolt, and currently popular explanations of the rising of the deprived and dispossessed against exploitation are equally "mystificatory". Imperial rule, Professor Kedourie argues, with all its defects, has in most cases brought much of value, both material and cultural, to the subject peoples, and if domination brought gain to the rulers, it also benefited the ruled. The immense influence and authority of the imperialist powers of Western Europe can be seen even in the manner in which their rule was opposed. In the eyes of Asian and African nationalists European civilization was inherently evil—yet every nation in Asia or Africa, in its own nationalist historiography, somehow claims the credit for having created that evil.

In Professor Kedourie's view not imperialism, but nationalism itself is the great Western offense against the Afro-Asian world. This doctrine is an essentially Western importation, which runs counter to the experience and realities of most of these countries. The introduction of these ideas and the attempt to remold polities and societies in accordance with them have brought immense harm to the peoples of Asia and Africa. In the course of this revolt against European domination, the old order has perished, but no new one has emerged.

European expansion, with the inevitable pressure of stronger on weaker societies, brought grave disturbance. "This pulverisation of traditional societies, this bursting open of self-sufficient economies could not fail to bring about in those who were subject to this process a serious and distressing psychological strain." The old order was disrupted, the old relationships undermined, and the individual, stripped of his traditional supports and loyalties, was impelled to an essentially European aspiration for intellectual, moral and economic independence. Failure to achieve this gives rise to feelings of "inadequacy and bewilderment" which sooner or later "erupt in violent and destructive action". Europe herself provides the ideas to express and direct this discontent; the imperial achievement of widespread literacy secures their rapid and extensive dissemination. Professor Kedourie asks why Europe has failed where Greece and Rome succeeded, in creating a new imperial civilization. He finds the explanation in the refusal of the European imperial masters—notably the British in India—to accept their assimilated imperial subjects as, in the last analysis, their equals. A Spanish or a Syrian provincial could rise to the highest office, even that of emperor, in Rome. The British in India refused to admit even Anglicized and loyal Indians to complete equality with themselves. In this refusal, in the mistrust which gave rise to it, and in the anguish and resentment which it engendered, Professor Kedourie sees the failure of imperialism and the beginnings of modern nationalism.

Professor Kedourie begins his series of excerpts from the writers of Asian and African nationalist movements with a passage from the great Greek scholar and patriot Adamantios Koraes. That a discussion of Afro-Asian nationalism should begin with Greece may seem at first strange, but it is right, for the Greeks were the first people outside Western Europe to accept the nationalist vision of identity and their place in history, and to try to give it political expression. This is followed by extracts from writers in Turkey, the Arab countries, India,

China, Africa, the Asian peoples of the Soviet Union and the Blacks of the Western hemisphere.

One of the themes discussed by Professor Kedourie and exemplified in his extracts is what he calls secular millenarianism. This, under the fashionable name of revolution, forms the theme of Mr Gerassi's very different collection.* For Professor Kedourie nationalism, with or without its millenarian aspects, is a false religion, which has brought untold suffering to mankind and of which Arabs and Jews, Indians and Pakistanis are equally the victims. For Mr Gerassi, revolutionary doctrine of almost any kind is the true faith of the redeemer. While Professor Kedourie offers us a collection of specimens for analysis, Mr Gerassi provides a canon of scriptures for our instruction. They are of varied provenance, including governmental statement of policy, the personal views of revolutionary leaders including that modern paradigm of the martyred god Che Guevara, and a number of passages from the manifestos of organizations, some of major importance, others enjoying in their own countries the status and influence of the SPGB in Britain. The Asian peoples of the Soviet Union are not represented. All the authors, except Lenin, have been edited and condensed. There are introductions to each section and a general introduction to the book as a whole. The flavor and quality of these may be judged from the following excerpts, the first from the general introduction, the second from the introduction to the section on Palestine:

> Freedom is not the right to say or do anything you want that does not infringe on [sic] the freedom of others. Freedom means having the material and psychological *power* to say or do that thing. Freedom is the real possibility of being relevant, of being meaningful, of being total.

> The governments of Jordan, Saudi Arabia, Kuwait and the Arab Gulf are feudal-fascist governments who are just as close to imperialism as is Israel. The Lebanese régime is run by a commercial and banking bourgeoisie in partnership with and dependent upon imperialism. The governments of Egypt, Syria and Iraq are petty-bourgeois—a class that, because it came to power without revolutionary struggle (via *coups d'état*)

* *Towards Revolution:* Vol. i, *China, India, Asia, the Middle East, Africa;* Vol. ii, *The Americas.* Edited by John Gerassi. (London, 1971)

has no revolutionary consciousness (but lots of revolutionary sounding rhetoric). In all these countries the masses are agitated. They want or need a socialist revolution.

That "want or need" sums it up beautifully.

Lenin once remarked that "the capitalists will sell us the rope with which to hang them". Capitalist publishers do not sell rope, but they are willing to supply, at a price, a manual on how to do the job. However, the danger is not great. Few genuine revolutionaries in Asia, Africa or Latin America can afford a ten-guinea revolutionist's manual. And no one hanged with rope of this quality is likely to come to much harm.

II

MUSLIM HISTORY AND HISTORIANS

6. *Sources for the Economic History of the Middle East*

The economic historian, even more than his colleagues in other fields of historical inquiry, has a liking for documentary evidence—a marked tendency to prefer archives to annals and other literature. The historian will of course be aware of the insights and even information that books can give him, and he will appreciate the relevance to his researches of the image of a society as reflected in the works of its authors and compilers. But whenever possible he will direct his main attention to the contemporary and immediate evidence or traces of historical events, in their original form, not as transmitted—and therefore transmuted—by a literary intermediary. The modern economic historian relies very largely on published and unpublished documentary and statistical materials. In the West, even the medievalist has at his disposal a mass of records, public and private, lay and ecclesiastical, central and local, on which to base his study of economic structures and economic change.

One of the classical difficulties of the historian of Islam is the lack of such evidence.[1] Without entering into the complex theoretical and philosophical problems of periodization, we may, for practical purposes, divide the history of the Middle East since the rise of Islam into three periods, defined by the availability and quality of documentary sources, and describe them by the neutral terms early, middle and late. In the late period, which in most areas begins in the 19th century and continues to our own day, our knowledge is enriched—if that is the right word—by the multifarious bureaucratic activities of the state and of other agencies. Research into the recent economic history of the Middle East can be based on material similar in form, if less so in content, to that appearing in other parts of the modern world, and can be pursued by similar techniques. Which parts, and which techniques, are for the researcher to determine, and it is possible that in time students of some Middle Eastern countries will develop a particular technique of their own, analogous to those used by specialists in other regions where only published plans, reports and statistics are available, and where these pose distinctive problems of acceptance and evaluation.

The middle period, corresponding roughly to what European historians call early modern history, is also illustrated by archives, though of a different—an early modern—kind. The most important by far is the Ottoman archives, the existence and range of which in effect define this period. Apart from the major collections in Istanbul, there are others in Ankara and in a number of Turkish provincial cities. Archival collections, of varying types and sizes, have also survived in Egypt and Tunisia, and in some of the former Ottoman lands in Europe and Asia. The Ottoman archives have already given rise to a considerable literature, much of it concerned with economic matters.[2]

In other parts of the region the position is much less satisfactory. There are Ottoman records for those provinces of Persia and Transcaucasia which for a time were incorporated in the Ottoman Empire;[3] for the rest of Persia, no archives have so far come to light. Outside the areas under Ottoman rule or suzerainty, there is only one region for which archives are known to exist. This consists of the Muslim Khanates of Central Asia, incorporated in the Russian Empire between 1865 and 1887. State archives and some private archives, dating for the most part from the period immediately preceding the Russian conquest, were preserved by the conquerors, and contain data on land-tenure, taxation, and related matters.[4]

In addition to these, there are two other groups of archives, of considerable but unequal interest to the economic historian. The first, and smaller group, consists of records preserved among the non-Muslim communities within the Muslim world. These, by virtue of their coherence and institutional structure, often enjoyed a continuity lacking in the larger and more fragmented Muslim society, and were thus able to accumulate and preserve records over long periods of time. The best known are the Armenian monastery of Ečmiadzin and the Greek Orthodox St Catherine's monastery in Mount Sinai, the documents of which have recently been studied and, in part, edited. Christian and Jewish ecclesiastical and communal archives exist in various centers, but have so far been little explored.[5] Published documents deal, among other things, with such familiar topics as the assessment and collection of taxes, land-tenure, and disputes of various kinds, usually over money or property.

The second, and very much larger, group consists of the archives of foreign governments, trading companies, religious orders, and other bodies that have been involved in or concerned with the Middle East—first in the Italian states, then Austria, Russia, the countries of Western Europe, especially Britain and France, and latterly also the U.S.A. These countries contain rich archive collections, almost all of which are freely open to researchers.

The Ottoman archives begin in the 15th century, and become really full in the 16th. For earlier periods of Middle Eastern history, and for areas outside the Ottoman Empire, there are, with certain limited exceptions, no archives at all.

This does not mean that there are no documents. Considerable numbers of documents have in fact survived, and may be found in public and private collections. But these collections are not archives; they are fortuitous assemblages of individual documents, discovered by chance and distributed haphazard, with no order other than that imposed on them by curators, editors, and historians. Their value may be very great, but it can never be the same as that of a genuine record office in which documents are preserved in their original form, order, and sequence, as they emerged from the work and served the needs of the institution that created them. Much of the value of such records lies in their comprehensiveness, continuity and cohesion. That such archives existed in medieval Islam is clear from the literary sources, but they have not survived. Archives are created and maintained for administrative use, not for the convenience of historians. The states of the medieval West survived and developed into the states of the modern West, and their archives, often still current, were preserved until a time when their historical importance was appreciated. This political continuity facilitated the survival of many other, local, institutions and the consequent conservation of their records. The church was another major element of stability and continuity, and the well-preserved and well-protected records of ecclesiastical offices and foundations are an invaluable source of information for the economic historian. The states of the medieval Middle East, with the exception of the Ottoman Empire, were destroyed, and their archives, ceasing to serve any practical purpose, were neglected, scattered and lost. Islam had no church, and the character of Islamic society did not favor the emergence of corporative bodies below government level, of such a type and of such duration as to produce and conserve records.

There are some exceptions to the statement, frequently repeated and generally accepted, that there are no archives for medieval Islamic history. The most important of these exceptions have already been mentioned—the archives of foreign and of minority institutions. These are naturally less plentiful than for the Ottoman period, but still contain much that is of interest. Italian and Spanish archives contain many documents relating to commerce, including a number in Arabic, which have received historically disproportionate attention from orientalists. Even the documents from St Catherine's, reflecting the concerns of the monks and their dealings with the outside world, are not without economic interest. They include rulings from the Egyptian chancery on disputes between the monks and their Bedouin neighbors, who claimed a share of their lands and crops (wheat, barley and fruit), and replies to appeals from the monks for the remission of taxes, tolls and services.

Another exception is the pre-Ottoman material preserved in the Ottoman archives, most of it, unfortunately, in Ottoman copies or adaptations. Ottoman policy in a newly conquered province was usually very conservative and normally maintained, at least for a while, the existing fiscal and administrative practice. The Ottomans also recognized existing *waqf*, and the *waqf* registers compiled after the Ottoman conquest of Syria include many *waqfs* of the Mamlūk and even of the Ayyūbid period. The administration of *waqf*, together with other matters arising out of the application of the holy law, also gave rise to small groups of pre-Ottoman documents that have been preserved in the Ministry of *Waqf* and the court of personal affairs in Cairo.[6]

The European archives are often of considerable size and importance, but, in view of their external origin, are inevitably limited in the range of information which they can offer. Such Middle Eastern archives as survive, from the pre-Ottoman period, are vestigial and restricted, and have on the whole been of more interest for diplomatics than for history.

In the absence of genuine archives, the surviving documents, despite their non-archival character, acquire considerable importance. There are several categories of such documents; most of them come from Egypt, where the dry climate on the one hand, and a relatively high degree of political continuity on the other, favored their preservation.

The first important group consists of some tens of thousands of miscellaneous documents and fragments, all but a few of them from Egypt, and written, for the most part, during the first four centuries of Islam. Some are in Greek, some in Arabic, some bilingual. A few are in other languages. They are known collectively as "the papyri", from the material on which they are written, and the special branch of scholarship concerned with their study is called papyrology.[7] This terminology, as Professor Claude Cahen has remarked, is unfortunate, and conveys a somewhat misleading impression of the scope and purposes of these studies. "In reality, papyrology, when it is concerned with mere deciphering, is a branch of palaeography; when interpretation is involved, it is exclusively a branch of history."[8] In fact, there has been a tendency to make a distinction—which for the historian is of no importance—between documents written on papyrus and documents written on paper, and to neglect the latter; there has also been undue separation between the study of Greek and of Arabic papyri, even where both date from the Islamic period and deal with similar topics.

Despite these limitations, and some others arising from the predominantly philological character of scholarship in this field, the study of the papyri has already significantly altered the accepted view of early Islamic history. Many of the papyri are administrative and financial documents. A comparison of these with similar documents from the late Byzantine period shows greater continuity and less change than was previously believed; a comparison of the evidence of the papyri with juristic expositions reveals the latter to be schematic and anachronistic, and has led to a perhaps rather exaggerated reaction from the earlier habit of complete reliance on such sources.

In the work that has so far been done on the papyri, the main attention has been given to the workings of government—to such matters as provincial administration, the assessment and collection of taxes, land surveys and accountancy, the administration of justice, the recruitment, equipment and supply of the armed forces. Much of this has an obvious relevance to economic history. Documents relating to the navy, for example, include information concerning the employment of skilled and unskilled labor in the shipyards, the supply of timber, nails, ropes and other materials to them, and the provision of food for the sailors and workers. In addition, there are numerous other papyri, of both official and private origin, dealing with the transfer of commodities by purchase, requisition or taxation, the employment of labor for wages or by *corvée*, and similar topics. After the pioneer work of Karabacek, Becker and Bell, published work on the papyri has, in the main, taken the form of editions, translations and evaluations of individual documents or groups of documents, with some work on administration, taxation, and law. The systematic use of the papyri by economic historians is still at a very rudimentary stage; given the unsystematic character of the evidence, and the arduous philological apprenticeship required for its study, this situation may well persist.

During the 10th century papyrus gradually went out of use, and was replaced, even in Egypt, by paper. Documents on paper, apparently of the same types as the papyri, have survived in considerable numbers. Not being papyri, these have been almost entirely disregarded by orientalist scholarship, and little is known about their range and content.

One important group of papers, also of Egyptian provenance, has received serious attention. These are the documents from the so-called *Geniza*, the repositories in which the Jews of Cairo placed written papers which were no longer required, to protect the name of God, which might occur in them, from desecration.[9] Leaving aside literary manuscripts and "mere scraps", the number of whole documents and self-contained fragments in the *Geniza* has been estimated by Professor S. D. Goitein at about 10,000. These date mainly from the Fāṭimid and Ayyūbid periods, with a small number from Mamlūk times. There is in addition *Geniza* material of the Ottoman period, which has not so far been used.

Like the papyri, the *Geniza* documents are subject to certain limitations. They are not archival; they all come from Egypt—and they are further limited, by their Jewish provenance, to such matters as concerned the members of one religious minority. The first of these limitations, the non-archival character of the documents, is of major importance and severely restricts the use that can be made of data on such matters as prices and wages, in the *Geniza* as in the papyri. The other limitations, though serious, are less so than would at first appear. The papyri, largely of governmental origin and concerned with such very local matters as taxation and provincial administration, tell us little about conditions outside Egypt; apart from the very few papyri found in South-west Asia,[10] the best they can offer is comparative material, which may occasionally be of use in elucidating data obtained from other sources. The *Geniza* includes documents of governmental origin, but the greater and most valuable part, for the economic historian, is of private origin—business and family correspondence, accounts, receipts, contracts and other commercial documents, and legal deeds and reports of various kinds. The commercial and social relations reflected in these documents are by no means limited to Egypt, but extend westwards to the Mediterranean lands, eastward to India.[11] They provide fuller information on the life and activities of the commercial classes in medieval Egypt that is available from any other source.

No third group of documents, comparable in scale and importance with the papyri and the *Geniza*, has so far been brought to light. Many documents exist, however, of which only a small proportion have been studied. As in the earlier periods, Egypt is the richest source. Besides the papyri, large numbers of Egyptian documents written on paper, and dating from the 10th century onwards, are kept in public collections; some 28,000 are reported in Vienna alone.[12] These documents, said to be of the same general type as the papyri, have hardly been touched by modern scholarship. A small group of documents from Damascus, discovered by D. and J. Sourdel, include some deeds of sale dated 310/922–3, the title-deeds of an estate, dated 604/1207–8, and a letter announcing the restoration of property previously confiscated by the sovereign.[13]

After Egypt, Iran and the neighboring lands in Transcaucasia and Central Asia provide the most important non-archival collections of documents. Original Persian documents from the pre-Mongol period are very few indeed. The earliest is a private letter from a Jewish merchant, written in Persian in Hebrew characters, possibly in the 8th century. It was found near Khotan. Others include a Judaeo-Persian law report of 1020 from Ahwāz, a deed for the sale of land, dated 501/1107, from the region of Khotan (?), and a group of six documents from Bāmyān of which one is dated 607/1211.[14] There are rather more documents from the period of the Il-Khāns and their successors, but it is not until the time of the Ṣafavids that we find them in any great numbers. Those that have already been found, in public and private collections in Iran and elsewhere, include many that deal with fiscal, commercial and other matters of economic interest.[15]

Besides all these, two other groups of documents have survived in the Middle East, because they were written on metal and on stone. Coins and inscriptions are available in great numbers, and have been extensively studied by numismatists and epigraphers.[16] The documentary information inscribed on coins is inevitably meager and repetitive, but even such modest data as the year and mint of issue can usefully contribute to the inferences drawn from the weight and metallic composition of coins, and from the place, quantity and company in which they are found. Probably the best known example is the series of hoards, containing many thousands of Muslim silver *dirhams*, that have been found in the countries around the Baltic, and especially on the Swedish island of Gotland, then an important commercial center. These coins come mainly from Iraqi, Persian, and Central Asian mints, and carry dates ranging from the turn of the 7th/8th century to the early 11th century. Until about the middle of the 10th century, the coins found in these hoards consist almost exclusively of Muslim *dirhams*. From the second half of the 10th century, the hoards include a growing proportion of other coins, Byzantine, West European, even Anglo-Saxon. Towards the middle of the 11th century Muslim coins disappear entirely from these silver hoards. These hoards, together with similar finds in Poland and Russia, especially in the regions of Kazan and Kiev, on the one hand, and in Western Europe on the other, have given rise to a vast literature on the trade between the Muslim lands and the North.[17] The problem, as Professor Tadeusz Lewicki has remarked, is still anything but clarified.[18]

Islamic inscriptions are extant in great numbers, with a very wide range of countries and periods of origin. Their range of content is, however, disappointingly narrow. One of the greatest of Arabic epigraphers, Max van Berchem, remarked that almost all of them "are centered on one of the two predominant ideas in the Muslim world: divine power and absolute political authority. On the one hand, the Koran, invocations, and pious phrases, confessions of faith, mystical allusions, and prayers for the dead; on the other hand, the names of the sovereign, his titles, exploits, and his perpetual praise."[19] Though some of us may wish to dissent from the particulars of Van Berchem's formulation, we must surely agree with his conclusion, that the inscriptions of Islam have far less documentary value than those of Greek and Roman antiquity. "In this world," said Benjamin Franklin in a famous phrase, "nothing can be said to be certain, except death and taxes."

The Muslim inscriptions may be said to reflect a parallel preoccupation with the two ultimate certainties, but differently expressed—as God and the government. It is at the point of contact or conflict between these two concerns that the inscriptions are most informative. Two groups of inscriptions are of particular interest to the economic historian. The first consists of the texts or summaries of *waqf* deeds, inscribed on pious foundations, to protect the service of God from the depredations of the state; the second deals with taxes, tolls and levies of various kinds—usually in the form of the pious abolition of illegal taxes by a pious new ruler.[20] Though never, as far as can be seen from the record, reimposed, these illegal taxes are re-abolished with monotonous frequency. Between the papyri and the Ottoman archives, inscriptions provide the best documentary evidence concerning taxation. Also of interest are the inscriptions on metrological objects (weights, coin-weights, measure-stamps, vessel-stamps, tokens), and trade-marks or certificates on manufactured articles, especially textiles and metalwork.[21]

For the second and third of the three periods we have considered, the economic historian of the middle East, apart from some problems of physical and linguistic access to documents, is not significantly worse off than his European colleague—indeed, he may find that the Ottoman archives offer material of a wealth and diversity not found elsewhere. For the first, or medieval, period, however, the documentary evidence available to him is very much poorer. In compensation, he has at his disposal a body of literary material of incomparable richness, "larger perhaps than any other civilization has produced until modern times."[22]

It would be pointless to attempt a survey of the literary sources for the economic history of the Middle East, which potentially include the whole vast literature of the area. It may, however, be useful to look at certain classes of writings, and to consider the type of information that they offer.

The first group of texts to be considered are those that deal directly and explicitly with economic questions, both theoretical and practical. The earliest prescriptive statements are in the Qur'ān itself, notably in the final pages of *Sūrat al-Baqara*. "God has permitted buying and selling, and forbidden usury . . . . O you who believe! Be pious towards God, and forgo what is owing to you from usury, if you are believers. If you do not do this, then expect war from God and the Prophet, but if you renounce [usury], your capital will remain with you, and you will neither inflict nor suffer injury."[23] Other passages confirm the lawfulness of honest trading, and touch on such matters as fair weights and measures, debts, contracts, and the like.[24]

Qur'ānic approval of buying and selling is amplified in a large number of sayings, attributed to the Prophet and to the leading figures of early Islam, in praise of the honest merchant and of commerce as a way of life. Some sayings go further, and defend the more expensive commodities which the honest merchants sold—such as silks and brocades, jewels, male and female slaves, and other luxuries. "When God gives wealth to a man," the Prophet is improbably quoted as saying, "He wants it to be seen on him." Even more striking is a story told in an early Shī'ite work. The Imām Ja'far al-Ṣādiq, it is said, was reproached by one of his disciples for wearing fine apparel (a variant says: clothes from Marw), while his ancestors had worn rude, simple garments. The Imām is quoted as replying that his ancestors had lived in a time of scarcity, while he lived in a time of plenty, and that it was proper to wear the clothing of one's own time.[25] These and similar attempts to justify luxurious living mark a reaction against the strain of asceticism in Islam, and no doubt reflect the interests of the luxury trades.

As in many other fields, the earliest known Muslim work on economic ethics consists very largely of a collection of sayings attributed to the Prophet and the early heroes of Islam entitled *Kitāb al-Kasb*, "On earning"; it was written by a Syrian of Iraqi *mawlā* ancestry called Muḥammad al-Shaybānī, who died in 804.[26] Shaybānī's purpose is to show that earning a livelihood is not merely permitted, but is incumbent on Muslims. Man's primary duty is to serve God, but to do this properly he must be adequately fed, housed and clothed. This can only be achieved by working and earning. Nor need his earnings be limited to providing for the bare necessities of life, since the acquisition and use of luxuries is also permitted.

Another point which Shaybānī is anxious to make is that money earned by commerce or crafts is more pleasing in God's eyes than money received from the government, for civil or military service. The same point is argued by al-Jāḥiẓ (d. 869) in an essay entitled "In praise of merchants and in condemnation of officials,"[27] and is echoed by many later writers. Jāḥiẓ stresses the security, dignity and independence of merchants in contrast with the uncertainty, humiliation and sycophancy of those who serve the ruler, and defends the piety and the learning of merchants against their detractors.

The discussion in ethical and religious terms of gainful employment, usually equated with commerce and crafts, was continued by a number of subsequent writers, occasionally in separate works, more frequently within the framework of more extensive treatises.[28] A 10th-century encyclopaedic work of Ismā'īlī inspiration includes a detailed survey of arts and crafts, classified in several different ways—by the materials they use, by the tools and movements they require and by "rank". Under the last heading crafts are divided into three main groups: The first, or primary, group provides basic necessities, and is subdivided into three subgroups—weaving, agriculture and building, providing the three basic needs for clothing, food and shelter. The second, or "ancillary", group consists of accessory and finishing trades, ancillary to the first. The third main group is concerned with luxuries such as silks, brocades and perfumes. A final cross-classification is by the "merit" of the crafts, which may derive from their indispensability, as agriculture; their precious materials, as jewellery; their skilled workmanship, as the making of astronomical instruments; their public utility, as the work of bath-attendants and scavengers, or, finally, the nobility of the craft itself, as painting and music.[29]

It would be easy to assemble other traditions, and writings of ascetic tendency, that say just the opposite and condemn commerce and those engaged in it. It is, however, noteworthy that centuries before Christian writers were prepared to defend and define the ethics of commerce against ascetic criticism, Muslim writers were willing to do so, and that even a major theologian like al-Ghazzālī (d. 1111) could include, in his religious writings, a portrait of the ideal merchant and a defense of commerce as a way of preparing oneself for the world to come.[30]

Besides religious writings on commerce, there are others, of a more practical nature. The best known is the *Kitāb al-Ishāra ilā maḥāsin al-tijāra* (Indication of the merits of commerce) written in the 11th or 12th century by Abū'l Faḍl Ja'far b. 'Alī al-Dimashqī. Greek philosophic influences are already apparent in the 10th-century encyclopaedia cited above. They appear again in al-Dimashqī's treatise, in a more specifically economic form—from Plato's *Politics*, Aristotle's doctrine of the golden mean and, in particular, the *Oikonomos* of the neo-Pythagorean "Bryson".

For al-Dimashqī, gain is a good thing for its own sake. Though he includes some theoretical and moralistic discussion, his main purpose is to provide practical guidance for merchants. He discusses, among other topics, the types, qualities and prices of merchandise, the roles of the three classes of merchants, the wholesaler *(khazzān)*, the exporter *(mujahhiz)*, and the traveling merchant *(rakkāḍ)*, the dangers of fraud and waste, and various problems such as the appointment of agents, the obtaining of information about market prices, the fixing of prices, the delivery of goods, and financial and commercial administration.[31]

Even more practical are works dealing with specific problems. "A Clear Look at Trade" *(al-Tabaṣṣur bi'l-tijāra)*, probably written in 9th-century Iraq, discusses the qualities, values and ways of evaluating gold, silver, pearls and precious stones, scents and aromatics, textiles, skins and other commodities, and lists the goods imported from the provinces of the Islamic Empire and from foreign countries.[32] An 11th-century author wrote "On the purchase of slaves"—a sort of slave-trader's vade-mecum, with a classification of slaves by race and country of origin and much fascinating information on the slave-trade in all its stages. This work is also, incidentally, a useful source for the history of Africa.[33] A common theme of the practical handbooks is the need for precautions against swindlers and fakers, whose methods are often described in fascinating detail.

A 13th-century Syrian author devotes a whole book to the subject of trickery and fraud. Beginning with false prophets, spurious priests, thaumaturges, alchemists, astrologers, mountebanks and the like, the author goes on to discuss the distinctive malpractices of dishonest grocers, cooks, horse-copers, money-changers, physicians and other trades and professions.[34]

Farmers seem to have been less articulate—or less represented in book-writing circles—than merchants. There is, however, a literature on agriculture, which deserves more attention than it has received. The earliest known work is the so-called "Nabataean Agriculture" *(al-Filāḥa al-nabaṭiyya)* written or translated into Arabic by Ibn Waḥshiyya in 291/904, and purporting to convey the agronomic knowledge of the pre-Arab inhabitants of Iraq. It was followed by a parallel compendium of Greek agronomy, *al-Filāḥa al-rūmiyya,* translated into Arabic from a Greek original. These and other, later, works deal with the different types and qualities of land, with agricultural implements and methods of work, with fertilizers, irrigation, animal and vegetable pests, and with the various problems of planting, tending and reaping crops, including cereals, vegetables, bulbs, fruits and flowers for perfume.[35]

Mining and metallurgy also received some attention. The South Arabian antiquary Ibn al-Ḥā'ik al-Hamdānī (d. 945) devoted a book to gold and silver, including a list of places from which they are obtained, with some information about the mines, and an account of the methods used in mining, smelting and assaying.[36] A 13th-century Egyptian mint official, Ibn Ba'ra, deals more specifically with the use of gold and silver for coinage. Besides much technical detail, he also offers useful information on monetary matters.[37]

A very rich source of information on economic matters is the vast bureaucratic and administrative literature of medieval Islam. Written by civil servants for civil servants, these works vary from manuals dealing with the working of one office or official to immense encyclopaedias of bureaucratic usage and procedure. A major concern of these writers is of course finance —revenue, financial administration, expenditure. The information they offer is by no means limited to the financial activities of the state. Discussions of tolls and customs-dues tell us something about trade and industry; works on the land-tax throw some light on agrarian conditions. To quote one rather striking example, an 11th-century handbook of mathematics written for the use of tax-assessors in Iraq deals with problems of money, wages, and prices, with trade and manufactures (work in gold, gold thread, fine stuffs) and with both the technical and administrative aspects of irrigation.[38]

Taxation and the regulation of commerce also take up much space in another major branch of Muslim literature—that of the law. At one time the jurists were treated with excessive respect, and their statements taken as a sufficient description of the functioning of Muslim institutions. A reaction followed, in the course of which scholars remarked that lawyers in general are concerned with what ought to be rather than with what is, and that Muslim lawyers in particular are inclined to construct ideal systems which may have little to do with the real facts of life. Recent scholars have adopted a more balanced attitude, neither accepting the statements in the law books at face value, nor rejecting them out of hand. Muslim law has not been static; it has undergone a long and complex development. A careful scrutiny of juristic texts can produce valuable information on the changing conditions, pressures and influences to which the jurists were subject.[39] Another body of legal material, of considerable value, is the Jewish Responsa—the answers given by rabbis to questions put to them. Many of these deal with matters of economic interest—disputes arising out of trade, manufacture, employment, partnerships, tenancies, inheritances and the like. The Rabbinic Responsa are very rich for the Ottoman period, and by no means negligible for earlier times.[40]

Most other branches of the scientific and scholarly literature of the area are potentially relevant—military writings, chemistry and physics, religion—especially heresiography and hagiography, geography, even philology. Among the most important are works of narrative history and biography. The value of the chronicles is self-evident. Of special value are the numerous local histories, which frequently record in detail such things as floods, earthquakes, famine and plague, as well as scarcities and gluts, harvests, market prices, and other data of economic interest. Useful information, independent of the Muslim historiographic tradition, may also be found in the chronicles and other literature of the Christian populations under Muslim rule.[41]

Biography offers particular promise and interest. In the biographical appendices to the annals, in the largely biographical local histories, and in the biographical dictionaries arranged by centuries or devoted to certain professions and other groups, Muslim literature offers us a great treasure-house of information for social, cultural and economic history. The possible contribution of these biographies to narrative history is obvious; less obvious, but far more important, is the cumulative value of these tens of thousands of life-histories, many of them of men of no great individual significance, in building up a picture of the society in which these men were born and educated, lived and died. In recent years, Western historians have made increasing use of the method of prosopography—that is, the approach to the study of historical phenomena through the examination and comparison of as many as possible relevant individual facts concerning as many as possible individual participants. This method, like any other, has its dangers and its limitations. It also has tremendous potentialities, especially for a society like that of Islam, where the mass of available biographical information goes far beyond the customary restricted oligarchies of power and privilege.[42]

Finally, there remains the vast mass of poetry and *belles lettres*, from which the historian can gather and piece together the countless fragments of information that he needs. The poet, in traditional Islamic society, often has an important public function. The political function of the poet—and the consequent political relevance of poetry—is well known. The economic uses of poetry are less explored. Two final examples, both from the Arabic Book of Songs *(Kitāb al-Aghānī)* must suffice. An Umayyad governor of Iraq, in the 8th century, forcibly expropriated a piece of land, needed for the extension of the irrigation system. The famous poet Farazdaq, on behalf of the landowner, composed a poem attacking the governor and accusing him of oppression. The second story also comes from Umayyad times. A merchant went from Kūfa to Medina with a consignment of veils, and sold all but the black ones, which the ladies apparently did not like. He complained to a poet, who obliged him by composing some verses, in which he spoke of his love for "the beauty in the black veil". The poem was set to music and sung all over Medina, every lady of refinement *(ẓarīfa)* bought a black veil, and the Iraqi merchant sold his entire stock. Thus, in a dark hour, with a black veil, the singing commercial was born.[43]

7. The Muslim Discovery of Europe

I suppose that most textbooks of European history or of world history—which in European textbooks is much the same thing—contain a chapter called "The Age of the Discoveries", or something of the kind, which deals with the period from the 15th century onwards when Western Europe set about discovering the rest of the world. My subject is another and earlier discovery, in which the West European was not the explorer going forth to discover the barbarian, but the barbarian discovered by the explorer—the Muslim explorer. My purpose is to outline, very briefly, the sources, nature, and stages of growth of Muslim knowledge concerning Western Europe, first in the obscure centuries before the Crusades, then during that great offensive of Western Christendom against Islam, of which the expeditions to Palestine were the easternmost expression.[1]

In the year 1068—that is, 30 years before the first Crusade, but after the Christian advance in Spain and Sicily was already under way—Ṣā'id ibn Aḥmad, Qāḍī of Toledo, wrote a book in Arabic on the categories of nations. He divides the nations of humanity into two kinds: those that have concerned themselves with science, and those that have not. The first group consists of the Indians, Persians, Chaldees, Greeks, Romans (including Byzantines and Eastern Christians), Egyptians, Arabs, and Jews. Of the remainder of humanity, he singles out the Chinese and the Turks as "the noblest of the unlearned nations", who are worthy of respect for their achievements in other fields. The rest of mankind Ṣā'id dismisses contemptuously as the northern and southern barbarians, of Frankish Europe and of Negro Africa.[2]

In this he was expressing the generally accepted view of Muslim scholars of his time. The centre of the world was the lands of Islam, stretching from Spain across North Africa to the Middle East, and containing almost all the peoples and centers of ancient civilization. To the north, the Christian Empire of Byzantium represented an earlier, arrested stage of that civilization, based on divine revelation, which had reached its final and complete form in Islam. To the east, beyond Persia, there were countries which had achieved some sort of civilized living, but of an inferior and idolatrous kind. Apart from that, to the north and to the south, there were only the white and black barbarians of the outer world. It is with the growth of Muslim knowledge of these northern barbarians that we are here concerned.

The first notions of the geographical configuration of Western Europe that have survived in Arabic literature date from the 9th century. They derive largely from Greek sources, and especially from the geography of Ptolemy, which was translated, or rather adapted, into Arabic at the beginning of the 9th century.[3] Soon Muslim scholars began to produce geographical works of their own; though generally they devote little space to so remote and unimportant a region as Western Europe, they do nevertheless illustrate the gradual extension of knowledge.

The first Muslim geographer whose work is extant was Ibn Khurradādhbeh, a Persian who wrote in Arabic towards the middle of the 9th century. He was employed in the state postal service in Persia and Iraq, and his book, like many classical Islamic geographical works, was in part inspired by the needs of that service. It is therefore mainly concerned with the territories under Islamic rule, but deals also with the Byzantine Empire, with which there was a postal link, and even, very briefly, with the remoter parts of Europe.

"The inhabited world," says Ibn Khurradādhbeh, "is divided into four parts: Europe, Libya, Ethiopia, and Scythia." Europe, which he calls Urūfa, consists of "Andalus, the lands of the Slavs, Romans, and Franks, and the country from Tangier to the border of Egypt."[4] On Andalus, then under Muslim rule, he is relatively well informed. On the countries beyond the Pyrenees he writes only a few lines, mentioning the merchants that come from those parts, and the commodities that they bring.

Similar accounts are to be found in the writings of other geographers of the time—though one of them, Ibn Rosteh (d. 910), adds this new detail: "In the northern part of the ocean are 12 islands, called the islands of Braṭīniya. After that one goes away from inhabited country, and no one knows how it is."[5]

All of them mention the city of Rome, of which they have some strange tales to tell. I shall return to these in a moment.

By the 10th century rather fuller information was available among well-informed circles in Baghdad. Thus al-Mas'ūdī (d. 956), far the greatest geographer of his time, was able to attempt a rather unflattering description of the northern peoples, a brief account of "the land of the Franks", and even a short history of its kings from Clovis to Louis IV, based, he tells us, on a book prepared by a Frankish bishop for the Andalusian prince (later Caliph) Al-Ḥakam, in the year 328/939. Mas'ūdī came across a copy of this book in Egypt in 336/947.[6]

From these and other Arabic and Persian writings it is possible to reconstruct some sort of picture of the European scene as it appeared to Muslim eyes before the Crusades. To the north of Muslim Andalusia, in the mountains of northern Spain and the foothills of the Pyrenees, were wild and primitive Christian tribes called Galicians and Basques. In Italy, north of the areas under Muslim control, was the territory of Rome, ruled by a priest-king called the Pope; and beyond it, the realm of a savage people called the Lombards. At the eastern end of the Mediterranean, north of the Muslim frontiers, was the Greek Christian Empire, and beyond that the broad lands of the Slavs. West of the Slavs, stretching all the way to the northern approaches of the Alps and the Pyrenees, was the vast kingdom of Franja, the land of the Franks. Among these, some authorities distinguished another people called the Burjān, or Burgundians. Yet further to the north, beyond the Franks, were the fire-worshipping Majūs or Magians—a name and description which the Arabs had quite arbitrarily transferred from the ancient Persians to the Norsemen. A few names of the remoter northern lands appear in Islamic writings: Britain, sometimes Ireland, and even parts of Scandinavia.

The literary sources of this information were chiefly Greek, probably with some meager additions from Syriac and Persian. As far as we know, only one Western book was actually translated into Arabic in medieval times—the late Latin chronicle of Orosius, dealing with Roman history, which was translated in Spain and was used later by Ibn Khaldūn and Münejjimbashî in their accounts of the Roman Empire.[7] One or two other works may have become known in one way or another, such as the account of the Frankish kings cited by al-Mas'ūdī.

One might have expected some knowledge of Western European affairs to percolate into the Muslim world through direct relations, for, after all, the two civilizations were in immediate contact all the way across the Mediterranean world from Spain through Italy to the Levant. But in fact the medieval iron curtain—if one may use the expression—between Islam and Christendom seems to have kept cultural exchanges at a minimum, and greatly restricted even commercial and diplomatic intercourse. The Muslim world, proud and confident of its superiority, and possessing its own internal lines of communication by land and sea, could afford to despise the barbarous and impoverished infidel in the cold and miserable lands of the north. But there were occasional merchants who crossed the religious frontiers, Christian pilgrims journeying from the West to Jerusalem and from the East to Rome, and sometimes diplomats too. No doubt because they had more leisure to observe and to record their impressions, these last are among our best authorities.

The earliest report we have purporting to describe a Muslim diplomatic mission to the north is the well-known and oft-cited story of the embassy of al-Ghazāl from Cordova to the lands of the Vikings in about 845. The late M. Lévi-Provençal cast doubt on the authenticity of this charming story, suggesting that it is a later fabrication based on an authentic account of al-Ghazāl's mission to Constantinople.[8] If such missions were rarities at the time, there were certainly other embassies besides that of the gallant gazelle. Eginhard, in a famous passage, tells of an exchange of embassies between Charlemagne and

Hārūn al-Rashīd, but it seems to have been of insufficient importance to attract the attention of the Arabic chroniclers, since they make no mention of it.[9] However, they do tell us something of a later Embassy from Bertha, Queen of Rome, to the Caliph al-Muktafī in Baghdad in 906 to offer friendship and even marriage.[10]

The mighty name of Rome was of course known to the Islamic world, though it was usually confused with Byzantium, to which the term *Rūm* was more commonly applied. Some scholars, however, were aware of the existence of a Rome in Italy too. The earliest named visitor to Rome from the Islamic world was Hārūn ibn Yaḥyā, whose description is cited by Ibn Rosteh.[11] Much of his information obviously comes from the collections of wonderful stories that circulated in medieval Rome, and was probably conveyed to him by Christian informants. Similar stories are to be found in the collection assembled by Ibn al-Faqīh (d. 903) and cited—with some reserve—by Yāqūt (d. 1229). They consist chiefly of descriptions of churches, with a great deal of fabulous and legendary matter.[12]

The only Muslim Embassy in medieval times that has really left any serious documentation was one sent from Andalusia in the mid 10th century. One of its members was the famous Ibrāhīm ibn Ya'qūb al-Isrā'īlī, whose account of the Slav lands, as preserved in the geography of Bakrī, has been known and studied since 1878, when it was first edited by Kunik and Rosen. Thanks to the brilliant analysis of the late Thaddeus Kowalski, it is now known that he is identical with the Ibrāhīm al-Ṭurṭūshī, parts of whose description of central, northern, and western Europe were preserved by 'Udhrī and thence cited by the 13th century geographer Qazwīnī.[13] There has been some argument as to the precise date and purpose of Ibrāhīm's visit to Otto, the most likely date being ca. 965. He may have traveled with an embassy sent by the Caliph of Cordova to Otto I, perhaps connected with the latter's embassy to Spain in 953, of which we know from the biography of John of Gorze.[14]

Ibrāhīm's account of France, Germany, and the Slav lands, with all its limitations, was far superior to those of his predecessors, and was made use of by later geographers. It is remarkable that this is the only personal description of Western Europe that we have, by a named traveler from the Islamic world, until the earliest Ottoman Embassy reports in the 17th century. True, there were unnamed pilgrims and merchants who went to Rome, and whose reports did enable Muslim geographers to devote a section to the one city in Europe whose name was known to them. But the Rome of the Muslim geographers is a shadowy, half-mythical place, interesting only because of its memories of the wonders of antiquity, and more often than not confused by Muslim writers with the far more real and immediate Rome that they knew on the shores of the Bosphorus—Constantinople, the capital of the living Roman Empire that was the great neighbor and adversary of Islam. As to the rest of Europe, it was hardly more than a wilderness, offering little interest or attraction to a Muslim visitor. Even the few intrepid travelers whom business or diplomacy took across the border seem to have been mainly Jews or Christians. The Muslim who wished to travel preferred to make his way across the spacious lands of Islam, or perhaps even to venture into the comparatively civilized countries of India and China, rather than brave the dangers and discomforts of darkest Europe.

But if the Mohammedans would not come to Europe, Europe was preparing to come to the Mohammedans. In the course of the 11th century the successive moves of Christian reconquest wrested much of Spain and all of Sicily from the Muslims, and at the end of the century reached out towards the heartlands of Islam. For over 200 years, Franks and Muslims were in close and daily contact with one another in the Levant—often in battle, but often also in trade, in diplomacy, even in alliance. In this period one will expect the Muslims to have more detailed and more accurate knowledge of their European Christian neighbors.

Certainly the Muslims of the 12th, 13th, and 14th centuries knew more about the West than did their predecessors, but we still cannot but be astonished at how little in fact they knew—or cared. What increase there is in their knowledge comes mainly from the Muslim far west—from Andalusian, Moorish, or Sicilian geographers like Idrīsī and Ibn Sa'īd. Idrīsī's geography, completed in 1154 in Norman Sicily, contains, as one would expect, much information on Italy, and also includes detailed descriptions of most of Western Europe. In these chapters Idrīsī pays some attention to earlier Muslim geographical writings, but seems to rely in the main on Western Christian informants and on Western, probably Catalan, maps.[15] His work and the later compilation of Ibn Sa'īd form the basis of most eastern accounts of the Franks. Here and there one has some personal impression of contact with the Franks in Palestine, in such justly famous works as the memoirs of Usāma and the travels of Ibn Jubair, but these are sporadic, exceptional, and without effect on subsequent writers. The eastern Muslim chroniclers have, of course, much to say about the military and political activities of the Crusaders in the East; they show, however, remarkably little interest in the internal affairs of the crusading states, still less in the differences between the various national contingents, and none at all in their countries of origin. The historians hardly ever troubled to correlate their knowledge of the Franks in Syria with the scanty information about Europe available in the writings of the cosmographers, geographers, and travelers. The idea that Frankish religion, philosophy, science, literature, or history might be of any interest hardly seems to have occurred to anyone at all. One striking exception was the great Persian historian Rashīd al-Dīn, who at the beginning of the 14th century included a brief account of Europe and an outline history of the Emperors and Popes in the universal history which he prepared for the Mongol Il-Khan of Persia. It is based, as Professor Jahn has shown, on the chronicle of Martinus Polonus, supplemented by information obtained in all probability from a papal envoy in Persia.[16]

But this venture in "occidentalism", made possible by the brief but significant interval of Mongol contacts with the West, had no successor. Apart from the brief sketch of the early Frankish kings given by Mas'ūdī, it seems to have been the only attempt made by a medieval Muslim historian at an outline of the history of the Christian West. The next was that given by the 17th-century Ottoman chronicler Münejjimbashi.

Even so great and original a thinker as Ibn Khaldūn—himself a native of Tunisia, one of the Muslim lands with most direct experience of the West, shared the general indifference. The second volume of his universal history, dealing with the pre-Islamic and non-Islamic peoples, includes ancient Arabia, Babylon, Egypt, Israel, Persia, Greece, Rome, and Byzantium. In Europe only the Visigoths are mentioned—a brief account of them is necessary as an introduction to the Muslim conquest of Spain, and is part of the tradition of Spanish-Arab historiography. Ibn Khaldūn's universal history did not extend north of Spain nor east of Persia—that is to say, it was limited to his own civilization and its direct predecessors, and thus resembled most of the so-called universal histories written in Europe until very recently. Only in the *Muqaddima* does he allude, very briefly and cautiously, to reports "heard of late" that the philosophic sciences were thriving in Europe. "But God knows best what goes on in those parts."[17] And this is at the end of the 14th century, and from no less a man than Ibn Khaldūn.

The great debate of the Crusades, so significant in Western history, stirred hardly a ripple of curiosity in the lands of Islam. Even the rapid growth of commercial and diplomatic relations with Europe after the Crusades seems to have evoked no desire to penetrate the secrets of the mysterious occident, as may be seen from the scarcity and vagueness of information about Europe in the late medieval chronicles, even in the manuals for chancery scribes.

This general lack of interest in the West is in sharp contrast with the earlier response of Islamic civilization to influences from Greece, from Persia, even from India. Many works were translated into Arabic from Syriac, Greek, and Persian—a few even from remoter languages. But with the solitary exception of the translation of the chronicle of Orosius, not a single translation into a Muslim language is known of any Latin or Western work before the 16th century, when historical works were first translated in Turkey. Nor was there any interest in the languages of Europe. As M. Colin has pointed out, from the whole eight centuries of Muslim Spain there is only one document that has come down to us indicating any sort of interest in a Western language outside the peninsula. It is a very late fragment—no more than a sheet of paper—containing a few German words with their Arabic equivalents. Of the mighty galaxy of scholars and philologists that flourished in Muslim Spain, only one—Abu Ḥayyān of Granada, who died in 1344—is reported to have interested himself in strange languages. He learnt Turkish and Ethiopic.[18]

It may well seem strange that classical Islamic civilization, which in its early days was so much affected by Greek and Eastern influences, should so decisively have rejected the West. But a possible explanation may be suggested. When Islam was still expanding and receptive, Christian Europe had little or nothing to offer, but rather flattered Muslim pride with the spectacle of a culture that was visibly and palpably inferior. What is more, the very fact that it was Christian discredited it in advance. The Muslim doctrine of successive revelations, culminating in the final mission of Muḥammad, led the Muslim to reject Christianity as an earlier and imperfect form of something which he himself possessed in its final and perfect form, and to discount Christian thought and Christian civilization accordingly. After the initial impact of Eastern Christianity on Islam in its earliest period, Christian influences, even from the high civilization of Byzantium, were reduced to a minimum. Later, by the time that the advance of Christendom and the decline of Islam created a new relationship, Islam was crystallized in its ways of thought and behavior, and had become impervious to external stimuli—especially from the millennial adversary in the West. Masked by the imposing military might of the Ottoman Empire, the peoples of Islam continued until the dawn of the modern age to cherish—as many in East and West still do today—the conviction of the immeasurable and immutable superiority of their own civilization to all others. For the medieval Muslim from Andalusia to Persia, Christian Europe was still an outer darkness of barbarism and unbelief, from which the sunlit world of Islam had little to fear and less to learn. It was a point of view which might perhaps have been justified at one time; by the end of the Middle Ages it was becoming dangerously obsolete.

8. The Use by Muslim Historians of Non-Muslim Sources

Herodotus, the father of history, wrote of the "great and wonderful actions" of both Greeks and Barbarians, and pursued his study into the past of alien lands and remote times. Though excluded by the hierophantic mysteries from access to oriental writings, he tried to make good the deficiency by travel and personal inquiry in Eastern lands. Some fifteen centuries later another European, William, Archbishop of Tyre in the states of Outremer, wrote a history of the Islamic Empires. He too sought his information from oriental sources, and, better placed than Herodotus, was even able to read them in the original.[1]

These first European students of oriental history were, however, exceptional. Herodotus, though acclaimed as the father of history, was not accorded the respect of classical historians, most of whom preferred to follow the precept and practice of Thucydides, and limit their concern to the deeds of their contemporaries and compatriots. The medieval European chroniclers were for the most part content to follow their example, and it is no accident that while William of Tyre's history of the Crusaders in the East—the *Historia rerum in partibus transmarinis gestarum*—was widely read and even translated into French, his *Gesta orientalium principum* has not, as far as is known, survived in a single manuscript. It was not until the Renaissance had awakened a new European curiosity and the Discoveries had whetted it with the sight of remote and alien peoples, that European historians began to show interest in other lands and societies, and to seek out and pass on information and opinions about them.[2] This universal historical curiosity is still a distinguishing, almost an exclusive, characteristic of Europe and her daughters. Oriental societies study their own history; perforce they also study the history of the West which has influenced or dominated them. They still show little interest in one another.[3]

The medieval Muslim, like the citizens of most other societies that have appeared among men, was profoundly convinced of the finality, completeness, and essential self-sufficiency of his civilization. Islam was the one true faith, beyond which there were only unbelievers—the Muslim equivalent of the Greek term barbarians. The Islamic state was the one divinely ordained order, beyond which there were only tyranny and anarchy. Universal history was the history of the Islamic community, outside which were lands and peoples whose only interest was as the settings and objects of Muslim action.

These lesser breeds were not unknown to Muslim historiography. Sometimes there were intrepid travelers who ventured among them. With many there were the normal exchanges of commerce, war, and diplomacy. From some there were acknowledged borrowings of useful knowledge and crafts. But none of these led to any interest in the history of the infidel peoples. To fight the Greeks it was necessary to have political and military intelligence; to learn from the Greeks it was useful to have philosophic and scientific training. For neither was there any need to inquire into the history of the Greek past. For centuries the Muslim Caliphate stood face to face with the Byzantine Empire—the House of War *par excellence* of medieval Islam. The Muslim chroniclers have much to say of the war on the frontiers; the Muslim geographers have ample information, probably drawn ultimately from secret service files, on the topography, administration, and strength of the enemy Empire, and even on the scandals of its court and capital. But at no time did they attempt to consult Greek historical sources, or to deal in a connected form with the history of the Greek Empire.

Still more striking is the case of the Crusades. For two centuries the Muslims of the Middle East were in intimate if hostile contact with groups of Franks established among them—yet at no time do they seem to have developed the least interest in them. As Professor Gabrieli has pointed out,[4] the Muslims, unlike the Christians, did not regard the Crusades as something separate and distinctive, nor did they single out the Crusaders from the long series of infidel enemies whom from time to time they fought. The chroniclers report in detail the smallest skirmishes between Muslims and Frankish troops—but they have little to say about the internal affairs of the Frankish states in the Levant, and even less about their countries of origin. The omission is the more remarkable in that the geographers and cosmographers have some information, mostly derived from western Muslim sources, about the Franks and their countries. Yet with one or two minor exceptions, the historians of Islam made no attempt to relate their narrative of the Syrian wars to this information, to trace the invaders back to their countries of origin, or to inquire into the mighty yet invisible movement that had launched them.[5]

The Crusades opened the way to closer diplomatic and commercial relations between the Muslim and Christian states of the Mediterranean. These are reflected in the manuals of civil service usage of the Mamluk period. In the encyclopaedic bureaucratic vade-mecum of Qalqashandī, and similar works, we find lists of the European sovereigns with whom the Sultans of Egypt had corresponded, with the correct names, titles, and forms of address for each, and some allusions to earlier exchanges of letters or embassies. We find nothing about the history of those countries.

All this does not mean that Muslim historians never concerned themselves with non-Muslim history. For the Muslim, the Islamic revelation is not a beginning but a completion, the final link in a chain of revelation—and the Islamic community is thus no new creation, but a revival and improvement of something that had existed long before. The history of Islam therefore did not begin with Muḥammad; it included the history of the earlier prophets and their missions, and something also of the peoples to whom they were sent. The earlier history is chiefly biblical and Arabian, within a framework defined by the historical allusions in the Qur'ān. The development of this history, and the use made of biblical sources and of Jewish and Christian informants, have been discussed by Professor Rosenthal.[6] The Prophet also speaks of Caesar and Chosroes, and here too some historical elaboration was permissible—

was even required for the explanation of the sacred tradition. For this too information was to hand—Persian converts to Islam, with memories of and access to Persian historical writings, Eastern Christians with knowledge of the histories of the pagan and Christian Roman Empires. Through them some accounts of Persian and Roman history found their way into the Arabic language, and, together with the Judaeo-Christian biblical material, became part of the common stock of Muslim universal history.

This stock, acquired in the early days when the Islamic community was still malleable and receptive, received few later accretions. It appears chiefly in the general introductory matter, leading up to the establishment of the Islamic oecumene; it is interesting to note that it is not normally supplemented by any discussion of the conditions in any specific country prior to the Islamic conquest. The Islamic community as a whole has some earlier history; the individual Islamic countries begin theirs with the advent of Islam.[7]

The external interests of Islamic historiography were thus limited to the prehistory of the Islamic community itself, and were moreover confined to the earlier period. With few and rare exceptions, they did not extend to the history of alien peoples or cultures, or even to the pre-Islamic history of the peoples and countries brought into Islam. In other words, Muslim historians were concerned only with their own civilization and its immediate ancestors—and in this they resembled the historians of most other human communities, including, until comparatively recent times, our own.

There were some exceptions. The universal curiosity of Mas'ūdī led him even to Frankish history, and enabled him to give a list of the Frankish kings from Clovis to Louis IV, based, he tells us, on a book prepared by a Frankish bishop for the Andalusian prince al-Ḥakam in 328/939.[8] The transcendent genius of al-Bīrūnī carried him across the impenetrable religious barrier of an alien script, to study Sanskrit and learn something of India—though his interests were philosophical and scientific rather than historical. These were however few and unrepresentative; even as great a historian as Ibn Khaldūn, in his universal history, does not go north of Spain or east of Persia.[9] Within that area he tried very hard to deal with non-Muslim as well as Muslim history, and made use of such non-Islamic sources as were available to him—as Orosius on Rome and Josippon on the Jews.[10] But he did not go beyond the limits of his own civilization and its known and recognizable predecessors—like the authors of most of the so-called universal histories written in Europe until very recently.

The first genuine universal history in Islam—probably in the world—is that of Rashīd al-Dīn. The Mongol conquests, by uniting for the first time under one dynasty the civilizations of South-west Asia and the Far East, created new opportunities for social and cultural contacts between societies previously separated by political and religious barriers. At the same time they opened the door to new contacts with Europe, as a number of Europeans availed themselves of the opportunity offered by the presence of non-Muslim rulers in the Middle East to explore the overland routes to China. The *Jāmiʿ al-tavārīkh*—a universal history prepared by Rashīd al-Dīn for the Mongol Ghāzān Khān—is a product of these new contacts. To carry out his task, he assembled a team of collaborators, including two Chinese scholars, a Buddhist hermit from Kashmir, a Mongol specialist on tribal tradition, and a Frankish traveler, probably a monk who had come as envoy from the Papal Curia. Through him Rashīd al-Dīn made the acquaintance of a European chronicle which has recently been identified as that of the 13th-century chronicler Martin of Troppau, also known as Martin Polonus. From this source, brought up to date by his informant, Rashīd al-Dīn was able to include a brief chronicle of the Holy Roman Emperors as far as Albert I and the Popes as far as Benedict XI. Both are correctly described as living at that time.[11]

Rashīd al-Dīn's venture into occidental and oriental scholarship, made possible by the brief interlude of Mongol power, found few imitators. His account of European history, the first since Masʿūdī's king-list, was the last until the 16th century, when the Ottoman need for political intelligence about Europe began to grow into an interest—albeit still a faint and disdainful one—in European history.

In the Saxon Landbibliothek in Dresden, there is a Turkish manuscript containing a history of France from the legendary Faramund to the year 1560. It was made by order of Ferīdūn Bey—compiler of the famous *Munshe'āt-i Selāṭīn* and Reis Efendi from 1570 to 1573—and was the work of two men, the *terjumān* Ḥasan b. Ḥamza and the *kātib* 'Alī b. Sinān. The book was completed in 980/1572.[12]

This work may well have been the first translation of a European historical work into Turkish. It was followed by an account of the discovery of the New World, adapted from European sources, which reflected the growing Turkish concern at the vast expansion of Western maritime power.[13]

During the 17th century several other Turkish historians show signs of an interest in European history and an acquaintance with European sources. Ibrāhīm Mülhemī (d. 1650) is said to have written a *Tārīkh-i Mulūk-i Rūm ve-Ifranj*, of which unfortunately no copy appears to have survived.[14] His more famous contemporary Ḥājjī Khalīfa (d. 1657) was also interested in Europe. Ḥājjī Khalīfa's researches into European geography are well known, and followed a line of inquiry opened, for practical reasons, by Ottoman map-makers and navigators in the previous century. Ḥājjī Khalīfa incorporated European material in his world geography, the *Jihānnümā*, and, with the assistance of a French priest, converted to Islam and known as Sheykh Meḥmed Ikhlāsī, prepared a Turkish version of the Atlas Minor of Mercator and Hondius. Probably with the help of this same Frenchman, Ḥājjī Khalīfa also prepared a Turkish translation of a history of the Franks—*Tārīkh-i Firengī*. Mordtmann, who believed this work to be lost, guessed that it was a translation of the Byzantine history of Chalcocondyles.[15] At least one copy, however, has survived in private possession in Turkey, and parts of it were actually published, in serial form, in the newspaper *Taṣvīr-i Efkār*, in 1279/1862–3. In his introduction Ḥājjī Khalīfa names his source—the Latin Chronicle of Johann Carion (1499–1537), which he used in the Paris edition of 1548.[16] In addition to these translations, Ḥājjī Khalīfa also wrote a brief "original" work on Europe, which has only recently come to light. It provides an outline of the Christian religion, some definitions of European forms of government, and a brief review of some of the states and rulers of Europe. Ḥājjī Khalīfa's purpose, he explains, was to rouse the Muslims from their "sleep of negligence" and give them accurate information about the numerous and powerful peoples of Europe, in place of the "lies and fables" told by the Muslim historians. His treatise serves, in the words of Professor Ménage, "by its very triviality, as an index of the ignorance of Europe which prevailed in his day among Ottoman men of learning."[17]

Of quite a different character was the use made of European sources by another Ottoman historian of the early 17th century, Ibrāhīm-i Pechevī (1572–1650). Pechevī was not concerned with universal history; still less was he interested in writing or translating the history of the infidel kings. His concern, like that of most Ottoman historians, was with the history of the Empire of which he was a subject, and more especially of the wars fought by the Ottoman armies in Europe. His history covers the events of the years 1520–1639. For the later period he relied to a large extent on his own knowledge or on the reports of old soldiers; for the earlier period he seems to have made use of the writings of his predecessors in Ottoman historiography. But in addition to those Pechevī had the revolutionary idea of consulting the historians of the enemy. He was interested above all in military history, and seems to have been fascinated by the stories of the great battles fought by the Ottoman Sultans and other rulers, dwelling with loving attention on every detail. But sometimes the Muslim chronicles were sadly lacking in details—and so Pechevī had recourse to the accounts written by the enemy. "In our country," he says, "there are men without number able to read and write Hungarian."[18] It was therefore a simple matter to have Hungarian chronicles read to him and to translate some of them into Turkish.[19] A number of passages, Pechevī says, he thought fit to incorporate in his own chronicle. These include an account of the battle of Mohacs, and other narratives of the wars in Hungary. Though Pechevī does not name his Hungarian sources, two of them have been identified by Kraelitz as Kaspar

Heltai and N. v. Istvanfy, whose histories were published in 1575 and 1623 respectively.[20]

Pechevī was not, as has sometimes been stated, the first Ottoman historian to use Western sources. He does however seem to have been the first to compare foreign accounts with native accounts of the same events, and to weave them into a single narrative. In this he can have had but few predecessors anywhere. He certainly had few successors.

Meanwhile, however, the more general interest in Western history continued. A lesser known historian of the late 17th century was Ḥüseyn Hezārfen (d. 1691), most of whose works are unfortunately still unpublished. Like Ḥājjī Khalīfa, whom he cites with admiration, he was a man of wide-ranging curiosity, and seems to have been especially interested in the geography and history of remote countries, as well as in the earlier history of his own. To an extent rare if not unique among Muslims of his day, he made the acquaintance of European scholars and men of letters, not a few of whom visited Istanbul. He is known to have been acquainted with Count Ferdinand Marsigli and Antoine Galland. It seems likely that he also knew Prince Demetrius Cantemir and Pétis de la Croix. It was perhaps in part through the good offices of these and other European friends that Ḥüseyn Hezārfen was able to gain access to the contents of European books, and incorporate them in his own works.

The most important of these, for our purpose, is his *Tenqīḥ al-tevārīkh*, completed in 1673. This is divided into nine parts, of which the sixth, seventh, eighth, and ninth deal with history outside the Islamic oecumene and its accepted predecessors. Part 6 deals with Greek and Roman history, including some account of the Greek philosophers; part 7 with the history of Constantinople since its foundation, including the Byzantine period; part 8 with Asia—China, the Philippines, the East Indies, India, and Ceylon; part 9 with the discovery of America. Oddly enough, Ḥüseyn Hezārfen does not seem to have included Europe in his survey, but his accounts of both Asia and America are based almost entirely on European sources, mostly via the *Jihānnümā* of Ḥājjī Khalīfa. His accounts of

Greek, Roman, and Byzantine history are also based on European works. These served to augment the meager stock of Islamic knowledge of classical antiquity.[21]

With the work of Aḥmed b. Luṭfullah, known as Müneǰǰimbashî (d. 1702), we return to universal history in the grand manner. His great *Jāmiʿ al-duwal*—the title is an obvious echo of Rashīd al-Dīn's *Jāmiʿ al-tavārīkh*—is a universal history of mankind from Adam to the year 1083/1672, based, so the author tells us, on some seventy sources. The Arabic original of the work is still unpublished, but a Turkish translation, prepared under the direction of the poet Nedīm, has been printed.[22] The bulk of the work, as one would expect, is concerned with Islamic history. A large part of the first volume, is, however, devoted to the history of the pre-Islamic and non-Islamic states. The former, as is usual, included the Persians and Arabians on the one hand, and the Israelites and Egyptians on the other, discussed on more or less traditional lines. Müneǰǰimbashî's ancient history, however, goes beyond the common Islamic stock. His accounts of the Romans and of the Jews clearly derive from Roman and Jewish sources, already in part available to him in the adaptation of Ibn Khaldūn. Müneǰǰimbashî has however much fuller information than Ibn Khaldūn, and is able to deal with such peoples as the Assyrians and Babylonians, the Seleucids and the Ptolemies, previously barely known to Islamic historiography. For these a European source must have been used. This becomes certain when we come to Müneǰǰimbashî's chapter on Europe, which includes sections on the divisions of the "Frankish" peoples and on the kings of France, of Germany, of Spain, and of England. The source of these would appear to have been the Turkish translation of the chronicle of Johann Carion, though, since Müneǰǰimbashî continues his narrative down to the reigns of Louis XIII of France, the Emperor Leopold in Germany, and Charles I of England, he must have had later supplementary material at his disposal. He reports the English civil war and the execution of King Charles. "After him the people of England (Anglia) did not appoint another king over them; we have no further information about their affairs" (i, 652).

Münejjimbashi's outside interests were not limited to Europe. For his account of the kings of Armenia, he tells us he made use of translations of Armenian chronicles (i. 652). For the ancient history of the Jews, he had recourse to Hebrew sources, made available to him by Jewish informants (i. 684). From his accounts of his dealings with these informants, and of his painstaking attempts to verify and compare material in languages unknown to him, we may get some idea of the far-ranging curiosity and meticulous scholarship of Münejjimbashi. Even China and Hindu India are included in the history, though here Münejjimbashi's information is meager and poor.

During the 18th century the nature of Ottoman interest in Europe underwent a radical change. The peace treaty of Carlowitz, signed 26 January 1699, marked the end of an epoch and the beginning of another. For a long time the growing internal crisis of Islamic civilization had been masked by the imposing military façade of the Ottoman Empire, protecting the Muslim heartlands both from foreign attack and from self-realization at home.

Now this façade was, for the first time, dangerously shaken. There had been unsuccessful campaigns and inconclusive wars before now. But the disastrous retreat that followed the second Ottoman failure at Vienna, in 1683, was the first clear and unmistakable defeat. At Carlowitz the Ottoman Sultan, for the first time since the foundation of the Empire, was compelled to accept terms dictated by a victorious infidel enemy.

A Turkish document, written shortly before the treaty of Passarowitz (1718), records an imaginary conversation between a Christian and an Ottoman officer, in which they discuss the military and political situation. The purpose of the writer seems to have been to prepare Ottoman ruling circles to accept defeat, by depicting as darkly as possible the unfavorable situation of the Empire. The conversation also makes a comparison between the Austrian and Ottoman armies, to the great disadvantage of the latter, and would appear to embody a plea for military reform.[23]

The impact of military defeat, and the resulting desire to seek out and make use of the talisman that had brought victory to the enemy, opened a new phase in the relations between Islam and the Western world—one which, with some important modifications, has continued until today. The new interest was at first limited to the weapons and military science of Europe, but it was inevitable that it should be extended at least to as much of European culture as seemed necessary for their effective application. In 1721, when the famous Yirmi Sekiz Meḥmed Sa'īd Efendi was sent as ambassador to Paris, his instructions were "to make a thorough study of the means of civilization and education, and report on those capable of application" in Turkey.[24] One of these "means of civilization" was printing, the establishment of which among the Turks owed much to the initiative and enthusiasm of the ambassador's son, Sa'īd Chelebi. Closely associated with him in this work was Ibrāhīm Müteferriqa, a Hungarian convert to Islam.

The first book appeared in February 1729. By the time the press was closed in 1742, seventeen books had been printed, most of them dealing with history, geography, and language. They included an account by Meḥmed Sa'īd Efendi of his embassy to France, a treatise by Ibrāhīm Müteferriqa on the science of tactics as applied in European armies, and a translation of a European account of the wars in Persia. Editions of earlier works included the 16th-century history of the discovery of the new world—*Tārikh al-Hind al-Gharbī*—and part of the geographical treatise of Ḥājji Khalīfa.

The new interest in Europe was primarily concerned with military matters. But once the barrier separating the two civilizations had been breached, it was no longer possible to keep a strict control over the traffic passing through. An interest in military science on the one hand, and a need for political and military intelligence on the other, led to an interest in recent European history which, desultory and sporadic at first, became more urgent as the realization spread that the very survival of the Empire might depend on an accurate understanding of European developments.

Besides the books printed at the Müteferriqa press, a small number of manuscripts in Istanbul collections testify to this new interest in European history. A manuscript of 1135/1722, entitled *Nemche Tārīkhi*, gives an outline history of Austria from 800 to 1662 A.D., and was translated from the German by the interpreter 'Os̱mān b. Aḥmed. Of rather a different kind are two anonymous manuscripts, written in about 1725, giving up-to-date and first-hand information about contemporary Europe. On internal evidence both appear to be the work of Ibrāhīm Müteferriqa himself.[25] Another report "on some historical circumstances of the states of Europe", dated 1146/1733–4, was made by the famous Aḥmed Pasha Bonneval, a French nobleman who joined the Ottoman service and was converted to Islam. It discusses events in Austria, Hungary, Spain, and France, and was translated into Turkish from the author's presumably French original. An outline survey of the major dynasties—the *Fihris-i Düvel* of 'Abd al-Raḥmān Münīf Efendi (d. 1742)—includes the pagan and Christian Roman emperors, the Byzantine emperors, the kings of France in Paris, and the kings of Austria in Vienna. Towards the end of the century a survey of European affairs—*Ijmāl-i aḥvāl-i Avrupa*—discusses Prussia under Frederick William II and France in the revolutionary period, and in 1799 an Istanbul Christian called Cosmo Comidas prepared, in Turkish, a handlist of reigning European sovereigns, with their dates of birth and accession, their capitals, titles, heirs, and other useful information.[26]

These works, or others of the same kind, became known to Ottoman historians, and some of the information they contained found its way into the main stream of Ottoman historiography. The first of the Imperial Historiographers who himself learnt a Western language and made use of Western sources was 'Aṭā'ullah Meḥmed, known as Shānīzāde (1769–1826). By education one of the ulema, he was a man of encyclopaedic knowledge, and became Imperial Historiographer in 1819. He seems to have learnt several European languages, and made a study of European medicine and other sciences. His major work was a Turkish translation, probably made from an Italian version, of an Austrian medical textbook. He also made a translation in 1220/1805, of the Instructions of Frederick the Great to his commanders—*Viṣāyānāme-i seferiyye*. It was therefore natural that, when called upon to write the history of the Empire for the years 1808–20, he should make some use of European sources.

The vast, swift campaigns of the Revolutionary and Napoleonic wars drove the lessons of the new warfare deep into the lands of Islam, while the new, secular ideas of the Revolution, untainted in Muslim eyes with any recognizably Christian origin, could for the first time penetrate the barrier that had hitherto excluded every movement of ideas from Europe, and thus provide the Muslim peoples, in their new liberalism and nationalism, with the ideological foundations of Westernization.

In the first half of the 19th century there were two main centres of Westernizing reform in the Middle East—Turkey and Egypt. In both of them the preparation and publication of translations of Western books played an important part. In Egypt under Muḥammad 'Alī Pasha there was an organized, state-sponsored program of translation, for the like of which we must go back to medieval times. Between 1822 and 1842, 243 books were printed at the Būlāq press, the greater part of them translations. Of these, rather more than half were in Turkish, most of the remainder in Arabic. Under Muḥammad 'Alī's rule Turkish was still the language of the ruling élite in Egypt, and we are therefore not surprised to find that works on military and naval subjects are almost all in Turkish. The same is to a large extent true of pure and applied mathematics, which were chiefly needed for military purposes. Works on medicine, veterinary science, agriculture, and grammar, on the other hand, are mostly in Arabic. History would seem to have been regarded as a matter for the Turkish-speaking rulers, since the few historical books issued from the press in the early period are all in Turkish. The first was a translation of Castera's *Histoire de l'impératrice Catherine II de Russie*, translated by the Greek Yakovaki Argyropoulo, and published in 1244/1829. It was reprinted in Istanbul in 1287/1870. Another early translation was an extract from the *Mémorial de Sainte Hélène*, published in 1247/1832 under the title *Tārīkh-i Napolyon Bonapart*. It is also known as *Napolyon sergüzeshti*. Then came versions of Botta's *Storia d'Italia* and of the memoirs of the Duc de Rovigo, both published in 1249/1834. These four books complete the historical translations from Western languages in the early period, though there were also one or two translations from Arabic into Turkish. Thereafter there was an interval of several years until the next historical translation appeared—a version of Voltaire's *Histoire de Charles XII*, published in 1257/1841. This time it was in Arabic, as were also a number of subsequent translations of historical works by Voltaire, Robertson, and others.[27]

In Turkey the movement began more slowly. The translations made in Egypt seem to have been known and studied, but it was not until the middle of the century that translations of European historical writings begin to appear in Istanbul. In 1866 a Turkish translation appeared, by Aḥmed Ḥilmī, of an English *Universal History*—probably the first world history in modern Turkish literature. Thereafter the translation movement developed quickly, especially in Turkey and Egypt, and rapidly altered the world picture as it appeared to Muslim students and readers.[28]

9. *The Cult of Spain and the Turkish Romantics*

Towards the end of the 19th century the Muslim Orient began to rediscover the lost and long-forgotten glories of Muslim Andalusia. The time was one of defeat and retreat for the Muslim peoples. The expansion of Europe—by sea from the west, by land from the east—was still bringing great and ancient Muslim cities under Christian rule. The French in North Africa, the British in India, the Russians in Central Asia, all seemed to be converging on the heartlands of Islam, and, at the same time, political and military defeats were matched by the retreat of traditional Islamic concepts and values before the advance of new notions emanating from Europe. Only the Ottoman Sultanate remained as an independent Muslim Great Power—by now the accepted leader and spokesman of Sunnī Islam; and even then the survival of the Ottoman Empire was gravely threatened by foreign invasion, domestic dissension, and the spread of new and disruptive ideas.

It was in these circumstances that the cult of Andalus emerged, and, responding to a deep emotional need, spread widely among Muslim intellectuals. In a time of humiliating weakness and backwardness, they could find comfort in the spectacle of a great, rich, powerful and civilized Muslim state in Europe—the leader and guide, as they saw it, of European civilization. In a time of decay, they could find a melancholy satisfaction in the contemplation of the sunset splendors of the Alhambra, in the long, sad epic of defeat and withdrawal. Before long, the rise and fall of Muslim Andalusia became favorite themes and settings of poets and novelists; the glories of Cordova served as a Golden Age for the romantic and apologetic school of Islamic historiography that was growing up in the Middle East and especially in India.

M. Henri Pérès, in his invaluable book on Muslim travelers in Spain, has dated the Muslim rediscovery of Andalusia from the year 1886.[1] It sprang, he says, from two sources—the attendance of Muslims at the international congresses of orientalists, where they made the acquaintance of European orientalist scholarship, including its work on Spain, and the action of the Ottoman Sultan Abdülhamid II, in sending prospectors to Spain in search of Arabic manuscripts.

Of the two, the latter had the more immediate effects. In 1886–7 the Sultan, at the suggestion of his minister of education Munīf Pasha, appointed and sent Ibn al-Talāmid al-Turkuzī al-Shinqīṭī, an Arabic scholar of Moorish origin, to Spain, to search for remnants of the bygone glories of Andalus.[2] He was the first of a long series of Muslim pilgrims, westward bound on a similar search.

The Sultan may well, as M. Pérès suggests, have been inspired by the Lebanese scholar Fāris al-Shidyāq, who was engaged in the search for and publication of Arabic texts at the time.[3] It is however more than likely that the Education Minister, Munīf Pasha, was himself actively concerned in the matter. Munīf Pasha (1828–1910),[4] a well-known Turkish publicist and public servant of the time, played an important role in the introduction and dissemination of modern knowledge and ideas in Turkey. Trained and for a time employed in the Translation Chamber of the Sublime Porte—Turkey's open window to the West—he published as early as 1859 a group of translations from Fontenelle, Fénélon, and Voltaire, and in 1860 founded the Ottoman Scientific Society (Jemiyet-i 'Ilmiye-i 'O̱smaniye), modelled on the Royal Society of England. Its journal, the *Mejmū'a-i Funūn*, includes a wide range of articles on history, geography, and philosophy as well as the natural sciences, and played a role in 19th-century Turkey in some ways analogous to that of the *Grande Encyclopédie* in 18th-century France. Munīf Pasha was a man of many interests and projects—even including a reform of the Arabic alphabet for typographical purposes. As Minister of Education from 1884 to 1888, he was at least formally responsible for al-Shinqīṭī's mission, which he himself appears to have suggested. Al-Shinqīṭī was invited to go from Arabia to Istanbul by one Haji Ibrahim, a Turkish professor of Arabic at the Dār al-Ta'līm in Istanbul, who had studied under him in the Hejāz when his father, Sherīf Pasha, was governor there. In Istanbul al-Shinqīṭī associated on familiar terms with many prominent Turkish officials and scholars, notably with Munīf Pasha, in whose house he lived as a member of the family.[5]

There is a further reason for believing that the project originated in Istanbul. In our time, when Turkey has abandoned all pan-Islamic activities and the Turkish language is little known in the eastern world, it is important to remember that in the 19th century Turkey was still generally recognized, by Muslims, as the leading Muslim power. It was in Turkey that the new problems of religion and nation, country and state, were first formulated and discussed. Turkish publications were read by the Turkish-educated Arab intellectuals of Aleppo, Damascus, and Baghdad; some too were published in now forgotten Arabic translations, and the ideas they contained filtered through to widening circles of Muslims in both Asia and Africa. Many of the characteristic themes and arguments of Arab literature towards the end of the 19th century are anticipated in Turkish some decades earlier, and the cult of Andalus is no exception.

The origin of this cult can be traced, with precision, to a book. It is the *Essai sur l'histoire des arabes et des Mores d'Espagne* of Louis Viardot, published in Paris in two volumes in 1833. A Turkish translation was prepared by Ziya Pasha and published in Istanbul, under the title *Endelüs Tarihi*, in 1280 A.H. (=1863–4). It was reprinted, in four volumes, in 1304–5/1886–7—that is, immediately before al-Shinqīṭī's mission.

The translator, Ziya (1825–1880) was one of the leading figures in 19th-century Turkish literature and notably among the group of liberal patriots known as the Young Ottomans.[6] The son of a clerk in the customs house at Galata, he was educated at the grammar school which Sultan Mahmud II had opened by the Süleymaniye mosque, and entered the civil service at the age of 17. In 1855, thanks to the influence of the great reforming minister Mustafa Reshīd Pasha, he joined the staff of the Imperial Household, as third secretary to the Sultan. There he attracted the attention of Edhem Pasha, then

Marshal of the Palace *(Mabeyn Ferīki)*, who urged him, allegedly as a cure for depression,[7] to learn French. Ziya set to work with a will, and before very long was ready to undertake the translation of Viardot's book. Edhem Pasha encouraged him and perhaps assisted him in this task.

The translation was not a distinguished effort. The original was of limited scholarly value; the translation the work of a beginner just mastering the language. Tanpînar has pointed to the translator's ignorance of history, Gibb to the heavy bureaucratic style which he adopted. Yet with all these defects the book had a great impact. Widely read at the time, it served to inspire a series of Turkish poems, plays, and stories which made the glories of Andalus familiar to a new generation of Turkish readers.

By far the most important of the writers concerned was the great poet and dramatist Abdülhak Hamid (1852–1937).[8] At the age of 11 he accompanied his father on a mission to Paris, where he went to school for a year. In 1876 he returned to Paris, as second secretary to the Turkish Embassy. It was at that time, in Paris, that he wrote his famous drama *Ṭāriq*, a passionate defence of the glory, greatness, and nobility of Islam. Its hero is Ṭāriq b. Ziyād, "the conqueror of Spain". In this drama of love, hate and jealousy, of war, death and glory, Hamid manages to assert his conviction of the profound ethical values of Islam, to express his ideas on patrotism and progress,[9] and to make some indirect comments on the political and social problems of the Ottoman Empire. It was, no doubt, because of these that the book was banned and seized after its publication in 1879. It was however reprinted and circulated secretly, and republished after the Young Turk Revolution.[10]

In the same year, 1876, Hamid dealt dramatically with a theme from the end of the Muslim history of Spain. *Nazife* is a one-act dialogue, in verse, between the Spanish King Ferdinand and Nazife, an Arab girl. The King, who loves Nazife, withdraws the permission he had previously given her to go to Morocco. The girl kills herself to save her honor. Some years later he wrote a sequel to this play, called *ʿAbdallah al-Saghīr*. Also in verse, it tells of the love of ʿAbdallah, the last Muslim ruler in Spain, for a Spanish girl called Carolina.

In 1879 Hamid wrote another drama on a Spanish theme—*Tezer*, also called *Melik Abdurrahman-i S̱aliṣ̱*. This play, also in verse, is situated in Cordova under the Umayyads, and tells the tragic story of a Spanish girl called Tezer (probably intended as Terez, Thérèse, Teresa). Loved by ʿAbd al-Raḥmān III, she allows herself to be used, in a plot against him, by her former lover Richard, the leader of an anti-Arab Spanish faction. Tezer, however, actually falls in love with ʿAbd al-Raḥmān, and in the ensuing dénouement loses her life.

In 1881, while living at Rize, on the Black Sea, Hamid returned to the theme of Ṭāriq, and produced a second full-length drama, in prose. *Ibn-i Mūsā*, or *Ẕāt al-jamāl*, continues the complex story of the conquerors of Spain, and follows them back to Syria and Arabia, to show the working-out of their destiny at the Umayyad court. Once again the themes are love, hate and jealousy, and the tragic clash of honor and passion.[11]

The influence of the French classical theatre on Abdülhak Hamid is obvious, notably of *Le Cid* and *Bérénice*. But if Corneille and Racine provided the manner, the humble Viardot provided the matter, and served as the starting point of a new and significant literary and intellectual trend.

Abdülhak Hamid was by no means the only Turkish author to turn to Viardot and the history of Andalus for inspiration. Muallim Nājī (1850–1893),[12] for example, wrote an historical poem called *Ḥamiyet*, describing the heroic Muslim defenders of Granada during the final struggle in 1492, and others could be added. He was, however, the most important and influential. Though in our time he has lost much of his influence, he was in his own day widely read and admired, not only in Turkey. His play *Tezer*, for example, is said to have been translated into Arabic and Persian, as well as into Serbian and Muslim Bosniak.[13] His three-year stay as Turkish consul-general in Bombay (1883–5) may also have brought his work and ideas to the attention of Indian Muslims. Following on Ziya's translation of Viardot, his work did much to popularize the romantic revival of interest in medieval Spanish Islam, and to encourage the cult of Andalus that is so noteworthy a feature of recent and modern Islamic writing.

III

MUSLIMS AND JEWS

10. The Pro-Islamic Jews

When Lord Beaconsfield, Prime Minister of England, returned from the Congress of Berlin, he received the somewhat mixed welcome which democratic societies usually offer to their leaders. His achievement, as he saw it, had been to save Turkey from dismemberment by the victorious Russians, and thus to preserve both the peace of Europe and the interests of Britain. For his supporters, he had indeed fulfilled his claim to "peace with honor"; for his opponents, he had brought shame and strife to his country, by pursuing policies which were harmful and wrong.

The dispute was an old and bitter one in English politics. On the one hand were those who believed, in Lord Palmerston's words, that "the integrity and independence of the Ottoman Empire are necessary to the maintenance of the tranquillity, the liberty, and the balance of power in the rest of Europe"—and, in addition, that the protection of Turkey against Russia was a vital British interest. On the other, there were those who rejected the Turks as infidels, barbarians, and aliens in Europe, and saw no reason to obstruct the Russians in the work of removing them. The quarrel between the Turcophiles and the Turcophobes aroused strong passions, and at times split not only the nation, but also parties and even families.

Nineteenth-century polemic was notoriously violent in tone, and the controversies on the Eastern Question in particular provide some really outstanding examples of political scurrility. Attacks on Disraeli sometimes contain hostile references to his Jewish origin. These are not on the whole frequent, and would not be remarkable in an age noted for uninhibited personal abuse. They can be easily paralleled by similar hostile references to other ethnic and religious groups in the country. It is, however, significant that the anti-Semitic theme occurs most frequently, most persistently, and most extensively in the discussion of Disraeli's Eastern policy, and takes the form of a specific accusation—that he was applying a Jewish, not an English policy, and was subordinating British interests to Jewish (or Hebrew, or Semitic) sentiments and purposes.

Disraeli's accusers give two reasons for regarding his pro-Turkish policies as Jewish. The first is that Russia persecuted the Jews and that Disraeli as a Jew was, therefore, determined to thwart Russia and help her enemies—a line of argument familiar in other times and places. The second, and in contemporary eyes far more important, reason was that Disraeli, as a Jew, was bound to rally automatically to the Turkish side. The Jew, even the baptized Jew, remained an Oriental; in the struggle over the Eastern Question, his loyalties were with Asia against Europe, with Islam against Christendom.

To the modern reader, such theories may seem fanciful to the point of absurdity. They were not so to Disraeli's critics, and commanded belief in surprisingly wide circles. The friendship of the Jew for the Muslim was taken for granted as a fact; the policy of Disraeli seemed to follow naturally from it.

A few examples may suffice to give the flavor of these writings. A Liberal member of Parliament, T. P. O'Connor, discussing the Russo-Turkish war of 1877, wrote:

> One of the most remarkable phenomena in the course of the war between Russia and Turkey was the extraordinary unanimity with which the Jews of every part of the world took the side of the Sultan against the Czar. People living within the same frontiers, speaking the same language, professing the same creed, with exactly the same interests, have held the most opposite views upon this Russo-Turkish question. In this country—to take the most striking example—the people, agreed for the most part on the main question of religion, of the same race, with the same great interests to conserve, differed with a bitterness almost unexampled in their domestic or in their foreign controversies. But here are the Jews, dispersed over every part of the globe, speaking different tongues, divided in nearly every sympathy,—separated, in fact, by everything that can separate man, except the one point of race,—all united in their feelings on this great contest! . . . For many ages—more in the past than in the present, of course—there has been among large sections of the Jews the strongest sympathy with the Mohammedan peoples. A common enemy is a great

bond of friendship, and as the Christian was equally the enemy of the Mohammedan and the Jew, they were thereby brought into a certain alliance with one another. This alliance has been most close on many occasions. In the time of the Crusaders, the Jews were the friends who aided the Mohammedans in keeping back the tide of Christian invasion which was floating against the East, and in Spain the Jews were the constant friends and allies of the Moorish against the Christian inhabitants of the country. The alliance must have been very close in the past indeed to have left such deep traces behind. . . . His [i.e. Disraeli's] general view then upon this question of Turkey is that as a Jew he is a kinsman of the Turk, and that, as a Jew, he feels bound to make common cause with the Turk against the Christian. . . . From first to last his policy was persistently, uniformly, without interruption, a policy of friendship to the Turk and the oppressor, and hate to the Christian and the oppressed.[1]

Such views were not confined to professional politicians and pamphleteers. They are also found in the writings of historians like J. A. Froude, Goldwin Smith, and E. A. Freeman. The last was particularly virulent:

But there is another power against which England and Europe ought to be yet more carefully on their guard. It is no use mincing matters. The time has come to speak out plainly. No well disposed person would reproach another either with his nationality or his religion, unless that nationality or that religion leads to some direct mischief. No one wishes to place the Jew, whether Jew by birth or by religion, under any disability as compared with the European Christian. But it will not do to have the policy of England, the welfare of Europe, sacrified to Hebrew sentiment. The danger is no imaginary one. Every one must have marked that the one subject on which Lord Beaconsfield, through his whole career, has been in earnest has been whatever has touched his own people. A mocker about everything else, he has been thoroughly serious about this. His zeal for his own people is really the best feature in Lord Beaconsfield's career. But we cannot sacrifice our people, the people of Aryan and Christian Europe, to the most genuine belief in an Asian mystery. We cannot have England or Europe governed by a Hebrew policy. While Lord Derby simply wishes to do nothing one way or another, Lord Beaconsfield is the active friend of the Turk. The alliance runs through all Europe. Throughout the East, the Turk and the Jew are leagued against the Christian. . . . We cannot have the policy of Europe dealt with in the like sort. There is all the difference in the world between the degraded Jews of the East and the cultivated and honourable Jews of the West. But blood is stronger than water, and Hebrew rule is sure to lead to a Hebrew policy. Throughout Europe, the most fiercely Turkish part of the press is largely in Jewish hands. It may be assumed everywhere, with the smallest class of exceptions, that the Jew is the friend of the Turk and the enemy of the Christian.[2]

The attempts of Freeman and Goldwin Smith to launch German-style intellectual anti-Semitism in England, like the later attempts by Chesterton and Belloc to import the French clerical variety, had very little success. But the belief in the "Semitism" of Disraeli's Eastern policy went far beyond such circles. "I have a strong suspicion," Gladstone told the Duke of Argyll, "that Dizzy's crypto-Judaism has had to do with his policy. The Jews of the East *bitterly* hate the Christians, who have not always used them well."[3] As late as 1924, in a paper which Sir James Headlam-Morley wrote as historical advisor to the Foreign Office, he remarked that Disraeli "in his sympathies . . . was consistently a Jew and a Zionist [sic] . . . . Not without reason did his enemies publicly attribute his Near Eastern policy to his 'Semitic instincts'. . . the conviction can scarcely be avoided that the charge contained part of the truth, and that if 'Semitic sympathies' be added we get yet nearer to Disraeli's inner personal motives."[4]

The charge against Disraeli's patriotism is obviously absurd. His policy of defending Turkey against Russia had been anticipated by such impeccably Christian and English gentlemen as Palmerston, Castlereagh, Canning and Pitt, and had long been an important, though not uncontested, principle of British diplomacy. But that is not the whole story. Disraeli's most recent biographer has reminded us that "historians do not always sufficiently weigh the influence of the conditions, prejudices and sympathies of early youth upon the choice of sides made by statesmen later, when they are confronted with the great political questions of the hour."[5] Like Churchill, Lloyd George, and so many others, Disraeli may well have been affected, in his mature attitudes and decisions, by the formative influences of his youth. Disraeli's pride in his Jewish ancestry is well known. His novels and letters amply attest his profound sympathy for the Turks, the Arabs and Islam, and his belief in the basic kinship between Jews and Muslims. Like so many Englishmen, he was fascinated by the desert and the Arabs; better than others, he was able to identify himself with both. Assertions of such identity recur frequently in his writings, in which the terms "Arabia" and "Arab" have an almost mystical significance. The Jews are "Mosaic Arabs" or even "Jewish Arabs", kinsmen and predecessors of the Muslim Arabs; "the Arabs are only Jews upon horseback". Judaism, Christianity and Islam are all Arabian religions: "On the top of Mount Sinai are two ruins—a Christian church and a Mohammedan mosque. In this, the sublimest scene of Arabian glory, Israel and Ishmael alike raised their altars to the great God of Abraham. Why are they in ruins?"[6]

Disraeli's sentimental Semitism, however well documented, does not explain his pro-Turkish feelings; still less does it throw any light on the general attitude of European Jews to the Turks and Islam. As his biographer Buckle remarked, had Disraeli been guided by racial feeling, "the race which that feeling would have led him to support would have been . . . the Arab, and not the Turk."[7] In any case, Disraeli's racialism—his obsession with race in general and the Jewish race in particular—owes more to his Christian education than to his Jewish ancestry, and has no parallel in the writings of authentic Jews of the time. It was in Christian Europe that the great racial myths, with the accompanying rejection of "inferior stocks", had begun to influence ideas and events; Disraeli's hymns, or rather fugues, on the theme of Jewish power and Jewish glory are no more than inverted anti-Jewish stereotypes, with as little foundation in reality as their originals.

Yet, beneath the distortions and slanders of Disraeli's political enemies, there was an important element of truth. Disraeli *was* an admirer of Islam, of the Persians and Turks as well as the Arabs, and in his youth had even thought of joining the Turkish army as a volunteer. Moreover, his pro-Turkish sentiments were connected with his vestigial Jewishness, and are typical of a good deal of Jewish opinion at the time. O'Connor, despite his malicious exaggerations, was not far wrong in speaking of the Jews in 19th-century Europe as a pro-Turkish, and more generally pro-Muslim, element.

One field in which the Jewish interest in Islam made a significant impact was that of scholarship. In the development of Islamic studies in European and, later, American universities, Jews, and in particular Jews of Orthodox background and education, play an altogether disproportionate role. In one of his early novels, Disraeli puts in his hero's mouth a lively plea for Oriental literatures: "Why not study the Oriental? Surely in the pages of the Persians and the Arabs we might discover new sources of emotion, new modes of expression, new trains of ideas, new principles of invention, and new bursts of fancy . . ." and praises "the Persians, whose very being is poetry, the Arabs, whose subtle mind could penetrate into the very secret shrine of nature."[8] Jewish scholars did much to bring these achievements of the Islamic genius to Western notice, and inculcate in the Western mind a less prejudiced and more sympathetic understanding of Islam.

One such scholar was Gustav Weil (1808–1889), a rabbinical student who became Professor of Arabic at Heidelberg. He mastered Persian and Turkish as well as Arabic, and spent some time in Algiers, Cairo and Istanbul. In 1843 he published his first major work—on the life and teachings of the Prophet Muḥammad. There had been many biographies of Muḥammad in Europe; Weil's was the first that was free from prejudice and polemic, based on a profound yet critical knowledge of the Arabic sources, and informed by a sympathetic understanding of Muslim belief and piety. For the first time, he gave the European reader an opportunity to see Muḥammad as the Muslims saw him, and thus to achieve a fuller appreciation of his place in human history. Weil's other publications on the beginnings of Islam include an historical and critical introduction to the Qur'ān, a translation of the major Arabic biography of the Prophet, and a five-volume history of the Caliphs. In terms of scholarship, these books have to a large extent been overtaken by subsequent research; in their day, however, and for long afterwards, they were standard works, and they remain as landmarks in the Western discovery of the East.

Many Jewish scholars came directly from Hebrew to Arabic studies, and made important contributions to both—particularly in the areas where the two overlap. Salomon Munk (1805–1867) and Moritz Steinschneider (1816–1917) were both specialists on Judaeo-Arabic literature, but their work was of great value to Arabic and Islamic studies generally. Munk's work on medieval Islamic philosophy, Steinschneider's studies and bibliographies on the translation movement—from Greece to the Arabs and from the Arabs to Europe—throw a flood of light on the cultural history of Islam and on the Muslim contribution to European civilization. Christians of Jewish origin also play a part. Karl Paul Caspari (1814–1892), a Lutheran theologian of Jewish parentage, wrote what was for long the standard European treatise on Arabic grammar. David Abrahamovitch Chwolson (1819–1911), a baptized Lithuanian Jew, became a professor at the newly founded faculty of Oriental languages at St Petersburg. Though primarily a Hebraist, he was also a competent Arabist, and through his writings and his influence as a teacher ranks among the founders of the Russian school of Arabic studies. To these may be added David Samuel Margoliouth (1858–1940), an Anglican clergyman who held the Laudian Chair of Arabic at Oxford University, and was one of the major Arabic and Islamic scholars of his day.

With the advance of emancipation during the later 19th and early 20th centuries, Jewish scholars play an increasing part in the European universities, notably in Oriental studies. A Turkish Jew, Joseph Halevy (1827–1917), and two Austrians, David Heinrich Müller (1846–1912) and Edward Glaser (1855–1908), were among the pioneers of South Arabian studies; a German rabbinical scholar, Hermann Reckendorf (1863–1923), whose father incidentally had translated the Qur'ān into Hebrew, wrote the standard work on Arabic syntax. Julius Hirschberg (1843–1925), Julius Lippert (1866–1911) and Max Meyerhof (1874–1945) devoted themselves to the recovery and study of Muslim science and medicine. Other important figures are the Iranist Wilhelm Bacher (1850–1913), Siegmund Fraenkel (1855–1909), Max Sobernheim (1872–1932), Josef Horovitz (1874–1931), Eugen Mittwoch (1876–1942), and the art historian Leo Aryeh Mayer (1895–1959), one of the pioneers of the new and flourishing school of Islamic studies in Jerusalem.

It was chiefly in Germany and Austria that Jewish scholars, half way between the traditionalism of the East and the emancipation of the West, were able to achieve the most effective combination of old-style learning and modern scholarship. But the Jewish role in Oriental studies can be seen very clearly in other countries too: David Santillana (1855–1931) and Giorgio Levi Della Vida (1886–1967) in Italy; Joseph Derenbourg (1811–1895), his son Hartwig Derenbourg (1844–1908), the Iranist James Darmesteter (1849–1894), the historian of Spanish Islam Evariste Lévi-Provençal (1894–1956) in France; the Persian scholar Reuben Levy (1891–1966) in England; Richard Gottheil (1862–1936) and William Popper (1874–1963), pioneers of Arabic studies in the United States. Probably the greatest of all was Ignaz Goldziher (1850–1921), a pious Hungarian Jew whose magnificent series of studies on Muslim theology, law and culture rank him, by common consent, as one of the founders and masters of modern Islamic studies.

The role of these scholars in the development of every aspect of Islamic studies has been immense—not only in the advancement of scholarship, but also in the enrichment of the Western view of Oriental religion, literature and history, by the substitution of knowledge and understanding for prejudice and ignorance. In recent years, the revival of learning in the East has given these scholars a new importance, as their works, in the original and in translation, are read by the Muslims themselves, and help to shape both their knowledge of past achievements and their awareness of present problems. It is said that when the Turkish historian Ahmed Refik, returning from a tour of Europe at the beginning of this century, was asked by his friends what was the most remarkable thing he had seen on his travels, he replied: "The University of Budapest, where I found a Jewish professor expounding the Qur'ān to a class of Christian pupils." The Jewish professor was of course Ignaz Goldziher. Since then, some of his writings have been translated into Arabic, and are used for teaching Muslim Arab pupils their own heritage. Not a few other Jewish scholars have been translated and adapted in the same way.[9]

Impact and influence are not always the rewards of accurate and original scholarship, and the reputation of these men rarely reached beyond the academic circles in which they lived and moved. There were others, however, whose impact was more strongly felt, and more extensive. Three in particular found readers and disciples in unexpected places.

The first of these was Arthur Lumley Davids (1811–1832), an English Jew who died of cholera shortly before his twenty-first birthday. An infant prodigy, he mastered Hebrew, Arabic, Persian and Turkish at an early age, and undertook a vast program of research. His most important work, published three weeks before his death, was his *Grammar of the Turkish Language*, the first in English since 1709. More significant than the grammar itself was the 78-page "Preliminary Discourse", in which, on the basis of an astonishingly wide range of learning, Davids surveys the origins and history of the Turkish peoples, the classification and characteristics of the Turkish languages, and the principal monuments of Turkish literature.

This "Discourse" was the first attempt of its kind to bring to the Western reader a balanced account of the Turks, their achievement and their place in history, and thus to correct the vulgar errors and prejudices that were current concerning them. It is inspired by a spirit of profound sympathy and admiration.

Davids' *Grammar* was published in English in 1832, and in a French translation, prepared by his mother, in 1836. Though no doubt a remarkable effort for so young an author, the book is of limited scholarly value, and was on the whole neglected by the world of Oriental scholarship. It was, however, greatly admired by the well-known Turcophile writer David Urquhart, who in his *Spirit of the East* (1839) quotes extensively from the "Preliminary Discourse".

Rather more important than Davids' influence on the Turcophiles was his influence on the Turks themselves, to whom his "Discourse" brought a new awareness of identity and a new pride of achievement. Already in 1851 Fuad and Jevdet Pashas, the co-authors of the first modern Turkish grammar in Turkish, drew on Davids' work. Their book, which was enormously influential in Turkey, has been regarded as the starting-point of the renovation of the Turkish language. In 1869 another Turkish author, Ali Suavi, wrote an article extolling the past glories of the Turkish race, for which his sole source was Davids' "Preliminary Discourse". This article was one of the earliest statements of an entirely new trend among the Ottoman Turks—that of nationalism. In adapting this new and essentially alien idea to their own needs, Turkish—and later also other Muslim—nationalists relied very heavily on Western literature. In this respect the most influential works were not necessarily the most scholarly.[10]

Another author, of rather doubtful scholarship and far greater influence, was David Léon Cahun (1841–1900), an Alsatian Jew who went on a tour of the Middle East in his youth and thereafter remained a passionate enthusiast. Cahun wrote and lectured extensively on the countries and peoples of the area, especially on the Egyptians and the Turks, and from 1890 gave courses at the Sorbonne on the history and geography of Asia. His writings include a number of romantic historical novels, several with Turkish and Muslim heroes; a wide range of geographical and ethnographical books and papers; and a number of books and articles on Islamic and Asian history. The best known of these was his *Introduction générale à l'histoire de l'Asie* (1896), a sustained hymn of praise to the greatness of the Turkish peoples, and their immense creative role in the history of Asia and indeed the world. A history of the Arabs remained unfinished at his death.

This *Introduction Générale* was published in a Turkish adaptation in 1899, and exercised a powerful attraction on successive generations of Turkish readers, not only in Turkey, but also in the Russian empire. Modern Turkish historians regard this book as one of the seminal influences in the development of pan-Turkism and of Turkish nationalism. Cahun's influence was not limited to his books. A committed liberal, he cultivated the Turkish and Egyptian émigrés in Paris, and served their cause both in person and through his writings.[11]

Among European Jews who became involved in Muslim countries and affairs, one was outstanding, both for his genuine scholarship and for his political influence. Arminius Vambéry (1832–1918) was the son of a Hungarian Talmudist, and was brought up in Orthodox Judaism and grinding poverty. His subsequent career was in every sense unorthodox. After an irregular and largely self-administered education, he went as a young man to Istanbul, where he lived from hand to mouth by giving lessons. In time he mastered Turkish so well that he became one of the leading authorities in Europe on Turkish studies, and one of the founders of the new science of Turkology. Between 1862 and 1864, disguised as a wandering dervish, he traveled in Persia and Central Asia; in 1865 he became professor of Oriental languages at the University of Budapest, where one of his pupils was Ignaz Goldziher. His numerous books and articles were read not only in Europe, but in Turkey where his friends included men in the highest positions. Both through his writings and his personality, he had a considerable influence on cultural and, to some extent, on political developments in Turkey.[12]

The Turks admired and responded to Davids, Cahun and Vambéry because they recognized, in all three, a genuine and deeply-felt sympathy for themselves. There is no evidence that their Turkish readers and disciples were particularly aware of the Jewish origin of the three men, or attached any importance to it; still less is there any sign of belief, among 19th-century Turks or Muslims, in a Muslim-Jewish bond of brotherhood such as was imagined by O'Connor, Freeman, and others. Yet the prevalence of Jews—and especially of conscious Jews—among Orientalists and Turcophiles is more than coincidental. Weil, Reckendorf, Vambéry, Goldziher and many others started with a Biblical and Talmudical training. Even such Westerners as Davids and Cahun had a more than nominal connection with Jewishness. Davids, his mother tells us, wrote on many subjects, "notably" on Jewish emancipation; Cahun wrote a book on the customs of the Jews of Alsace, with a preface by the Chief Rabbi of Paris.[13] Even converts like Disraeli and Chwolson show an active concern, not only in their writings but also in their actions—the one by his stand for Jewish emancipation, the other by his testimony against the blood-libel.

Why then did these Jews and ex-Jews rally to the Islamic and Turkish side, to such an extent that in Europe, though not in

Turkey, their pro-Turkish attitude was treated as an acknowledged fact? Certainly not because of any agreement or alliance, for the devotion of some Jews to Muslim studies and causes aroused no corresponding interest or sentiment on the other side.[14] Some romantics, however, like the young Disraeli, seem to have dreamed of such an alliance, and seen its fulfillment in the golden age of Muslim Spain, "that fair and unrivalled civilization" in "which the children of Ishmael rewarded the children of Israel with equal rights and privileges with themselves. During these halcyon centuries, it is difficult to distinguish the followers of Moses from the votary of Mahomet. Both alike built palaces, gardens, and fountains; filled equally the highest offices of the state, competed in an extensive and enlightened commerce, and rivalled each other in renowned universities."[15]

This kind of romanticism affected a number of Jewish writers of the time, and has a curiously mixed origin. Basically, it was part of the romantic cult of Spain, which reached its peak in Victor Hugo's *Hernani* (1830), and was extended to the Muslim Middle Ages by Washington Irving's highly successful *Chronicle of the Conquest of Granada* (1829) and *The Alhambra* (1832). Jewish romantics found an additional point of interest in the tragic fate of their own ancestors in Spain—a fate which was becoming better known through the labors of historians. One of these was Disraeli's cousin Elias Haim Lindo, whose *History of the Jews in Spain and Portugal* appeared in 1846.[16] The broad outlines of the story, in the simplified and dramatized form in which great historic events so often reach the popular imagination, were well defined. The Jews had flourished in Muslim Spain, had been driven from Christian Spain, and had found a refuge in Muslim Turkey.

The reality was of course more complex, less idyllic, less one-sided. There had been times of persecution under the Muslims and times of prosperity under Christian rule in Spain—and many Christian states, as well as Turkey, had given shelter to the Spanish Jewish refugees. Even at its best, medieval Islam was rather different from the picture provided by Disraeli and other romantic writers. The golden age of equal rights was a myth, and belief in it was a result, more than a cause, of Jewish sympathy for Islam. The myth was invented by Jews in 19th-century Europe as a reproach to Christians—and taken up by Muslims in our own time as a reproach to Jews.

Like most powerful myths, this story contains an element of historic truth. If tolerance means the absence of persecution, then classical Islamic society was indeed tolerant to both its Jewish and its Christian subjects—more tolerant perhaps in Spain than in the East, and in either incomparably more tolerant than was medieval Christendom. But if tolerance means the absence of discrimination, then Islam never was or claimed to be tolerant, but on the contrary insisted on the privileged superiority of the true believer in this world as well as in the next. The great conflict of the Crusades, and later the European counter-attack against the Turks, brought a harshening of Muslim attitudes, directed primarily against the Christians, but to a lesser extent also against the Jews. Both minorities suffered from the decline in Muslim power, prosperity, and standards. In more recent times the position of the Jews had become relatively worse, since unlike the native Christians they were unable to invoke the protection of the Christian powers. European travelers to the East in the age of liberalism and emancipation are almost unanimous in deploring the degraded and precarious position of Jews in Muslim countries, and the dangers and humiliations to which they were subject.

Jewish scholars, acquainted with the history of Islam and with the current situation in Islamic lands, can have had no illusions on this score. Vambéry is unambiguous: "I do not know any more miserable, helpless, and pitiful individual on God's earth than the *Jahudi* in those countries. . . . The poor Jew is despised, belabored and tortured alike by Moslem, Christian and Brahmin, he is the poorest of the poor, and outstripped by Armenians, Greeks and Brahmins. . . ."[17]

In view of this, it is the more striking that Jewish scholars and writers should in general have felt and expressed so much sympathy for Islam. In part this was based on a well-grounded feeling of gratitude. In medieval Spain there had indeed been a great age of Jewish creativity, which owed much to Muslim tolerance; in modern Turkey many Jews, fleeing from Christian persecution, had found a new home under Muslim rule.

To the European Jews of the early 19th century, facing the opportunities and frustrations of emancipation, there were some further points to note. In medieval Spain, at least so it appeared, there had been a degree of social and cultural communication between Jew and Gentile such as was impossible in medieval Christendom, and was only just becoming possible, against many obstacles, in Europe in their own day. In the world of Islam, governments might discriminate against non-Muslims, including Jews; but they rarely persecuted them. There might be contempt, degradation, even occasional repression, but there was nothing in Islam to compare with the specific hatred, both theoretical and popular, that was directed against the Jews in Christendom.[18] In the age of secularism, theological anti-Judaism was far from dead; the newer, racial anti-Semitism was already making itself felt.

Although the term anti-Semitism was not invented until 1862, the racial ideology that gave rise to it was already well established in the early 19th century. Instead of—or as well as—an unbeliever and "Christ-killer", the Jew was now labelled as a member of an alien and inferior race, variously described as Semitic, Asiatic, and Oriental. The old-style religious Jew, secure in his faith, was untroubled by religious hatred, except of course in so far as it endangered his life and liberty; the new-style emancipated Jew was deeply disturbed by racial rejection, which wounded his spirit even when it spared his body. Told that he was a Semite or an Asian, he looked to other Semites and other Asians for comfort—just as the Czechs and Serbs looked to their Slavic big brother in Russia. The obvious choice was Islam—which in the 19th century meant the Ottoman Empire, the last surviving Muslim great power. In Europe, the collocation of Jews and Moors, Jews and Saracens, Jews and Turks was bitterly familiar from a thousand pogroms and Crusades, bans and banishments, inquisitions and persecutions —familiar, that is, to the Jews, who were the nearer and easier victims of the anger directed against both. The worst massacres of Jews in medieval Christendom were perpetrated by Crusaders on their way to fight the Saracens; the expulsion of the Jews from Spain was the climax of the reconquest from the Moors; the deadliest enemies of the Turks were the Russians, the most inveterate Jew-haters of modern Europe. A fellow-feeling, even if unreciprocated, was understandable.

Gratitude, sentiment, fellow-feeling—all play their part in the growth of pro-Muslim sentiment among Jews. But underlying them all there was something more powerful—an affinity of religious culture which made it possible for Jews, even emancipated, liberal West European Jews, to achieve an immediate and intuitive understanding of Islam. It is fashionable nowadays to speak of the Judaeo-Christian tradition. One could as justly speak of a Judaeo-Islamic tradition, for the Muslim religion, like Christianity, is closely related to its Jewish forerunner. Judaism has more in common with each of its two successors than either has with the other, and thus in many ways occupies an intermediate position between the two. The Judaeo-Christian affinities are well-known, and are at last being recognized. The Judaeo-Islamic affinities include such things as inflexible monotheism, austerity of worship, the rejection of images and incarnations and, most important of all, submission to an all-embracing divine law, enshrined in scripture, tradition, and commentary, which regulates and sanctifies the most intimate details of daily life.[19] Not only were the sacred texts similar in spirit, but they were written in cognate languages. The same word, *din*, means religion in Arabic, law in Hebrew. The connection between the two meanings is obvious to any Jew or Muslim. A Hebraist could learn Arabic, a Talmudist understand the *Sharīʿa*, with greater ease and with greater sympathy than his Protestant or Catholic colleagues. This feeling of affinity was expressed by the most illustrious of Jewish Islamicists, Ignaz Goldziher, in a letter written shortly before his death, to an Arab pupil: "It is for your people and for mine that I have lived. When you return to your country, tell this to your brothers."[20]

11. Semites and Anti-Semites

In the *Economist* of 9 November 1968, a reviewer of two books on Jerusalem reminded the Jewish authors that "the Arabs too are Semites, and have the long Semitic memory". A few weeks earlier, on 26 October 1968, another or possibly the same reviewer, discussing a collection of essays by the late Isaac Deutscher, remarked that "he [Deutscher] might have added that Palestinians, Jew and Arab, are all Semites, and that both races have a noble heritage of supra-nationalism from which to work".

Deutscher would not of course have added anything of the kind. Though frequently misguided, he was a sensitive and a literate man, and would no more have called a Jew or an Arab a Semite than he would have called a Pole or an Englishman an Aryan.

The Semite, like the Aryan, is a myth, and part of the same mythology. Both terms—Semite and Aryan—originated in the same way, and suffered the same misuse at the same hands.[1] Primarily linguistic, they date from the great development of scientific philology during the late 18th and early 19th centuries, when European scholars made the momentous discovery that the languages of mankind were related to one another and formed recognizable families. The term Aryan, of Indian origin, was first applied to a group of languages spoken in south Asia, to which Sanskrit and its derivatives belonged, and then extended to a larger group of languages in Europe and Asia, more commonly known as Indo-European. Semitic was applied at about the same time to another family of languages including Hebrew, Arabic, Aramaic, and, later, some other languages of the Middle East and North Africa. The name of course comes from Shem, one of the three sons of Noah, from whom, according to the Book of Genesis, the Jews and most of their ancient neighbors were descended. The term Semite in this sense seems to have appeared in print for the first time in 1781, in a contribution by A. L. von Schlözer to J. G. Eichhorn's *Repertorium für biblische und morgenländische Literatur*.

Though these terms were strictly linguistic in origin and use, nevertheless confusion between language and race seems to have appeared at quite an early date. The German philologist Max Müller is quoted as saying that one can no more speak of a Semitic or an Aryan race than one can speak of a brachycephalic or dolichocephalic dictionary. Scholars did in fact speak of Semites, but as a convenient shorthand for people speaking a Semitic language and having a culture expressed in a Semitic language. In this sense—of the speakers of a language, the carriers of a culture, "Semite" was frequently and respectably used as a substantive. Scholars have never failed to point out—repeatedly and alas ineffectually—that this linguistic and cultural classification has nothing to do with the anthropological classification of race, and that there is no reason whatever to assume that people who speak the same language are of the same racial origin. Indeed, if one looks at the speakers of Hebrew and of Arabic at the present time—not to mention English—such an assumption is palpably absurd. Speakers of Arabic include the racially highly diverse peoples of Syria, Lebanon and Iraq on the one hand, and of the Sudan and North Africa on the other; and even the small state of Israel, after the "ingathering of the exiles" from all over the world, shows a diversity of racial type even greater than that of the Arab world. One may call the Arabs and Israelis fellow-Semites in the sense that both speak Semitic languages, and that is all. To assume or imply any further content would be rather as if one were to describe the English and, say, the Bengalis as fellow-Aryans, and to suggest that they have some common identity because of that.

Racialist mythologies, based on certain false assumptions concerning Semites, Aryans and other groups, became very popular during the 19th century, when they provided, for those who needed it, an ideological justification for rejecting Jews, to replace the religious rationalization which was ceasing to satisfy secularized Christians. If Jews could no longer decently be persecuted because they were unbelievers, then they might be persecuted because they were members of an alien and inferior race. Religious prejudice was old-fashioned and obscurantist; racial discrimination in contrast appeared, to the 19th century, as modern and scientific. The important thing was of course that the Jews should be kept down, and that some intellectually and socially acceptable reason should be found for this. A further advantage of the new, racial dispensation was that it deprived the Jew of the opportunity, open to him under religious persecution, of deserting his own side and joining the persecutors. The present, third phase, in which politics has superseded both race and religion in anti-Jewish action and propaganda, has restored this option.

Anti-Jewish propaganda in Western and Central Europe had long had racial overtones. In 16th-century Spain the forced mass conversion of Jews and Muslims gave rise to a virulent racialism directed mainly against "new Christians" of Jewish origin and their descendants, and an obsession with purity of blood—*limpieza de sangre*. Racial themes appear occasionally in the 18th century, in the writings of the French Enlightenment. They became commoner during the 19th century, and were given a more systematic form in Germany, where the term anti-Semitism was first used.[2]

Hatred of the Jews has many parallels, and yet is unique. In some respects it resembles the normal hostility which one may find among people for neighbors of another tribe, another race, another faith or from another place, or the attitude which majorities sometimes adopt towards minorities. There are many examples all over the world of minority groups, often of alien origin, who play some specific economic role, and arouse hostility in consequence. Such are the Lebanese in West Africa, the Asians in East Africa, and the Chinese in South-east Asia. Hostility to Jews often arises or is aggravated by similar causes, but nevertheless anti-Semitism—in its persistence and extent, its potency and results, is without parallel. The one other persecution that is at all comparable, the massacre of the Armenians, is of a different order. The persecution of the

Armenians was limited both in time and in place—to the Ottoman Empire, and to the 19th and 20th centuries. It was in reality a struggle between two different peoples for the same country. It was not associated with either the demonic beliefs or the deep, almost physical hatred which inspire and direct anti-Semitism in Central and Eastern Europe and sometimes elsewhere. It may perhaps be described as an outstanding example of normal conflict. The uniqueness of anti-Semitism lies in the peculiar relationship of the Jews to Christianity, and in the role assigned to the Jews in Christian beliefs concerning the genesis of their faith. Some years ago, an American Secretary of State made a very revealing remark. Speaking of Arab hostility to Israel, he observed that it was not really surprising, since the Jews had murdered Muḥammad. They did not, of course, but it is quite obvious what he had in mind.

What then is the relevance of all this to the Arab-Israel dispute? How far is this dispute a racial problem? Before attempting to answer this question, I should like to clarify two important points. The first is the meaning of the term race. This word has been used and misused in many ways in our time, and much misunderstanding has been caused by unrecognized differences of definition. It is not my purpose here to define the nature of race or of racial identity, but it may be useful to explain what I mean by the word in the context of the present discussion. Race, then, is a quality, possessed or ascribed, which is or is believed to be involuntary, immutable, and hereditary, and thus essentially different from such forms of identity as religion and nationality, which can be adopted or relinquished at will. (I speak of course of the Anglo-American term nationality, not of the German *Nationalität* or the Russian *Natsionalnost*, both of which are racial in content.)

My second point is that I am here concerned only with the racial aspects of the problem; not with the rights and wrongs of the Arab-Israel conflict, and not with those aspects, by far the most important, that have nothing to do with race at all.

The argument is sometimes put forward that the Arabs and their friends, in opposing Israel or Zionism, cannot be anti-Semitic because the Arabs themselves are Semites. This argument is doubly flawed. First, the term Semite has no meaning as applied to groups as heterogeneous as the Arabs or Jews, and indeed it could be argued that the use of such terms is in itself a sign of racialism. Secondly, anti-Semitism has never anywhere been concerned with anyone but Jews. The Nazis, who may be accepted as the most authoritative exponents of anti-Semitism, made it quite clear that their hostility was limited to Jews only, and did not include the other so-called Semitic peoples. On the contrary, the Nazis found and still find no difficulty in simultaneously hating Jews and courting Arabs; they made a considerable and on the whole successful effort to cultivate the Arabs, and won the friendship and support of many Arab leaders, including some who still hold high office.[3]

Jews and pro-Jews have often tended to identify enmity to Israel or to Zionism with anti-Semitism, and to see Nasser as a new but unsuccessful Hitler and the *Fatah* as the present-day equivalent of the S.S. This is a false equation. The Arab-Israel conflict is a political one—a conflict between peoples over real issues, not a matter of prejudice and persecution. It is not necessary to assume that Arab hostility to Israel is a result of anti-Semitism—there are other adequate reasons by which it can be explained.

Nevertheless, since Israel happens to be a Jewish state inhabited largely by Jews, and since there are people who hate Jews independently of the Palestine conflict, anti-Semitism may sometimes be a factor in determining attitudes—on occasion even in determining policy and action. How far and in what circumstances is this so? It may be useful to examine this question in relation to some of the different groups involved.

The first and most important of the opponents of Israel are obviously the Arabs. In general it is true that the Arabs are not anti-Semitic—not because they themselves are Semites, a meaningless statement, but because for the most part they are not Christians. Anti-Semitism in its modern form is the response of the secularized Christian to the emancipated Jew—but with theological and psychological roots going back to the very origins of Christianity. In Islam, the Gospels have no place in education—and the processes of secularization and emancipation have barely begun. This being so, we shall not be surprised to find that Christian Arabs have often been anti-Semitic, and indeed played a leading part in introducing European-style anti-Semitism to the Arab world. That characteristic expression of Christian anti-Semitism, the blood-libel, has appeared from time to time in the history of the Middle East, as well as in Europe. When it did, it was, until recent years, almost invariably Christian in origin.[4] The most notable case among many in the 19th century was the famous Damascus affair of 1840, when Jews in that city were accused of the ritual murder of a Franciscan father. The accusers were his fellow monks and the French consul.

This does not of course mean that Jews under traditional Muslim rule lived in the inter-faith Utopia invented by modern myth-makers. Jews, like Christians, were in both theory and practice second-class citizens. This situation was however by no means as bad as the modern associations of this term would suggest. As members of a protected community, they enjoyed limited but substantial rights, which were at most times effectively maintained. In return, they owed—and gave—loyalty to the state, and accepted certain disabilities which were not normally very onerous. They were expected to keep their place, and the rare outbreaks of violence against Jews or Christians almost always resulted from a feeling that they had failed to do so.[5] They have conspicuously failed to do so in recent years.

The spread of anti-Semitism in the Arab lands in modern times has been due to three main causes. The first, chronologically, is European influence. A few Arabic translations of anti-Semitic tracts were published as early as the 19th century. Others followed, including the *Protocols of the Elders of Zion*, which first appeared in Arabic in Cairo in about 1927. There are now more versions and editions in Arabic than in any other language. There are also numerous other works, translated, adapted, and even original, dealing with the iniquities of the Jews through the millennia and the universal Jewish conspiracy against mankind, and including the old charges of blood-lust, ritual murder and the like, as well as the standard modern myths of power and money. There are even writings which defend and justify the Nazi persecution of the Jews. Some contemporary Arab comment on the Eichmann trial in Jerusalem is significant in this respect.[6]

From 1933 onwards the spread of anti-Jewish propaganda among the Arabs was no longer left to chance or to private enterprise. Nazi Germany made a truly immense effort in the Arab countries, and won many converts. This work was continued by Nazi émigrés after the war. In a sense, the final destruction of the Jewish communities in Arab countries was a long-term result of the Nazi effort.

The second factor is the Palestine question. As we have seen, Arab hostility to Israel has in its origins nothing to do with anti-Semitism as such. But Israel is Jewish, and there are Jewish minorities in Arab countries. In a time of crisis, the ready-made themes, imagery and vocabulary of anti-Jewish abuse that were offered to the Arabs proved too tempting to resist.

Jews in Arab countries had in general been indifferent or hostile to Zionism. They were converted, like others, by persecution. The first outbreak in modern times occurred in Baghdad on 1 and 2 June 1941, during the last hours of the pro-German Rashid Ali régime. According to official sources, 110 Jews were killed and 240 injured, 586 business premises sacked, and 911 houses destroyed. Unofficial estimates are higher. The next wave came in November 1945, with riots and attacks on synagogues and Jewish shops in Egypt and Syria, and a massacre in Libya, where 130 Jewish dead were officially counted and so many houses, shops and workshops destroyed that much of the community was left homeless and destitute. A third wave followed in December 1947, with massacres of Jews in Aleppo and Aden. In the latter, official estimates gave 82 dead, a similar number injured, 106 shops sacked, 220 houses destroyed or damaged.[7]

These events, with lesser outbreaks in some other places and increasing pressure almost everywhere, began the liquidation of the ancient Arab-Jewish communities and incidentally contributed greatly to the creation of Israel. The armed struggle in Palestine in 1947–48, the proclamation of Israel, and the subsequent Arab-Israeli conflict completed the process.

It has sometimes been argued that the outbreaks of violence against Jews in Arab countries and the subsequent flight of Arab Jews from their homes were due entirely to Zionism and the Arab reaction against it. This explanation has some plausibility, and there can be no doubt that the Palestine problem is an important element in the growth of Arab hostility to Jews. But it is not a sufficient explanation. In two countries with large Jewish minorities, Iraq and Yemen, the governments of the time not only permitted but positively facilitated the transfer of their Jews to Israel; other Arab governments too have shown more interest in the departure of their Jews than in their ultimate destination. The first post-war pogrom, in November 1945, was touched off by demonstrations on the anniversary of the Balfour Declaration, and might be explained by concern for the fate of Palestine, then under consideration. The same cannot be said of the earlier massacre in Baghdad. At the beginning of June 1941, Hitler ruled Europe, and Stalin was still his loyal helper; America was neutral, and Britain was strictly enforcing the 1939 White Paper in Palestine. Zionism—which was in any case rejected by most Iraqi Jews—could hardly have seemed a serious threat, and one needs great faith to believe that the Baghdad mobs in June 1941 were moved to fall upon their Jewish compatriots because of a problem 600 miles away and a threat six years in the future.[8]

The reaction against Zionism and the response to European anti-Semitism both had their effect. But what finally sealed the fate of the Arab Jews was the third, and in many ways the most important, factor—the general worsening of the position of minorities, both ethnic and religious, in the Middle East. In a time of violent change, the old tolerance has gone, the new equality has proved a fraud. All are insecure, some are persecuted—and the Jews, as so often, suffer in an acute and accelerated form the ills of the society of which they are a part.

From the outpouring of official and private anti-Semitic propaganda in Arabic—not only in books, but also in newspapers, magazines, films, radio and television—one might gather that the Arabs were going through a wave of anti-Semitism similar to that of the Nazi period. Such an impression would be mistaken. Unlike German anti-Semitism, or that of Poland or Russia, this anti-Semitic literature in the Arab countries does not rest on any real popular feeling, and has no roots in the past; indeed, it is doubtful whether one can really speak, even now, of anti-Semitism among Muslim Arabs—though of course there are always exceptions. Even across the battle lines, personal relations are still possible between Jews and Arabs, of a warmth and sincerity inconceivable to many Westerners. The anti-Semitic literature is overwhelmingly foreign in content and style—even the anti-Jewish cartoons have to use German and Russian stereotypes. In the Arab lands anti-Semitism is not, as in Europe, exploited by politicians, but is created by them. It has, so to speak, been switched on; it could as easily be switched off.

This does not of course mean that there has been no antagonism to Jews in the Arab countries in the past, or that Arab hostility today is purely political and ideological. Those Arab experts who know some Arabic are aware that it is only in the last few years that Arabs have begun to refer to their adversary as "the Zionists". Previously the enemy was *al-Yahūd*, the Jews, and to a large extent remains so now, except in public and in print. But this is not racial, nor does it resemble Christian anti-Semitism. It rests on no theology of guilt, no scriptural condemnation, no assumption of racial distinctness and inferiority. Rather is it the anger of a dominant group at a formerly tolerated minority which has signally failed to keep its place in the proper order of things. The Jew—in the East even more than in the West—has defaulted on his stereotype. An important factor in the Arab response to Israel is surely a sense of shock and outrage at the appearance of the Jew—familiar, tolerated, and despised—in this new and strange role, as soldier, administrator, and ruler.[9] Such resentments are by no means directed against Jews only. They also touch other communities which have somehow offended against the proprieties of the traditional order, and at the present time offer more of a threat to the Christian minorities—emancipated, assimilated and affluent—than to the few remaining Jews in the Arab East.

All this has nothing to do with anti-Semitism in either its religious or its racial form, but belongs rather to the category of normal conflict. European opponents of Israel—the Russians, the Poles, the East Germans and the rest—are quite a different matter. The Soviet Union no doubt has good political reasons for its present policy towards Israel. Unlike the Nazis, the Russians would be perfectly capable of changing sides if they thought it desirable. Indeed, for a brief period some 20 years ago they supported Israel against Britain, and it was arms from the Eastern bloc which enabled the infant state to withstand the Arab armies in 1948. Since then, however, the Soviet Union has turned the other way, and has, with its satellites and followers, pursued a policy of unrelenting hostility to the Jewish state.

While this policy can be explained on political grounds, certain features are noteworthy.

One of these is the violence of the language used both *to* Israel and *about* Israel, in both diplomatic and propaganda utterances. Even by the standards of communist political vituperation, the invective used in condemning Israel and Israeli actions is remarkable. One may observe striking similarities both in argument and in expression between East Germany and West Germany, in the condemnation of Israel—in East Germany by the official press and radio, in West Germany by the two groups of extremists—of the right, the neo-Nazis, and of the left, both old and new. Their hostility to Israel and the manner in which they express it are of course not the only points that these groups have in common.

Perhaps even more noteworthy is the fact that the Soviet Union has on two different occasions broken off diplomatic relations with Israel. This is a step which the Soviets have not taken since early times, even with their most dangerous and avowed enemies. They were careful to maintain diplomatic relations for as long as possible with Pilsudski's Poland—even after the murder of a Soviet ambassador in Warsaw; with Fascist Italy, and with Nazi Germany, even after the *Anschluss* with Austria and the German occupation of Czechoslovakia. Nor have they found it necessary in more recent times to break off diplomatic relations with states which are opposed to them, or which they accuse of being imperialist puppets or communist heretics, in Europe, Asia, Africa or the Americas. They did not, for example, break off relations with Yugoslavia in 1949, with China or the U.S.A. at any time, or with the new anti-communist rulers of Indonesia and Ghana. Only with Albania, in 1961, did the Soviet Union break off relations, under extreme provocation, and then only *de facto*, not *de jure*. Most of the satellites retained their diplomatic relations, and a few years later the Soviet Union tried unsuccessfully to restore them. They have however twice broken off diplomatic relations with Israel. The first occasion was in 1953, at the time of the "Doctors' Plot" in Moscow, when a small bomb was exploded in the courtyard of the Soviet Embassy in Tel Aviv. There was never the slightest suspicion that this was anything but an irresponsible private operation. Diplomatic relations were restored after a while, but were broken off again in 1967, this time by almost the whole Soviet bloc. This disparity is very striking, and leaves one wondering what peculiar characteristic of Israel, lacking in other countries, has twice required a rupture of diplomatic relations. The vocabulary and iconography of Soviet anti-Zionism, with their covert and sometimes overt appeals to old-fashioned racial and even religious prejudice, may suggest an answer.

A third group of opponents of Israel and Zionism are the non-communist supporters of the Arab cause in the "free world". Because these lack the obvious motives, whether political or ideological, of the Arabs on the one hand and the communists on the other, they are the ones most frequently accused of being moved by anti-Semitic motives. Often, this accusation is an injustice. There are many who support the Arab cause out of a sincere conviction that it is a just one; others who support it for good practical, personal, political or commercial reasons unconnected with any kind of prejudice. The fact must however be faced that there are some—what proportion would be difficult to say—for whom the Arabs are in truth nothing but a stick with which to beat the Jews.

In England and in other English-speaking countries, there has never developed a tradition of intellectual anti-Semitism such as has at different times flourished in France, Germany, and Russia. The attempts by Goldwin Smith and E. A. Freeman to launch German-style racial anti-Semitism in the 19th century, like the later attempts by Belloc and Chesterton to import the French clerical variety, had little or no success. This is the more remarkable in that English literature offers what is probably a richer gallery of mythic Jewish villains than any other literature in Europe—a gallery that begins with Chaucer's murderers of St Hugh of Lincoln, and includes such varied figures as Shylock, Barabas the Jew of Malta, Fagin, Melmotte, Svengali, the sophisticated stereotypes of Graham Greene and T. S. Eliot and the penny-plain stereotypes of John Buchan and Agatha Christie.[10] Prejudice against Jews has of course always existed, and has on occasion—very infrequently—amounted to a factor of some political importance. But it has never in modern times reached the point when anti-Semitism could be openly avowed by anyone with serious intellectual pretensions or political ambitions. Anti-Semitism is on the whole furtive, disguised, and hypocritical. Where openly expressed, it is usually a lower-middle-class phenomenon—the petty snobbery of the provincial golf club, whose members can find no other way of giving themselves status. In the working class it conflicted with the standards of brotherhood and internationalism, to which all paid at least lip service and often much more. In the upper middle class, the intellectual and professional classes and the upper class, its open expression conflicted with accepted standards of good taste. In the English-speaking countries in particular, therefore, the Palestine conflict provided a heaven-sent (if that is the right word) opportunity to be anti-Jewish with a good conscience inside oneself and a good appearance towards others. This was a political conflict, not a racial prejudice, and an anti-Jewish position could be justified on the highest ethical and political grounds. I stress again—this is not true of all pro-Arabs, perhaps indeed not of any great number of them, but it is certainly true of some, for whom the Palestine problem and the sufferings of the Arabs provide perfect cover for prejudices which they would otherwise be ashamed to reveal.

Some are easy to detect. The openly fascist and racialist groups still active in various parts of the world are almost without exception pro-Arab—and their literature makes their real sentiments and purposes abundantly clear. Some Arabs have disdained the support of such tainted allies; others, including both governments and revolutionaries, have made good use of it.[11]

In more respectable circles, it is by no means easy to distinguish between those who are pro-Arab and those who are merely anti-Jewish. There are however some symptoms which, though not infallible, are a fairly good indication. One of the characteristics of the anti-Jew as distinct from the pro-Arab is that he shows no other sign of interest in the Arabs or sympathy for them, apart from their conflict with the Jews. He is completely unmoved by wrongs suffered by the Arabs at the hands of anyone other than Jews—whether their own rulers or third parties. He shows no interest in the history or achievements of the Arabs, no knowledge of their language or culture. On the contrary he may speak of them in a way which is in reality profoundly disparaging. No one in his right mind would claim to be an expert on, say, France or Germany without knowing a word of French or German. The claims to expertise of our self-styled Arabists without Arabic rest on the assumption that Arabs are somehow different from—and inferior to—Frenchmen and Germans, in that what they say and write in their own language can be safely disregarded. In the same spirit, some so-called pro-Arabs explain away the more extreme statements of certain Arab leaders by attributing the quality of what they say to the inevitable vagueness and violence of the Arabic language. Arabic is one of the noblest instruments that the human race has ever forged for the expression of its thoughts. It is a language rich in poetry and eloquence, two arts whose practitioners are not always to be taken as saying exactly what they mean or meaning exactly what they say. But that is only one side of Arabic. It is also a language which has been used with remarkable clarity and precision. As a medium of philosophical and scientific literature, its only peer, until modern times, was Greek. At once poetic and accurate, Arabic was for a very long time one of the major languages of civilization. To offer such excuses for the utterances of individual Arabs is an expression not of sympathy but rather of ignorance and, ultimately, of contempt, If anyone had tried, in the '30s, to excuse Hitler's speeches by saying that this was the only way in which one could speak in the German language, would he have been accepted either as an expert on Germany—or as a friend of the German people?

A second characteristic of the anti-Jew as opposed to the pro-Arab is his tendency to harp on Jewish power and influence, which he usually greatly exaggerates, and to complain of Jewish double loyalty. There are about 450,000 Jews in Britain. The anti-Jew proceeds on the assumptions (a) that they are all as rich as Rothschild, as efficient as Marks & Spencer, as clever as Isaiah Berlin, as articulate as Bernard Levin, as resourceful as John Bloom; (b) that they are all working together for Israel; (c) that they are committing some offense in doing so.

In fact of course the great majority of Jews in Britain, as elsewhere, are as ignorant, inept, and inert as anyone else. Like others again they are sharply divided, some for Israel, some, no doubt fewer but not unimportant, against Israel, and the great mass at best sympathetic but inactive. The question of double loyalty takes different forms. In democratic and open societies, like Britain and the U.S.A., Jewish double loyalty is in the main a problem only for Jews and anti-Jews, not for the great mass of the population who are neither the one nor the other. Most non-political Englishmen and Americans find it normal that Jews should sympathize with Israel, and are indeed slightly puzzled or even disturbed when they do not. As citizens of a free country, Jews have the same rights as anyone else to be pro-Israel, pro-Arab, or pro-whatever they please. A selective restriction of this right, imposed on Jews but not on others, on support for Israel but not for other foreign causes, would put them, in effect, in a separate and inferior category of citizenship. This line of thought has won little support in free countries.

In countries with an authoritarian tradition, like Russia or Poland, or a centralist tradition, like France, the position is different, and opposition by a group of nationals—Jews or others—to a foreign policy pursued by the government is regarded as a form of dissidence verging on treason. In France, some have seen Zionist Jews as a modern equivalent of the Huguenots and the Ultramontanes; the resemblance is remote, and its effect very limited, though it has already caused some concern to French Jews.[12] In Poland and Russia, where this kind of argument is more familiar, the pressures and penalties to which the Jew is subject are incomparably greater. Russian and Polish Jews must not merely refrain from supporting Israel; they must actively oppose her. The point was well made—in private—by a distinguished Polish Jewish writer during the 1967 war. "I agree," he said, "that a man can have only one country to which he owes allegiance—but why does mine have to be the United Arab Republic?"

In our time, anti-Zionism has come to have a wider range and relevance, often quite unconnected with the Middle East and its problems. In the 19th century, religiously-expressed anti-Judaism was regarded as reactionary and outmoded, and gave way, in more modern and secular circles, to racially-expressed anti-Semitism. In our time racialism in turn has been discredited, and has, for some, been duly succeeded by an anti-Zionism in which politics takes the place previously occupied by religion and then race. The change is one of expression and emphasis rather than of substance, since all these elements have been and still are present. Even now, if one wishes to attack or discredit a Jew, one may call him an unbeliever, a Semite, or a Zionist, depending on whether the atmosphere and prevailing ideology of the society in which one operates is religious, ethnic, or political. In Poland, I am told, people are dismissed from their posts for having a Zionist grandmother.

Racial feelings can work both ways, and may underlie non-Jewish support for Israel, as well as non-Arab hostility. One group, the approximate rather than exact counterpart of the Jew-hating Arabophiles, are those who favor Israel because they hate Arabs. Such motives were at one time evident in France, where the war in Algeria gave rise to a quasi-alliance with Israel against the common Arab enemy, and where the final French withdrawal left a feeling of bitterness for which the Israeli victories provided some solace. This feeling was however specific and transitory; it was political and psychological rather than racial, and is of declining importance. In the English-speaking countries hostility to the Arabs as such is not a factor, though there are some who include the Arabs in a generalized dislike of lesser breeds. For these, the choice between Jew and Arab may present an agonizing dilemma.

Two other groups, among the supporters of Israel, are the inverted and repentant anti-Semites. By inverted anti-Semites I mean those who basically accept the anti-Semitic myth of the secret Jewish world power, but see it with respect and admiration rather than with hatred and fear. A classical example is Benjamin Disraeli, whose view of the role of the Jews does not differ greatly from that of the anti-Semites, but is presented in positive instead of negative terms, with pride instead of hate. The same kind of awestruck belief in Jewish power can be found in some gentile sympathizers with Zionism—even, for example, among some of the promoters of the Balfour Declaration, who saw in it a device to win "international Jewry" to the Allied cause.[13] This belief still appears occasionally even at the present day, though it has lost most of its cogency in view of the manifest inability of "international Jewry" to do anything against either Hitler or his successors in enmity to Judaism. Awe for the mysterious power of Jewry has given place to respect for the political and military power of Israel—but this is not a racial consideration.

The repentant anti-Semites—usually vicarious—are another matter. There can be no doubt that one of the most important sources of support for Israel in the period following the fall of Hitler was guilt—guilt, that is, in the modern sense, a psychological state rather than a legal fact. The true anti-Semite is rarely repentant, and feelings of guilt for crimes against the Jews are often in inverse proportion to the degree of personal responsibility. They were, nevertheless, a factor of importance, and the response of many Christians to the emergence of Israel was determined by the feeling that they, their countries, and their churches were accessories to the Nazi crimes, if not by active complicity, then by acquiescence or indifference.

Such feelings are a dwindling asset to Israel, and must inevitably die away as the memory of Nazi crimes recedes into the past. In the Soviet Union, official propaganda has even tried to conceal the fact that the Nazis persecuted Jews; to reveal it might arouse sympathy for either the Nazis or the Jews, and both responses would in different ways be undesirable. In the West one can almost hear the sigh of relief with which some persons and institutions have, after more than 30 years of unease, resumed their posture of moral superiority to the unredeemed and unbelieving Jews.

Finally, what of the Jews themselves? For the Jews are by no means unanimous in their support for Israel. The universal Jewish conspiracy, whether for Israel or any other purpose, is of course a figment of anti-Semitic imagination and has never had any reality. Many Jews are pro-Israel to varying degrees and a minority of them are active in Israel's support. There is, however, a by no means insignificant number of others who are active opponents of Israel—certainly more than in the past. These Jewish opponents of Israel are of several kinds. Some, as with non-Jews, are believers in the justice of the Arab cause; some are moved by internal Jewish religious considerations. Of the remainder, the most important are supporters of the old and new lefts, whose reactions to this as to most other problems are determined by political decisions, not necessarily their own, and by the current position of the ideological hemline. Many in particular proceed on the fashionable progressive assumption that any cause or any state which is supported by the United States must be an evil one; Israel, enjoying such support, must therefore necessarily be in the wrong in any dispute in which she is involved.

This is not a racial question. In the case of Jewish leftists old and new, however, there is an additional factor which should not be underrated. This is the phenomenon of Jewish self-hate—the neurotic reaction which one finds among some Jews to the phenomenon of anti-Semitism by accepting, sharing, expressing, and even exaggerating some of the basic assumptions of the anti-Semite.[14] In the 19th and early 20th centuries this kind of response could be found, in particular, among assimilated German Jews, of both left and right. A classical example is Karl Marx's essay on the Jewish question, now enjoying a new popularity in Arabic translation. Another is the posture of some German Jewish conservatives, who adopted the standards and outlook, as far as they could, of the German Nationalist right, and repeated their accusations against Jews, particularly Jews other than those of Germany. This did not of course help them in any way when the Nazis came to power and imposed their own solution of the Jewish problem. Today the phenomenon of Jewish self-hate is found chiefly on the far left, where hostility to Israel provides, or appears to provide, an opportunity of freeing oneself from ancestral and, more immediately, parental bonds, and passing from the minority to the majority. This may help us to understand some of the tortured utterances of the claustrophobic or rather claustrophiliac world of Jewish left-wing Marxism, and the curious phenomenon of Jewish supporters of black anti-Semitism in the U.S.A.—the American children of survivors of European ghettoes and death camps, who accept, or rather demand, a share of guilt for the enslavement of the African in America, and thus tacitly assert their membership of the dominant even if guilty majority.

All this—Gentile anti-Semitism or philo-Semitism, Jewish loyalty or self-hate—has nothing whatever to do with the rights and wrongs of the Arab-Israel dispute. It does however influence and sometimes determine the attitude of important groups of observers and participants from outside, including journalists, politicians, officials, and hence even governments. There are several familiar, sometimes pathetic figures—the Jew driven one way or the other by tribal solidarity or the desire to escape; the old-style white racialist, trying to decide which he hates more, Arabs or Jews; the tormented American WASP liberal, who sees the Palestine conflict as, ultimately, one between Harlem and the Bronx, and makes a choice determined by his own personal blend of prejudice and guilt; the anxious politician, now as in the '30s, seeking to avoid even the appearance of serving a Jewish purpose, and falling over backwards into other, less mythical, dangers. The fear of serving Jewish purposes was a not unimportant factor in the appeasement of Hitler, long after the point when self-interest clearly required that he be resisted. The advance of Soviet power in the Middle East has been eased by similar anxieties on the part of some who might otherwise have opposed it.[15]

Race is topical at the moment, and the racialist is the fashionable enemy. It is therefore good propaganda to present one's problem as racial, and to call the adversary a racialist. This has given rise to a series of accusations, some grotesquely comic—such as the insult "Nazi", hurled by Hitler's allies at Hitler's victims—others merely false.

At first sight it might seem that some at least of the accusations on both sides are true. Have not the Arab governments persecuted their Jewish subjects? Is not Israel a self-proclaimed Jewish state, to which Jews and only Jews have a right of entry? Yes indeed. But "Jewish" is a racial category for anti-Semites and those who have been misled by them, including some Jews. It is not and never has been such for authentic Jews, nor for that matter for most Arabs. Legal decisions in Israel have confirmed that a Jew converted to another religion ceases to be a Jew while a Gentile converted to Judaism becomes a Jew. This is not a racial definition. Correspondingly, Arab hostility to Jews, whether directed against the Jewish state or against the Jewish community, in whatever words and actions it may find expression, is fundamentally not racial in character.

Fortunately—for the Palestine problem is difficult enough without injecting racialism—all this has little real effect on either the Arabs or the Israelis. The problem is political and strategic, social and economic, national, communal, and perhaps even religious—but not, despite all the efforts that have been and are being made, racial. Neither Arabs nor Israelis are completely free from racial feelings and prejudices, and both have racial tensions of a sort within their own societies. But these are comparatively minor and, what is more important, are not directed against one another. The Middle East has its racial problems, and in the past these have sometimes caused trouble, but it does not share the obsessive concern with race that affects its neighbors in Europe, Asia and Africa. However difficult the Palestine problem may be, it is not as yet poisoned by the bitterest conflict of our time—and in this there is some faint cause for hope.

12. An Ode Against the Jews

Little is known of the life of Abū Isḥāq.[1] His name is given as Abū Isḥāq Ibrāhīm b. Masʿūd b. Saʿīd al-Tujībī al-Ilbīrī. Tujībī indicates that he was descended from the famous Arab family of Tujīb, which played a role of some importance in the history of Muslim Spain; Ilbīrī suggests that he came from Elvira. He appears to have been born towards the end of the 10th century, and probably moved to Granada, along with the rest of the inhabitants of Elvira, when that city was sacked by the Ṣanhāja Berbers during the insurrection of 1010. In 1012 Zāwī b. Zīrī, the founder of the Berber Zirid dynasty, made Granada his capital.

A jurist by training, Abū Isḥāq served as secretary to the *qāḍī* of Granada, and also acted as a teacher. His career coincided with the reign of Bādīs b. Ḥabbūs (reigned 1038–1073), the Zirid monarch who was the patron of Samuel ibn Nagrella, known in Jewish literature as Ha-Nagīd, and of his son Joseph. At some point Abū Isḥāq seems to have fallen foul of authority; by order of Bādīs he was banished from Granada and went to live in a convent called Rābiṭat al-ʿUqāb, in the Sierra de Elvira. According to Ibn al-Khaṭīb, he was banished because of the slanders of the Jewish minister Joseph ibn Nagrella, but a poem which Abū Isḥāq composed at al-ʿUqāb suggests that other influences may have been at work:

I settled there and it dispelled my troubles,
and soothed me, and I did not feel estranged there.
Though there are many wolves around it, yet
I find the wolf less dangerous than the jurist (faqīh)
Nor do I regret the absence of any brother, for
I have seen that a man's ruin comes on him from his brother.
What has made me despair of our times is that
honor does not go to the honorable.[2]

From these verses it would seem that Abū Isḥāq blamed his misfortunes on co-religionists and colleagues—on brother Muslim jurists, rather than on Jews. Later, however, he turned his anger against these, and composed his famous *qaṣīda*, or ode attacking Joseph ibn Nagrella in particular and the Jews of Granada in general. He lived long enough to witness, and presumably enjoy, the death of Ibn Nagrella and of many other Jews in Granada on 30 December 1066, and himself died shortly after, in 1067.

The poem was first made known to modern scholarship by the Dutch orientalist Reinhart Dozy, who found a biography of Abū Isḥāq, including this and some other poems, in a Berlin manuscript of the *Iḥāṭa fī ta'rīkh Gharnāṭa*, by the 14th-century Granadan author Ibn al-Khaṭīb, and published the Arabic text of this passage, with a French translation.[3] This was used by Heinrich Graetz[4] and subsequent Jewish historians. The poem, with some lines omitted, appears again in another work by Ibn al-Khaṭīb, the *Aʿmāl al-aʿlām fī man būyiʿa qabl al-iḥtilām min mulūk al-Islām.*[5] A unique manuscript of Abū Isḥāq's *Dīwān*, preserved in the Escorial library, was published by E. García Gómez, with an introduction.[6] The anti-Jewish poem was reprinted and partially translated into English by A. R. Nykl,[7] and again partially translated and analysed by M. Perlmann.[8]

The following is a new translation of the poem.

Go, tell all the Ṣanhāja[9]
the full moons of our time, the lions in their lair
The words of one who bears them love, and is concerned
and counts it a religious duty to give advice.[10]
Your chief has made a mistake
which delights malicious gloaters
He has chosen an infidel as his secretary
when he could, had he wished, have chosen a believer.
Through him, the Jews have become great and proud
and arrogant—they, who were among the most abject
And have gained their desires and attained the utmost
and this happened suddenly, before they even realised it.[11]
And how many a worthy Muslim humbly obeys[12]
the vilest ape[13] *among these miscreants.*
And this did not happen through their own efforts
but through one of our own people who rose as their accomplice.[14]

Oh why did he not deal with them, following
the example set by worthy and pious leaders?
Put them back where they belong
and reduce them to the lowest of the low,
Roaming among us, with their little bags,[15]
with contempt, degradation and scorn as their lot,
Scrabbling in the dunghills for colored rags[16]
to shroud their dead for burial.
They did not make light of our great ones
or presume against the righteous,
Those low-born people would not be seated in society
or paraded[17] *along with the intimates [of the ruler].*
Bādīs! You are a clever man
and your judgment is sure and accurate.
How can their misdeeds be hidden from you
when they are trumpeted all over the land?
How can you love this bastard brood
when they have made you hateful to all the world?
How can you complete your ascent to greatness
when they destroy as you build?
How have you been lulled to trust a villain
and made him your companion—though he is evil company?
God has vouchsafed in His revelations
a warning against the society of the wicked.[18]
Do not choose a servant from among them
but leave them to the curse of the accurst!
For the earth cries out against their wickedness
and is about to heave and swallow us all.
Turn your eyes to other countries
and you will find the Jews there are outcast dogs.
Why should you alone be different and bring them near
when in all the land they are kept afar?
—You, who are a well-beloved king,
scion of glorious kings,
And are the first among men
as your forbears were first in their time.
I came to live in Granada
and I saw them frolicking there.
They divided up the city and the provinces
with one of their accursed men everywhere.
They collect all the revenues
they munch and they crunch[19]
They dress in the finest clothes
while you wear the meanest.
They are the trustees of your secrets
—yet how can traitors be trusted?

Others eat a dirham's worth, afar,
while they are near, and dine well.
They challenge you to your God
and they are not stopped or reproved.
They envelope you with their prayers[20]
and you neither see nor hear.
They slaughter beasts in our markets[21]
and you eat their trefa.[22]
Their chief ape has marbled his house
and led the finest spring water to it.
Our affairs are now in his hands
and we stand at his door.
He laughs at us and at our religion
and we return to our God.[23]
If I said that his wealth is as great
as yours,[24] *I would speak truth.*
Hasten to slaughter him as an offering,
sacrifice him, for he is a fat ram
And do not spare his people
for they have amassed every precious thing.
Break loose their grip and take their money
for you have a better right to what they collect.
Do not consider it a breach of faith to kill them
—the breach of faith would be to let them carry on.
They have violated our covenant with them
so how can you be held guilty against the violaters?
How can they have any pact[25]
when we are obscure and they are prominent?
Now we are the humble, beside them,
as if we had done wrong, and they right!
Do not tolerate their misdeeds against us
for you are surety for what they do.
God watches His own people
and the people of God will prevail.

Abū Isḥāq's verse tirade is of interest in two respects—as an example of the public and social function of poetry, and as evidence on the position of a Jewish community in a medieval Muslim society.

According to a 9th-century Arabic author, poetry has four functions—to command, to forbid, to give information and to elicit it. These functions are discharged in eulogy, satire, elegy, apology, love-making, comparison, and "reports of happenings".[26]

The modern observer might describe many of these functions of the medieval poet as journalism, publicity, propaganda, public relations—even as broadcasting. Medieval Islam society was, by comparison with contemporary Christian Europe, highly literate and sophisticated; the Arabs, at all times, have shown a unique skill in the art of words, a ready appreciation, and a swift response.[27] In such a society, information and image could be of great significance, and the success, even the survival of a ruler or minister might depend on their manipulation. Lacking the mass media which serve the present-day holder or seeker of power, the medieval had recourse to his poet who, in return for a consideration, produced a version of events, a statement of opinions, or an image of a person which was vivid, memorable, and conducive to his patron's requirements. Eulogy served to present the patron to the public in the most favorable light, satire to tarnish the images of his rivals and opponents. Politics, opinion, and news were not the only concerns of this kind of poetic journalism. The poet could also provide a social column, by celebrating or commemorating in verse the births, marriages and deaths of the great; he could promote special interests of various kinds; he could even, in a prefigurement of the singing commercial, advertise goods for sale—and, anticipating another type of modern journalism, he could extort money by the threat of scurrilous abuse.[28]

The poet may seek to advance his own personal interests; or those of a patron whom he serves or hopes to serve; or those of a group or faction to which he feels himself to belong.[29] This group may be tribal or ethnic, religious or sectarian, political or personal—sometimes, though rarely, even local. Normally, the poet's aim is propagandist—that is to say, he seeks to influence men's opinions and attitudes, to persuade or dissuade, to win or divert their support. Sometimes, his aim is more direct and immediate—incitement to action rather than mere suasion. Probably the most famous instance recorded in Arabic historiography is the massacre of the Umayyad princes after the accession to power of the Abbasids. In several different versions, an inflammatory poem declaimed by a hostile poet is said to have been the cause of the massacre, or at least the signal for the killers to begin their work.[30]

Such stories are no doubt exaggerated and dramatized—but they do reflect an important aspect of the function of poetry and the poet in public life. The anti-Jewish *qaṣīda* of Abū Isḥāq is clearly intended to produce results, and not merely to relieve the author's feelings. The form and style are noteworthy. The meter is short and sharp, the language simple and direct, the statements forceful and concrete—aimed at the Ṣanhāja Berber soldiery, who could not be expected to appreciate or even understand the intricate prosody, abstruse vocabulary, elaborate imagery, and recondite allusions that were customary in formal Arabic poetry.[31] This time Abū Isḥāq wanted to be understood by a wide public—and it seems that he got what he wanted.

Abū Isḥāq, says Ibn al-Khaṭīb, brought about the destruction of Joseph ibn Nagrella, by means of "a poem, which was memorized, in which he incited the Ṣanhāja against him . . . so that they killed him, and also attacked his people."[32] "This *qaṣīda*," he concludes, "was the cause of their extirpation."[33]

The rather vague statements of Ibn al-Khaṭīb have been taken to mean that the poem was the immediate cause of the outbreak in which Joseph ibn Nagrella and thousands of his co-religionists perished.[34] This seems unlikely. The Jewish accounts of the massacre make no mention of Abū Isḥāq or his poem;[35] neither do the earlier Arabic sources, which give a more detailed account of the outbreak, explaining the circumstances in which it occurred, without reference to the poet agitator.[36] The story that the poem was the direct and immediate cause may be dismissed as dramatic exaggeration, of a familiar kind; it may however safely be assumed that this piece of verse propaganda, with its fierce and plain appeal to hate, envy and violence, will have helped powerfully to prepare the way.

Abū Isḥāq speaks for himself, not a patron. His immediate objective was a powerful Jewish statesman against whom he appears to have had a personal grudge, and Dozy and García Gómez are probably right in attributing his rage to frustrated personal ambition.[37] But his invective and his accusation are aimed at the Jews in general, not merely at Ibn Nagrella as an individual; and it is upon the Jews as such that he invokes the vengeance and punishment of the outraged Muslims.

Outrage is the dominant theme of the poem. In striking contrast to the anti-Judaism and anti-Semitism of Christendom, Abū Isḥāq does not deny the right of the Jews to life, livelihood, and the practice of their religion. On the contrary, he is well aware that these rights are legally guaranteed by the *dhimma*, the contract between the Muslim state and the tolerated non-Muslim communities to which it extends its protection and which are thence known as *dhimmīs*. Abū Isḥāq was, it will be recalled, a jurist. He does not seek to deny or to minimize the contract; indeed, even in his fury, he is at some pains to reassure his hearers (and no doubt himself) that in killing and robbing the Jews they will not be acting illegally, i.e. violating the provisions of a contract sanctified by the Holy Law of Islam. The contract, he argues, has already been violated by the Jews, and has therefore ceased to be operative. The Muslims and their ruler are therefore absolved from their obligations under the contract, and are free to attack, kill and expropriate the Jews, without illegality—i.e., without sin.

Abū Isḥāq indicates how, in his judgment, the Jews have broken the contract. In the simplest terms, they have failed to keep their proper place—to remain in the station which is assigned to them. The law relating to the *dhimma* makes it clear that the protected communities must recognize the primacy of Islam and the Muslims of this world as well as the next, and must accept certain fiscal disabilities and social limitations, in token of their submission. These conditions are specified in the law-books, but were in general not very strictly enforced by Muslim governments. In contrast to the treatment of parallel problems in Christian countries, in Islam practice was usually more tolerant than precept, and Christians and Jews enjoyed greater rights and opportunities than would have been accorded to them with the strict enforcement of the law.[38]

There was nevertheless a very definite feeling that the non-Muslim communities had their place, and should not be allowed to exceed it. Abū Isḥāq makes clear, if with some exaggeration, what that place was to be. Diatribes like his, and massacres like that of Granada in 1066, are of very rare occurrence in Islamic history. When they do occur, the circumstances are almost invariably the same. Members of a minority community, sometimes Jews, more often Christians, have waxed rich and powerful; they are accused of flaunting their wealth and abusing their power, and thus forfeit their rights and bring retribution on themselves.[39] The word most commonly used of the Jews is *dhull*, which means humility, abasement,[40] and Abū Isḥāq clearly expected his Jews to remain poor, humble and degraded. In practice, considerable latitude was allowed to Jews, as to other minority groups, but too striking and visible a departure from the approved condition of *dhull* was apt to arouse popular anger.

The position of Jews and Christians under traditional Muslim rule certainly fell a long way short of the inter-faith utopia imagined by modern romantics and apologists, but it was one which enabled them to survive and at times to flourish. To the modern ear, "second-class citizen" has a harsh and evil sound—yet second-class citizenship which is rooted in tradition, respected by law and custom, and effectively maintained, is better than first-class citizenship on paper only. Constitutional rights, in countries where such concepts have little meaning, are a poor substitute for entrenched privileges. To the citizen of a liberal democracy, the status of *dhimmī* would no doubt be intolerable—but to many minorities in the world today, that status, with its communal autonomy and its limited yet recognized rights, might well seem enviable.

13. *The Sultan, the King, and the Jewish Doctor*

One of the most popular motifs in the saga of Maimonides as a Jewish culture hero is the story of how he was invited to go and treat the King of England, Richard Lionheart, who had gone to Palestine with the Third Crusade—and refused the invitation. This story, which appears in almost every biography of Maimonides and in most popular histories of the Jews, assumes several forms. The simplest version merely states that on some occasion King Richard sought the services of Maimonides as a physician. Others develop this into an offer of employment as body-physician, sometimes with the further suggestion that Maimonides accompany the King back to London. The reason given for his refusal is, usually, his satisfaction with his court-post in Cairo; sometimes also disquiet about conditions in London.[1]

The birth, growth, and luxuriance of this story provide a curious and instructive example of the methods and validity of popular historiography. It derives from a single source—the *Ta'rīkh al-Ḥukamā'*, or *History of Physicians*, of the Egyptian Muslim writer Jamāl al-Dīn Abu'l-Ḥasan ʿAlī ibn Yūsuf al-Qifṭī (1172–1248). He was born in Qifṭ, in upper Egypt, to a family of scholars and officials. When he was 15 years old his father was appointed first assistant to the chief minister al-Qāḍī al-Fāḍil, the patron and benefactor of Maimonides. Later his family moved to Palestine, and after many travels al-Qifṭī eventually settled in Aleppo, where he remained until his death. Among his closest friends there was the Jewish physician Joseph ibn Yaḥyā ibn Shimʿōn, a pupil of Maimonides, who may possibly be identical with the famous Joseph ibn ʿAqnīn. Al-Qifṭī thus had the opportunity of collecting information for the biography of Maimonides which he included in his book.

This work, a biographical dictionary of physicians, was written between 1230 and 1235. The full text is unfortunately lost, but an abridgment made by Muḥammad ibn 'Alī al-Zawzanī about a year after al-Qifṭī's death has survived. An edition of the Arabic text did not appear until 1903,[2] and the work has not yet, so far as I am aware, been translated into any European language. The passage relating to Maimonides, however, became known to European scholarship very much earlier, when the Maronite scholar Casiri (Al-Ghazīrī) published the Arabic text, together with a Latin translation, in his catalog of the Arabic manuscripts in the Escurial library, printed in Madrid in 1760.[3] This Latin version was used by Heinrich Graetz and other 19th-century writers on Maimonides.

The relevant passage in al-Qifṭī's text may be rendered as follows:

> . . . He left Spain and travelled to Egypt with his family, and settled in the town of Fusṭāṭ, among the Jews there. He revealed his religion publicly and lived in the quarter called al-Maṣīṣa. He earned a living by dealing in precious stones and the like, and people studied philosophy under him. This was in the last days of the Egyptian 'Alid dynasty. They wanted to employ him among the other physicians and to send him out to the king of the Franks in Ascalon, who asked them for a physician. They chose him, but he refused this service and refrained from participating in this affair. And when the Ghuzz ruled in Egypt and the dynasty of 'Alī collapsed, the Qāḍī al-Fāḍil 'Abn al-Raḥīm b. 'Alī al-Baysānī took him under his wing and showed him favor and assigned a salary to him.[4]

Since Casiri's Latin version has, directly or indirectly, formed the basis of most subsequent writing on the subject, it may be useful to quote that part of it that deals with the Frankish king:

> Interea Philosophicas disciplinas publice praecepit; adeoque in Medicorum album adscriptus, & Francorum Regis *Ascaloniae* ipsum maxime optantis Medicus electus est: quod tamen munus & honorem omnino recusavit.

It will be noted that Casiri's translation is rather different in form and emphasis from the original. Moreover, both his text and translation omit the important phrase: وذلك فى أواخر أيام الدولة المصرية العلوية —"This was in the last days of the Egyptian 'Alid dynasty."[5]

From this reference back to the primary source, several important points emerge:

1. The name of the Frankish king is not given.
2. There is nothing to show whether permanent employment or merely a visit was involved.
3. There is no suggestion whatever of accompanying the Frankish king back to his own country in Europe.
4. No reason is given for Maimonides' refusal.
5. No date is given for the episode, but there is a strong implication that it took place early in Maimonides' career in Egypt—before the fall of the Fatimids in 1171, and before he had established himself as a successful physician in Cairo.

Who then was the Frankish king? Casiri, assuming that the incident took place during the first Frankish occupation of Ascalon (1153–1187), contents himself with noting that there are four possibilities—the four kings who reigned in the Latin kingdom of Jerusalem in that period. Graetz seems to have been the first to assert that it was Richard Lionheart, and was sufficiently confident of this identification to incorporate it, without qualification, in the text of his narrative, where we read:

> Maimuni's Ruf war so gross, dass ihn der englische König Richard Löwenherz, die Seele des dritten Kreuzzuges, zu seinem Leibarzte ernennen wollte. Maimuni schlug aber diesen Antrag aus.[6]

In a footnote to this sentence Graetz cites the Latin version of al-Qifṭī, and remarks:

> Dieser מלך אלפרנג בעסקלאן kann nur Richard Löwenherz bedeuten, welcher Askalon wieder aufbauen liess und zum Stützpunkte für die kriegerischen Unternehmungen gegen Jerusalem machte.

It will be seen that Graetz is not responsible for the invitation to London, which would seem to be a gloss by Yellin and Abrahams to Graetz's hypothesis, nor did he put forward any of the reasons later adduced for Maimonides' refusal. He did, however, make, with a confidence which I hope to show was quite unjustified, the identification of the unnamed Frankish king with Richard Lionheart, and also introduced two other elements to the story for which the original source provides no foundation.

We may at once set aside Graetz's assumption that it was Maimonides' reputation that led King Richard to wish to appoint him as his physician. From our text it seems clear that the Frankish king merely asked for *a* physician, and that it was "they"—the authorities in Cairo—who chose Maimonides. It has already been pointed out that the text speaks merely of sending a physician, and says nothing whatever of an appointment as body-physician. This, too, therefore must be set aside as pure imagination.

Nor, despite Graetz's confidence and the repetition of so many subsequent writers, is there any certainty—or even likelihood—that the Frankish king in question was really Richard Lionheart.

If we accept the authenticity of al-Qifṭī's narrative—on which the whole story rests—then the episode must have taken place between two dates: 1165, when Maimonides arrived in Egypt, and 1192, when under the peace-terms signed in that year Richard withdrew from Ascalon and the fortress was demolished. From the wording of al-Qifṭī's narrative there is, moreover, a strong probability that the limits must be drawn more narrowly. "This was in the last days of the Egyptian Fatimid dynasty. *They* wanted to employ him among the other physicians and to send him out to the king of the Franks in Ascalon, who asked *them* for a physician. *They* chose him, but he refused. . ." The identity of the "they" who did these things is not quite clear from the text, but it would seem that these events took place before the coming of the Ghuzz. Max Meyerhof assumed that it was the Fatimid court, and therefore inferred that Maimonides was already a court-physician under the last Fatimid Caliph, al-'Āḍid.[7] Claude Cahen has taken it to be the guild of physicians in Cairo, to whom, he assumed, such a request would have been referred.[8] In either case, the text would seem to make it fairly clear that it was under the Fatimids that "they" wanted to employ Maimonides; that it was under the Fatimids that a request was received from the Frankish king for a physician, and that "they" chose Maimonides to go to him. If we accept this, then the *terminus ad quem* for the incident is the year 1171, when the Fatimid dynasty was finally overthrown by Saladin—twenty years before King Richard Lionheart set foot in the Holy Land. Meyerhof, in a passing allusion, did in fact place the incident in the Fatimid period, and suggested that the Frankish king was probably Amalric.

This is, however, not in itself conclusive. The text that we possess of al-Qifṭī's work is not the original but a later abridgment. Though al-Qifṭī was in general an accurate and conscientious scholar, his biography of Maimonides does contain some errors, and it is therefore just conceivable that the story of the request from the Frankish king in Ascalon, though authentic in itself, has fallen out of its proper place in the chronological sequence. We may therefore, for the time being, retain Richard Lionheart, together with other later kings, as possible candidates, though their candidature will seem weak in comparison with that of the Frankish king who came to Ascalon before the fall of the Fatimid Caliphate in 1171.

At this point it may be useful to digress briefly in order to review the history of the town of Ascalon in this period. It first came into prominence in the year 1099, when, after the capture of Jerusalem by the Crusaders, the retreating Egyptian army entered and held Ascalon. For the next half-century it was an Egyptian fortress, and was used by them as a bridgehead and a base for raids into the Frankish-held territory in Palestine. With its population swollen by Muslim refugees from the areas conquered by the Crusaders, and with its garrison maintained and regularly reinforced from Egypt, it became a major military center, and a key objective in the struggle between the Crusaders and the Muslim rulers of Egypt. The Crusaders, gravely perturbed by Egyptian raids from Ascalon, built a ring of fortresses round it to neutralize the threat which it offered to Jerusalem. Finally, in 1153, after a siege of seven months, the Crusaders captured the town by a combined sea and land attack.

Having previously been a base of Egyptian action against the Franks, it now became a springboard for Frankish political and military adventures in Egypt. The Fatimid Caliphate was tottering to its end, and the rival viziers who disputed for power in Cairo, in their desperate struggle for allies, had no hesitation in calling on Frankish as well as Muslim help from Syria. In the '60s of the 12th century the Crusaders were even able to exact an annual tribute from Cairo, and on two occasions, in 1164 and 1167, the King of Jerusalem, Amalric, led an army of Crusaders into Egypt, ostensibly to come to the rescue of the vizier or the Caliph. A third Frankish expedition set out in December 1168, but this time the rival Egyptian factions joined forces and compelled the Franks to withdraw. Thereafter, with the consolidation of Saladin's power, the Crusaders fell back on the defensive, and in 1187, after their defeat by Saladin at the decisive battle of Ḥaṭṭīn, they were compelled to surrender Ascalon, together with most of their other strongholds in Palestine, to the victorious leader of the Muslim counter-Crusade.

The second, and very brief, Frankish occupation was a result of the Third Crusade. After his defeat at Arsūf in 1191, Saladin found himself unable to hold Ascalon against Richard Lionheart. He therefore destroyed the town and evacuated its population. Richard arrived at the desolate site in January 1192, and at once began work on rebuilding the fortress. He demolished it and withdrew, in accordance with the peace terms signed in the autumn of the same year. A third occupation by the Franks in the 13th century does not concern us, as it took place after Maimonides' death.[9]

Within the wider period determined by the arrival of Maimonides in Egypt and the withdrawal of Richard Lionheart from Ascalon, four kings reigned over the Latin kingdom of Jerusalem: Amalric (1163–1174), Baldwin IV (1174–1185), Baldwin V (1185–1186), and Guy de Lusignan (1186–1192). To these we may add two other names: Count Raymond III of Tripoli, who acted as Regent of the kingdom from 1174 to 1177 and again in 1185–1186, and might easily have been described as king (*malik*) by a Muslim author; and, finally, King Richard Lionheart of England.

Of all six candidates Richard Lionheart is the least likely. He is the latest of them, and came to Ascalon at a time when Maimonides was already an established and celebrated figure in Cairo—yet both the wording of al-Qifṭī's text and the inherent probabilities of the situation imply that the incident took place when Maimonides was an unknown newcomer. Richard, newly arrived from the West, would be less likely than the acclimatized Syrian Franks to seek the services of an Eastern physician. His stay in Ascalon was brief, lasting only a few months—and most of that time he was engaged in active hostilities against the Muslims. Finally, Richard was well-known to Arabic historiography under the name of al-Inkitār ("the king of England"), and is therefore less likely than a king of Jerusalem to be described simply as "the king of the Franks".

In August 1192 King Richard fell sick, probably of typhus fever. This illness is mentioned both by Richard's biographer Richard of Devizes, and by Saladin's secretary and biographer Bahā' al-Dīn. Both of them agree that the Muslim leaders took a sympathetic interest in Richard's welfare; Richard of Devizes tells a story, probably apocryphal, of how Saladin's brother al-'Ādil came to visit him and commiserate with him; Bahā' al-Dīn says that Richard kept on sending messengers to Saladin to ask for fruit and snow, for which he craved in his fever. "The Sultan," says Bahā' al-Dīn, "granted him this, hoping to obtain intelligence through the relays of messengers."[10]

It was no doubt of this occasion, though he does not specifically mention it, that Graetz was thinking when he assumed a request from Richard to Cairo for the services of a physician. The fact remains, however, that although Richard's sickness is discussed by both Frankish and Muslim sources, none of them, to my knowledge, gives any hint of any such request—an omission which is the more remarkable in view of the liking of the chroniclers for the theme of the mutual, chivalrous respect of Richard and Saladin, and the friendly contacts between them.

Of the other kings, all had some connection with Ascalon. Amalric was often there, and used it as the base for his expeditions to Egypt. Baldwin was present at the defense of Ascalon against Saladin in 1177. Guy de Lusignan held the fief of Ascalon before becoming king.

Of all the candidates, Amalric is by far the most probable. Already on the throne when Maimonides arrived in Egypt, he continued to reign for three years after the deposition of the last Fatimid Caliph, and is thus the only one who would qualify for consideration if, as seems most likely, we must place the incident between 1165 and 1171.

There are other arguments to support this identification. Amalric, unlike any of the others, was active in Egyptian affairs, and took part in an Egyptian civil war, in alliance with one of the Egyptian factions. The period of his political and military association with the vizier Shāwar provide the likeliest set of circumstances when such an invitation from the Muslim authorities in Cairo to attend a Frankish king in Ascalon might have been issued.

That the Franks established in Syria and Palestine respected the superior medical knowledge of the East and at times consulted Eastern physicians is in general known from other sources. In the particular case of Amalric, we have actual references to two such consultations. One of them is the story told by William of Tyre, of how when Amalric was dying he called for physicians "of the Greek, Syrian, and other nations noted for skill in diseases."[11] It is conceivable that this was the occasion when Maimonides' services were sought, though it should be noted that this death-bed consultation took place three years after the end of the Fatimid Caliphate.

On the whole it seems more likely that the incident was connected with Amalric's Egyptian adventure. For this we find indirect confirmation in a story related by the author of another biographical work on physicians, the Syrian Ibn Abī Uṣaybiʿa (1203–1270). Speaking of the Christian physician Abū Sulaymān Da'ūd, born in Jerusalem but resident in Egypt, he says:

> The physician Rashīd al-Dīn Abū Ḥalīqa, the son of al-Fāris, the son of this Abū Sulaymān, told me when King Amalric came to Egypt he was astonished at my grandfather's medical skill, and asked the Caliph for him. Then he took him and his five children to Jerusalem. . . .[12]

The pious Rashīd al-Dīn's attribution of Amalric's choice to his wonderment at Abū Sulaymān's skill is strikingly reminiscent of Graetz's story of Maimonides' fame reaching Richard

Lionheart. Perhaps the two may be explained as examples of the same kind of ancestral piety. What seems most likely is that Amalric simply asked for a doctor—and got Abū Sulaymān Da'ūd. May we guess that on this occasion Maimonides was asked, and refused, and that Abū Sulaymān was then asked—and accepted? The Jew might well have hesitated before placing his life in the hands of the Crusaders. The expatriate Christian need have had no fear of returning to his native city under Christian rule.

Amalric went twice to Egypt, in 1164 and 1167. Ibn Abī Uṣaybi'a does not say on which of the two occasions Abū Sulaymān was invited. If the occasion was the same as that described by al-Qifṭī, then it must have been the second visit. In 1164 Maimonides had not yet arrived in Egypt. In 1167 he had been there for two years.

One final question may now be considered—that of Maimonides' service with Saladin. Several of the modern writers who have told this story assert that, after becoming the physician of al-Qāḍī al-Fāḍil, Maimonides also won the favor of Saladin, who appointed him as his court- and body-physician. Some even adduce this appointment as the reason for his refusal of Richard's invitation.

If, as has been suggested, the Frankish king in question was Amalric, then it will be obvious that neither Saladin nor al-Qāḍī al-Fāḍil can have played any part in the story, since neither of them achieved a position of power or eminence until several years later. It may be that Maimonides was already at that time a court-physician to the last Fatimid Caliph, as has been suggested by Meyerhof; but this is purely a hypothesis based on an interpretation of a line in al-Qifṭī's text.

There is no doubt that at a later stage Maimonides served as physician to al-Qāḍī al-Fāḍil, who was his friend and patron, and who enjoyed great power as the chief minister of Saladin. It also seems fairly certain that in his last years Maimonides attended patients in the royal household, as he says himself in his letter to Samuel ibn Tibbon, dated 30 September 1199:

> The Sultan lives in Cairo and I live in Fusṭāṭ, a distance of two Sabbath-days journey. Every morning I must call on the Sultan, and if he, or one

of his children, or one of his wives is sick, I spend the whole day there. Even when there is nothing special I never get home before the afternoon. . . .[13]

But Saladin himself had left Egypt in 1174 and again, finally, in 1182. Was Maimonides ever in his personal service?

The story of Maimonides' service with Saladin, unlike that of his invitation by Richard Lionheart, does at least rest on an early text. It occurs in one of the earliest biographical notices on Maimonides—that of Ibn Abī Uṣaybi'a, a contemporary and colleague of Maimonides' son Abraham. Ibn Abī Uṣaybi'a, in the course of a very laudatory account of Maimonides, says: "The Sultan al-Malik al-Nāṣir (that is, Saladin) held him in high regard, and was attended medically by him. So, too, was his son al-Malik al-Afḍal."[14]

That Maimonides was a court-physician under the successor of Saladin is confirmed by other sources, not least by Maimonides himself. Neither he, however, nor any other early source alludes to service with Saladin, and it is difficult to believe that so distinguished a patient would have escaped mention either by Maimonides—who was not averse to speaking of his professional successes—or by his admirers.

Ibn Abī Uṣaybi'a's book was first published in 1884. His remarks on Maimonides were, however, briefly cited, in a French translation, by Silvestre de Sacy in 1810,[15] and again used in 1840 by Wüstenfeld, who incorporated the Saladin story in his own account of Maimonides.[16] From these sources the story was repeated by many later authors.

It is, however, almost certainly untrue. The first to doubt it was Graetz, who points out that it is in effect contradicted by Maimonides' letter to Ibn 'Aqnīn.[17] In this letter, written some years after Saladin had left Egypt, Maimonides speaks with satisfaction of his successful practice among the great: "I must tell you that in the practice of medicine I have achieved much fame among the great, such as the chief judge, the amīrs, the house of al-Fāḍil, and other great ones of the city. . . ."[18]

The implication of the passage would seem to be that this success is fairly recent—and, moreoever, it contains no allusion to a court-appointment. The letter is dated *Marheshvan* 1503

Sel. (October 1191). As Munk, the editor of the letter, pointed out,[19] the date must be erroneous, and most subsequent authorities have agreed on an earlier date. The earliest would be 1187, when Ibn 'Aqnīn, to whom the letter is addressed, left Cairo. The most probable dates are 1187 or 1190. It would thus seem clear that Maimonides' appointment as an Ayyubid court-physician must be placed some time between the letter to Ibn 'Aqnīn—when it had not yet happened—and the letter to Ibn Tibbon of 1199. It seems likely that the appointment took place towards the end of this period, since Saladin's son al-Afḍal, who is named as Maimonides' patron and to whom he dedicated a book, did not seize power in Egypt until 1198. In any case, the appointment must have taken place after Saladin's final departure from Egypt in 1182, and probably after his death in 1193.

Maimonides, the story-books tell us, the court-physician of Saladin in Cairo, was invited by Richard Lionheart, but refused, preferring his appointment in Cairo. That Maimonides ever served Saladin rests on a single, unsupported statement, almost certainly untrue; that he was ever invited by Richard rests on a guess, almost certainly mistaken. The subsequent popularity of both are an interesting confirmation of the words of the great American poet Robert Frost:

A theory, if you hold it hard enough
And long enough, gets rated as a creed.

IV

TURKS AND TATARS

14. The Mongols, the Turks and the Muslim Polity

Ten years ago a well-known Swiss writer on Middle Eastern affairs published an article on patriotism and nationalism among the Arabs. Discussing the attitude of nationalists to the past, and their tendency to substitute fanciful constructions for serious history, he quotes "a high Syrian government official" as saying, "in deadly earnest": "If the Mongols had not burnt the libraries of Baghdad in the 13th century, we Arabs would have had so much science, that we would long since have invented the atomic bomb. The plundering of Baghdad put us back by centuries."[1]

This is of course an extreme, even a grotesque formulation, but the thesis which it embodies is not confined to, and was not invented by, romantic nationalist historians. Deriving ultimately from the testimony of contemporary sufferers, it was developed by European orientalists, who saw in the Mongol invasions the final catastrophe which overwhelmed and ended the great Muslim civilization of the Middle Ages. As the barbarians had destroyed the Roman Empire, it was thought, so the Mongols destroyed the Caliphate—except that the destruction was more terrible and more permanent, and the new masters, unlike the Germanic barbarians in Europe, could neither learn from others, nor themselves create anything new. This judgment of the Mongols, sometimes extended to include the Turkish invaders who had preceded them out of the steppe, was generally accepted among European scholars, and was gratefully, if sometimes surreptitiously, borrowed by romantic and apologetic historians in Middle Eastern countries as an explanation both of the ending of their golden age, and of their recent backwardness. It was expressed with characteristic force by the famous English orientalist Edward Granville Browne, who saw in the Mongol invasion "a catastrophe which . . . changed the face of the world, set in motion forces which are still effective, and inflicted more suffering on the human race than any other event in the world's history of which records are preserved to us."[2]

To Browne, writing in Cambridge in the early years of this century, it may well have seemed that the Mongol conquest was a calamity of unparalleled magnitude, and that a civilization so stricken could never fully recover. But for the less innocent historians of a less tranquil age, the horrors of the past assumed a milder aspect. The great Russian orientalist V. V. Bartold, writing in Moscow in 1917, was able to achieve a more tolerant view of Mongol destructiveness, and a more robust assessment of the recuperative powers of their victims.

> It would be a mistake, however, to consider that cultural life could only continue in these localities which had escaped the inroads of the Mongol troops. It is true that a cultured land had been conquered by a wild people still believing in the efficacy of human sacrifice. When a town was taken, except for the artisans who were needed by the conquerors, the inhabitants were sometimes subjected to total massacre. People, who had survived these horrible experiences, naturally thought that the country will [sic] not arise again for another thousand years. Influenced by the opinion of writers contemporary to that epoch, European scholars have believed that the Mongols dealt a heavier and more devastating blow to the cultural life of Asia and Eastern Europe than, for example, was dealt to the cultural life of Southern Europe by the Great Migration of Peoples. In reality, the results of the Mongol invasion were less annihilating than is supposed. . . . Besides a not numerous military contingent the Mongol Khans brought with them their cultured councillors [sic] who helped them to establish their rule and to apply to the new country that harmonious and well-constructed governmental and military organization which had been elaborated at the time of Chenghiz Khan himself.[3]

Since then, a more intimate experience of catastrophe on the one hand, and a deeper knowledge of Islamic history on the other, have confirmed some—though not all—of Bartold's insights. In our own time we have seen, in the heart of Europe, rulers and armies compared with whom the Mongol Khans and the Tatar hordes appear almost as angels of mercy—and we have seen the swift recovery of the lands they ravaged. Not all scholars would now fully accept Bartold's views on the benevolent and progressive character of Mongol rule. They were well received in Mongol, Tatar and Turkish circles—others however have suggested some revisions, and among Russian scholars in particular there has in recent years been a sharp reaction against them, and against what is called the "racialist-nationalist idealization of the Turco-Tatar nomads" by pan-Turkist writers. Professor I. P. Petrushevsky has formally declared that Bartold's evaluation of the consequences of the Mongol invasions for the economic development of Iran and neighboring countries "cannot be accepted by Soviet historiography".[4] This statement is obviously prescriptive, not descriptive, and, like other such decisions recorded on behalf of Soviet historiography, may not be determined exclusively by the findings of historians and the evidence of the sources. A clue may be found in hostile allusions, without citation of authors or titles, to "pan-Turkists", i.e. those who ascribe a common identity and purpose to the Turkic peoples inside and outside the U.S.S.R. Bartold is declared innocent of complicity in such villainy. His errors are attributed to his lack of Marxist discipline, not to sinister pan-Turkist motives. But even Professor Petrushevsky affirms that the processes of development, interrupted by the catastrophe of the 13th century, were resumed and completed in the 14th, and concedes that Bartold had some reason to react against the one-sided presentation of the Mongols as destructive savages. Most scholars would now agree that the harmful effects of the Mongol conquests were not as great, as lasting, or even as extensive, as was once thought.

The reconsideration of the impact of the Mongols on the Islamic world has been concerned with three periods, before, during and after their irruption, and with three questions; what did they destroy, what did they achieve, and what did they leave behind them? The traditional answer to the first of these questions is that they destroyed the Caliphate, and with it the great Arabic-Islamic civilization that had flourished under its aegis. "Islam," says a contemporary Syrian historian, "has never suffered a greater and more decisive disaster than this,"[5] and other historians, of that and later ages, have shared this opinion. The destruction of the Caliphate, still, even in its decay, the legal center of Islam and the symbol of its unity, and the establishment of a heathen domination in the Islamic heartlands, were indeed a bitter blow to Muslims, and it is not surprising that their anguish has echoed through the centuries. But the real significance of this act of destruction has been much exaggerated. The golden age of classical Islamic civilization had long since ended, and the Mongols conquered a society that was far advanced in decay. The Caliphs had lost most of their effective power, and by abolishing the Baghdad Caliphate the Mongols did little more than lay the ghost of something that was already dead. Even some modern nationalist historians, their perceptions sharpened by more recent reverses, have begun to appreciate this. "Some of us still believe," says Professor Constantine Zurayk, "that the attacks of the Turks and the Mongols are what destroyed the Abbasid Caliphate and Arab power in general. But . . . the fact is that the Arabs had been defeated internally before the Mongols defeated them. . . ."[6]

In another respect, too, the effects of the Mongol conquests have been exaggerated—in the extent and consequences of the material damage done by them. Certainly, the damage was great. The immediate blows of the Mongols, though no doubt trivial by modern standards, were terrible and overwhelming. Even the Persian historian Juvaynī, a servant and admirer of the Khans who sees in them the instruments of God's purpose, tells how they destroyed whole cities and massacred or deported their inhabitants. Their ravages were not confined to the cities; in many areas the extirpation of the military aristocracy, the death or flight of the peasantry, left vast lands untenanted, uncultivated and unclaimed, often permanently abandoned to nomadic herdsmen. Recent studies have shown that the damage done by the Mongols to the economy of Persia was not limited to the actual destruction during the campaigns of conquest. The ill effects of depopulation and the neglect of irrigation works were aggravated by harsh and extortionate policies, which degraded and impoverished the peasants, and set back the development of agriculture and of the rising feudal society of the immediately preceding period.[7]

Yet these effects, however terrible, were limited both in extent and duration. Egypt, which by this time had become and has ever since remained the chief center of Arab Islam, was never conquered by the Mongols, and was thus only indirectly affected by their coming. Syria suffered only raids, and after the defeat of the Mongols by the Mamluk army of Egypt at 'Ayn Jālūt in Palestine in 1260, was incorporated in the Egyptian Sultanate and protected by Mamluk power from Mongol attack. Arab Africa was never invaded; Turkish Anatolia was long dominated by the Mongol state in Persia, but suffered little direct interference, and survived to cradle the last and greatest of the Islamic Empires—that of the Ottomans. Persia, indeed, was hard hit—but even here by no means the whole country was affected. In South Persia, the local dynasties submitted voluntarily to the Mongols, and their cities, not looted by the invaders, continued to flourish. Even in those parts of Persia which were actually overrun and devastated, there was some recovery, and before long some Persian cities were again centres of industry, trade and culture.

Only in one country did the Mongol conquest leave permanent injuries—in Iraq, once the metropolitan province of the Caliphate. Here, as elsewhere, the immediate effect of the invasion was the breakdown of civil government; in Iraq this also meant the decline of the elaborate irrigation works on which the prosperity, even the life of the country depended. But whereas in Persia there was a partial recovery once the new régime was firmly in control, in Iraq there was hardly any.[8] The Mongol Il-Khans of South-west Asia, like the Seljuks before them, made Persia, not Iraq, the center of their power; Tabriz, their residence, grew into a great and wealthy city. Even before the Mongol conquests, Iraq had lost much of her importance; the coming of the Mongols, the destruction of the Caliphate, and the emergence of new centers, finally ended it. The Mongols conquered Persia and Iraq, but failed to conquer Syria and Egypt; these, under the Mamluk Sultans, formed the base of the most important Muslim military power of the day, and the most dangerous adversary of the Il-Khans. Iraq now became an outlying frontier-province, abandoned to the destructive inroads of the Bedouin, who moved into the breaches made by the Mongols and, unlike them, did not pass on, but stayed. The valley of the Tigris and Euphrates was cut off from the Mediterranean lands by the Mongol–Mamluk conflict; it was overshadowed by the rise of the new Persian center to which it was subordinated, and outflanked by the flourishing Turkish states in Anatolia, now under Mongol suzerainty. Iraq could no longer serve as a channel for east–west trade, which now passed through two other, competing routes—the Mongol northern route, through Anatolia and Persia, and the Mamluk southern route, through Egypt and the Red Sea. Bereft of the Caliphate and ruled by a Mongol governor, Baghdad could no longer be the center and the rallying point of Islam. This role passed to Cairo and later to Constantinople, leaving the fallen city of the Caliphs to centuries of stagnation and neglect.

The dethronement of Iraq and the partial devastation of Persia are the significant exceptions in the general picture of gradual recovery and renewed activity in the Muslim Middle East. Clearly, such a revival could not have been accomplished under the heel of destructive and unteachable savages, such as the Mongols of the conventional image. The opposite extreme is expressed, in a lyrical passage, by the Polish Altaist Wladyslaw Kotwicz.

> *Dans leur empire,* [he says] *les Mongols firent régner l'ordre et le droit, organisèrent une administration uniforme, entreprirent l'œuvre de reconstruction des pays en ruines, de relèvement de l'industrie et du commerce, développèrent des rapports culturels avec les territoires les plus reculés de l'ancien monde.*
>
> *Leur autorité énergique fit effectivement régner, sur la plus grande surface de cet ancien monde, une vraie* Pax mongolica.[9]

Even allowing for the natural affection of a Mongolist for the Mongols, and for the revisions imposed by more recent research, there is a certain element of truth in this picture. Once the conquests, with their attendant horrors, were completed, the Mongols were quick to appreciate the advantages of peace and order, and the *pax mongolica* became a reality in their vast dominions.

Some beneficial effects of Mongol rule in Persia are discernible almost immediately. Once firmly established, the Khans brought a measure of security and stability. In contrast to barbarian Europe, there was no permanent reversion from a money economy to barter, from an urban to a rural way of life. The merchants raised their heads again, and the Il-Khans, for their own good reasons, gave them every encouragement. Their interest was more than that of the greedy savage who has learnt to tend instead of killing his dairy cattle—though even to learn that, in so short a time, would have been no small achievement. The Il-Khans gave active help to what they regarded as useful sciences, such as medicine, astronomy and mathematics; after their conversion to Islam at the end of the 13th century, they extended their patronage to Islamic learning, and by the 14th century Muslim Khans were raising magnificent edifices for Islamic worship and scholarship.

In one respect the Mongol conquests actually brought some advantage to the lands of Islam—through the broadening of Muslim horizons. The Mongol world was not limited to the familiar Muslim lands of the Middle East and Central Asia. It included southern Russia and, most important of all, the Far East, with which Muslim Western Asia was now united for the first time in a single imperial system. In this way Persia was opened to Chinese influence, notably in art and technology. The Mongols also exposed the Muslims to other contacts, as Europeans seized the opportunity offered by their presence to explore the land and sea routes through Persia to China and India. The benefits of these journeys, it may be noted in passing, are more apparent in Europe than in the Middle East.

A good example of the wide outlook and interests of the Mongol era in Persia is the *Jāmiʿ al-tavārīkh*, the Assembly of Histories, by the Persian historian Rashīd al-Dīn (1247–1318). Rashīd al-Dīn was a Jewish convert to Islam, a physician, scholar and minister, who was entrusted by the Il-Khans with the task of preparing a universal history. He assembled a team of collaborators and informants, including two Chinese scholars, a Buddhist hermit from Kashmir, a Mongol specialist on tribal tradition, and a Frankish monk, as well as a number of Persian scholars, and with their help composed a vast history of the world, from Ireland to China. In thus attempting a universal history, going beyond the confines of their own civilization and its accepted precursors, Rashīd al-Dīn and his colleagues anticipated European historical scholarship by half a millennium.

The Mongols, then, though they ravaged some of the lands of Islam and abolished the Baghdad Caliphate, did not destroy Islamic civilization, which was far advanced in the decline before they came and which, in new forms, rose again after their coming. But their advent marked the turning-point in a process of change which, in the course of time, transformed the whole pattern of society and government in the Middle East. The Mongols were relatively few in number; their direct rule in the Middle East was limited to the northern tier, and to a brief period. They bequeathed neither a language nor a religion to the lands they conquered, and whether their dominion was "historically progressive" or "historically reactionary", as Russian scholars of successive generations have argued, its effects in either direction were exhausted within a century. Yet the historical instincts of those who, from contemporaries onwards, saw in the Mongol conquests the end of one era and the beginning of another, were fundamentally sound; their error was the common one of telescoping a long and complex evolution into a single dramatic event. The great change in medieval Islam cannot be understood only in terms of the brief episode of Mongol conquest and domination; it must be seen against a broader background, involving a longer period than the reign of the Khans, and the movement of more numerous peoples than the Mongol tribesmen of Jenghiz and his heirs.

Professor Zurayk, it will be recalled, links the Turks with the Mongols as the invaders of the collapsing Arab Caliphate. The association is not new. "It is a remarkable thing," says a 13th-century Damascene chronicler, discussing the defeat of the Mongols by the Mamluks at ʿAyn Jālūt, "that the Tatars were defeated and destroyed by men of their own kind, who were Turks."[10] Rashīd al-Dīn also links the two together. The Assembly of Histories begins, as one would expect, with "the present masters of the world". Volume I is in two parts, the first dealing with the steppe peoples in general, the second with Jenghiz Khan and his successors. The first, concerned with the divisions, genealogies and legends of the tribes of the steppe, includes Turks as well as Mongols, and in time became a source-book for Turkish heroic and historiographic myths. Even a Turkish tribal origin-myth, as Professor Hatto has remarked, is "fused with a wishful travesty of the saga of the more dazzling Mongols . . . at the poetic level of myth and folk-tale."[11]

The Turks and the Mongols were ethnically, culturally and linguistically distinct; yet they had much in common. Both came into the Middle East from the steppe-lands of Central and North-east Asia, where they shared a common way of life and were subject to similar influences. These affinities brought the Mongols closer to the Turks than to any of the other peoples they had conquered. Jenghiz Khan himself made use of Uygur Turkish advisers, and ordered the adoption of the Uygur script for the Mongol language. The Mongols, few in number, leaned heavily on Turkish support in both war and government. In time, the Mongols in the Islamic lands were merged into the mass of their Muslim subjects, and even lost their language, adopting various forms of Turkish in its place. The very name Tatar, once that of a section of the Mongols, has for a long time been applied to the Turkish-speaking Muslim inhabitants of the territories that were once ruled by the Mongol Khans of the Golden Horde.

The great migrations of the steppe peoples into the Middle East began in the 10th century, when the Turkish tribes of Central Asia crossed the Jaxartes and began their march of conquest westwards. They ended in the period after the death of Timur or Tamerlane, the last of the great Turkish world-conquerors, in 1405. Even then, the trickle of Central Asian tribes continued for a while, until it was stopped by the double barrier of Safavid and Ottoman power on the plateaux of Iran and Anatolia.

In the establishment of Turkish power and the spread of Turkish customs over the lands of Islam, two periods are particularly significant. One was that of the Seljuk Great Sultans, who ruled for about a century from the conquest of Baghdad in 1055 to the death of Sultan Sanjar in 1157. The other was that of the Mongol conquests of the 13th century and the period of Mongol supremacy and influence that followed them.

The Seljuks had entered Islam as condottieri, and had served various Muslim rulers, including the Ghaznavids, before they carved out an independent state of their own. They were devout and earnest Muslims, and, as their Russian historian has remarked, "it is quite natural that the first Saljuqids . . . were better Muslims than [the Ghaznavids] Maḥmūd and Mas'ūd, just as Saint Vladimir was a better Christian than the Byzantine Emperors."[12] They were also free Turks, with their roots in Central Asia, and with memories both of the older Turkish kingdoms and of the tribal traditions of the Oghuz. We can point to many Turkish elements among the titles, ranks and emblems of the Seljuk Sultanate; we can also see the first phases of a profound transformation of Islamic state and society, part of which must surely be attributed to the incursion of the steppe peoples.

The transformation is completed with the second and greater of the steppe Empires—that of the Mongols. Their rule, though of brief duration, was of great significance, for it was at this time that the main characteristics of the post-Mongol phase of Islamic government were formed. The first Mongol rulers of Persia were pagans—the first to rule over an important Islamic territory since the beginnings of Islam. Their system of government was avowedly non-Islamic—based on the so-called *Yasa* of Jenghiz Khan. This seems to have been a complex of Mongol rules and customs; it was held to be binding on the Khans themselves as well as on their subjects, both Mongols and others. Even after the conversion of the Il-Khans of Persia to Islam, the Mongol laws remained effective, and Mongol practices were only gradually and partially modified under the influence of Muslim administrative and legal traditions.

The Mongol influence was of course strongest in those areas where the rule of the Mongol Khans persisted—in Central Asia, in Persia and in the territories of the Golden Horde in Russia. It was, however, by no means limited to these areas. The Syro-

Egyptian Empire of the Mamluks, though it escaped Mongol conquest, was profoundly influenced by the Mongol example and by the Mongol deserters and refugees who migrated to Egypt. During the 13th and 14th centuries the Mongols enjoyed the immense prestige of victory and conquest; they were in consequence imitated in warfare, even in dress—as Europe was imitated in the 19th and 20th centuries. The Mamluk emir of 13th-century Egypt wore his Tatar coat and hat in much the same way and for much the same reasons as his modern equivalents wear fitted tunics and peaked caps. Both are alien to Islam—but both were the symbols of power and victory.

Far stronger than in Egypt was the Mongol influence in Turkish Anatolia. After conquering Persia, the Mongol horsemen had swept on to Mesopotamia and Anatolia, where they had dealt the Seljuk Sultanate of Rūm a blow from which it never recovered. After dragging out an attenuated existence for some fifty years, it finally disappeared at the beginning of the 14th century. Most of eastern and central Anatolia became subject to the Il-Khans of Persia and was ruled either by Mongol governors or by Turkish vassals. Even after the decline of Il-Khan power had permitted the development of local autonomies, the administrative and financial system which the Il-Khans had impressed on the country continued to function. It was still working under the Anatolian princes and survived to exercise a formative influence on the institutions of the Ottoman state.

After the death of the Il-Khan Abū Sa'īd in 1336, the Mongol dominions in the Middle East broke up, and a number of smaller states, ruled by Mongol or Turkish dynasties, appeared in Persia, Mesopotamia and Anatolia. Those of Persia were of short duration. Farther east, Timur had succeeded in making himself ruler of the Mongol successor state in Central Asia. In 1380, already master of Transoxania, he invaded Persia and in the next seven years over-ran the whole of it. He twice defeated the Khan of the Golden Horde, raided India, annexed Iraq and then over-ran Syria and exacted homage from the Mamluk Sultan. In 1394 and 1400 he invaded Anatolia, and in 1402 inflicted a crushing defeat on the Ottomans at the battle of Ankara, capturing the Ottoman Sultan Bayezid. He died in 1405 while preparing an invasion of China.

Timur was a Muslim from a Turcicized tribe—but he was proud to relate himself to the Mongol Imperial house by marrying a princess of the line of Jenghiz Khan. He led mixed Mongol and Turkish armies, in which the former were the dominant element but the latter the great majority. His career has been variously represented as a reaction of Islam against the Shamanism of the Mongol Khans and as the last convulsion of the Altaic invasion. Unlike the Khans of the earlier conquests Timur was, or claimed to be, a pious Muslim, and amid the enormous destruction he wrought he was careful to show deference to the places and personnel of the Islamic faith. But despite the noticeable Islamizing tendency, his system of government was still in the Mongol tradition.

With his death, the great movement of the steppe peoples that had begun in the 10th century seems to have come to an end—though the infiltration of tribes continued and, what was more important, the penetration of nomads already in the Middle East into the structure of urban life and civilization.

Of the great changes that can be discerned in Islamic government and society during and after the invasions of the steppe peoples, how much can be attributed to the influence of the invaders? The question is by no means easy to answer. The Turks, after their conversion to Islam, had surrendered themselves to their new religion almost completely. Partly because of the simple intensity of the faith as they encountered it on the frontiers of Islam and heathendom, partly perhaps because their conversion to Islam at once involved them in Holy War against their own unconverted kinsmen beyond the borders, the Muslim Turks sank their national identity in Islam as the Arabs and Persians had never done.

Yet something of the Turkish past survived. The Turkish language, brought from Central Asia by the first migrants and invaders, lived on and emerged triumphant in a new Muslim dress. Turkish rulers, even in lands of old Islamic traditions, used titles and symbols of authority that go back to pre-Islamic

Turkish antiquity. Even in the Ottoman Empire, the symbols of the bow and the arrow and the horsetail remain to commemorate the mounted archers from the steppe that had first crossed the rivers from Central Asia into the lands of Islam; the Altaic titles of Khan and Beg were used or conferred by a sovereign whose roots of power led back to the Mongol Khans as well as to the Sultans of Islam.

The persistence of these old Turkish titles and emblems, long after the Islamization of the Turks, symbolizes the survival, at a deeper level, of habits, practices, and beliefs inherited from an earlier age. The identification and evaluation of these survivals is however a task of no small difficulty. The evolution of Islamic and Persian notions and practices of government is well documented and has been fairly well studied. Those of the Turks, however, are still little known and have formed the subject of some dubious theorizing.

The attempt has been made by some historians to explain the whole structure of Ottoman administration in the Imperial age by reference to the nomadic herdsmen who invaded Anatolia in the 11th century—rather as at one time a school of historians in the West tried to trace the British parliamentary system to the alleged practices of primitive Germanic tribes. In avoiding fanciful and exaggerated hypotheses on steppe origins, we should not however fall into the opposite error of underrating them. Both the Turkish and the Mongolian dynasties that ruled over Islam during the formative period between the 11th and 14th centuries were of steppe origin, and even when they had been long assimilated in the cities and river valleys of the Middle East, new waves of nomadic invaders from the steppe were still breaking into the lands of Islam and seeping into the apparatus of government. When the Mongol victories had brought a new aristocracy and a new law from the steppe, the Turks rediscovered their pride in their ancestors and their ancestral way of life, and sought more self-consciously after the emblems and prerogatives of a specifically Turkish sovereignty.

The cultural and political baggage of the steppe peoples when they entered the world of Islam was not limited to their own native inheritance. They had for long been in contact with other sedentary civilizations—for example, with the ancient, little-known but highly important Iranian cultures of Central Asia, the influence of which can be traced through pre-historic Iranian borrowings in the Turkic languages. Easier to observe, and more relevant to our present inquiry, is the influence of China—clearly visible on both the pre-Islamic Turks and the Mongols. It is from Chinese sources that we first hear of the Turks, as a tributary people among the barbarians beyond the North-west frontier of the Chinese Empire. The earliest Turkish records—the 8th-century Orkhon inscriptions—reveal profound Chinese influence, and in a sense express a kind of Turkish national revolt after a long period of subjugation to China.

Several of the later Turkish tribes and peoples which entered the Islamic world were still strongly affected by Chinese civilization. Still more so were the Mongols and their kin. The first important group of these to become known to the Muslims were the Kara Khitay, who appeared on the North-eastern frontiers of the Empire of the Great Seljuks. Of Mongol or Tunguz stock, they had conquered Northern China in the 10th century and founded a Chinese dynasty. The name Cathay commemorates their period of rule. In the early 12th century they were driven out of China by another related people, and began to move westwards. Towards the middle of the 12th century they conquered Transoxania from the Karakhanids and set up a vast Empire stretching from the Oxus to the Yenissei and the border of China. The Seljuk Sultan Sanjar, trying in vain to stem their advance, suffered a humiliating defeat at the battle of the Katvan steppe in 1141.

This little-known engagement must rank among the decisive battles of Asian history. In Persia, it accelerated the decline of Seljuk power and the break-up of the Seljuk Great Sultanate into a number of small states. In Central Asia it confirmed the domination, over what was now old Muslim territory, of a dynasty of Far Eastern origin, with Chinese Imperial experience. Their language of government, we are told, was Chinese, and they introduced many elements of the Chinese administrative and fiscal system.

With the great Mongol conquests, Muslim South-west Asia passed under the control of a people of East Asian origin, dominated since the childhood of their race by the vast majesty of China. Jenghiz Khan himself leaned heavily on Chinese precedent and advice; in his first expedition in 1219 across the Jaxartes into the lands of Islam, he was accompanied by his Chinese counsellor, Ye-lu Ch'u ts'ai, a high Chinese official and, incidentally, a descendant of the former Kara Khitay ruling house. By the time Jenghiz Khan's grandson, Hülegü Khan, advanced across the Oxus, on a new campaign of westward conquest, the Mongols had conquered China itself—and the subjugated lands of Islam were incorporated in an Empire that, from 1267, had its capital in Peking.

Far to the west, the Khan of the Golden Horde in South Russia and the Il-Khan in Persia were autonomous territorial rulers, but they were subject to the supreme authority of the Great Khan, the head of their family and overlord of their Empire. In time, the Khanates of the West became independent and Islamic—but by that time the oriental civilization of the united Mongol Empire had profoundly affected them.

In the period following the destruction of the Caliphate, a fundamental division becomes apparent in the Middle East, between two great cultural zones. In the north was the zone of Perso-Turkish civilization with its centre in the plateau of Iran, extending westwards into Anatolia and beyond into the lands conquered by the Ottomans in Europe, eastwards into Central Asia and the new Muslim Empire of India. In these countries Arabic survived only as the language of religion and the religious sciences; culturally it was supplanted by Persian and Turkish, which became the media of a new form of Islamic civilization. To the south lay the countries where Arabic was spoken—the derelict province of Iraq, and the new center in Egypt, with its Syrian and Arabian dependencies, and its African hinterland. Here, behind the defenses of a Mamluk Byzantium, the older Arabic culture survived, and entered on its long-drawn-out Silver Age. Persian was not known and, except in art and rather more in architecture, the new cultural developments in the north had little effect.

Politically, however, the Turk and the Mongol were everywhere dominant. Mongol or Turkish dynasties ruled all the countries from the Mediterranean to Central Asia and India, and even the Syro-Egyptian Empire of the Mamluks was governed and defended by a ruling class of imported slaves of Turkish speech, mainly from the Kipchak country north of the Black Sea.

In the 14th century the greatest of Arab historians, the Tunisian Ibn Khaldūn, observed the almost universal supremacy of the Turks, and saw in their coming a proof of God's continuing concern for the welfare of Islam and the Muslims. At a time when the Muslim Caliphate had become weak and degenerate, incapable of resisting its enemies, God in His wisdom and benevolence had brought new rulers and defenders, from among the great and numerous tribes of the Turks, to revive the dying breath of Islam and restore the unity of the Muslims. By the providential dispensation of the Mamluk system, he affirms, they were constantly reinforced by new importations from the steppe, who embraced Islam with enthusiasm, yet retained their nomadic virtues unspoilt by the corrupting influences of civilization.[13]

In this interpretation of events, Ibn Khaldūn is applying his own well-known version of the myth of the noble savage. His praise of the steppe peoples as the saviors of Muslim power is however by no means without foundation. The military prowess of the Turks and Mongols has never been questioned; their political contribution to the recovery, stability, and, for a while, expansion of the Muslim world deserves more attention.

It is perhaps in the forms and functioning of government that the great transformation wrought by the invaders from the steppe can most clearly be seen. In the Mongol kingdom of the Il-Khans, and in the states which followed it in Persia and Anatolia, new patterns appear that differ sharply from those of the old Caliphate. The extent of the change may be measured against those countries which knew Turkish but not Mongol rule —as Egypt and India, and those that knew neither—as Morocco.

The first and most striking feature of the new era is the reinforcement of political power. The states of the post-Mongol era are stronger, more stable, and more enduring than those of the past—and the states of the plateaux of Anatolia and Iran are stronger than those of the countries less directly affected by Turco-Mongol rule. In the six centuries before the Mongol invasions, few states in Islam had lasted for much more than three or four generations. The patriarchal Caliphate had perished within forty years of the Hijra; the kingdom of the Umayyads had lasted for less than a century; even the Abbasid Caliphs, though they reigned in name for five centuries, wielded effective power for little more than the first of them, and were thereafter forced to yield it to an unending series of dynasties, some of them great and powerful, but all of them ephemeral in the form, the extension and the duration of their dominion. Even in the periods of their greatness the authority they wielded, though vast, was fragile. Institutions, régimes, realms—all were shifting and impermanent, liable to sudden and total upheaval.

In the Turco-Mongol age all this is changed. In Egypt, the Mamluks, recruited for the most part from the Khanate of the Golden Horde and deeply influenced by the statecraft of their Mongol neighbours, established a state and a government that lasted for two and a half centuries—certainly the most stable and powerful régime that Egypt had known since the Muslim conquest. In Persia, lying on the main high road of invasion, things were more difficult—but even there the heirs of Timur and the various dynasties that followed them succeeded in maintaining the stability and continuity of government—out of which, in time, the territorially and administratively coherent modern kingdom of Persia emerged. And in Anatolia, these same traditions of government helped to maintain the various Turkish principalities and the Ottoman state which eventually swallowed them all.

An important contribution of the steppe peoples to this stability was a workable principle of dynastic succession. The juristic doctrine of Islam was that the headship of the state was elective. In fact the elective principle remained purely theoretical, and Islam was ruled by a succession of dynasties, ranging from those of the Caliphs themselves to the petty hereditary autonomies of the provincial governors. But the elective principle remained strong enough to prevent the establishment of any regular and accepted rule of succession. With the Caliphate, the fiction of election was maintained on each accession, and beyond the general principle that the Caliph should be chosen among the members of the reigning family, there was no restriction of choice. In the secular dynasties which held the real power, authority was personal and military—and rarely survived the grandson of the founder. Besides Islamic influences, Persian influences were also powerful—but they came from the late, degenerate phase of the Sasanid Empire of Persia, just before its collapse under the shock of Arab invasion. The example it offered was of a personal absolutism, unrestrained—and therefore unsupported—by any entrenched rights or interests; depending on fear rather than on loyalty. In the classical manuals of statecraft the possibility of loyalty—by family, faith or estate—seems to be discounted altogether, and kingship is based unashamedly on punishment and reward.

The Turks introduced a new conception. Already in the Orkhon inscriptions we find the notion clearly expressed of a family singled out by God to rule over the Turks, and, more vaguely, other peoples and lands beyond them. The same idea reappears in an Islamic form in the correspondence of the Great Seljuks, with their claim to an inherited and divinely sanctioned imperial sovereignty, and again, in a pagan form, in the chancery protocol of the Mongol Khans. For the Persians, the sovereign was the sole autocrat; for the Turks and Mongols, sovereignty was a family possession, and the whole family of the Khan or Sultan had a right to share in it. In the kingdoms of the Karakhanids and Seljuks we see the principle at work, whereby the brothers and cousins of the sovereign are admitted to a share of sovereignty. Under the Mongols, the whole vast Empire won by the conquests was divided up into family appendages, each of which was given to a son or grandson of Jenghiz Khan. We see it again among the Anatolian principalities, and perhaps also in the Seljuk and early Ottoman practice of appointing the sons of the Sultan to provincial governorships, in which they held miniature courts.[14]

A ruling family, held together and sustained by strong ties of tribal loyalty; a divine grant of authority, so sacrosanct that defaulting members of the family were put to death by strangling with a bow-string, to avoid the sacrilege of shedding their blood—these were no small advantages in setting up a régime that was secure and accepted. But to make it permanent, in lands of ancient culture and jaded loyalty, more was needed.

It was found. In the Turkish kingdoms there was a clarity and cohesion in the institutional structure of state and society that is in marked contrast with the looseness and vagueness of classical Islamic times. The power of the state rests on and is exercised through well-established and well-organized institutions and social orders—army, bureaucracy, judiciary, and men of religion, with well-defined powers and functions, with regular recruitment and hierarchic promotion. The emergence of these new features has been variously attributed—to the steadiness and sobriety of the new ruling groups, to changes in the system of land tenure, to the transformation of Islamic belief and attitudes through the new orthodoxy, to the influence of Chinese—and Byzantine—Imperial administration, to the introduction and acceptance of fire-arms. All no doubt played their part—though the determining of their relative importance is very much a matter of argument. What is clear is that in these states, and notably in the Ottoman Empire, land ownership and taxation, justice and religion, government and war are better organized and better correlated than ever before in Islam, and give to the Turkish rulers an assurance, a competence and above all a permanence that are new to the Islamic world.

With the consolidation of the Turkish states came an important change in the nature of the realms over which they ruled. Their territories were wider, their frontiers more permanent. The constant rise and fall of petty principalities—regional or personal, military or tribal, forming and reforming in ever different shapes—had come to an end. After the Mongol invasions, three great states, based on Egypt, Persia and Turkey, with more or less stable frontiers, divided the Middle East between them. With the Ottoman conquest of the Mamluk sultanate in 1517 their number was reduced to two—two great dynastic monarchies, which confronted one another from the Caucasus to the Persian Gulf, as the Sasanid and Byzantine Empires had done a thousand years earlier. One of them, Persia, has survived to our own day; the disappearance of the other has left many uncertainties that are not yet resolved.

15. Ottoman Observers of Ottoman Decline

In May 1541 the Grand Vizier Lûtfi Pasha, after a brief but successful term of office, was dismissed by Sultan Süleyman the Magnificent, apparently because of a dispute arising in the harem. He retired with a pension to his estate in Dimotika, where he died a number of years later. In his enforced leisure he occupied himself with scholarship and especially history, and composed various works, one of which was a history of the Ottoman Empire up to his own day. Another of his writings was a booklet called the *Âṣafnāme*—the Book of Asaph, after the Biblical figure who in Muslim legend was the vizier of King Solomon and the ideal model of the wise and loyal minister.[1]

Lûtfi Pasha's book, however, is more than a Mirror of Ministers, of the kind common in Muslim literature since early times. When he became Grand Vizier, he tells us, he found the High Divan in great disorder, and many things contrary to the fundamental laws of the Empire. He, therefore, felt it his duty to set down the results of his own experience, for the guidance of those who, after him, would be called upon to fill this great office beyond which there is nothing to which a subject can aspire, and to give both practical advice and ethical principles for the conduct of the affairs of state, while he himself sought peace in retirement. "The Kingdom of this mortal world is swift in passing and full of death. It is better to find wise but not heedless repose in the corner of leisure and the enjoyment of gardens and meadows. May God, from Whom we seek aid, and in Whom we trust, secure the laws and foundations of the house of Osman from the fear and peril of fate and the evil eye of the foe."[2]

It was with these premonitions of mortality that Lûtfi Pasha set down his rules of what Grand Viziers should do and—more urgently—of what they should avoid. First and foremost, the

Grand Vizier should be disinterested, without any private aim or spite. "Everything he does should be for God and in God and for the sake of God."[3] This should be possible for the holder of an office that is the peak of ambition. He should not make free with requisitions for the support of couriers, but should limit them to those occasions when their absence would be harmful to the affairs of state, for "in the Ottoman realms there is no such inequitable exaction as the courier service".[4] He should preserve the sovereign from love of money and from its evil consequences, and see that the property rights of the subjects are respected, "for the summary annexation of the property of the people to the property of the sovereign is a sign of decay in the state".[5] The Grand Vizier should be frank and honest in his dealings with the Sultan and without fear of dismissal. "It is better to be dismissed and admired among men than to render dishonest service."[6] He should observe the five daily prayers in his house; he should be accessible and try to give satisfaction. Above all, he must beware of gifts from tainted sources. "For officers of the state, corruption is a disease without remedy . . . beware, beware of corruption; O God! save us from it."[7] After this sudden note of passion Lûtfi Pasha observes, rather more practically, that the emoluments of the Grand Vizier amount to about 2½ million aspers—"which, thank God, is, in the Ottoman state, a sufficient bounty".[8] When Lûtfi Pasha himself was Grand Vizier, he says, he spent 1½ million on the expenses of his kitchen and his suite, and half a million on charity, leaving half a million in his personal treasury.

Lûtfi Pasha was also concerned about the cost of living. "The control of prices is an important public responsibility, and the Grand Vizier must devote special care to it. It is not right if one high official is a rice merchant or if the house of another is a drug-store. The fixing of prices is in the interests of the poor."[9]

Lûtfi Pasha returns again and again to the question of government appointments. The Grand Vizier should make appointments and promotions solely on the basis of merit and competence, without favoritism or interest. He should give only few and small fiefs to his own followers. He should maintain discipline, and respect the order of precedence and seniority.

He should submit to no influence or pressure in making appointments, but follow his own judgment. He should investigate complaints against minor officials and judges, and, when necessary, reprimand or even dismiss them.

The final responsibility, however, belongs to the Sultan, who must from time to time be reminded of this fact: "The Grand Vizier in speaking to the world-protecting Sovereign should repeatedly say: 'My Sovereign, I have cast the yoke off my neck. On the Day of Judgment henceforth thou wilt answer'."[10]

In the second chapter, on the military function of the Grand Vizier, Lûtfi Pasha draws special attention to the need to strengthen the navy. He quotes with approval a remark of Kemalpashazade (*d.* 1533-4), to Selim I: "My Lord, you dwell in a city whose benefactor is the sea. If the sea is not safe no ships will come, and if no ship comes Istanbul perishes." He himself had said to Sultan Süleyman, "Under the previous Sultans there were many who ruled the land, but few who ruled the sea. In the conduct of naval warfare the infidels are ahead of us. We must overcome them."[11]

The third and fourth chapters deal with finance and with the peasants; "The Sultanate stands on its treasury. The treasury stands by good management. By injustice (*ẓulm*) it falls."[12] The Grand Vizier must see that revenue is greater than expenditure, and must beware of inflating his own staff. The army should be good rather than large, and the army pay-lists should be kept accurate and up-to-date. A standing paid army of 15,000 men is quite sufficient—and to pay it regularly no mean achievement. Tax-revenues should be assigned to government commissioners rather than to tax-farmers, and the amounts fixed by the Chief Treasurer. The extraordinary taxes levied from the peasantry should be neither too heavy nor too frequent, and steps should be taken to prevent the depopulation of the countryside.

Thus, in the middle of the 16th century, when the Ottoman Empire was at the very peak of its power and glory, a perceptive Turkish statesman was already deeply concerned about its fate and welfare, and was able to lay his fingers unerringly on what became, in the years to follow, the characteristic signs of Ottoman decline. Inflation and speculation, venality and incompetence; the multiplication of a useless and wasteful army and bureaucracy; the vicious circle of financial stringency, fiscal rapacity, and economic strangulation; the decay of integrity and loyalty; and beyond them all, the growing, menacing shadow of the maritime states of the West—all these were already seen by Lûtfi Pasha as he cultivated his garden in Dimotika.

The long debate on the reasons for the decline of the Roman Empire began, we are told, when the sack of Rome by Alaric and his Visigoths first made plain the weakness of the Roman state. The debate on the decline of the Ottoman Empire began when the Empire was at its zenith—and it began among the Ottoman Turks themselves. The percipience of Lûtfi Pasha, his ability to perceive and relate cause and effect in the historical process of which he was a part, his anxious awareness of weakness and decay in the body politic find clear expression in his manual for ministers where, in contrast to the normal euphory of oriental historiography, he points not merely to the errors and failings of his ministerial colleagues and successors—which is fairly common—but also to the cracks that have appeared in the pillars of state and society.

This awareness of process and capacity for analysis were by no means unique in Ottoman annals. On the contrary, Lûtfi Pasha's work was the first of a long series of similar writings, in which the urgent and hopeful demand for reform gives way to a profoundly pessimistic longing for a lost Golden Age, as the faith of the Turks in their ability to restore the greatness of the past faded.

Not all these writings had the form of statesmanly memoranda. One of the most remarkable is in the form of a poem by an obscure poet called Veysi, written in about 1608. The poet gives a stark picture of Turkish government and society, in a manner more reminiscent of an Old Testament Prophet than of an Ottoman office-holder. The poet threatens the judgment of God on a tyranny worse than that of Pharaoh. The Law of God is disregarded, and its professed exponents are hypocritical and self-seeking—"were no pay given for it, the word of God would not be read". The Qadis and Qadi-'askers are corrupt and oppressive, the age is dominated by women or young boys; the great are interested only in money; the feudal cavalry are neglected and fiefs given to favorites of the Vizier or of the harem; the Janissaries and their commanders have become a cause of disorder and sedition; the high officers of state are all corrupt and tyrannical; in fine " 'the fish stinks from the head', they say; the head of this evil is known".[13]

The crises of the late 16th and early 17th centuries gave rise to a number of political and ethical tracts and treatises, the most famous of which is the memorandum of Kochu Bey, an Ottoman official of Macedonian or Albanian birth. After being recruited by the *devshirme*, he followed a career in the Saray. He became the intimate adviser of Sultan Murad IV (1623-1640), and in 1630 composed for him the treatise on the state and prospects of the Ottoman Empire which has led scholars to call him the Turkish Montesquieu.[14] In this Kochu Bey analyses, with courage and penetration, the defects that had led to the decline of Ottoman power since the time of Süleyman the Magnificent, and advises the Sultan on how to remedy them. "It is a long time since the high-chambered household of the lofty Sultanate (may it remain under the protection of eternal grace) was served by solicitous, well-intentioned, worthy ulema and by obedient, self-effacing, willing slaves. Today the state of affairs having changed, and evil, upheaval, sedition and dissension having passed all bounds, I have sought occasion to observe the causes and reasons of these changes, and bring them to the Imperial and august ear."[15]

Kochu Bey paints a glowing picture of the golden age of the Ottoman past, which reached its summit under Süleyman the Magnificent. It was, however, during his reign that the deterioration began; it advanced rapidly under his immediate successors. In nineteen chapters, Kochu Bey describes, with somber detail and astonishing frankness, the causes and processes of Ottoman enfeeblement and impoverishment, of material and moral decline.

He attributes the decay of Ottoman power and integrity to four principal, interrelated causes. The first of these is the withdrawal of the Sultans, from the time of Süleyman, from the direct supervision of the affairs of state. In former times the Sultans were present at meetings of the Imperial Council, and interested themselves actively in the state of the people and the provinces. After Süleyman the Sultans secluded themselves in the harem, and thus broke off the indispensable intimacy between the sources of power and those entrusted with its exercise.

At the same time the office of Grand Vizier, the keystone of the edifice of Ottoman government, was debased and debilitated. In former times the Grand Vizier was the supreme administrator. He rose to his high office through the ladder of administrative employment and experience, and was promoted for his competence and merit. Once appointed, he enjoyed absolute discretion and power, and was free from any kind of illicit pressure or influence. His tenure was virtually permanent, and he was dismissed only for grave dereliction of duty. The trouble began when Sultan Süleyman in 929/1523 made Ibrahim Pasha, a palace favorite, Grand Vizier in defiance of the old system. Thereafter it became normal for Sultans to advance their personal favorites to this office. Such Grand Viziers had neither experience nor competence, and brought the office into disrepute. After 992/1584 the Grand Viziers lost both their powers and their security. They were subject to all kinds of interference by palace favorites, and liable at any moment to summary dismissal, confiscation, and even execution. This degradation of the highest office of state adversely affected the morale and the efficiency of both the civilian and the military servants of the Ottoman House.

The withdrawal of the Sultan and the degradation of the Grand Vizier left the way open to the pernicious régime of palace favorites—of women, eunuchs, hangers-on, speculators, intriguers, and self-seekers, men of every religion and none, without loyalty, integrity, or virtue of any kind. Both the imperial household and the corps of Janissaries had been overrun with outsiders and interlopers, the former with "Turks,

Gypsies, Jews, people without religion or faith, cutpurses and city riff-raff", the latter with "townsmen, Turks, Gypsies, Tats, Lazes, muleteers and camel-drivers, porters, footpads, and cutpurses".[16] And these in turn had opened the way to corruption, the blight which, if unchecked, would destroy every branch of the civil, military, economic, social, political, and religious life of the Empire.

Kochu Bey demonstrates point by point how palace intrigue and venality were corroding the pillars of the Ottoman state. The Imperial household had been corrupted and had become a source of contamination to the rest of the apparatus of government. The military fief system, which once provided the backbone both of the army and of the countryside, was being undermined and destroyed. The feudal sipahis were being crushed out of existence, and their fiefs given to courtiers and harem women, who sometimes accumulated as many as fifty of them in a single holding. The result was both military and agrarian breakdown.

If the army's feudal cavalry was disintegrating, its paid infantry and artillery were in no better shape. The corps of Janisseries, once a select *corps d'élite*, had swollen in size beyond all reason by enrolling any riff-raff willing to pay a bribe. They had become a useless and destructive nuisance, terrorizing and exploiting the civil population, and performing no military duty other than drawing their pay. With the army in such poor shape, it was not surprising that the Empire had lost nineteen provinces since 1591, and was unable to maintain order in those that remained.

Appointment to office by purchase or favor had become general—even in religious offices such as judgeships. No dynasty in Islam had been as loyal to the Holy Law and as respectful to its representatives as the House of Osman. The chief Mufti of the capital, the Sheykh al-Islam, had been chosen as the wisest, best and most pious of the ulema and usually held his office for life. Other judges were pious, conscientious and modest, and held office for many years. Dismissals were rare, and only for good cause. Now, appointments and promotions among the ulema were made without reference to merit, scholarship, or seniority. All went by favor. Tenure of office was brief and insecure, the holders unworthy and grasping. The judges were hated and despised by the people.

The treasury was empty. Taxes, instead of being collected by trustworthy government commissioners, were leased to tax-farmers. Even the revenues of crown estates were squandered and dissipated. Kochu Bey cites as an example the crown lands on the eastern borders, which formerly brought an income of 48,400,000 aspers. "Part had been lost to the enemy; part given away, contrary to law, as freehold (*temlik*), pious foundation (*vakif*), or slipper-money;[17] part has simply gone to rack and ruin; part has gone into the appanage of the Viziers."[18]

To meet the deficiency the government had sharply raised both the rate and the frequency of the special taxes on the peasantry. The poll-tax on non-Muslims, for example, had been raised from 40-50 aspers per house to 240 aspers per head, as well as many other imposts.[19] How could the peasants bear this? "In fine", says Kochu Bey, "the like of the present oppression and maltreatment of the poor peasantry has never been at any time, in any clime, or in the realm of any king. If in any of the lands of Islam an atom of injustice is done to any individual, then on the Day of Judgment not ministers, but kings will be asked for a reckoning, and it will be no answer for them to say to the Lord of the Worlds, 'I delegated this duty'.... The world can go on with irreligion, but not with injustice."[20] Such sentiments are commonplace in Islamic manuals of ethics and politics. It is not however usual to find them coupled with so clear a denunciation of the existing state of affairs—or expressed in a memorandum from an official to a sovereign.

With this note of passion Kochu Bey's careful restraint breaks down, and the profound feelings that inspired his book come to the surface. He remains however practical and specific, and prescribes a remedy besides diagnosing the disease. Despite his gloomy picture, Kochu Bey is basically optimistic. He believes that by swift and resolute action the Sultan can stop the rot and restore the old order to its perfection. "And then the enemies of the faith, seeing the good order and stability... will say, in helpless fear and envy: 'The House of Osman lay for sixty years in neglectful sleep, but now they are wide-awake, and have begun to make good the shortcomings of past days'."[21]

Writing in 1630, Kochu Bey, the loyal servant of the state, could still think of the previous sixty years as an evil interlude to be ended by a resolute Sultan, and look forward to the renovation of an Empire which, by its extent, its mineral and other resources, and its masses of valiant men, was without equal in the world. Only 23 years later, in 1653, another Ottoman writer, of very different formation, surveyed the state of the Empire in a somewhat different spirit.

Mustafā ibn Abdüllah, variously known as Kâtib Chelebi and as Hajji Khalifa (1608-1657), was also an officer in the Ottoman service, and served in various capacities in the Finance Department. Unlike Kochu Bey, he was not a slave of the Porte recruited by *devshirme* but a free Muslim, born in Constantinople, to a father who himself held a palace appointment. His vast and miscellaneous learning, his far-ranging intellectual curiosity, and his versatile and unconventional mind made him one of the outstanding figures in Turkish cultural and intellectual history. He was, incidentally, one of the first Ottoman scholars to show an interest in Western learning.

In 1063/1653, we are told, the Sultan Mehmed IV called a meeting of high dignitaries to discuss the reasons for the persistent deficit in the state finances. "Under the rule of my late father", said the Sultan, "as also earlier, the revenue was sufficient to cover expenditure or even exceeded it. My expenditure is not as great as that of my father, and the revenues are the same. What then is the reason that the income of the state no longer suffices to cover the expenditure, and why is it that money cannot be raised for the fleet and other important matters?" Each present gave his answer, beginning with Grand Vizier, who replied that in fact the expenditure of the state had increased considerably, and that this was why the revenues no longer sufficed. After this meeting some inconclusive investigations of the state finances were made, and some ineffective palliatives adopted. Kâtib Chelebi, as a finance official, was present at some of the discussions, and set down his own views on the causes and remedies of the chronic financial crisis, in an essay entitled "*The Rule of Action for the Rectification of Defects*".[22]

Kâtib Chelebi begins with a brief account of the circumstances that had led him to compose his essay, and then sets forth a theory, clearly derived from the *Muqaddima* of Ibn Khaldūn, of the rise and fall of human societies. States and societies, like individuals, are organic, and are subject to the laws of growth and decay. The life-span of a state, like that of an individual, falls into three phases; the first of growth, the second of stasis, the third of decline.[23] With states, again as with individuals, the relative lengths of these three phases vary according to the health and strength of any one state. The Ottoman Empire, thanks to the strength of its constitution and the soundness of its limbs, had lived for a long time, and the phase of stasis had passed slowly. The approach of the third stage was indicated by certain symptoms, which could be recognized and treated in individuals by physicians and in states by statesmen.[24]

Kâtib Chelebi then goes on to give his own diagnosis and suggested treatment of the ills of the Ottoman state in three chapters, dealing with the peasantry, the army, and the treasury. The peasantry corresponds to the black gall in the body, and is disordered by undernourishment. The Sultans of the first phase were careful to protect the peasantry from oppression and extortion, and not a single village fell into ruin. During the second phase some peasants lost their livelihood through risings and disturbances, and fled from the villages to the towns. Now Constantinople was packed with people. In twelve years of travel through the Empire, from 1622 to 1634, he had found most villages deserted. On a visit to Persia, on the other hand, he had traveled fifteen to twenty stages without seeing a single deserted village, since the Persian state was then still at the end of its phase of stasis. The ruin of the Ottoman countryside was well-known. One cause was fiscal extortion, but the basic cause was the sale of offices, which had lowered the standard of loyalty and integrity in the public services and which forced the purchasers to practise extortion in order to recoup themselves. In former times officials were dismissed, dispossessed, or even executed on charges of corruption; but now this damnable practice, contrary both to common sense and to religion, and outlawed even by the kings of the infidels, had become the very axis of the affairs of state. At one time it had at least been disguised and surreptitious. Now it was open and universal. The treasury had been impoverished and the army demoralized, and while formerly the infidels fled before the soldiers of Islam the reverse now happened. "So that, if the tyrannical excess of taxation and the deleterious sale of offices are not abandoned; if by return to justice that which was lost is not recovered and penance is not done; then it is certain that the curse of disobedience to the law and the burden of injustice and violence will ruin the Empire. From God we come and to Him we return (Qur'ān ii, 151."[25]

After this terrible warning Kâtib Chelebi goes on to discuss the army, which, he says, corresponds in the social body to the phlegm in the physical body. It performs a useful and necessary function, but is harmful in excess. Excess of phlegm is a characteristic disorder in old men, and so is an excessive army in ageing states. This is a natural development of old age, and it is wasted effort to try and keep the phlegm—or the army—down. It will inevitably grow back. The most one can hope for is to keep it under control and reasonably harmless. Under Süleyman the Magnificent in 970/1562–3 the total number of paid troops was 41,479 men with an annual pay of 122,300,000 aspers; in 974/1566–7 it had risen to 48,316 men for 126,400,000 aspers; in 997/1588–9 to 64,425 men for 178,200,000 aspers; in 1004/1595–6 to 81,870 men for 251,200,000 aspers; in 1018/1609–10 to 91,202 men for 310,800,000 aspers; and under Osman II (1618–22) and Mustafa I (1617–18) the troops rose to 100,000 men. Thereafter a vigorous attempt was made to reduce their numbers, which fell by 1050/1640–1 to 59,257, at a cost of 263,100,000 aspers, but they soon rose again and reached and surpassed the previous level. It would be useless to try and keep their numbers down to the level at which they were under Süleyman, but efforts should be made to keep the cost within limits.[26]

The treasury, says Kâtib Chelebi, is the stomach of the social body, and all classes of society are affected, directly or indirectly, by its intake and maintenance. When the peasantry are oppressed, the treasury becomes empty, and the whole social body suffers. The signs of old age are lethargy and digestive disorders. Just as in the physical body the hair and beard turn white, so in the social body the phase of decline produces luxury and ostentation. Titles and honors are spread ever wider, more and more classes ape the clothing and household furnishings of the sovereign, so that the expenditure both of the individual and of the community becomes larger and larger. Kâtib Chelebi illustrates this with some figures of the income and expenditure of the Ottoman treasury, of which the following are examples:

Date	*Income*	*Expenditure*
972/1564–5	183,000,000	189,600,000
1000/1591–2	293,400,000	363,400,000
1006/1597–8	300,000,000	900,000,000 [*sic*]
1058/1648	361,800,000	500,500,000
1060/1650	532,900,000	687,200,000

To preserve a permanent balance by reducing expenditure and increasing income is very difficult, and is regarded by financial experts as impossible. It may, however, be possible to procure an interval of stability and recuperation.[27]

Kâtib Chelebi then sums up his conclusions and recommendations. There are four ways in which the state might be saved and restored to health: by a man of the sword *(sahib-i sayf)*; by the dignitaries *(a 'yan-i devlet)*; by the army commanders; or by high officers of state *(vükela-i devlet)*. The three last are unlikely, since in all three groups loyal and just men are but few; most are concerned only with their personal satisfactions. The solution must, therefore, come from a man of the sword.

The immediate tasks of this military dictator would be to remedy the deficit in the treasury, the excessive size of the army, the increase in expenditure, and the poverty of the peasants. Here Kâtib Chelebi makes some suggestions for fiscal reform, military and budgetary economy, the abolition of the sale of offices, and the restoration of the rule of law.[28]

Despite the pious formulae with which Kâtib Chelebi ends his essay, it is clear that he had little hope of success. Indeed, in another of his works, he remarks of this essay: "As I knew that my conclusions would be difficult to apply, I took no further trouble about it. But a Sultan of some future time will become aware of it, and put that into operation, which will bring him the best results."[29]

The same note of pessimism may be heard in the memoranda of Hüseyn Hezarfen,[30] written in 1669, and of Sarî Mehmed Pasha,[31] written in 1703. Like Kâtib Chelebi, Hezarfenn showed some interest in the West, and had read European history. He was acquainted with such Western visitors to Istanbul as Marsigli and Antoine Galland, and may have provided some of the material for Prince Kantemir's *History of the Ottoman Empire*.[32] His analysis is along the same lines as those of his predecessors, with discussions of the seclusion and incompetence of the later Sultans, the weakness of the Grand Vizier, the sale of offices and resulting evils. He lays rather more stress than Kochu Bey and Kâtib Chelebi on the need for good and conscientious provincial governors and is more inclined than they are to insist on force. The Sultan should maintain a staff of spies to watch his servants as well as his enemies, and should not hesitate to use fear as law to maintain his authority. "The Sultans must submit to the noble Sharīʿa, and must not kill anyone except by judgment according to the Sharīʿa . . . but let them not abolish discretionary bodily punishment altogether, for punishment is a condition of kingship. If the fear of such punishment were to pass away from people's hearts, this would make the evildoers more numerous and more insolent. The right thing is that there should be fear among the bad and trust among the good people. Permanent fear and permanent trust are both harmful. While the people are between fear and hope, let the Sultanate be well-ordered and let the Sultan be generous."[33] In the same spirit Hezarfen insists strongly on the investigation and punishment of delinquent officials, officers, and ulema. He lays great stress on the moral responsibility of the Sheykh al-Islām and the corps of ulema for the welfare of the state and the people, and urges them to live up to their high calling.

Sarî Mehmed Pasha was a high official of the Ottoman state who no less than seven times was appointed to—and dismissed from—the high office of Defterdar, or chief of the treasury. His lifelong experience of the intimacies of government in his time gives added point to his strictures on corruption and incompetence and his urgent yet hopeless demand for a strong hand at the helm and for a civil service with competence, integrity, and security of tenure. Though he does not differ in essentials from his predecessors, he adds to them the fruits of his own personal experience.

The modern reader of these 16th- and 17th-century memorialists, while respecting their perspicacity and their integrity, will no longer be entirely satisfied with their historical interpretations, and even while accepting their facts and some of their judgments will question the stress and value they lay upon them. To quote but two examples: in reading Kochu Bey's strictures on Ottoman fiscal rapacity, we shall be less impressed by the rise of the poll-tax from 40 to 240 aspers, when we remember that the rate of exchange of the asper to the gold ducat had fallen in about the same proportion. We may also ask whether corruption can really be considered as a major cause of the decay of the Empire, and whether it is not rather a pervasive and corrosive manifestation of a deeper ill. For Kochu Bey and his successors, corruption and favoritism, rapacity and oppression were the root causes of Ottoman decline. The different philosophic presuppositions and historical methods of our time may lead us to regard these as symptoms rather than as causes, and to seek their origins in deeper and vaster changes.

Our present concern, however, is not with the decline of the Ottoman Empire but with the interpretations of it propounded by contemporary Ottoman observers.[34] In reading their works, we cannot but be astonished at the clarity with which they saw and the lucidity with which they described the decline and stagnation of the Empire of which they were loyal and devoted subjects. With a degree of self-knowledge rare in any society, and with a moral courage the more striking in an autocratic monarchy, they did not hesitate to describe and condemn the faults and crimes of those who, so they believed, were responsible for the ruin of the country and the state. The fundamental analysis of Ottoman decline was that of Kochu Bey, whose diagnosis and prescriptions were reproduced, with varying sophistication of exposition, by most of his Ottoman successors in the 17th and 18th centuries.[35]

Ottoman statesmanship was still looking backward to the golden age in the past, and earnest reformers saw the only hope of salvation in a restoration of Islam and of the pure and ancient traditions of the house of ʿOsman. In 1792, when Selim III asked a score of eminent Ottomans for their advice on how to run the Empire, there were many who still gave the same answer. There were some, however, who had found another way.[36]

V

HISTORY AND REVOLUTION

16. *The Significance of Heresy in the History of Islam*

For the medieval Muslim, the significance of heresy was religious: it was related, that is to say, to differences of belief, opinion or practice concerning divinity, revelation, prophecy, and matters deriving from these. These matters, in Islam, extended to include the whole range of public and political life, and any further explanation, beyond the religious one, was unnecessary, even absurd, for what could be added to the greatest and most important of all the issues confronting mankind? The grounds and terms of argument between opposing religious factions were almost invariably theological. That is not to say that Muslim polemicists always accepted the good faith of their opponents. Very often they accuse those whose doctrines they dislike of pursuing ulterior motives—but usually these ulterior motives are themselves religious. The commonest of them is the recurring theme of a plot to undermine Islam from within in favor of some other faith. This is usually connected with some more or less fabulous figure, of superlative malignity and perversity, who functions as a *diabolus ex machina*, to explain dissension and heresy in the community. This is in part due to the general tendency of Islamic historical tradition to attribute to the limitless cunning and multifarious activity of an individual the results of a long development of thought and action; in part also to the tactic, familiar in other times and places, of discrediting critics within the community by associating them with enemies outside the community. The two classical examples are ʿAbdallāh ibn Saba' and ʿAbdallāh ibn Maymūn al-Qaddāḥ. The first, a convert from Judaism and a contemporary of the Caliph ʿAlī (reigned 656–661), is credited with devising most of the beliefs and policies of the extremist Shīʿa in the first centuries of Islam. On the second, an associate of Ismāʿīl ibn Jaʿfar aṣ-Ṣādiq (disappeared ca. 755–762), is fathered the whole complex development of the Ismāʿīlī religion and organization up to Fatimid times. He is variously described as a Jew, as a follower of the Mesopotamian Christian heretic Bardaisan, and, most commonly, as an Iranian dualist; like his predecessor, he is alleged to have sought to destroy Islam from within in the interests of his previous religion. Modern criticism has shown that the roles attributed to these two, together with many of the doctrines ascribed to them, are exaggerated, distorted, and in many respects fictitious.

The medieval European, who shared the fundamental assumptions of his Muslim contemporary, would have agreed with him in ascribing religious movements to religious causes, and would have sought no further for an explanation. But when Europeans ceased to accord first place to religion in their thoughts, sentiments, interests, and loyalties, they also ceased to admit that other men, in other times and places, could have done so. To a rationalistic and materialistic generation, it was inconceivable that such great debates and mighty conflicts could have involved no more than "merely" religious issues. And so historians, once they had passed the stage of amused contempt, devised a series of explanations, setting forth what they described as the "real" or "ultimate" significance "underlying" religious movements and differences. The clashes and squabbles of the early churches, the great Schism, the Reformation, all were reinterpreted in terms of motives and interests reasonable by the standards of the day—and for the religious movements of Islam too explanations were found that tallied with the outlook and interests of the finders.

To the 19th century, obsessed with the problems of liberalism and nationality, only a struggle for national liberation could adequately explain the religious cleavage in Islam, the bitter controversies between doctrine and doctrine, the armed clash of sect with sect. The intuition of Gobineau and Renan, the insight of Dozy and Darmesteter helped to create a picture of Shiʿism as a liberal revival of the Persian national genius, as a resurgence of the Aryanism of Iran in generous revolt against the alien and constricting Semitism of Arabian Islam. Increased knowledge among scholars of Shīʿa literature and close acquaintance by travellers with Shīʿa practice soon exploded the legend of a liberal reformation. But the identification of Shiʿism with Iran was more persistent, and derived some support from the adoption of Shiʿism as the state religion of Persia from the 16th century onwards, as well as from the frequent statements by early authors attributing Shiʿite doctrines and activities to Persian converts.

Nevertheless this hypothesis is now generally abandoned. Wellhausen, Goldziher, Barthold and others have shown that the main centres of early Shiʿism were among the mixed, predominantly Semitic-speaking population of southern Iraq; that Shiʿism was first carried to Persia by the Arabs themselves, and for long found some of its most enthusiastic supporters there among the Arab soldiers and settlers, and in such places as the Arab garrison city of Qumm—even today one of the most vigorous centers of Shiʿite religion in Persia. Though racial antagonisms played their part in these struggles—and the 19th-century scholars made a lasting contribution in discerning them—they were not the sole or even the most potent factor. The accusations of the early polemicists are directed against the old Persian religion, not against the Persian nation —and the charges of Iranian dualist infiltration can be paralleled by similar tales of Jewish and Christian attempts to insinuate their own doctrines into Islam under the cover of Islamic heresy. It was in North Africa, Egypt, and Arabia that Shiʿism won its earliest and most resounding political successes. Only two of the important independent dynasties of Muslim Persia professed the Shiʿite religion. The first, the 10th-century Buyids, came from the peripheral and untypical Persian province of Dailam, by the Caspian Sea. Despite their Shiʿism they were willing to preserve the Sunnī, Arab Caliphate, and their fall was followed by an effortless Sunnī restoration. The second, the 16th-century Safavids, were a Turkish-speaking family from the North-west, relying on Turkish support and professing doctrines that derive from the religious ideas of Turkish Anatolia and Adharbayjan, not from the Persians. Their success in forcibly imposing these doctrines on a country that was still predominantly Sunnī must be explained in terms of the moral and political condition of Iran in the 16th century. It has no bearing on the schisms and conflicts of earlier times.

The advance of knowledge and of understanding thus brought the abandonment of a theory which in any case had ceased wholly to satisfy. For the 20th century, in the West at least, the problems of nationality and national liberation were no longer the main themes of the historic process. The expansion and contraction of societies, the clash of interests and classes, economic change and social upheaval, class war and cataclysm—these were the basic truths which the 20th-century historian saw in the mirror of history. Kharijism, Shiʿism, and the other movements in Islam were now interpreted in terms not of national but of social categories, not of race but of class. In the first quarter of the 20th century, the Russian progressive Barthold, the German conservative Becker, the Italian positivist Caetani, the French Catholic Massignon looked around them, and achieved a new understanding of the revolutions of early Islam—both of those that succeeded, and of those that failed.

At this point it may be useful to describe briefly the picture that Orientalist scholarship at present offers of the causes and phases of heresy in Islam. While there are certainly differences of opinion or interpretation on many specific issues, the current pattern of thought is broadly as follows.

During the period between the death of the Prophet in 632 and the fall of the Umayyad Caliphate in 750 two main heretical groups developed, expressing in religious terms the opposition of certain parties to the existing social and political order and to the orthodox faith that was its moral and public expression. One of these, the Kharijites, drew on largely Bedouin support, and expressed the resentment of the untamed nomads against the encroaching state—not so much against the Umayyad state specifically, as against the very fact and notion of the state, of a constituted authority exercising constraint and even coercion, and curtailing the total freedom of tribal society. The Kharijite theory of the Caliphate carries the doctrine of consent to the point of anarchy, and the Kharijites have indeed been described as the anarchist wing of the revolutionary opposition.

The second, and far more important opposition group was the *Shīʿat ʿAlī*, the party of ʿAlī, commonly known as the Shīʿa. This began as a political group supporting the claims of ʿAlī to the Caliphate, but rapidly developed into a religious sect. As such, it reflected the outlook and aspirations of an important social class—the *mawālī* (singular *mawlā*)—those Muslims who were not full members by birth of an Arab tribe. The greater part of these were the non-Arab converts to Islam. These were to be found especially in the industrial and commercial quarters which grew up around the garrison cities planted by the Arabs in the conquered provinces. Around the cantonments where the Arab warriors were stationed, new cities appeared, full of *mawlā* craftsmen and merchants, purveying to the growing and diverse needs of the conquerors, and thriving on the flow of gold brought by the conquests. Soon *mawlā* soldiers themselves took part in the wars of conquest, while their superior skill and experience gave them a predominant place in the day-to-day administration of the Empire. Conscious of their growing importance, they became increasingly resentful of the economic and social disabilities imposed upon them by the Arab aristocratic régime, and rallied readily to a form of Islam that challenged the legitimacy of the existing Arab aristocratic state. Their aspiration was for an order in which all Muslims would be equal and Arab birth would no longer carry privileges. Their religious doctrines were adapted from their previous faiths. Judaeo-Christian and Persian messianism and legitimism prepared them to accept the claims of the descendants of the Prophet, who promised to overthrow the Empire of tyranny and injustice and establish an Empire of equity and justice.

Within the Shīʿa camp there were two main trends—a moderate one, with much Arab support, and limited political objectives; an extremist one, with mainly *mawlā* support, and with revolutionary policies and tactics. The existing régime was Arab; Persians were prominent among the revolutionaries, and some elements of racial conflict were injected into the struggle.

But the *mawālī* were by no means exclusively Persian; many of them, including their leaders, were Arab, and the conflict was basically social rather than national.

The ʿAbbasids rode to power on the crest of one of these religious opposition movements, and their victory was a social as well as a political revolution. In the first century of ʿAbbasid rule the exclusive hegemony of the Arab aristocracy was ended, and men of many races found equal opportunity in a new social and political order. Renouncing their disreputable revolutionary antecedents, the ʿAbbasids strove to formulate and inculcate a new orthodoxy, no longer the tribal cult of a race of alien conquerors, but the universal religion of a universal empire. After some early and unsuccessful experiments with other religious ideas, the ʿAbbasids eventually adopted the consensus of the theologians, which in time became orthodox, Sunnī Islam. Orthodoxy was once more the religion of the state and the existing order—and new heresies arose to meet the spiritual needs and material aspirations of the dissatisfied.

The first to oppose the ʿAbbasids, their state, and their faith was the disappointed extremist wing of the movement that had brought them to power. Later, the great economic and social changes of the 8th and 9th centuries created new centres of discontent, especially among the artisans and workpeople of the swarming cities, and among the dethroned and dispossessed Arab tribes of the desert borderlands. These discontents found expression in a welter of small radical sects, each with its own local and sectional support. Most of these sects accepted in one form or another the claims of the house of ʿAlī, and are thus loosely classified as Shiʿite. By the beginning of the 10th century most of them had coalesced about one of two main groups. One of them, the Ithnāʿasharī or Twelver Shīʿa, continued the moderate, limited opposition of the early Arab Shīʿa; the other, the Ismāʿīlī sect, resumed the interrupted development of the earlier extremist *mawlā* Shīʿa. This second group carried through a successful revolution and established the Fatimid Caliphate, which reigned in Egypt for two centuries.

By the 11th century social and political change in the East had once more created a revolutionary situation. The growth of feudal and military rule, accelerated and consolidated by the Seljuq invasions, brought massive upheavals. Arab and Persian landowners, dispossessed or subjugated by Turkish feudal lords, merchants ruined by the shortage of minted money and the decline of trade, bureaucrats chafing under the bridle of foreign military masters, all helped to swell the ranks of the discontented and rebellious. To these Isma'ilism, in a revived and modified form, brought a seductive doctrine of moral and political revolution, now associated with a new and effective strategy of attack.

For a time the activities of the Ismā'īlī Assassins were subordinate to the Fatimid capital in Cairo, but soon, as the Fatimids themselves fell under the domination of their Turkish military commanders, relations between Cairo and the Assassins were broken off, and the latter were free to pursue their radical ideas and policies uncontaminated by any links with state or empire. The Seljuqs were well aware of the danger, and endeavoured to meet it. As their soldiers guarded the bodies of their servants from Assassin daggers, so their theologians and teachers guarded the minds of their subjects from Ismā'īlī ideas. It is in this period that the *madrasa* appears—the theological seminary, founded as a center for the formulation and dissemination of orthodox doctrine, to meet the Ismā'īlī challenge that came first from the colleges and mission-schools of Fatimid Egypt, later from the Assassins' castles in the mountains. At the same time the religious genius of al-Ghazālī (*d.* 1111) evolved a new form of orthodoxy, in which the cold, flat dogmas of the theologians drew warmth and contour from the intuitive and mystical faith of the Ṣūfīs. The tide of popular piety, given new channels and new impulses, began to flow towards and not away from the schools and the dynasty—the nearest Muslim equivalents of Church and State.

By the time of the great Mongol invasions of the 13th century, extremist Shi'ism had ceased to be a vital force in Islam. Here and there, in remote fastnesses of mountain and desert, or isolated and immobilized amid alien surroundings, it dragged on an attenuated and fossilized existence. But in the main Islamic centres of the Middle East, the theologians and the people, driven towards one another by the double shock of Christian and Mongol invasion, henceforth professed the same orthodox Sunnī religion; the same, that is, in its essential central doctrines, though still varying greatly in belief and still more in practice and organization, from place to place and from group to group.

Since the 13th century the religious history of Middle Eastern Islam has been chiefly concerned with the interplay of dogmatic religion and popular piety. Though the great synthesis of al-Ghazālī and his successors brought the two into communion, they remained distinct—sometimes in alliance, sometimes in conflict, always modifying and influencing one another by alternate clash and compromise. For the people—as distinct from the State, the schools, and the hierarchy—the characteristic expression of religious life has remained, until our own time, the Ṣūfī brotherhood, with its mystical and ecstatic faith, its dervish saints and leaders, its latent hostility to the established theological and political order. Though the Ṣūfī orders in time became formally Sunnī and politically quietist, many of them remained suspect in the eyes of Sulṭāns and ʿUlamā—and occasionally, as in the great revolt of the Ottoman dervishes in the early 15th century, the buried embers of discontent burst into conflagration.

The above summary of the genesis and evolution of Islamic heresy is obviously incomplete and necessarily schematic and personal. But it reflects broadly the findings of modern scholarship; and indeed, as truth is dealt with by historians, it is in all probability substantially true—that is to say, it represents as much as can be seen in the evidence at present available by the present generation of observers, though in the future new sources may yield greater knowledge, new experience bring deeper insight.

But what after all do we really mean when we say that such-and-such an interest or motive "underlies" a religious movement—or, approaching the problem from the opposite angle, that one or another sect or doctrine "represents" or "expresses" a social group or aspiration? Does it mean, as the cruder disciples of our time would have it, that scheming men made unscrupulous use of religion as a mask or cloak behind which they hid their real purposes from their deluded followers? Does it mean, in Marxist terms, that the sect was the ideological exponent of the economic conditions and interests of a class—or, in the subtler language of Max Weber, that once an appropriate form of religion appeared in a certain stratum, the conditions of that stratum gave it the maximum chance of survival in the selective struggle for existence against other, less appropriate forms? The problem is of more than purely historical interest, since in our own day, in Persia, in Egypt and in other Islamic countries, new religious movements are stirring beneath the secularized surface; sects and creeds are replacing the wrecked parties and programs that have never really responded to the needs and passions of the peoples of Islam.

It may bring us closer to an understanding of the meaning of heresy in Islam if we look at what the classical Islamic authors themselves said on the subject, and in particular examine the precise import of the various technical terms used.

It is curious, even astonishing, that among the very few loan-words of European or Christian origin used in modern literary Arabic are the words *hartaqa*—heresy and *hurtūqī* (or *hartīqī*)—heretic. This word first appears in the Christian Arabic literature of Syria, as far back as medieval times, and no doubt came by way of Syriac and the Eastern Churches. During the 19th century it began to pass into common Arabic usage. At first it appeared chiefly in translations of Western books, and in Western Christian, or non-religious contexts. But in our own day it is used by Muslim writers on Muslim history—not, admittedly, by those brought up on traditional theological lines, but by western-trained historians seeking to apply to their own history the principles and methods learnt elsewhere. Can it be that Islam, with its 72 and more named heresies, has no name for heresy, and is thus in the position of the Red Indian tribe which, we are told, has a score of verbs for different ways of cutting, but no verb "to cut"? Or is the notion of heresy in the Christian sense so alien to Islam that a loan-word was needed to describe it?

There are in fact several Islamic terms which are tendered as "heresy" by western scholars. They are by no means synonyms. Each has its own meaning, and none of them, as modern Arabic writers have found, can properly express that which in the Christian Churches is called heresy.

The first of these in order of appearance is *bidʿa*, meaning innovation, and more specifically any doctrine or practice not attested in the time of the Prophet. The term is thus the converse of *Sunna*. It is used currently by the early theologians, and even appears in the traditions attributed to the Prophet, who is quoted as saying that "the worst things are those that are novelties; every novelty is an innovation, every innovation is an error and every error leads to hell-fire". In its extreme form this principle meant the rejection of every idea and amenity not known in Western Arabia in the time of Muḥammad and his companions, and it has indeed been used by successive generations of ultra-conservatives to oppose tables, sieves, coffee and tobacco, printing-presses and artillery, telephones, wireless, and votes for women. It soon became necessary to distinguish between "good" or licit innovations, and "bad" or illicit innovations, the latter being such as were contrary to the Qur'ān, the Traditions or to the *ijmāʿ*, the consensus of the Muslim community. This last meant in effect that the acceptance or rejection of an innovation was determined by what in modern parlance would be called "the climate of opinion" among the learned and the powerful, and that, since the climate of opinion changes, the *bidʿa* of today may become the *sunna* of tomorrow, opposition to which is itself a *bidʿa*. Moreover, since no machinery exists for the consultation or formulation of a universal *ijmāʿ* for all Islam, there may be differing *ijmāʿ*s influenced by different traditions and circumstances in different parts of the Islamic world, and the dividing-line between *sunna* and *bidʿa* may thus vary with place as well as time. Islam has in fact absorbed a great deal that was foreign to the religion of the Companions, sometimes in concession to new ideas, sometimes by way of compromise with the existing practices of the peoples to which it came. But these innovations of doctrine and practice were always restrained and modified by the action of *ijmāʿ*, and from time to time drastically curtailed by a wave of religious conservatism. The gravamen of the charge of *bid'a* levelled against a doctrine was not primarily that it was false or bad, but that it was new—a breach of habit, custom, and tradition, respect for which is rooted deep in the pre-Islamic tribal past, and reinforced by the belief in the finality and perfection of the Muslim revelation.

It will readily be seen that there are many contexts in which the word *bid'a* can reasonably be translated as heresy, but the two terms are far from being exact equivalents. Theological polemicists are ready enough to hurl accusations at those whose doctrines they disapprove of, but they are often reluctant to pursue their charges to their logical conclusion. Even so fanatical an opponent of all innovations as the Syrian jurist Ibn Taymiyya (d. 1328) prefers a sort of quarantining of suspect groups and individuals, followed where necessary by admonition and even coercive action. Only when a *bid'a* is excessive, persistent, and aggressive are its followers to be put beyond the pale of the community of Islam.

The idea of excess is also expressed in another theological term—*ghuluww*, from an Arabic root meaning to overshoot, to go beyond the limit. Underlying this is the notion, deep-rooted in Islam, that a certain measure of diversity of opinion is harmless, and even beneficial. "Difference of opinion in my community is an act of divine mercy," says a tradition attributed to the Prophet. The Holy Law of Islam is expounded in four versions, by four schools of jurisprudence, each with its own principles, text-books, and judiciary. All four are different, yet all are valid, and live in mutual toleration. Even Shi'ism was in its origin a *tashayyu' ḥasan*—a lawful partisanship, one not exceeding the limits of permitted disagreement—and only later left the common ground of orthodoxy. This almost parliamentary doctrine of limited disagreement and common basic assumptions, despite periods of lapse, survives right through the history of Islam, and explains the mutual toleration of Twelver Shī'ī and Sunnī in 'Abbasid Iraq, of dervish and 'Ulamā in post-Mongol Islam. The followers of the four schools, and of some others that have disappeared, are all considered orthodox. Even the Shiʿites, the Kharijites and others, though held to be in manifest error on important points of doctrine and Holy Law, were still Muslims, and enjoyed the privileges of such in this world and the next. Only certain groups, who carried their divergence to excess *(ghuluww)* are excluded from Islam. Such are the exaggerators *(ghulāt*—singular *ghālī)* among the Shīʿa, who in their veneration for ʿAlī and his descendants ascribe divine powers to them, and are thus guilty of polytheism. Such too are the other groups of extremists among the Shiʿites, Kharijites, Murji'ites, Muʿtazilites, even among the Sunnīs, who deny prophecy, revelation, or Holy Law, or preach such doctrines as reincarnation, metempsychosis, or antinomianism. These, in the view of the majority of the theologians, are to be excluded from Islam—though, characteristically, opinions differ as to where the line should be drawn.

The term most commonly translated as heresy is *zandaqa*—the faith of the *zindīq*. This word is of uncertain origin—possibly Syriac, more probably Persian. In Sasanid times it seems to have been applied to Manichaeans, and more generally to followers of ascetic and unorthodox forms of Iranian religion. In Islamic times too the word was at first applied to Manichaeans and related groups, more especially to those who held dualist doctrines while making nominal profession of Islam. Later it was generalized to cover all holders of unorthodox, unpopular and suspect beliefs, particularly those considered dangerous to the social order and the state. At the same time it was applied loosely to materialists, atheists, agnostics, and the like, and came to have the general meaning of free-thinker and libertine.

Despite its etymological obscurity and semantic vagueness, the word *zindīq* had, in another respect, a terrible precision. For unlike the other terms discussed, it belonged to administrative rather than theoretical usage. A charge of *bidʿa* or *ghuluww*, uncomplicated by any act of overt rebellion, meant no more than being consigned by some theologian to hell-fire. A charge of *zandaqa* meant being taken by a policeman to prison, to interrogation, perhaps to execution. The first recorded prosecution is that of Jaʿd ibn Dirham, a forerunner of the Muʿtazila, who in 742, during the reign of the Umayyad Caliph Hishām, was condemned, mutilated, and crucified on a charge of *zandaqa*. Generally speaking, however, the Umayyads repressed only those doctrines that openly challenged their own title to the Caliphate. They were not greatly concerned with deviations from dogma as such, the less so since orthodox dogma was still in process of formulation.

The ʿAbbasids were more keenly aware of the potentialities of seditious religious teachings. The repression of *zindīqs* began during the reign of al-Manṣūr (754–775), and some were condemned to death. The Caliph attached sufficient importance to this question to include an injunction to extirpate *zandaqa* in his political testament to his successor, al-Mahdī (775–785), under whom the really serious repression began. In 779, while passing through Aleppo, the Caliph ordered a *zindīq*-hunt, in which many were caught, condemned, beheaded and quartered. Thereafter the repression proceeded with vigor, and a regular inquisition was established, under the control of a Grand Inquisitor called *ʿArīf* or *Ṣāḥib al-Zanādiqa*. There seems little doubt that among the many victims claimed by the inquisition under al-Mahdī and al-Hādī (785–786) the Manichaeans provided the main bulk. But, as one would expect, the inquisitorial net caught other fish too. Some, like the poets Bashshār ibn Burd and Ṣāliḥ ibn ʿAbd al-Quddūs—both executed for *zandaqa* in 783—were hardly more than earnest enquirers with inadequate respect for authority. Others, too numerous to mention, were good Muslims whose removal, for political or personal reasons, was deemed opportune by the Caliph, his ministers or his inquisitors.

After the time of al-Hādī the direct threat of Manichaeism seems to have subsided, and the persecutions of the *zindīqs*, though they continue, are intermittent and on a smaller scale. At the same time the word *zindīq* loses its connotation of Manichaeism and dualism, and comes to be applied to any extreme or seditious doctrine—to some forms of Ṣūfī belief—or no belief at all. In legal parlance the *zindīq* is the criminal dissident—the professing Muslim who holds beliefs or follows practices contrary to the central dogmas of Islam, and is therefore to be regarded as an apostate and an infidel. The jurists differ as to the theoretical formulation of the point of exclusion, but in fact usually adopt the practical criterion of open rebellion.

More or less synonymous with *zandaqa* in its later, generalized application is the word *ilḥād*, originally meaning deviation from the path. The word appears in this general sense in the Qur'ān, but was not part of the technical vocabulary of the earliest jurists and theologians. In the first few centuries of Islam the *mulḥid*—deviator—is the man who rejects all religion, the atheist, materialist or rationalist of the type of the notorious Ibn al-Rāwandī (9th–10th centuries). In this sense the word was misapplied by orthodox theologians, as a term of abuse, to a number of sects, and especially to the Assassins in Persia. By Mongol times it had become the common appellation of the Assassins, so that both Chinese and European visitors to Persia call them by it. In post-Mongol times, and especially in Ottoman usage, *mulḥid* and *ilḥād* tend to replace *zindīq* and *zandaqa* as the common terms for subversive doctrines among the Shīʿīs, the Ṣūfīs, and elsewhere. In the 19th century an Ottoman historian used both *ilḥād* and *zandaqa* to describe the ideas disseminated in Turkey by the emissaries of the French Revolution.[1]

From the days when the seeds of Islam were first flung by the Arab hurricane on to the soil of many lands, strange flowers have often appeared in the garden of the faith—doctrines and practices that were aberrant, discordant, incongruous. Some of them were perhaps native growths in Arabian Islam—weeds and tares brought by the self-same wind of conquest. Others, the majority, were grafts and hybrids from alien stocks—beliefs and customs from pre-existing cults, foreign teachings from Plotinus, Mazdak and Mani, later from Voltaire, Rousseau and Marx. These were duly recognized and condemned by the guardians of the faith as innovatory, exaggerated, intrusive, and erroneous. Though they brought some modifications to the main stock and local sub-varieties of Islam, most of them were in the course of time quietly extruded by the action of the slowly evolving consensus of the Islamic community.

But how far do these amount to heresy in the strict, technical sense of the word? The Greek word αἵρεσις originally meant "choice", then a school or sect that represents the "choice" of its adherents. Finally, in the Christian Church, it is specialized to mean a religious error, contrary to the truth as authoritatively defined and promulgated by the Church, and condemned as such by a competent ecclesiastical authority. By this definition, there has been and can be no heresy in Islam. As Goldziher says:

> The role of dogma in Islam cannot be compared with that which it plays in the religious life of any of the Christian Churches. There are no Councils and Synods which, after lively controversy, lay down the formulae, which henceforth shall be deemed to embrace the whole of the true faith. There is no ecclesiastical institution, which serves as the measure of orthodoxy; no single authorized interpretation of the holy scriptures, on which the doctrine and exegesis of the Church might be built. The Consensus, the supreme authority in all questions of religious practice, exercises an elastic, in a certain sense barely definable jurisdiction, the very conception of which is moreover variously explained. Particularly in questions of dogma, it is difficult to determine in unanimity what shall have effect as undisputed Consensus. What is accepted as Consensus by one party, is far from being accepted as such by another.[2]

In the absence of an apostolic tradition and of a supreme pontiff, orthodoxy and heterodoxy in Islam could at first sight be determined only by making the teachings of one school the touchstone for the rejection of the others. The difficulties and absurdities of such a standard are well summarised by al-Ghazālī. Is al-Bāqillānī a heretic for disagreeing with al-Ashʿarī, or al-Ashʿarī for disagreeing with al-Bāqillānī? Why should truth be the prerogative of one rather than the other? Does truth go by precedence? Then do not the Muʿtazilites take precedence of al-Ashʿarī? Because of greater virtue and knowledge? In what scales and with what measures shall the degrees of virtue be measured, so that the superiority of one or another theologian may be established? . . . "If you are fair, you will soon realise that whoever makes truth the preserve of any one theologian is himself nearest to heresy . . . because he gives his master a rank that belongs only to the Prophet, considering him immune from error, so that orthodoxy consists in following him and heresy only in opposing him."[3]

In this passage, the Arabic words translated as heretic and heresy are not any of those discussed above, but *Kāfir* and *Kufr*, unbeliever and unbelief. And with these terrible and unequivocal words we perhaps come nearest to an Islamic equivalent of heresy. The sectarian, though some of his doctrines may in time be excluded by the cumulative force of the Consensus from the main stream of Islam, is still a Muslim. In the eyes of the jurists, he is still entitled to the status and privileges of a Muslim in society—property, marriage, testimony, the holding of public office, even to treatment as a believer, though a rebel, in insurrection and war. In the eyes of the theologians, he is a Muslim though a sinner, and may aspire to salvation in the life to come. The vital barrier lies, not between Sunnī and sectarian, but between sectarian and unbeliever. And unbelief, as al-Ghazālī observes, is a legal question, like slavery and freedom, to be determined by legal rules and processes, and involving legal consequences.[4] The excommunicated unbeliever is not only damned in the world beyond; he is outlawed in this world. He is deprived of all legal rights and barred from all religious offices; his very life and property are forfeit. If he is born a Muslim, his position is that of an apostate, a dead limb that must be ruthlessly excised.

In this as in so many other respects the practice of Islam was less severe than its theory. In theological circles, it is true, charges of unbelief were readily bandied about, and the word *kāfir* was part of the small change of religious polemic. "The piety of theologians," observes al-Jāḥiẓ, "consists of hastening to denounce dissidents as unbelievers."[5] Al-Ghazālī speaks with withering contempt of those "who would constrict the vast mercy of God to His servants and make paradise the preserve of a small clique of theologians."[6] But in fact these loose accusations had no practical effect. The victims were for the most part unmolested, and many held high office—even legal office—in the Muslim state.

As the rules and penalties of Muslim law were codified and brought into application, charges of *kufr* became rarer and rarer. There are two versions of the last words of al-Ash'arī (d. 935–6), one of the greatest of Muslim dogmatists. According to the one, he died cursing the Mu'tazila. According to the other, his last words were: "I testify that I do not consider any who pray towards Mecca as infidels. All turn their minds in prayer towards the same object. They differ only in expression."[7] This statement, even if it be apocryphal, is a true expression of the attitude of Sunnī Islam to the problem of *takfīr*—the denunciation or excommunication of the unbeliever. Many definitions were attempted of the basic minimum of belief—but most inclined, in practice if not always in theory, to accept as Muslims any who testify to the unity of God and the apostolate of Muḥammad. This standard was the more acceptable to jurists, since the only religious transgressions for which the *Sunna* of Muḥammad prescribes the death-penalty are polytheism and the reviling of the Prophet. Outward performance is sufficient, according to a tradition of the Prophet, since God alone can judge a man's sincerity. Thinkers as diverse as the tolerant and mystical al-Ghazālī and the fanatical and puritanical Ibn Taymiyya agree in stretching the limits of Islam to the utmost.

A dictum of the jurists lays down that in a trial for apostasy, any legal rule or precedent, even a weak one, which would give an acquittal must be followed. Even open rebellion did not automatically involve *takfīr*. In 923 the chief *Qāḍī* Ibn Buhlūl refused to denounce the Carmathian rebels as unbelievers, since they began their letters with invocations to God and the Prophet, and were therefore *prima facie* Muslims. The Shāfiʿī law insists that the sectarian, even in revolt, is entitled to be treated as a Muslim; that is to say, that his family and property are respected, and that he cannot be summarily despatched or sold into slavery once he becomes a prisoner. Only the most persistent and outrageous error or misconduct was condemned as *kufr*, or as the more or less equivalent crimes of *zandaqa* and *ilḥād*. The accused was then summoned to recant and repent, and, if he failed to do so, was put to death. Some jurists refused the opportunity to recant, since the good faith of a *zindīq* could not be accepted.

All this does not of course mean that persecution of heresy was unknown in Islam. From time to time heretics were tried and condemned, with or without *takfīr*, and punished by imprisonment, whipping, decapitation, hanging, burning, and crucifixion. Inquisitions were rare, but the ordinary Islamic judiciary could be empowered to deal with the discovery and punishment of religious error. The suppression of *zindīqs* by the early ʿAbbasids has already been mentioned. Under al-Ma'mūn a new inquisition, known as the *miḥna*, was used to impose the official Muʿtazilite doctrine; with the restoration of Sunnī orthodoxy under al-Mutawakkil (847–861), the same means were used against the Muʿtazila themselves and against the Shīʿa.

Repression of dangerous doctrine continued sporadically under the ʿAbbasids, the most striking being that of the extremist Shīʿa. At the same time mystical teachings, the menace of which to the state was less immediately obvious, were kept under surveillance. In 922 the God-intoxicated Ṣūfī al-Ḥusain ibn Manṣūr al-Ḥallāj suffered martyrdom in Baghdad for proclaiming his union with God, and thus endangering the established order in heaven and on earth. Two and a half centuries later the illuminist al-Suhrawardī suffered a similar fate in Aleppo. The Seljuqs used all possible means to meet the threat of the Assassins—Saladin stamped on the embers of the Ismāʿīlī Fatimid Caliphate and compulsorily restored Sunnism in Egypt. In post-Mongol times the threat of Shiʿism had for a while subsided, and mystic and dogmatist were drawn closer by adversity. A few executions of individual Shiʿites are recorded in Syria under the Mamluks—most of them seem to be due to the deliberate provocations of would-be martyrs.[8]

In Turkey the growth of the Ottoman principality to statehood and empire constricted the erstwhile religious freedom and eclecticism of the frontier, and provoked the armed resistance of groups on or beyond the limits of orthodox tolerance. The Bekṭāshīs, strongest among the mixed populations of Western Anatolia and Rumelia, made their peace with the Empire, and received tolerance and even favor. The Shīʿa were mostly to be found among the Turcomans in Central and Eastern Anatolia, and had close affinities with the Shīʿa Safavids who ruled Persia from the beginning of the 16th century. The Anatolian Shiʿites were thus potential or actual enemies of the state, and the Ottoman Sultans used both repression and re-education to render them harmless. At the same time a far more effective repression was carried out in Persia, this time of Sunnism, resulting in its virtual extinction in that country.

The one constant criterion was subversion. The followers of doctrines and practices which threatened the state, the dynasty, or the fabric of society were outlawed and repressed. Others—be they as remote from Islam as the Nuṣayrīs, Druzes and Yazīdīs—were accorded tolerance, and even allowed the name and status of Muslims.

It has been observed as a curiosity that the word religion does not occur in the Old Testament. This is not because the ancient Hebrews had no religion, but because they did not distinguish a separate part or compartment of their personal and public lives for which they might require this special term. Religion embraced the whole of life—man's dealings with his fellow men, with society and with the state, as well as his dealings with God. Even the simple, basic acts of working and resting, eating, drinking, and procreation were sanctified as the fulfillment of a divine command and a divine purpose. Islam too has no words to distinguish between sacred and profane, spiritual and temporal, for it does not accept or even know the dichotomy that these pairs of antonyms express—the cleavage and clash of Church and State, of Pope and Emperor, of God and Caesar. The Islamic state is in theory and in the popular conception a theocracy, in which God is the sole source of both power and law, and the sovereign His viceregent on earth. The faith was the official credo of constituted state and society, the cult the external and visible symbol of their identity and cohesion; conformity to them, however perfunctory, the token and pledge of loyalty. Orthodoxy meant the acceptance of the existing order; heresy or apostasy, its criticism or rejection. The same sacred law, coming from the same source and administered through the same jurisdiction, embraced civil, criminal, and constitutional as well as ritual and doctrinal rules. The sovereign was the supreme embodiment of the Holy Law, maintained by it, and maintaining it. Where Church and State are inextricably interwoven, so too are religion and politics, and religion provided the only possible expression, in public and social terms, of sustained opposition. Whenever a group of men sought to challenge and to change the existing order, they made their teachings a theology and their instrument a sect, as naturally and as inevitably as their modern western counterparts make ideologies and political parties.

Yet even this explanation, based on the local characteristics of Semitic law and faith, cannot be more than partial. Beyond it lies a profounder relationship between heresy and revolt, one that is bound up with the ultimate meaning of religion in human life.

17. The Revolutions in Early Islam

In a sense, the advent of Islam itself was a revolution. The new faith, hot from Arabia, overwhelmed existing doctrines and churches; the new masters who brought it overthrew an old order and created a new one. In Islam there was to be neither church nor priest, neither orthodoxy nor hierarchy, neither kingship nor aristocracy. There were to be no castes or estates to flaw the unity of the believers; no privileges, save the self-evident superiority of those who accept to those who willfully reject the true faith—and of course such obvious natural and social facts as the superiority of man to woman and of master to slave. Even these inferiorities were softened by the new dispensation. The slave was no longer a chattel but a human being, with recognized legal and moral rights; woman, though still subject to polygamy and concubinage, acquired property rights not equalled in the West until modern times, and even the non-Muslim enjoyed a tolerance and security in sharp contrast with the lot of non-Christians in medieval—and sometimes modern—Christendom.

In the Roman world, neither the advent of Christianity nor the coming of the barbarians brought any sudden revolutionary impact comparable with that of Islam. Both movements were slower and more gradual than the Arab-Islamic conquests. Christianity, after more than three centuries of opposition, captured the Roman Emperor, and itself became enmeshed with the Roman Empire and government; the Germanic barbarians accepted and took over both the Christian faith and the Roman state, and adapted both to their own ways and purposes. The Arab conquerors brought their own religion and created their own state; much of the conflict of early Islamic times arises from the clash between the two.

All the Arab warriors shared—though not equally—in the tribute of the conquered lands. Many of them sought further—sometimes conflicting—advantages. There were tribesmen in search of pasturage, oasis-dwellers looking for estates, and Meccan merchants avid to exploit the rich commerce of great cities. To many it seemed that the government of the Caliphs, especially the third Caliph 'Uthmān, was more responsive to their needs than to those of Islam.

The needs of Islam were variously understood and interpreted. For the nomads, deprived of the free use of the lands they had conquered and subjected to the irksome and unfamiliar control of organized authority, the wealth and power of the Meccans were an affront, a betrayal of the cause for which they had fought. Islam meant the brotherhood and equality of the believers, limited only by their freely given and revocable loyalty to their chosen leader. Wealth and the status which it gave, power and the authority which it conferred, were regarded as a derogation from the authentic message of Islam, and charges of robbery and tyranny evoked a ready response.

Achievement rarely accords with aspiration. The Islamic Caliphate was established to serve the cause and spread the message of Islam. Instead, it seemed to serve the interests of a small group of rich and powerful men, who maintained it by methods that approximated, to an increasing and disquieting extent, to those of the ancient Empires that Islam had superseded. Pious and earnest men denounced the Caliphs as worldlings, usurpers and tyrants; angry and ambitious men joined them in seeking to overthrow this tyranny, and the state and community of Islam were convulsed by a series of bitter civil wars. The declared issues were the Caliphate—who should rule, and how—and the restoration of authentic Islam. Each victory, whether of the rebels or of the defenders, ended with a reinforcement of the sovereign power, and a further step in the direction of a centralized autocracy in the old Middle Eastern style. By a tragic paradox, only the strengthening of the Islamic state could save the identity and cohesion of the Islamic community—and the Islamic state, as it grew stronger, moved further and further away from the social and ethical ideals of Islam. Resistance to this process of change was constant and vigorous, sometimes successful, but always unavailing—and out of this resistance emerged a series of religious sects, different in their ideologies and their support, but alike in seeking to restore the radical dynamism that was being lost. At first, when Arab and Muslim were still virtually synonymous terms, the religious struggle was a civil war of the Arabs; later, as Islam spread among the conquered peoples, converts began to play an increasing and sometimes a dominant role. It is a striking testimony to the universalist appeal and surviving revolutionary power of Islam that the great revolutionary movements in the Islamic Empire were all movements within Islam and not against it.

The first civil war ended in 661 with the victory of Muʿāwiya and the establishment of a new Caliphate, in his own family, that lasted for 90 years. The discipline and order of Muʿāwiya's régime, in contrast to the anarchic factionalism of many of ʿAlī's supporters, seemed to offer a better prospect for the unity and survival of Islam and its protection against the forces of disruption, and many even of the pious transferred their allegiance to the less attractive but more effective Umayyad. The Umayyad Caliphate, in its successive phases, represented a series of compromises—of interim arrangements which preserved the unity of the Islamic polity, at the cost of establishing a predominance of the Arab aristocracy and an imperial system that gradually borrowed more and more of the structure and methods of the defeated empires.

The process was not unresisted. One group of ʿAlī's supporters, the Kharijites, had turned against him during his lifetime, and continued to oppose the Umayyads and after them the ʿAbbasids. The Shīʿa, or party of ʿAlī, transferred their allegiance after his death to other members of the Prophet's family, not necessarily his descendants, and followed a series of rebels and pretenders who attempted to overthrow the Umayyads and take their place.

The dramatic martyrdom of the kin of the Prophet at Karbalā' in 680, more than any other single event of the time, helped to transform the Shīʿa from a political faction—the supporters of a candidate for office—to a religious sect, with strong messianic overtones. Another contribution came from the new converts, who brought with them, from their Judaeo-Christian and Iranian backgrounds, many religious ideas alien to primitive Islam. These new converts became Muslims; they did not become Arabs, still less aristocrats, and the expectations aroused in them by their new faith made them deeply resentful of the inferior social and economic status accorded to them by the dominant Arab aristocracy. These feelings were shared by both pious and discontented Arabs, especially those who suffered from the sharper economic and social differentiation that came with conquest and riches. Many of the new converts were familiar with both political and religious legitimism. They were readily attracted by the claims of the house of the Prophet, which seemed to offer an end to the injustices of the existing order and a fulfillment of the promise of Islam.

The early history of Shīʿism is still very obscure. Most of the expositions that have come down to us are the work of theologians, both Sunnī and Shīʿite, and are presented according to a theological, not an historical classification, determined by types of doctrine rather than by the sequence of events. They were all written at later dates, and often read back into the past the ideas and conflicts of later times. In doing so, they tend to systematize and stabilize much that was shifting and chaotic. In time, the Shīʿa crystallized into a sect, or group of sects, with clearly defined doctrines, marking them off from Sunnī Islam on the one hand and from other sects on the other. In early times this had not yet happened. The Muslims were still a single community, in which various groups formed and broke up, following different doctrines and leaders, and changing them with bewildering ease.

It was during this early and obscure period that certain doctrines, which came to be characteristically Shīʿite, were gradually formed. One was the belief in an *Imām*—a divinely chosen leader, of the house of the Prophet, who was the sole rightful head of the Islamic community. Another, closely linked with it, was the belief in a *Mahdī*, a messianic *Imām* who, in God's good time, would overthrow the rule of the impious usurpers who held sway, and would "fill the earth with justice and equity as it is now filled with tyranny and oppression."

Behind the luxuriant myths, the exotic doctrines, the passionate and violent outbursts, powerful forces were at work. Their nature has been variously interpreted, and the attempt to explain them, first in national and then in socio-economic terms, has encountered many obstacles.

One difficulty has arisen from the terms and categories used by Western scholars, and derived from Western experience—that is, from Christian theology and European society. Explanations of Muslim "sects" by means of Muslim "classes" tend to be explanations of an analogy by means of another analogy—with results that are highly abstract and remote from reality. Another, more practical problem is the lack of hard, factual knowledge concerning economic and social developments in early Islam. It is difficult enough to relate religious movements to social conditions when both are well documented and thoroughly explored; very much more so when one is trying to relate the little-known to the unknown—and with intellectual tools forged for another purpose.

Nevertheless some progress can be recorded. Explanations in terms of a simple conflict between rich and poor, between the possessors and the dispossessed, are seen to be as inadequate in themselves as the purely ethnic explanations which preceded them. The class structure of medieval Islamic society was of bewildering complexity. There were, for example, nomads, countrymen and townsmen—but with countless sub-divisions and cross-classifications. The nomads included powerful and weak tribes, noble and base tribes, Northern and Southern, rich and poor. Within the tribe, too, there were important distinctions of birth, wealth and status. In the countryside there were gentry and peasantry, large and small landowners, free peasants, sharecroppers and serfs. In the towns there were freemen, freedmen and slaves; notables and populace; courtiers, government officials, tax-farmers, soldiers, scholars, men of religion, merchants great and small, artisans, and the mass of the urban poor. Occupations were by no means clearly differentiated—governors and soldiers drew profits from commerce as well as pay from the state, while merchants might qualify for salaries and pensions. In addition there were social distinctions and disputes—gentilic, tribal, etc.—which were deeply felt and bitterly contested, yet to which it would be very difficult to assign any clear economic origins or consequences; similarly the effect of religious and ethnic divisions should not be discounted, and cannot be fully explained. Finally there were very important regional variations and divisions, between the cities and provinces of a newly assembled Empire, with vast differences both in their previous history and subsequent development.

The sources are rich in references to economic and still more to social conflict—often between interest groups that are relatively small and locally defined. Some are manifestations of wider conflicts. Tribesmen complain of an unfair distribution of land and other booty, in which their tribe has not received its proper share; nomads object to the use of conquered lands for cultivation instead of grazing. Bedouin debtors speak bitterly of merchants and moneylenders, both Arab and Persian; Iranian gentlemen retain their well-born contempt for commerce and those who engage in it. There is general resentment of taxation, unfamiliar to the nomads, demeaning to the conquerors—but becoming more effective and more onerous as the Islamic state establishes itself. That resentment is intensified by inequalities in assessment, and the emergence of fiscally privileged elements. Much is said of the grievances of the *mawālī*, who adopt the faith of the conquerors and join the brotherhood of Islam, but are denied the fiscal and some other privileges of Muslims.

The *mawālī* are to be found especially in the new cities, the rapid growth of which is one of the most important developments of the Arab Caliphate. In the former Byzantine provinces, where city life was old and familiar, the change was relatively slight, In the former Sasanid lands, where urbanization was much less advanced, the swift and sudden development of the Muslim cities brought tension and conflict.

The economic and social history of the early Islamic Empire is still little known or explored, but certain significant developments can be perceived or reasonably inferred. The Arab conquests displaced important possessing and dominating groups; the impact of this change must have been far greater in the

Eastern than in the Western provinces. From Syria and Egypt the defeated and dispossessed Byzantine magnates could withdraw to what was left of the Byzantine Empire, leaving their former subject provinces to new masters. No such escape was open to the magnates of the fallen Persian Empire, who had to remain where they were, endure the new domination, and find their place in it as best they could. It is not surprising that these elements, with their reserves of skill and experience and their recent memories of lost greatness, should have played a more decisive role in the development of Islamic society and government than the inert residue of population in the long-subject Byzantine cities. At first they seem to have made their accommodation with the Arab conqueror, and retained something of their functions and privileges under his rule. But with the consolidation of Arab power, the massive settlement of Arab tribes in Iran, and the growth of cities, new conflicts and new alignments can be discerned.

The conquests also restored to circulation great accumulated riches which had been frozen in private, public and church possession. The sources are full of stories of rich booty, wide distribution, and lavish expenditure. They also tell of great new fortunes, built up by members of the Arab aristocracy.

> On the day 'Uthmān was killed [says al-Mas'ūdī] he possessed, in the hands of his treasurer, 100,000 dinars and a million dirhams. The value of his estates in Wādī 'l-Qurā, Ḥunayn and elsewhere was 100,000 dinars, and he also left many horses and camels. In the time of 'Uthmān a number of the Companions of the Prophet acquired houses and estates. Al-Zubayr ibn al-'Awwām built his house in Basra, where it is well known at the present time, the year 332 of the Hijra [=943-4 A.D.], and provides lodgings for merchants, sea-going traders and the like. He also built houses in Kūfa, Fusṭāṭ and Alexandria. These houses and estates are well known to the present day. The value of al-Zubayr's property at his death was 50,000 dinars. He also left a thousand horses, a thousand slaves, male and female, and lands in the cities we have mentioned. Similarly, Ṭalḥa ibn 'Ubaydallah al-Taymī built a house in the Kunāsa quarter in Kūfa, which is well known at the present time as "the house of the Talḥīs". His income from his estates in Iraq amounted to a thousand dinars a day, and some say more; from his estates in the region of al-Sharāh he received more than that. He built himself a house in Madīna, made with plaster, bricks and teakwood. Similarly, 'Abn al-Raḥmān ibn 'Awf al-Zuhrī built a house and made it wide. In his stables were tethered 100 horses, and

he owned 1,000 camels and 10,000 sheep. At his death, a quarter of his property was worth 84,000 dinars. Sa'd ibn Abī Waqqās built his house in al-'Aqīq. He made it high and spacious, and put balconies around the upper part. Sa'īd ibn al-Musayyab said that when Zayd ibn Thābit died he left ingots of gold and silver that were broken up with axes, in addition to property and estates to the value of 100,000 dinars. Al-Miqdād built his house at the place called al-Jurf, a few miles from Madīna. He put balconies round the upper part, and plastered it inside and outside. When Ya'lā ibn Munya died, he left half a million dinars, as well as debts owed to him by people, landed property and other assets, to the value of 300,000 dinars.[1]

With their share of the spoils, their generous endowment in lands and revenues, their monopoly of military commands and their indirect control of administration, the Arab aristocracy of conquest acquired immense riches; amid the opportunities and delights of the advanced countries in which they found themselves, they spent their wealth with abandon. Among the conquered peoples, and before that among their own Arab compatriots, there were growing murmurs of discontent. There must, however, also have been others who profited.

The Arab conquests finally ended the Perso-Byzantine conflict across the Middle Eastern trade routes, and, for the first time since Alexander, joined the whole region from Central Asia to the Mediterranean in a single imperial system. It seems likely that these changes favored the growth of trade and industry, for which the newly rich *conquistadores* provided markets. Like the Vikings in medieval Europe, the wealthy Arabs in the Middle East spent money on high grade textiles, in which the Umayyad court and aristocracy showed a particular interest. The textile industry may well have been the most important single factor leading to the growth of a commercial and industrial society. The construction of royal and private palaces and other buildings, and the manifold needs of the well-paid Arab soldiers and settlers in the garrison cities, will also have encouraged this development.

These new, rapidly growing cities became centres of discontent, which seems to have been due to dislocation and frustration more than to actual hardship. Among the wealthy, the arrogance of the conqueror aristocracy and the disabilities imposed on those who did not belong to it became increasingly irksome; among the poor, ripped from their protective village systems and adrift in the cities, the unaccustomed spectacle of wealth aroused new desires which could not be satisfied. If, as in both earlier and later times, the population of cities grew more rapidly than was justified by their economic development, there will also have been an unstable, disoriented, precariously surviving populace of unskilled laborers, runaway peasants, vagabonds, paupers and beggars—uprooted, frustrated and resentful.

In the pious and sectarian opposition to the Umayyad system, various gradations can be discerned; in the degree of their sophistication, their extremism, their radicalism—their divergence from Islamic norms, and their readiness to use violence. Many attempts have been made to relate these gradations to ethnic and social groups, and some conclusions may, very tentatively, be accepted. Northern Arabs tend to be less radical than Southern Arabs, Southern Arabs less than *mawālī*. From the time of Mukhtār (d. 686) the radical Shīʿa tend to draw increasingly on *mawlā* support, though their leaders remain Arab, usually from Southern or from assimilated border-tribes. Ethnic identifications are relatively easy, since the sources express themselves more readily in ethnic terms; this does not necessarily mean that they are more important.

Among early exponents of *ghuluww*, extremist doctrines, the sources mention a weaver, a seller of barley and a dealer in straw. These and a few other references to artisans and shopkeepers among the *ghulāt* hardly suffice to document any statement of the social composition of their support. A better indication may be obtained from their teachings and aspirations—what they wanted, and what they opposed. They were against aristocracy—against the system of privileged exclusiveness, which distinguished even between two sons of the same father, where one was born of a free Arab mother and the other of a slave-woman. There were many such sons of concubines, whose families added to the numbers of the discontented. They were against autocracy and the growing power of the state, especially in the imposition and collection of taxes. God had sent His Prophet to reveal the truth, not to collect taxes, and merit lay in the observance of God's command, not in noble birth. If there was to be an order of priority, it should be by precedence in Islam, not by descent, by wealth, or by power.

Their political program usually consisted of the overthrow of the existing Caliphate and the installation of their chosen Imam. It is more difficult to speak of any social or economic program, though their activities—and such successes as they managed to achieve—are clearly related to social and economic discontents, antagonisms, and aspirations. There are scattered references to the promises made by agitators and rebel leaders—to defend those who are not noble, to distribute the booty fairly, to give grants to those who are deprived, even to liberate slaves who rally to the cause. Some idea of the hopes that were aroused may be gathered from the messianic traditions telling of what the Mahdī would do when he revealed himself. Apart from a variety of picturesque personal, topographical, and military details, these traditions give a fairly accurate idea of what needs the Mahdī was expected to meet. Part of his task was Islamic—to bring men back to true Islam, spread the faith to the eastern and western limits of the earth, and conquer the Christian city of Constantinople. More urgently and more insistently, he was to establish justice—"to fill the world with justice and equity as it is now filled with tyranny and oppression". Some versions are more specific; he would establish equality between the weak and the powerful, bring plenitude and security, and a prosperity so great that money would be unconsidered and uncounted—"like that which is left on the ground to be trampled on;" the heavens would not withhold rain; the earth would give bountiful crops and surrender her precious metals. In that time a man would say "O Mahdī, give!" and the Mahdī would say "Take", and would pour into his garment as much as he could carry.

To a growing extent these political, religious and social aspirations were focused about the claims of the kin of the Prophet, the Hashimids, to an inheritance which, so it seemed, had been misappropriated and misused by the representatives of the nobility of Quraysh. After many failures, this inheritance was successfully claimed by the house of 'Abbās.

With the fall of the Umayyads, the old order had been overthrown. A new order had been established, with the kin of the Prophet at its head. The victory had been won by a brotherhood of dedicated religious revolutionaries, working, preaching and growing for more than 30 years. Great hopes and great expectations had been aroused. Their fulfillment was now due.

It was not long before the new masters of the Empire confronted the dilemma which, sooner or later, faces all successful rebels—the conflict between the responsibilities of power and the expectations of those who brought them to it. For a while the 'Abbasids did indeed try to persuade the Muslims that their accession really represented the achievement of the promised millennium. The adoption of black flags and then black robes as the emblems of the dynasty were one attempt to comply with the pattern of the coming of the righteous ruler, as depicted in the prophecies. Another was the adoption of regnal titles of messianic import. The Umayyads had used no honorific or other titles, being known simply by their personal names. The first 'Abbasid too was known in his own day simply as Abu'l-'Abbās, without a title—but the second was called al-Manṣūr, the appellation of the awaited redeemer of the Southern Arabs, and his son and grandson bore the still more obviously messianic titles of al-Mahdī and al-Hādī. Only with the fifth 'Abbasid Caliph, Hārūn al-Rashīd, does this messianic note disappear from the official nomenclature of the dynasty.[2]

There was more to show for the successful revolution than a variation in royal titulature. An immediate and striking change was the abandonment of the aristocratic principle of descent. The Umayyad Caliphs had all been the sons of free Arab mothers, as well as of Umayyad fathers; the son of a slave-woman, however able, was not even considered as a possible candidate for the succession. Abu'l-'Abbās too was the son of a free and noble mother, and it was for this reason that he had been preferred to his brother Abū Ja'far, the son of a Berber slave-girl, as Imām and then Caliph. But on his death it was Abū Ja'far who, despite reproaches from some of his followers, succeeded as Caliph with the title al-Manṣūr. Al-Mahdī's mother was, appropriately, a Southern Arabian woman, said to be a descendant of the ancient kings of Ḥimyar; but his successors al-Hādī and Hārūn al-Rashīd were the sons of a slave-girl of uncertain origin. Of Hārūn's two sons who warred for the succession, al-Amīn, the loser, was born to an 'Abbasid princess, al-Ma'mūn, the winner, to a Persian concubine. Thereafter most of the 'Abbasid caliphs were the sons of slave mothers, usually foreign, and such parentage ceased to be an obstacle to wordly success or social prestige.

The Arab aristocracy and the aristocratic principle suffered other defeats. During the first half-century of 'Abbasid rule, noble birth and tribal prestige ceased to be the main titles to positions of power and profit, and the Arab tribes gradually withdrew into insignificance. Instead, the favor of the Caliph was now the passport to success, and more and more it was given to men of humble and even of foreign origin. The *mawālī* were at last acquiring the equality that they had craved, and with their success the very name and status of *mawlā* lost their significance. A new multi-national ruling élite emerged, of officials, soldiers, landowners, merchants and men of religion. Their common characteristic was Islam, which replaced Arabism as the first-class citizenship of the Empire.

The 'Abbasids laid great stress on the Islamic character of their rule and purpose. The impious and worldly Umayyads had gone, and in their place had come the pious kin of the Prophet, to restore and preserve the equality and brotherhood of the believers. Though their own personal way of life was rarely if ever better than that of the Umayyads, the 'Abbasid Caliphs were careful to preserve the outward decencies of religion—a due show of respect for the cult, the law, and above all the personnel of the Muslim faith.

To maintain this posture required a position much closer to the central Sunnī consensus than was afforded by the Hāshimiyya sect, which had been the main instrument of the 'Abbasid bid for power. The militant missionaries and leaders who had contributed so greatly to the 'Abbasid victory were, in one way or another, removed, and a religious group which hailed the Caliph as divine was ruthlessly crushed by the Caliph's troops.

The disavowal by the 'Abbasids of origins which they now regarded as disreputable was completed by the Caliph al-Mahdī, who abandoned the claim to the Imamate derived from Muḥammad b. al-Ḥanafiyya and Abū Hāshim, and instead announced that the Prophet had appointed his uncle al-'Abbās as successor, thus conferring a hereditary right on his descendants and, incidentally, excluding the 'Alids.

The conversion of the 'Abbasids to empire and to orthodoxy inevitably disappointed the hopes of some who had followed them. There were also other sources of resentment. The changes in Islamic society that were taking place generated new tensions and gave rise to new discontents, which sought an outlet. Several such changes can be discerned, beginning before the 'Abbasid accession, and continuing for a long time after it. As with other revolutions, the change of régime did not mean a sudden, immediate and total transformation in the order of society, in the vulgar sense of the term revolutionary; rather did it mark the point when a new political order emerged as part of the profound and extensive changes that were already taking place, and then itself helped to carry these changes further.

One of these changes is the growth of commerce and the rise, in wealth, power and status, of the merchants—the bourgeoisie of the growing Muslim cities. The prosperous and respected merchant was not a new figure. Unlike other conquering aristocracies, the Arab nobility did not despise trade; on the contrary, many of them engaged in it, to great advantage—though most of them found government and war more lucrative and more attractive. The merchant community, however, continued to grow, and was reinforced by *mawālī* and even by non-Muslims. In 'Abbasid times the merchants became an important class—wealthy, confident and self-reliant; they were proud of their membership of an honorable profession, and were even inclined to look down on the servants of the state as engaged in tasks that were morally inferior and as recipients of moneys that were morally tainted. To no small extent, the theologians and jurists who were formulating the rules of Islamic orthodoxy were drawn from the merchant class, and their writings often tend to reflect the ethos and the needs of the Muslim bourgeoisie.

Numerous traditions were cited or invented to show that commerce is an occupation pleasing in God's eyes, and wealth a sign of God's favor. Even conspicuous consumption enjoyed divine approval, for "when God gives riches to a man, He wants it to be seen on him." This and similar traditions are cited to justify the wearing of fine clothes, and the building and furnishing of luxurious dwellings. One dictum, improbably attributed to the Prophet, even asserts that "poverty is almost like apostasy". Under the early 'Abbasids, the role of the merchants is limited, and they are overshadowed by the bureaucrats, many of them Iranians with an aristocratic tradition of contempt for commerce. By the 9th century, however, they appear among powerful figures at the court, on terms of intimacy with the rulers themselves.

Agriculture and stockraising remained the source of livelihood of the overwhelming majority of the population, and the main source of revenue of the state. The techniques of industrial production showed little improvement on those of antiquity; the organization and extent of production, however, show considerable development, while commerce, both within and beyond the far-flung Muslim Empire, expanded vastly in scope and scale. A stable and internationally accepted specie coinage and an elaborate system of credit facilitated trade and encouraged the growth of large-scale commercial and financial enterprises. This emergent capitalism affected other layers of society. Not only merchants and financiers, but also officials, landowners, literati, generals, and even princes ventured their capital in commercial undertakings—while merchants for their part sometimes invested part of their savings in landed estates and in tax-farms.

In contrast to Europe in the same period, there was a great development of cities, which became larger, more numerous and more sophisticated. The main centre of town life shifted from the citadel and cantonments, which had been the core of the early cities, to the residential and commercial suburbs. There were artisans, apprentices and journeymen, often organized in large-scale enterprises under public or private ownership, laborers, shopkeepers and itinerant vendors, and a floating population of uprooted and unemployed. Slavery was of limited economic importance—slaves appear mainly in domestic functions, as craftsmen, or as agents or stewards of landowners and entrepreneurs.

Our sources are of urban origin, and tell us little about the countryside. The impression they leave is that, by and large, the changes of the times had little effect on the lot of the peasant and nomad. Agricultural techniques remained substantially unchanged, though new crops and new methods of irrigation were sometimes introduced from one region to another. The country supplied food and raw materials to the cities, but the return seems to have gone in the main to city-dwelling landowners and tax-farmers. Trade was between cities; there is little evidence of the movement of goods or services from the city to the countryside, which supplied its own simple needs. The concentration of ownership in the hands of rich merchants and military chiefs brought larger estates and stricter control, and a harder life for the peasants. In earlier 'Abbasid times there were still peasant smallholders and more or less independent lessee sharecroppers. There even seems to have been some attempt to amend the system of tax assessment to their advantage. In later times, however, they were compelled by fiscal and other pressures to make over their holdings to large landowners, and remain on them as tenants. Islamic law did not recognize serfdom, but the debtor could pay his debt only by personal labor, and was pursued if he fled. Some found a refuge in banditry, which became rife. Others joined the rabble of the cities.

The eastern provinces, taken from the former Persian monarchy, had special problems. Here city life was relatively new, and the tensions resulting from the growth of new urban centers more keenly felt. The old Iranian gentry had survived the Arab conquest with much of their power and influence, in local affairs, intact, and with a proud memory of the recently fallen Sasanid Empire. Under the early 'Abbasids, men of this class, converted to Islam, were able to play a role of some importance in the administration of the Muslim state. Later, when discontents arose, they could provide a coherent and competent leadership lacking in the socially fragmented western provinces.

The changes which prepared, accompanied and followed the 'Abbasid revolution brought release and opportunity to some, hardship and disappointment to others. In some respects, the aims of the radical sectarians were fulfilled. The privilege of birth and, to a large extent, of race was gradually abolished, and the road to preferment opened to all—or almost all—Muslims. Despite the inevitable and recurring tendency to the formation of aristocracies, this social egalitarianism has remained characteristic of Islam to the present day. True, the non-Muslim was still subject to certain disabilities, but this was felt to be reasonable; the disabilities were not oppressive, and submission to them was in a sense by choice, since the brotherhood of Islam was now open to all who chose to join it. In theory and to no small extent even in practice, Islam was the common citizenship of the community, the source of its ethos and its law, the ultimate determinant of identity, loyalty, and status.

Despite these improvements, old discontents survived and new ones appeared. In general, the millennium had failed to materialize; more specifically, rapid economic and social development had brought distress to many. Socially the revolution had achieved notable successes, though these were often uneven in their effect in different regions and among different classes. Politically, things were worse then before. The aristocratic Umayyad state had been limited by the need to gain and retain the loyalty of the great Arab aristocrats—powerful and influential men whose power and influence derived from sources independent of the Caliph and to a large extent beyond his reach. The bureaucratic 'Abbasid state, with its well-ordered civil service and its professional army, suffered no such limitation. Despite the trappings of Islamic piety with which the 'Abbasids adorned themselves and their court, their government was in effect more distant from Islamic political ideals than was that of the Umayyads—and far closer to the imperial polity of ancient Iran. The sovereign was no longer a first among equals, but a remote and inaccessible autocrat, wielding immense power over his subjects through an apparatus of government that was becoming more complex and more oppressive. Small wonder that a poet exclaimed:

> *Would that the tyranny of the sons of Marwān would return to us,*
> *would that the justice of the sons of 'Abbās were in hell!*[3]

18. Islamic Concepts of Revolution

In the middle of the 8th century the Umayyad Caliphate was overthrown and the 'Abbasid Caliphate established in its place. Among modern scholars it has become customary, when speaking both of the actions which brought about this change and of the results which followed from it, to use the term *revolution*. Among contemporaries, the term commonly used to denote the 'Abbasid victory was the Arabic world *dawla*, which in later times came to mean dynasty and then simply state. This was not however its original meaning. The basic meaning of the root *d-w-l*, which also occurs in other Semitic languages, is to turn or to alternate—as for example in the Qur'anic verses "These [happy and unhappy] days, we cause them to alternate *(nudāwiluhā)* among men" (Qur'ān, iii, 134/140), and "what God has assigned as booty to His Prophet, from the people of the cities, belongs to God and the Prophet and the kinsmen, the orphans, the poor, and the wayfarer, that it may not become a perquisite circulating *(dūlatan)* among those of you who are rich" (lix, 7). Other early texts confirm the meaning of "turn" —the time of success, power, office or ownership enjoyed by an individual or a group. Sometimes the word is used in the context of the vicissitudes of fortune. "*Al-dunyā duwal*" says an early author—roughly, the world is full of ups and downs—and continues: "What is for you will come to you in spite of your weakness; what is against you, you cannot prevent by your strength."[1] In an essay by Ibn al-Muqaffa' (ca. 720–ca. 756), the Persian adviser of the first 'Abbasid caliphs, he urges caution on a ruler whose power is newly established, and uses the phrase "*Idhā kāna sulṭānuka 'inda jiddati dawla*"—if your rule is at the beginning of a turn.[2] It is in this sense that Ibn al-Muqaffa', speaking of the accession of the 'Abbasids, says: "Then came this *dawla*", and that the first ʿAbbasid Caliph al-Saffāḥ, addressing the people of Kūfa after his accession, says to them, "You have reached our time, and God has brought you our *dawla*."[3] In another passage, al-Saffāḥ is quoted as speaking of the *dawla*, i.e. the time of power and success, of Abū Muslim[4]—a servant and not a member of the dynasty. In time, the term *dawla* came to be used more particularly of the reigning ʿAbbasid house, and thus acquired the meaning of dynasty and ultimately of state.

It is possible that cyclical theories of politics, derived from Greek or Persian sources, may have contributed to this use of the word *dawla*. Though no early statements of such theories in Arabic have so far come to light, they appear in slightly later writings, as for example in an astrological essay by the 9th-century philosopher al-Kindī and, more extensively, in the 10th-century encyclopaedic work called *Rasā'il Ikhwān al-Ṣafāʾ (Epistles of the Sincere Brethren)*. According to these, *dawla*, which is associated with *mulk*, kingship, passes from nation to nation, from country to country, from dynasty to dynasty. Such a change occurs at intervals of 240 years. Significantly, the *Rasā'il* were composed about 240 years after the accession of the ʿAbbasids, and their authors were connected with the Ismāʿīlīs, an activist Shiʿite group which aimed at the overthrow of the ʿAbbasids and their replacement by a new line of Imam-Caliphs, descended from the Prophet through his daughter Fāṭima.[5] Cyclical interpretations of history are central to the doctrines of the Ismāʿīlīs and related sects, and are often adduced to support the claims of Messianic pretenders and rebels.

The troubles of the ʿAbbasids did not end with the defeat of the Umayyads and their own enthronement as supreme sovereigns of Islam. They still had to face a series of opposition movements and even armed rebellions by groups which challenged their right to rule, and sought to install others in their place. The most active and best known among them were those who felt that the change had not gone far enough—that the ʿAbbasid régime too closely resembled that which it had replaced, and should give way to one which would bring a more radical transformation of the political and social order. Some of them, loosely designated by the general name of Shīʿa, hoped to achieve this result by transferring power to the kin of the Prophet; others, the Kharijites, rejected all forms of legitimism, and sought to establish a truly elective caliphate based on the voluntary and revocable consent of the ruled.

A quite different point of view was represented by the group who are sometimes called al-Nābita, roughly the young upstarts. Politically, these were supporters of the deposed Umayyads—that is, legitimists who believed in the rights of the old caliphal dynasty, and questioned the arguments adduced by the ʿAbbasids and their spokesmen to justify their violent supersession. In an essay written in about 840, the great Arabic prose-writer al-Jāḥiẓ briefly reviews the political history of Islam to his own time, and attempts to justify, on religious grounds, the action of the ʿAbbasids in overthrowing the reigning Caliph. He specifically rejects the doctrine of unconditional obedience which, he claims, is implicit in the arguments of the Nābita:

> The wrong-doer is accursed, and whoever forbids the cursing of the wrong-doer is himself accursed. But the Nābita of our time and innovators of our age allege that to abuse bad rulers is sedition *(fitna)* and to curse tyrants is an innovation *(bidʿa)*, even if these rulers . . . terrorize the good and encourage the bad, and rule by favoritism and wilfulness, the flaunting of power, contempt for the people, repression of the subjects, and accusations without restraint or discretion. If this misconduct reaches the degree of unbelief, if it passes beyond error to irreligion, then it becomes a greater error even than that of whoever refrains from condemning them and dissociating himself from them. . . . The Nābita agree that anyone who kills a believer, whether with clear intent or with specious pretexts, is accursed; but if the killer is a tyrannical ruler or a fractious amir, they do not consider it lawful to curse him or depose him or banish him or denounce him, even if he has terrorized the good, murdered the learned, starved the poor, oppressed the weak, neglected the frontiers and marches, drunk fermented drinks and flaunted his depravity.[6]

Al-Jāḥiẓ's position in this essay is clear. The sovereign is a human being, and may be guilty of some human error and sin while retaining his right to rule and his claim on the obedience of his subjects. But if his error reaches the point when he is neglecting his duties and abusing his powers as sovereign, then the duty of obedience lapses, and his subjects have the right—or rather the duty, since it is with duties, not rights, that Islamic jurisprudence and politics are concerned—to denounce him, and if possible to depose and replace him.

The Western doctrine of the right to resist bad government is alien to Islamic thought. Instead, there is an Islamic doctrine of the duty to resist impious government, which in early times was of crucial historical significance. This doctrine is enshrined in the traditions of the Prophet, particularly in two sayings: "There is no [duty of] obedience in sin", and "Do not obey a creature against his Creator." The intention of these two oft-quoted sayings and of other similar dicta[7] is fairly obvious. Normally, the subject owes a duty of complete and unquestioning obedience to the Imam, the head of the Islamic state and community. If, however, the Imam commands something that is contrary to God's law, then the duty of obedience lapses, and instead it is the duty of the subject to disobey—and resist—such a command.

At first sight this principle looks like a basis for doctrines both of limited government and of justified revolution. Its effectiveness, however, was reduced by two fatal flaws. In the first place, the jurists never explained how the lawfulness or sinfulness of a command was to be determined; in the second place no legal procedure or apparatus was ever devised or set up for enforcing the law against the ruler. In fact, social and political pressures were usually sufficient to enforce formal respect for the basic precepts of Islamic observance—and for little more. This interpretation is expressed in a number of sayings ascribed to the Prophet. According to one undoubtedly spurious tradition, the Prophet adjured his followers: "If you have rulers over you who ordain prayer, the alms-tax, and the Holy War, then God forbids you to revile them and allows you to pray behind them." Another tradition, equally spurious, conveys the message of quietism—and its limits—in a more vivid form: "The Imams are of Quraysh [the Arabian tribe to which the Prophet belonged] . . . if Quraysh gives a crop-nosed Ethiopian slave authority over you, hear him and obey him, as long as he does not force any of you to choose between his Islam and his neck.

And if he does force anyone to choose between his Islam and his neck, let him offer his neck."[8]

In time, the duty of disobedience was hedged around with restrictions and qualifications, and was in effect forgotten in the general acceptance, in theory as well as in practice, of the most complete quietism. A 14th century *qāḍī*, al-Ījī, still mentions, somewhat obliquely, the duty of resistance to sin; it only applies, however, if two conditions are met. First, a man must be satisfied that his action will not stir up sedition *(thawarān fitna)* and that it will achieve its purpose. (If he thinks it will not achieve its purpose, then resistance is meritorious, but not obligatory.) Second, there must be no snooping *(tajassus)*.[9] In other words, don't look for trouble; if you meet it, try to avoid it, and do not resist until success is a foregone conclusion.

In earlier times, when this defeatist and quietist attitude had not yet been adopted, the duty of disobedience was still a political and religious factor of importance. It was of particular concern to the early 'Abbasids, who felt the need to justify, in Islamic terms, both their acquisition of power by revolution, and their retention of it against any further challenge. The question was discussed by Ibn al-Muqaffa', in an essay addressed to the Caliph al-Manṣūr, ca. 757–8. There are some people, he says, who cite the saying that a creature should not be obeyed against his Creator, and who give it a false and distorted interpretation. According to them, if the Imam commands us to disobey God, he must be disobeyed; if he commands us to obey God, he must be obeyed. But if the Imam is to be disobeyed in disobedience, and others beside the Imam are to be obeyed if they command what God commands, then there is no difference between the Imam and anyone else in the right to obedience. This doctrine, says Ibn al-Muqaffa', is a device of the devil to subvert obedience and disrupt order, so that men may be equal *(naẓā'ir)* and leaderless, and defenseless against their enemy. Another group, he says, go to the opposite extreme. According to them, we must obey the Imams in all their commands, without inquiring whether these commands are in obedience or disobedience to God. None of us can call them to account, for they are the masters of power and knowledge, and we are their subjects, bound to obey and submit. This doctrine, says Ibn al-Muqaffaʻ, is as harmful as the first in degrading authority and undermining obedience, since it leads to foul wickedness in rule, and to clear and public licence for sin. The truth lies between the two. It is right to say that there should be no obedience in sin; it is wrong to undermine the authority of the Imam by giving licence to disobey him. The limitation of the duty of obedience applies only to the major precepts of religion. If the Imam forbids fasting, prayer and pilgrimage, prevents the fulfilment of God's commands and permits what God has forbidden, then he has no authority to do this. He has however the right—moreover the exclusive right—to be obeyed in all matters of governmental judgment, discretion and administration, such as beginning and ending military campaigns, collecting and expending moneys, appointing and dismissing subordinates, discretionary decisions, based on Qur'ān and Sunna, in matters where there is no binding precedent, making war and peace, etc.[10] Most later writers agreed in limiting the duty of disobedience to clear violations of major prescriptions of the ritual law; many go further, and specify that this does not apply to the personal conduct of the ruler, who presumably may violate the law with impunity, but only to the orders which he issues to his subjects.

A recurring theme in discussions of the duty of disobedience is the imperative need to avoid *fitna*—the term normally used for a movement which tends to disrupt the religious, social and political order. The word has an interesting history. The basic meaning of the root is a test or proving, hence by extension a temptation, which tests a man's faith and his loyalty to the community. The word occurs frequently in the Qur'ān in the sense of temptation or trial of faith, against which the believer is warned to be on his guard. Often, the context indicates that the danger is public and social rather than private and personal —a temptation to disaffection as much as to unbelief. "Expel them [the Meccans] from whence they have expelled you, for *fitna* is worse than killing . . . fight them until there is no more *fitna*, and the religion of God prevails" (Qur'ān, ii, 191, 193).

It is this meaning—of disturbance or disaffection—that predominates in post-Qur'anic usage, and is reflected back in some of the apocryphal sayings attributed to the Prophet. The Islamic conception of *fitna* is a natural consequence of the Islamic conception of conformity. Orthodoxy, in Christianity, means in the first instance belief in an officially defined creed and submission to ecclesiastical authority. Sunnism, in Islam, basically implies loyalty to the community and acceptance of its traditions—and, since religion and politics in Islam are inextricably intermingled, this in turn involves obedience to the Caliph as the accredited head of both state and community. Religious dissent is a private matter as long as it is concerned only with theological beliefs; it becomes a *fitna*, dangerous and punishable, when it involves a rupture of social and political bonds—separation from the community *(mufāraqat al-jamāʿa)*, and the withholding of allegience from the Caliph.

The archetypal *fitna*, often called the "great *fitna*", arose in connection with the murder of the Caliph ʿUthmān in 656 A.D. and the civil war which followed it. The Caliph had been murdered by Muslim mutineers, and another was installed in his place. He in turn was challenged by others, who denied his right to his office and accused him of condoning a crime. According to one side, ʿUthmān was the rightful Caliph; those who killed him were rebels and murderers whose crime must be punished; those who condoned their offence were themselves offenders. According to the other side ʿUthmān had violated the law of God, and forfeited his right to rule; his death was an execution, not a murder, an act of justice, not a crime. The civil war was a time of great trial and temptation, in which the faith and loyalty of all the Muslims was put to the test.

Thereafter *fitna* became the normal term for seditious dissent or violent opposition to established authority, It is for example the term used by al-Kindī in his astrological epistle for the troubles and upheavals that bring a cycle of power to an end. It is used of religious groups whose deviation from tradition goes beyond the permitted limits of difference—particularly of such militant groups as the Kharijites and the Ismāʿīlīs. In this context, it is often associated with the idea of *bidʿa*—innovation, which is a departure from or violation of the *Sunna*. Later it is applied to almost any outbreak of violence—military mutinies, city riots, provincial rebellions. It is invariably a term of abuse, used of other groups, never of one's own. It was the term used by the first Muslim writers to speak of the French Revolution of 1798.[11]

Classical Arabic has a number of words to denote rebellion or insurrection. The commonest verbs are *kharaja*, literally to go out,[12] *qāma*, to rise or stand up, and *nazā*, to leap, leap out, hence break loose, escape. In the derived form *intazā* this root is used, especially in western (i.e., North African and Spanish) texts, in the sense of to revolt against one's sovereign, to make oneself independent. The 10th-century Spanish author Ibn Faraj of Jaen is said to have written, while in prison, a history of rebels and insurgents in Muslim Spain (*Ta'rīkh al-muntazīn wa'l-qā'imīn bi'l-Andalus wa-akhbāruhum*). This book is unfortunately—but not surprisingly—lost.[13]

A word with a rather different history is *baghā* (active participle *bāghī*, plural *bughāt*). Starting from the basic root-meaning of excess, abuse, the *bāghī* comes to be a law-breaker, a violator of legal, social, religious or moral standards. As well as a rebel, he may be a tyrannical ruler who abuses his power; he may also be a sexual debauchee or pervert. Inevitably, the word can also be used of a high-spirited or refractory camel. In the technical language of the Muslim law, *bughāt* is the normal term for rebels.

The jurists give careful consideration to the legal problems of rebellion—the regulation of warfare against rebels, their rights as belligerents and as prisoners, the sanctity of their property, the validity of legal judgments made under their jurisdiction.[14]

As so often, the terminology and argumentation of the jurists cloak a purpose other than the apparent one. In the strict theory of the Muslim law, there could be only one Muslim state, the universal *Dār al-Islām* (House of Islam), and only one Muslim sovereign, the Caliph. Juristic discussions of international law—of warfare, diplomacy, etc.—could therefore only deal with relations between the Muslim state and a non-Muslim state or states. In fact of course the Muslim world was divided into many autonomous or independent states, and it was necessary to regulate, legally, the relations between them. This was achieved by the legal fiction that a state other than the Caliphate was an established group of rebels. The *bughāt* of juristic literature are assumed to be Muslims; they have at their disposition organized armed forces, and control a territory in which they maintain (Muslim) law and order. Their rebellion consists of withholding obedience from the Caliph. From all this, it is clear that what the jurists have in mind is not an attempt to overthrow the régime, but merely to withdraw from it and establish an independent state within a certain territory. In a word, their concern is not with revolution, but with secession.

During the 19th and 20th centuries the need to discuss European revolutions, and later also domestic revolutions, brought three more terms into use. *Ikhtilāl*, though Arabic in origin, is mainly confined to Turkish usage. Originally meaning disorder or upheaval, it is commonly used by Turkish authors of the 18th century for revolts, riots, mutinies, and disturbances of public order of any kind.[15] It was the term used by contemporary Turkish writers to designate the great French Revolution.[16] Since then, it has been specialized in modern Turkish usage to denote revolutionary upheavals which lack the user's respect or approval. Thus, it is never used of the Young Turk or Kemalist revolutions, occasionally but not frequently used of the Russian Revolution, and almost invariably used of the anti-Young Turk rising of 1909. It is also used by the 19th-century Turkish historian Jevdet, in what must be one of the earliest Muslim accounts of the American Revolution.[17]

In the Arabic-speaking countries a different word was used for revolution—*thawra*. The root *th-w-r* in classical Arabic meant to rise up (e.g. of a camel), to be stirred or excited, and hence, especially in Maghribī usage, to rebel. Already in medieval times the word occurs in political contexts. Thus al-Saffāḥ, the first 'Abbasid Caliph, using the active participle, calls himself *al-Thā'ir* in his address to the people of Kufa, and an Alid leader in 10th-century Persia even adopts it in his title—

al-Thā'ir fi'llāh, the *thā'ir* in God. Certainly in the first and in probably the second the significance of *thā'ir* is one who brings disturbance and upheaval. In a negative sense it is used by Saladin's biographer to denote a plot to overthrow him and restore the deposed Fatimids.[18] Often, it connotes the establishment of a petty independent sovereignty; thus, for example, the so-called party kings who ruled in 11th-century Spain after the break-up of the Caliphate of Cordova, are called *thuwwār* (sing. *thā'ir*). The noun *thawra* at first means excitement, as in the phrase, cited in the *Ṣiḥāḥ*, a standard medieval Arabic dictionary, "*intaẓir ḥattā taskun hadhihi 'l-thawra*" (wait till this excitement dies down)—a very apt recommendation. The verb is used by al-Ījī, in the form *thawarān* or *ithārat fitna*, stirring up sedition, as one of the dangers which should discourage a man from practicing the duty of resistance to bad government. *Thawra* is the term used by Arabic writers in the 19th century for the French Revolution,[19] and by their successors for the approved revolutions, domestic and foreign, of our own time.

In current Arabic usage, the noun *thawra* and the adjective *thawrī* are the terms accepted by the revolutionary socialist régimes in Egypt, Syria, Iraq and elsewhere to describe their own actions, intentions and ideologies. Apart from the rejection of hereditary monarchy and the assertion of a form of socialism, these terms are not identified with any specific political system. The converse of *thawrī* is *raj*ʿ*ī*, a neologism[20] meaning reactionary and used especially of monarchical, conservative, and liberal régimes in Arab countries. The specialization of the term *thawra* to denote governments, their ruling groups, and their aulic ideologists, has opened new lines of semantic development. For some, the antithesis *thawra/raj*ʿ*iyya* (revolution/reaction) replaces the earlier antithesis Islam/Unbelief, with the same suggestion of perpetual conflict and inevitable ultimate victory. For others, *thawra* has simply become a synonym for authority, and is thus repeating the semantic evolution of the medieval word *dawla*. Another possibility, if relations with the Communist powers continue to develop on present lines, is that the word *thawra* will acquire much the same connotation as comprador—or perhaps native prince.

One last term remains to be considered. The classical Arabic root *q-l-b* means to turn or revert. The seventh form, *inqalaba*, usually means to be altered, changed, or turned upside down and occurs in a famous verse of the Qur'ān (xxvi, 227) "*Wa-saya'lamu'l-ladhīna ẓalamū ayya munqalibin yanqalibūn*"— "Those who have done wrong will know to what end they will revert". Al-Kindī in his astrological writings[21] uses it of the predetermined cyclical turn of power, *inqilāb al-dawla*. The use of the verbal noun *inqilāb* as the equivalent of the European term revolution seems to have been introduced by the Young Ottoman exiles, notably by the radicals Mehmed Bey and Vasfi Bey, who published a journal called *Inqilāb* in Geneva in 1870. Thereafter this became the accepted Turkish word for revolution, and is applied to the political changes of 1908, 1919–23, and 1960. Its use in Arabic is rare, and when it occurs it is usually derogatory.

VI

NEW IDEAS IN ISLAM

19. *The Idea of Freedom in Modern Islamic Political Thought*

In traditional Islamic usage freedom was a legal, not a political concept. The Arabic terms *ḥurr*, free, and *ḥurriyya*, freedom, with their derivatives and equivalents in the other languages of Islam, denoted the status of the free man in law, as opposed to the slave. In some periods and places, words meaning free were applied to certain privileged social groups which were exempt from taxes and other burdens to which common people were subject. This social usage is however exceptional and untypical, and the term *ḥurr* was normally used only in a juridical sense, with little social and no political content. When Muslim writers discussed, as they often did, the problems of good and bad government and denounced the latter as tyranny, they were distinguishing between just and unjust, lawful and wilful rule. Good government was a duty of the ruler, not a right of the subject, whose only recourse against bad government was patience, counsel and prayer. The converse of tyranny was justice, not freedom; the converse of freedom was not tyranny but legal and personal slavery.[1]

The first examples in Islamic lands of the use of the term freedom in a clearly defined political sense come from the Ottoman Empire in the late 18th and early 19th centuries, and are patently due to European influence, sometimes to direct translations from European texts. Significantly, the word chosen by the Turkish translators to render this unfamiliar notion was not the legal term for non-servile status, but a quite different term, previously used mainly in fiscal and administrative contexts. *Serbestiyet* (later also *Serbestī*) is an abstract formed from *serbest*, which in Ottoman official usage denoted the absence of certain limitations or restrictions. Thus, in the Ottoman military feudal system, a special kind of *timar* (a form of grant or fief) was called *serbest*. This meant that all the revenues of the *timar* went to the holder, as against an ordinary *timar* in which certain revenues were reserved to the imperial exchequer.

In its first known appearance in an official political document, the word *serbestiyet* denotes collective rather than personal freedom—i.e. independence rather than liberty in the classical liberal sense. This is in the third article of the Russo-Turkish treaty of Küčük Kaynarja (1774), which ended Ottoman suzerainty over the Khan of the Crimean Tatars and recognized their independence from both Turkey and Russia (as a preliminary to their absorption into the Russian Empire in 1783). The two states agree to recognize the Tatars as "free and entirely independent of any foreign power"; the Sultan is regarded as their religious head, "but without thereby compromising their political and civil liberty as established". The forms of words in the Italian original of the treaty for these two phrases are "*liberi, immediati, ed independenti assolutamente da qualunque straniera Potenza*" and "*senza pero mettere in compromesso la stabilita libertà loro politica e civile*". The language and content of these clauses, so reminiscent of the free cities of the Holy Roman Empire, must have presented some difficulty to the dragomans of the Sublime Porte, who at that time were Phanariot Greeks. The Turkish text, containing concepts and expressions new to Ottoman usage, reveals their ingenuity.[2]

The French Revolution gave the word *serbestiyet* a new meaning. Moralî El-Sayyid Ali Efendi, the Ottoman ambassador in Paris under the *Directoire,* uses it several times in his report on his embassy to translate *liberté*, chiefly in relation to symbols and ceremonies.[3] The Chief Secretary Atîf Efendi, in his memorandum of 1798 on the political situation resulting from the activities of revolutionary France, shows a clearer understanding of the new political content of the term, and of the danger which it represented to the established order, in the Ottoman Empire as elsewhere. In his introductory account of the Revolution, he tells how the revolutionaries had enticed the common people to follow them with promises of equality and freedom as a means of obtaining complete happiness in this world. More specifically, he is alarmed by the actions of the French in the former Venetian possessions which they had acquired, the Ionian islands and four towns on the Greek mainland. By evoking the forms of the government of the ancient Greeks and installing "a form of liberty" he said, the French had made clear their hostile intentions.[4]

Before the end of the year the French had landed in Egypt, where General Bonaparte, on arrival, addressed the Egyptians on behalf of the French Republic, "founded on the basis of freedom and equality".[5] The word used for freedom is *ḥurriyya* which, however, was still far from being a commonly accepted equivalent to the European term in its political sense. Ruphy's French-Arabic word-list, printed in 1802,[6] renders *liberté* by *ḥurriyya*, but with the restriction *"opposé à l'esclavage"*; in the sense of *"pouvoir d'agir"* he prefers *sarāḥ*, from an Arabic root meaning to roam or graze freely. In classical usage it also denoted the dismissal of a wife by divorcement.

Early references to freedom in works of Muslim authorship are hostile, and equate it with libertinism, licentiousness, and anarchy. A significant change can, however, be seen in a passage in which the Ottoman chronicler Shanizade (d. 1826), under the year 1230/1815, discusses the nature of council meetings, which became frequent at this time. Neither Islamic tradition nor Ottoman policy favoured the assertion of new political ideas, and Shanizade is careful to base the holdings of such consultations on Islamic precedent and "ancient Ottoman practice", and to give warning against its misuse; at the same time he points out that such consultations are normally held, with beneficial effects, in "certain well-organized states"—a striking euphemism for the states of Europe—and attributes to the members attending the councils a representative quality entirely new to Islamic political thought. The members of the councils consist of two groups, "servants of the state" and "representatives of the subjects"; they discuss and argue freely (*ber vejh-i serbestiyet*) and thus arrive at a decision.[7] In this indirect and unobtrusive way Shanizade was able to introduce to his readers such radical and alien ideas as popular representation, free debate, and corporate decision.

In the decades that followed, the notion of political freedom became more familiar through discussions of European affairs and translations of European works, as for example the Turkish version of Carlo Botta's *Storia d'Italia*,[8] which abounds in references to liberal principles and institutions, It was also discussed and developed by several Muslim writers, who were influenced more especially by the rather conservative constitutionalism of the post-Napoleonic era—the idea of the *Rechtsstaat*, or state based on the rule of law, in contrast to both the unbridled absolutism of Napoleon and the licence of the Revolution.

One of the most important of these was the Egyptian Shaykh Rifā'a Rāfi' al-Ṭahṭāwī (1801–1873), a graduate of al-Azhar who lived in Paris from 1826 to 1831 as religious preceptor to the Egyptian student mission. His account of what he saw and learnt was first published in Egypt in Arabic in 1834 and in a Turkish version in 1839; it includes a translation with commentary of the French constitution and a description of parliamentary institutions, the purpose of which is to secure government under law and "the protection of the subject from tyranny". What the French call freedom (*ḥurriyya*) says Shaykh Rifā'a, is the same as what the Muslims call justice and equity (*al-'adl wa'l-inṣāf*)—that is, the maintenance of equality before the law, government according to law, and the abstention of the ruler from arbitrary and illegal acts against the subject.[9]

Shaykh Rifā'a's equation of *ḥurriyya* with the classical Islamic concept of justice helped to relate the new to the old concepts, and to fit his own political writings into the long line of Muslim exhortations to the sovereign to rule wisely and justly, with due respect for the law and due care for the interests and welfare of the subjects. What is new and alien to traditional political ideas is the suggestion that the subject has a *right* to be treated justly, and that some apparatus should be set up to secure that right.

With remarkable percipience, Shaykh Rifā'a sees and explains the different roles of parliament, the courts and the press in protecting the subjects from tyranny—or rather, as he points out, in enabling the subjects to protect themselves. What is far from clear is the extent to which he felt these ideas and institutions to be relevant to the needs of his own country. In his later writings there is little suggestion of any such relevance; even his commendation of the Khedive Ismāʿīl for setting up a consultative assembly in 1866 shows a traditional concern with the duties of the ruler—justice and consultation—rather than a liberal concern with the rights of the ruled. In his book *al-Murshid al-amīn* (*The Faithful Guide*)[10] he defines freedom under five sub-headings, the last two of which are civic (*madanī*) and political (*siyāsī*). Both are defined in relation to social, economic and legal rights, without any specific reference to *political* rights in the liberal sense. The first three sub-headings are natural, social (i.e. freedom of "conduct"), and religious. Political freedom is the assurance of the state to the individual of the enjoyment of his property and the exercise of his "natural' freedom—that is, the basic innate power of all living creatures to eat, drink, move, etc., limited by the need to avoid injury to himself or to others.[11]

Shaykh Rifāʿa's Turkish contemporary Sadîk Rîfat Pasha (1807–1856), though vaguer in his theoretical notions of the meaning of freedom, is more specific on its immediate application at home. In an essay first drafted while he was Ottoman ambassador in Vienna in 1837—and in close touch with Metternich—he discusses the essential differences between Turkey and Europe, and those respects in which Turkey might profitably seek to imitate Europe. Sadîk Rîfat is deeply impressed by European wealth, industry, and science, in which he sees the best means of regenerating Turkey. European progress and prosperity, he explains, are the result of certain political conditions, of stability and tranquillity, which in turn depend on "the attainment of complete security for the life, property, honor and reputation of each nation and people, that is to say, on the proper application of the necessary rights of freedom." For Sadîk Rîfat, as for Shaykh Rifāʿa, freedom is an extension of the classical Islamic idea of justice—an obligation of the ruler to act justly and in accordance with the law; but it is also one of the "*rights* of the nation", and the establishment of these rights in Turkey is a matter of "the most urgent necessity".[12] Similar ideas are expressed by another Turkish writer,

Mustafa Sami, a former Embassy secretary in Paris, who in an essay published in 1840 speaks with admiration of the political and religious liberties of the French.

Such ideas find official expression in the first of the great Ottoman reforming edicts—the Rescript of the Rose Bower (*Gülhane*) of 1839, which recognizes and seeks to establish the rights of the subject to security of life, honor and property, and to government under law. There are two specific references to freedom—in the clause guaranteeing that "everyone shall dispose of his property in all freedom (*serbestiyet*)," and in the clause concerning the Councils, in which everyone present "shall express his ideas and observations freely (*serbestçe*) and without hesitation".[13]

These ideas of freedom are still very cautious and conservative; one would expect no other from Shaykh Rifāʿa, the loyal servant of the rulers of Egypt, or from Sadi̊k Ri̊fat, the disciple of Metternich and coadjutor of the reforming minister Mustafa Reshid Pasha. The subjects were to be treated justly by the government; indeed, they had a right to be treated justly, and laws should be promulgated to secure such treatment. But there is still no idea that the subjects have any right to share in the formation or conduct of government—to political freedom, or citizenship, in the sense which underlies the development of liberal political thought in the West.

While conservative reformers talked of freedom under law, and some Muslim monarchs even experimented with councils and assemblies, government was in fact becoming more and not less arbitrary and oppressive. The modernization of government and the abrogation of intermediate powers at once strengthened the autocracy of the state and removed or weakened the traditional limitations on its functioning. More authoritarian government provoked more radical criticism; the newly created and rapidly expanding press provided a medium for its expression; 19th-century Europe offered a wide range of inspiration and example.

The suggestion has been made that some of the Lebanese movements of the periods 1820–1 and 1840 may have been inspired or influenced by French Revolutionary ideologies of national liberation and political democracy. The documents on which these suggestions rest[14] are few and uncertain, and may reflect the activities of French agitators more than any genuine local movement. A more definite expression of libertarian ideas occurs in an account of the revolt of the Maronites of Kisrawān in 1858–9, led by Ṭanyūs Shāhīn; he is said to have aimed at "republican government" *(ḥukūma jumhūriyya)*, probably meaning some form of representative government.[15]

The intensification of Western influence during and after the Crimean War on the one hand, and the growing internal political and economic pressures on the other, both helped to bring a revival of libertarian thought and activities in the 1860s. The press provided a platform of a kind previously unknown. The first privately owned newspaper produced by a Turk, the *Terjüman-i Ahval*, began publication in 1860, and was followed in 1862 by the better-known *Tasvir-i Efkâr*. The poet and journalist Ibrahim Shinasi, in his introductory editorials to the first issues of both newspapers, laid great stress on the importance of freedom of expression.

The topic was by no means academic. As far back as 1824, a Frenchman had established a French-language monthly in Izmir which, despite some difficulties with the authorities, grew into a weekly and played a role of some importance in the affairs of the Empire. Its vigorous comments sometimes got the editor into trouble—with foreign powers rather than with the Turkish authorities. A contemporary Turkish historian quotes an intervention by the Russian ambassador:

> Indeed, he said, in France and England journalists can express themselves freely, even against their kings, so that on several occasions, in former times, wars broke out between France and England because of these journalists. Praise be to God, the divinely-guarded realms [i.e. the Ottoman Empire] were protected from such things, until a little while ago that man appeared in Izmir and began to publish his paper. It would be well to prevent him. . . .[16]

Official regulation of books and pamphlets was introduced in 1857; the first press law was promulgated in 1864. There was reason, for libertarian ideas were in the air. In Syria in 1866 the Christian author Francis Fatḥ Allāh al-Marrāsh wrote an

Arabic allegorical dialogue[17] which includes a philosophic and political discussion of freedom, and of the conditions which are required to maintain it. More directly political in content was the work of a Muslim writer, the famous Khayr al-Dīn Pasha, one of the authors of the Tunisian constitutional enactment of 1861.[18] In this rather conservative programme of reform, Khayr al-Dīn examines the sources of European wealth and power, and finds them in the political institutions of Europe, which secure justice and freedom. Identifying the two, he makes some cautious and rather obscure recommendations on how to secure them in the Islamic state without violating or departing from Islamic traditions and institutions, by reliance on "consultation", since the consultation of ministers, ulema, and notables is the authentic Islamic equivalent of the European system of representative and constitutional government. It may be noted that neither as chief minister in Tunisia in the years 1873–7, nor as Grand Vizier in Turkey in 1878–9, did he do anything to restore the constitutions which had been suspended in both countries.

Already in 1856, in an ode addressed to Reshid Pasha on the occasion of the Reform Edict of that year, Shinasi tells the reforming Pasha: "You have made us free, who were slaves to oppression", and continues: "Your law is an act of manumission for me, your law informs the Sultan of his limits."[19]

The radical implications of these words—the replacement of justice by freedom as the antithesis of tyranny, and the suggestion of a constitutional restriction of the sovereign's powers—were developed and made clear in the late '60's and '70s by the group of liberal patriots known as the Young (strictly "new") Ottomans. The political ideas of the Young Ottomans, though couched in Islamic terms and related, sometimes with visible effort, to Islamic traditions, are of European origin, and express an Ottoman-Islamic adaptation of the liberal patriotism current in Europe at that time. Their ideal was the British parliament at Westminster, their ideology was drawn from the liberal teachings of the French enlightenment and revolution, their organization and tactics were modelled on the patriotic secret societies of Italy and Poland.

In the political writings of the Young Ottomans the two key words are *Vatan*—fatherland, and *Hürriyyet*—freedom. The latter was the name of the weekly journal which they published in exile (London, June 1868–April 1870; Geneva, April–June 1870). In this journal, and in other writings, the Young Ottoman ideologists, above all Namîk Kemal (1840–1888), expounded their interpretation of liberty—the sovereignty of the people, to be secured by constitutional and representative government.[20] For Kemal as for earlier Muslim writers, the primary duty of the state is still to act justly—but justice means not only care for the welfare of the subject, but respect for his political rights. These rights must be safeguarded by appropriate institutions:

> To keep the government within the limits of justice, there are two basic devices. The first of them is that the fundamental rules by which it operates should no longer be implicit or tacit, but should be published to the world.... The second principle is consultation, whereby the legislative power is taken away from the government.[21]

Like his predecessors, Namîk Kemal tries to present these imported ideas as natural developments from traditional Islamic notions; in this way justice grows into freedom and consultation into representation.

Thus far, Namîk Kemal and his associates had been anticipated by earlier 19th-century writers, and even to some extent by rulers, who had summoned councils and issued edicts. But the Young Ottomans, in both thought and action, went far beyond their cautious forerunners. For Namîk Kemal, a consultative assembly, even an elected one, is not enough. The essence of the matter is that this assembly be the exclusive possessor of the legislative power, of which the government would thus be deprived. This doctrine of the separation of powers, to be expressed in and maintained by a written constitution, is supported by the even more radical idea of the sovereignty of the people, which Namîk Kemal identifies with the classical *bayʿa*, the juridical term for the process by which the accession of a Caliph, according to Islamic law, was proclaimed and recognized.[22]

> The sovereignty of the people, which means that the powers of the government derive from the people, and which in the language of the Holy Law is called *bay'a* . . . is a right necessarily arising from the personal independence that each individual by nature possesses.[23]

He was not deceived by the apparently liberal and constitutional aspects of the Ottoman reforms. The reform edict of 1839 was not, as some had claimed, a fundamental constitutional charter, but a measure of administrative westernization.

> Had the Rescript not confined the general precepts of law set forth in its preamble to personal freedom alone, which it interpreted as security of life, property and honor, but also proclaimed such other basic principles as freedom of thought, sovereignty of the people, and the system of government by consultation [i.e. representative and responsible government], then only could it have taken the character of a fundamental charter. . . .[24]

In 1876, with the promulgation of the first Ottoman constitution, the liberal and parliamentary program of the Young Ottomans seemed to be on the point of realization. Article 10 of the constitution lays down that personal freedom is inviolable, and subsequent articles deal with freedom of worship, the press, association, education, etc., as well as with freedom from arbitrary violations of the rights of the person, residence and property. In its political provisions, however, the constitution is less libertarian. It derives not from the sovereignty of the people but from the will of the sovereign, who retains important prerogatives and all residual powers; it gives only perfunctory recognition to the principle of the separation of powers. Its effective life was in any case brief. In February 1878 Parliament was dissolved; it did not meet again for thirty years.

Under Sultan Abdülhamid II freedom was a proscribed word, and the ideals which it connoted became all the more precious. For Turkish modernists of that generation, the fountainhead was the West, which provided both material examples of the benefits of freedom, and intellectual guidance on the means of attaining it. "When you look upon this fascinating display of human progress," wrote a young Turkish diplomat from the Paris Exhibition of 1878, "do not forget that all these achievements are the work of freedom. It is under the protection of freedom that peoples and nations attain happiness. Without freedom, there can be no security; without security, no endeavour; without endeavour, no prosperity; without prosperity, no happiness. . . ."[25] As an earlier generation had turned to Voltaire, Rousseau and Montesquieu, so the new generation read the writings of Haeckel, Büchner, Gustave Le Bon (specially favored because of his sympathy for Islam), Spencer, Mill and many others.

> If there are today [wrote Hüseyn Rahmi in 1908], men who can think, can write, and can defend freedom, they are those whose minds were enlightened by these sparks [of European culture]. In those dark and melancholy days, our friends, our guides were those intellectual treasures of the West. We learned the love for thinking, the love for freedom, from those treasures.[26]

In more practical political terms, freedom meant constitutional and representative government—the ending of autocracy, the restoration of the constitution, and the safeguarding of the rights of the citizen by free elections and parliaments.

But freedom was no longer a purely political matter. For some, the exponents of materialist and secularist ideas, it involved an intellectual liberation from what they saw as the shackles of religious obscurantism. Perhaps the first to conceive of liberation in social and economic terms was Prince Sabaheddin (*c.* 1877–1948), who sought to lead Turkey from a collectivist to an individualist social order by a policy of federalism and decentralization and by the encouragement of private enterprise. In 1902 he founded a society dedicated to the achievement of these purposes. Similar ideas inspired the Liberal Entente, which appeared in 1911 as a rival to the Young Turk Union and Progress Party. An interesting example of the use of the word in a social and individualist connotation is in the Egyptian author Qāsim Amīn's famous book *Taḥrīr al-mar'a (The Liberation*—i.e. emancipation—*of Woman.)*[27]

After the Young Turk revolution of 1908 the establishment, for a while, of effective freedom of thought and expression initiated a period of vigorous debate, in which the problem of freedom, with others, was examined, analysed, and discussed from many points of view; political, social, economic and religious freedom all found their exponents and defenders. But as the bonds of autocracy and censorship were wound tighter by the Young Turks, the debate dwindled into insignificance. In the new Turkey that emerged under the first and second republics, the discussion of freedom does not differ significantly from that of Europe, and does not belong to the history of Islamic thought.

Ottoman subjects from the Arab lands played a certain role in the libertarian movement almost from the beginning. On 24 March 1867, the Egyptian prince Muṣṭafā Fāḍil Pasha published in the French newspaper *Liberté* an open letter to the Sultan, advising him to grant a constitution to the Empire.[28] Besides endowing them with their first manifesto, the Pasha also helped the Young Ottoman exiles financially, and was later succeeded in this by his brother the Khedive Ismāʿīl, who saw in them a useful instrument of his political purposes.

In Hamidian times, one of the first libertarian journals published in exile was started by Salīm Fāris, a son of the Sultan's Arabic journalist Aḥmad Fāris al-Shidyāḳ. Published in London in January 1894, it was entitled *Hürriyet*—a significant evocation of the earlier Young Ottoman weekly. He was later induced by agents of the Sultan to cease publication. Other exiles included the Lebanese amir Amīn Arslān, who published an Arabic journal in Paris in 1895, and a former Syrian deputy in the Ottoman parliament of 1876, Khalīl Ghānim, who became active in Young Turk circles. The ideas and arguments of the Young Ottomans and of the Young Turks found their echoes also in Arabic publications, which at this period tend to offer a provincial adaptation of ideas circulating among the Turkish ruling groups.

In Egypt, under Khedivial and then British rule, political thought evolved along different lines, more directly influenced by Europe, and less directly affected by events and movements in the Ottoman Empire—though even here these had their effect. Many of the leaders of thought were Arabic-speaking émigrés from the Ottoman lands; the occasional presence and activity in Egypt of such Turkish personalities as Prince Sabaheddin and Abdüllah Jevdet (1869–1932) cannot have passed unnoticed. Walī al-Dīn Yakan (1873–1931), of Turkish origin and a participant in Young Turk politics, wrote extensively in Arabic on political and social problems. A work of some influence was Abdüllah Jevdet's Turkish translation of Vittorio Alfieri's *Della Tirannide*. Entitled simply *Istibdād* (Despotism), it was first printed in Geneva in 1898 and reprinted in Cairo in 1909. This translation appears to underlie the famous Arabic adaptation of Alfieri's book by the Aleppine exile in Egypt, ʿAbd al-Raḥmān al-Kawākibī (1849–1902), entitled *Ṭabāʾiʿ al-istibdād (The Characteristics of Despotism)*.[29]

One of the earliest discussions—little noticed at the time—of freedom in Egypt, after Shaykh Rifāʿa, is that of the Azharī Shaykh Ḥusayn al-Marṣafī. In his *Risālat al-kalim al-thamān (Essay on Eight Words)*,[30] he examines and interprets, for the benefit of "the intelligent young men of these times", eight political terms "current on the tongues of men".[31] One of them is *ḥurriyya*[32] which the Shaykh explains in natural and social terms—the difference between men and beasts, the human habit of social specialization and association, and hence the need for social cooperation and the mutual recognition of rights. The Shaykh recognizes the necessity of freedom in its natural and social sense, but rather obscurely warns his young readers against untoward extension of the concept into the realm of politics.

Despite such warnings, the influence of European liberal political thought continued to grow, and found frequent expression in Arabic as well as Turkish writings. The merits of freedom are variously presented and defended. For some, a vaguely understood freedom is still the secret talisman of Western prosperity and power; its adoption is therefore desirable in order to achieve the same results. For others, freedom means the overthrow of tyranny, usually identified with Sultan Abdülhamid, and the establishment of a constitutional régime in its place.

Perhaps the last and most cogent exposition of the classical liberal position in Arabic is that of the Egyptian Aḥmad Luṭfī al-Sayyid (1872–1963). A declared disciple of John Stuart Mill and other 19th-century liberals, Luṭfī al-Sayyid gives a central position to the problem of liberty in his political thought.

Freedom, basically, means the rights of the individual—his inalienable natural freedom, defined and safeguarded by civil rights, which in turn are secured by political and legal arrangements and institutions. The action and interference of the State must be kept at the minimum; the freedom of the individual and of the nation must be secured by a free press, an independent judiciary, and a constitutional régime guaranteeing the separation of powers.

Luṭfī al-Sayyid is concerned not only with the freedom of the individual, but also with that of the nation, which has corporate natural rights distinct from and additional to the aggregate of the rights of the individuals composing it. Rejecting pan-Islamism and disapproving of Arab nationalism, he sees the nation as Egypt, and argues for her liberation from both foreign rule and native authoritarianism.[33]

The liberal interpretation of freedom continued to find exponents, particularly after the Young Turk revolution of 1908 and again after the military victory of the democracies ten years later. But in the meantime a new interpretation of freedom was gaining ground, resulting from the spread of imperialism and the rise of nationalism. In nationalist usage, freedom is a synonym for independence—the sovereignty of the nation state untrammeled by any superior, alien authority. In the absence of any such subordination to aliens, a nation is called free, irrespective of the political, social and economic conditions prevailing within it. This interpretation of freedom had less impact among the Turks, whose independence though threatened was never lost, than among the Arab peoples for whom the main theme of political life was the ending of alien rule.

During the period of British and French domination, individual freedom was never much of an issue. Though often limited and sometimes suspended, it was on the whole more extensive and better protected than either before or after. The imperial régimes conceded freedom but withheld independence; it was natural that the anti-imperialist struggle should concentrate on the latter and neglect the former.

In the final revulsion against the West, Western democracy too was rejected as a fraud and a delusion, of no value to

Muslims. The words liberty *(ḥurriyya)* and liberation *(taḥrīr)* retained their magic, but were emptied of that liberal individualist content which had first attracted Muslim attention in the 19th century. A few voices still spoke of personal individual rights, and some writers used a word from the same root, *taḥarrur*, to denote psychological self-liberation, or emancipation (from the shackles of tradition and the like). But for most users of the word, freedom was a collective, not an individual attribute; it was first interpreted politically, as independence, and then, when this by itself proved inadequate, reinterpreted in quasi-economic terms, as the absence of private or foreign exploitation. In the 1950s and '60s the idea of political freedom in the classical liberal sense seemed to be dead in most Arab countries, and dying elsewhere in the world of Islam. The beginning of the 1970s saw signs of a revival of interest, linked with a certain disillusionment with the other interpretations of freedom which had been imposed on them.[34]

20. *On Modern Arabic Political Terms*

During the past hundred years the Arabs, like many other peoples in Asia and Africa, have had to find new words for a series of political concepts and institutions alien to their own traditions, and imposed or imported from outside. Drawn from European history, and expressed in terms of European thought, the new political language was strange and difficult, and remained so even when the structures themselves began to change. Arab history offered no precedents for the new facts and ideas; the wealth of the Arabic language seemed to lack words to denote or even adequately to describe them.

In devising its vocabulary of modern politics, Arabic has resorted to four main methods—borrowing, neologism, semantic rejuvenation, and loan-translation.

Of these, borrowing is the least important. In contrast to other languages such as Turkish and even colloquial Arabic, modern literary Arabic has accepted very few loanwords, and even these, while remaining lexically foreign, have usually been grammatically assimilated. Political loanwords came in the main with identifiably foreign referents. These may be institutions, like *barlamān*, parliament, presumably via French; functions, like *qunṣul*, consul (with *qunṣuliyya*, consulate); political movements or ideologies, like *balshafī*, Bolshevik, and *fāsh*[*ist*]*ī*, fascist. The former is now of rare occurrence; the latter is very extensively used, usually in a standardized collocation with *nāzī*, as a non-specific term of abuse for political and national opponents. Two loanwords of more general application are *diktātūrī* (also *dīktātūrī*), dictatorial, and *dīmūqrāṭī*, democratic, each with its corresponding abstract noun ending in *iyya*. *Diktātūrī*, a pejorative term for authoritarian government, is of limited usefulness in the Arab countries at the present time.

Dīmūqrāṭī on the other hand is widely used, with a very variable range of meaning, including elements derived from Eastern and Western Europe, and from North and South America, as well as from indigenous tradition and experience.[1]

At first sight it may seem surprising that Arabic should have borrowed the word *dīmūqrāṭī*. The notion was not altogether new, and could have been known to scholars through the Arabic versions and adaptations of Greek political writings, in which "democratic polity" is rendered *madīna jamāʿiyya*. This literature was however little read in the 19th and early 20th centuries, and those who did read it may be excused for failing to perceive the connection between the systems described by ancient and medieval philosophers and the ideas and practices which were called democratic in their own day.

The same observations can be made of such neologisms as *jumhūriyya*, republic. In classical Arabic, the usual equivalent of the Greek *polīteía* or Latin *res publica* was *madīna*, a word of Aramaic provenance which originally meant a jurisdiction, then a country or district, and finally a city. This word was obviously too vague for precise political description. When, in late medieval times, the Arabic-speaking countries encountered functioning republics in Venice and elsewhere, they seem to have felt no need to devise any special term for them. It was not until the French Revolution that the Muslims, recognizing the emergence of a new political phenomenon, coined a new word to denote it.

This term, like many of the Arabic neologisms of the 19th century, was an Ottoman rather than an Arab creation. The Turks were the first Muslim ruling group to encounter the facts and read the literature of modern politics, and therefore to feel the need for a new vocabulary for both discussion and administration. Turkish was the dominant language in the Ottoman Empire, in Central Asia and for a while even in Egypt and part of North Africa. When it gave way, it was usually to European languages—French, Russian, English or Italian. Modern Arabic was thus a comparative latecomer, and was able to make use of an important new vocabulary coined by Ottoman scholars, officials and journalists. For educated Turks, Arabic was a classical language, on which they drew in the same way as West Europeans drew on Latin and Greek. Lexically, metaphysics and telephone are both Greek loanwords in English—but the historical and cultural difference between the two cases is obvious. Both have their equivalents among the Arabic words in Ottoman Turkish. Many, like metaphysics in English, are words borrowed from an earlier culture along with the ideas and objects which they denote. Others, like telephone, are new coinages for new referents. When such words are adopted back into their languages of etymological origin, they are lexical natives, but semantic intruders. Such are *têlephônon* and *têlegraphima* in modern Greek; such too are a wide range of new terms in modern Arabic.

These repossessed neologisms comprise an important part of the modern Arabic political vocabulary. *Jumhūriyya*, at first republicanism and then simply republic, is an Ottoman coinage of the late 18th century. An Arabic term for republic produced at the time of the French occupation of Egypt, *mashyakha*, was not accepted into common usage, and soon disappeared in this sense. Today *jumhūriyya* is the universally recognized word for republic in all the Arab lands.[2]

Two other Ottoman neologisms of great popularity at the present time are *qawmiyya*, nationalism, and *ishtirākiyya*, socialism. Both date from the 19th century, and appear to be products of Turkish journalism. *Kavim* (from Arabic *Qawm*) is used in Turkish in the sense of tribe or people, often with a somewhat derogatory implication, rather like the French *peuplade*. *Kavmiyet* was at first used in a pejorative sense, to mean tribalism, and thence factional, particularistic or disruptive nationalism. Thus in 1870 Ali Suavi uses it when arguing against nationalism. For Muslims, he says, only religious identity is important. Religion unites them; nationalism would divide them.[3] The same line of argument is pursued by other anti-nationalist Turkish writers, of both pan-Islamic and Ottomanist opinions, and in 1913 Mehmet Akif gave it vigorous poetic expression.[4] In the same year Ahmed Naim published a book denouncing nationalism *(kavmiyet)* as "a foreign innovation as deadly to the body of Islam as cancer is to man."[5] Even the theoretician of Turkish nationalism, Ziya Gökalp, used *kavîm* and *kavmiyet* to denote identity and solidarity based on ethnic affinity, and thus at a more primitive level than nationality based on religion *(ümmet)* or culture *(millet)*.[6]

In Turkish *kavmiyet* remained on the whole derogatory, and gradually fell into disuse. In Arabic, however, the word entered on a new phase of development. It appears in the proclamation published by the Sharīf Ḥusayn of the Hijaz in 1916,[7] and thereafter becomes standard Arabic usage. More recently, it has been specialized to denote pan-Arab nationalism as against the national or rather patriotic loyalties of the individual Arab countries.

Socialism in 19th-century Tûrkish was *ishtirāk-i emvāl*, literally "sharing of property", whence *ishtirakjî*, a socialist, and *ishtiraki*, socialistic. In Turkish the term fell into disuse, and was replaced by *Sosyalist*. Adopted in Arabic, it soon gained universal acceptance.

Other Ottoman Arabic neologisms include learned expressions, such as *iqtiṣādī*, economic, and a wide range of public administrative terms, such as *khārijiyya*, foreign affairs; *dākhiliyya*, home affairs and *baladiyya*, municipality.

Apart from Ottoman usage, Arabic neologisms come from two main sources—Egypt and the Arabic-speaking Christians, especially the Maronites in Lebanon and elsewhere. They include such terms as *ʿalamānī* (earlier *ʿālamānī*), secular (from *ʿālam*, world, whence worldly); *shuyūʿī*, communist (from *shuyūʿ* or *shiyāʿ*, a legal term for community of property ownership); *duwalī*, international (derived, contrary to accepted grammatical usage, from the broken plural of *dawla*, state); *iqṭāʿī*, feudal (from *iqṭāʿ*, a grant of revenue to an officer or functionary in medieval Islamic states); *rajʿī*, reactionary (from *rajaʿa*, to return or turn back); *diʿāya*, propaganda (from *daʿā*, to call or summon, a term technically applied to the preaching of certain sectarian missionaries in medieval Islam). Most of these words date from the late 19th or early 20th century.

Another method of devising new terms is by a process of semantic rejuvenation or resemanticization. This occurs where an old word, which may or may not be obsolete, is given, more or less arbitrarily, a new meaning different from those which it previously expressed. Two examples, both from the 19th century, are *ḥukūma*, government, and *dustūr*, constitution.[8] In classical Arabic *ḥukūma* was a noun of action, meaning the act, later also the function, of adjudicating, of dispensing justice, whether by an arbitrator, a judge, or a ruler. After some semantic development, it was adopted in early 19th-century Turkish to express the European notion of government, i.e., the group of men exercising the authority of the state, as distinct from the abstraction of the state on the one hand and the person of the sovereign on the other. In this sense it passed into Arabic, and became common usage in the late 19th century.

Dustūr comes from a Persian word, originally meaning a person exercising authority, more particularly a member of the Zoroastrian priesthood. In classical Arabic usage, it had several meanings, but commonly meant a rule or set of rules, especially in the craft-guilds. Its modern use in the sense of constitution is no doubt a development of this last meaning.

Other more recent refurbishments of old words include *shuʿūbiyya*, local (i.e. not pan-Arab) particularism (originally an anti-Arab faction in medieval times); *fidāʾī*, guerrilla or commando (literally one who offers his life as ransom, especially used of the terrorists sent out by the medieval Islamic sect known as the Assassins); *thawra*, revolution, originally rising, from the verb *thāra*, to rise, at first in the physical sense, e.g.—to quote examples given by classical lexicographers—a camel rising to its feet, a swarm of locusts rising into the air, and thence by extension an insurrection.

It is tempting to include such words as *umma*, nation, and *shaʿb*, people, in this category, since their content at the present time differs radically from classical and even early modern Arabic usage. They might however more properly be placed in the fourth category, of loan-translation or calque.

This is, at the present time, by far the most usual method of procuring new terms, and accounts for the greater part of the modern Arabic technical vocabulary, of politics as of other fields of activity and themes of discussion. Briefly, loan-translation means that an Arabic word is given a change of meaning or an extension of range of reference, borrowed from the historical development of the equivalent word in another language. Loan-translations occur even in classical Arabic—e.g., in the terms *umm al-qurā*, "mother of towns", from the Greek *mêtropolis*, and *tadbīr al-manzil*, "management of the house", economy, from the Greek *oikonomía*. In modern times they have hitherto usually been drawn from English or French. One or two simple examples may suffice to explain the process. *Kahrabā'* in classical Arabic means amber, in modern Arabic electricity. This reproduces the development of the western word, which comes from the ancient Greek *êlektros*—amber. *A͟dhā'a* in classical Arabic means to spread or disseminate news or information, i.e. to broadcast in the pre-technical English sense of the word. In modern Arabic it has imitated the development of the English word, and acquired the meaning of public radio transmission.

Loan-translation of political terms takes several forms. The earliest examples are common Islamic political terms, used with a change of meaning of which the users were probably unaware. Thus, according to the dictionaries, *malik* means king and *wazīr* means minister—but the use of these words for 19th-century European or European-style monarchs and the members of their governments represented a substantial modification of the hitherto accepted connotation of these terms among Arabic-speakers. The same is true of such other terms as *umma*, religio-political community, nation; *dawla*, dynasty, government, state; *ra'īs*, head, chief, president, *ḥizb*, faction, group, party; *istiqlāl*, unrestricted rule, independence; *za'īm*, surety, pretender, leader.

The last of these is particularly interesting. In early classical Arabic *za'īm* had the meanings of leader, spokesman, or surety. In medieval practice, it was used chiefly of rulers or claimants whose claims the user did not recognize. It was thus applied by Sunnī authors to the chiefs of the Ismā'īlī sectaries in Persia and Syria and to the head of the Jewish community in Baghdad; it was also used by scribes in the service of the Egyptian Mamluk Sultanate to designate the Zaydī and Almohade "Caliphs" in the Yemen and North Africa, whose title to the Caliphate was not admitted. This meaning of pretender or false claimant is confirmed by an Arabic-Spanish vocabulary of 1505, which explains *zaʿīm* as "*hablador de sobervias, vanaglorioso*".[9] The word *zaʿīm* came into general use in the 1930s, when an Arabic equivalent for *Duce* or *Führer* was required.

In all these, the new meaning is an extension rather than a replacement of the old political content, which still remains and can affect the use and understanding of these terms in Arab political life, often to the confusion of outside observers. In another type of loan-translation, the political meaning is wholly new. Thus, the word *inqilāb*, in classical Arabic, means revolution in the literal sense—i.e., revolving, turning round. In 1870, probably for the first time, the Turkish émigré activist Mehmed Bey used the word in its modern sense.[10] In Turkish, *inqilāb* became and has remained the "good" word for revolution, used of revolutions of which the user approves; in Arabic on the other hand it has acquired a pejorative meaning, and is used in a sense which might be translated by the French *coup* or German *Putsch*—English experience happily provides no suitable equivalent.

There are many other words, previously non-political, which have acquired a new political significance, drawn from pan-occidental usage. They include such terms as *ḥurriyya*, freedom;[11] *al-ra'y al-ʿāmm*, public opinion; *majlis nuwwāb*, chamber of deputies; *majlis shuyūkh*, Senate; *istiʿmār*, colonization, *muḥāfiz*, conservative; *waṭan*, country, *patrie*; *intikhāb*, election; *taʿāyush*, co-existence; and *taṣāʿud*, escalation.

The emergence of the modern Arabic political vocabulary is an important aspect of the political and cultural life of the Islamic world. A careful study of its development is essential to the evaluation of texts and documents; an appreciation of the layers of content of the current language of politics can contribute greatly to the decipherment of political symbols and kennings, and thus to the better understanding of political thought, purpose, and process.

21. Islam and Development: The Revaluation of Values

The term "developing countries" is at the present time applied, by polite convention, to a large group of countries in Asia, Africa and elsewhere, which differ very widely among themselves in culture, background, social and political structure, and degree of development, but have this in common—that they are classified as undeveloped or under-developed in relation to the societies of Europe and the lands of European settlement overseas. In addition, they have shared the traumatic experience of the impact, influence and, sometimes, domination of the alien civilization of the West, which brought immense and irreversible changes on every level of social existence. Some of these changes were the work of Western rulers and administrators. Such foreigners, however, tended on the whole to be cautiously conservative in their policies; while they brought many great changes in practical and material things, their influence on institutions and ideas was far less radical than that of the native Westernizers. These were of many kinds—rulers who sought to acquire and master the Western apparatus of power; men of affairs, anxious to adopt Western methods and techniques for the creation or acquisition of wealth; men of letters and of action, fascinated by the potency and efficacy of Western knowledge and ideas.

The acceptance of modern civilization by a developing country may involve the installation of a modern-style political and administrative structure, the adoption of modern social and cultural patterns and institutions, the acquisition of modern economic and technical methods and skills. But in addition to these and other borrowings, and as an essential concomitant to their successful assimilation, it must involve the acceptance, implicitly or explicitly, of the modern values and standards that underlie and accompany the growth and functioning of these things.

The revaluation of values was, and has remained, a problem at every stage of development in the West itself. The process of borrowing values from another society poses additional difficulties, especially when the borrower is itself a society of ancient civilization, with cherished and deep-rooted values and standards, sustained by high achievement, of its own. There are some values that are no doubt common to all mankind—such as truth, wisdom, valor, and loyalty; but the social application and interpretation of these values may vary greatly from one society to another, and even present the appearance of a contradiction. Such a conflict—between the traditional values assumed in the family, the community, the home and social surrounding, and the new values proclaimed in the public life of the school, college, university, and government—may set up dangerous tensions in the individual and in society. Officially, the old values are abandoned, even discredited and derided, and are replaced by the values and standards of the modern West; in fact they survive, with sufficient power and vitality to exact submission, even from the most modernized of citizens. When a society adopts a new religion, the gods of the old faith sometimes survive as devils in the new theology. In the same way, when a society adopts new values, the old values may survive, in a vestigial and surreptitious form, as vices in the new order. The citizen, while obeying his instincts and traditions, will nevertheless feel guilt at flouting the new values on which the new order rests, and thus imperilling its success; he will also feel shame vis-à-vis the outside world, which he feels will despise him for failing to live up to its—now also his—standards.

A good example of this is the value of loyalty—a social virtue prized by all mankind, and essential to the survival of any kind of society. But the basis of identity and cohesion may vary greatly from society to society. In the Muslim Middle East the two strongest claims on loyalty were those of kinship and religion. These have been displaced, in the official scale of values, by new public, civic, and legal loyalties—to political principles and ideals, to nation and country, and, on a different level, to specific obligations, codes, and institutions. The old loyalties to kin and faith live on; but instead of being virtues, they are now condemned, in the new political morality, as vices. The old virtue of family loyalty has become the vice of nepotism; the old virtue of religious loyalty has become the vice of fanaticism—and both are despised, sometimes even by those who obey them, as retrograde and uncivilized. There is no ascertainable moral difference here—the protection of one's political associates is not notably superior to the patronage of one's cousins; blind and unreasoning nationalism is not markedly more attractive than fanatical religious zeal—but the former are considered modern and progressive, the latter backward and barbarous, out of accord with the needs and purposes of the modern state; and indeed there is no doubt that religious fanaticism often divides the nation, which is the modern political unit, and delays development, or that the vague but potent loyalties of kinship lead to the fragmentation of capital and the limitation and diffusion of effort, and thus inhibit economic growth. Their persistence, in the modern state, creates grave problems of adjustment and even survival.

Even some of the old, high religious ideals have been condemned as hostile to development. Such for example is asceticism, which tends to reduce and limit human needs instead of satisfying them, and thus discourages effort; the virtue of renunciation leads too easily to the vice of indolence. Similarly, the great importance attached to the virtue of charity—in the sense of alms-giving—in the traditional Islamic scale of values has been criticized, in that it gives an accepted—even an honorable—place to the beggar in society, and thus discredits and discourages honest toil. The charge that the Islamic religion is innately hostile to economic development is difficult to sustain; the social and cultural causes of economic backwardness in Muslim countries must be sought in a complex of factors, of which historic Islam is a part and, to some extent, an expression. In the Middle Ages, the Muslim Empires achieved a real flowering of economic life; in more recent times, as Becker remarked, Christian Ethiopia has been at least as handicapped as the Muslim lands.[1] There is nothing in Islamic doctrine to oppose economic progress, though there is much in the social and legal practices of Muslims that needs careful reconsideration from this point of view.

While the old virtues have become vices, some of the old vices are becoming virtues—and moreover virtues which are necessary for the growth of a modern society. An example of this may be found in the traditional and modern—or bourgeois—views of generosity and meanness. In the old scale of values generosity is a great personal and social virtue; meanness a low and contemptible vice. Anecdote, historiography and social comment unite in extolling the open-hearted and open-handed individual or ruler, who bestows his largess freely and unstintingly without inquiring too closely into the claims and merits of the beneficiary or the purposes of the benefaction. To withhold such largess, or to make such inquiries, brings charges of meanness—even of avarice. The modern world, reared on the bourgeois virtues of thrift and industry, takes a different view. The 'Abbasid Caliph al-Manṣūr, whom the Muslim tradition condemned for his miserliness and nicknamed Abu'l-Dawāniq—the father of farthings—is praised by modern historians for his careful and provident economic policies. Other rulers, famous for their generosity, are now condemned as reckless and ruinous spendthrifts. It would be easy to multiply examples of the same process, from both public and private life, in our own time.

Associated with the traditional contempt for thrift is an attitude towards the acquisition of wealth in general, and certain occupations in particular. In the Muslim Middle East a number of crafts and professions were originally followed, in the main, by members of religious or ethnic groups regarded as social inferiors. The stigma of inferiority remained even after this specialization had ceased to operate. Trade and finance came to be despised, and those engaged in them suspect; thrift was confused with avarice, and enterprise with greed. The worthiest occupations were the service of God and the State; the most esteemed persons were the ulema, the military, and the civil servants. These alone, according to the traditional scale of values, were engaged in noble pursuits, which were honorable and dignified even if not always very remunerative.

All others were either vile mechanics or grasping hucksters. To work with one's hands, in particular, was contemptible, and the possession of manual skills, outside the artisan classes, carried no prestige or esteem. This had a harmful effect on the development of science and technology, in which progress often depends on a combination of intellectual training and manual—even, in a sense, artisanal—dexterity. Muslim landowners in the old days might be cultivated gentlemen or working farmers. They were rarely both and were therefore unable to produce anything resembling the technical and agrarian improvements introduced by the gentlemen-farmers of England in the 17th and 18th centuries. The same attitude is noticeable in the time of the 19th-century Turkish and Egyptian reforms, when graduates of the new schools of agronomy and medicine preferred to work in offices rather than soil their hands with earth or with patients. Of the first classes of graduates of the medical schools established in the early 19th century, it was in the main only the failures who actually became doctors. The successes became administrators, officers, officials and statesmen. Even today, economic and technical progress can be held back by the survival of traditional evaluations of attainment and achievement, and traditional definitions of prestige, honor and dignity. Such, for example, is the old and deep-rooted attitude to work, power and status which makes the Middle Eastern motorist a bold and resourceful driver but a reluctant and unpredictable mechanic.

Development and progress are the basic needs of the developing countries—the needs in relation to which they are so defined and classified; yet development requires certain qualities—of enterprise, experiment, and originality—which are condemned as vices and defects in the old scale of values. In traditional societies the very concepts of development and progress are lacking. Improvement, according to traditional ideas, is achieved by trying to conform to a model or pattern—the perfect man, the perfect city, the perfect state. This model is, so to speak, external and given, and the effort towards improvement is thus basically an attempt at imitation. The more successful and sustained the imitation, the better. The modern idea of development—of a process of growth and maturing, whereby the innate qualities and aptitudes of an individual or a society are fostered and cultivated and brought to a higher level, is lacking.

In the self-view of traditional society there is no progress and no development; there can, however, be change, and change is usually for the worse. The ideal model is usually situated in the past, in terms of a mythology, a revelation or master-philosophy, or a semi-historical golden age. Given this original perfection, all change is deterioration—a falling-away from the sanctified past. Virtue, in society, means the acceptance and observance of tradition; departure from it is the major social offense. The true path is the doctrine and practice of the ancestors, as preserved and recorded by tradition—in a word, the Sunna. Departure from it is *bidʿa*—innovation, the Islamic theological term which is the nearest equivalent to the Christian concept of heresy.[2] A *bidʿa* can be good, and can be admitted as such by the religious authorities—but this is the exception rather than the rule. Normally, an innovation is assumed to be bad unless specifically accepted as good or permissible. There could be no more striking contrast with the attitude of modern society—the insistent and often fatuous pursuit of novelty as something necessarily and intrinsically good for its own sake. In the modern world, political and ideological as well as commercial salesmen try to market old wares by disguising them as new. In traditional society, on the contrary, new ideas and doctrines can only be made acceptable, if at all, by presenting them as a return to the pure and ancient tradition.

This tendency springs in part, of course, from a kind of cultural or communal nationalism—from a desire to soften the humiliation of accepting an alien practice or doctrine by disguising its alien provenance and ascribing it to long-lost, newly-discovered indigenous origins. But such nationalism, though widespread, is by no means the sole or even the main source of this historical romanticism. Another derives from the conscious attempts of would-be innovators to make their innovations more palatable by relating them to familiar and accepted things. Thus, when constitutional and representative government was in fashion in the Middle East, a series of attempts were made to relate it to Islamic origins, culminating in the speech from the throne at the opening of the Ottoman parliament on 14 November 1909, which referred to the "parliamentary form of government prescribed by the Holy Law". In the same spirit, now that socialism has become popular in the Arab lands, and official in Egypt, a shaykh of al-Azhar has been found to proclaim that Islam is the true socialism, and that Muḥammad was the first socialist. The purpose of this, of course, is not to convert socialists to Islam, but to make socialism acceptable to Muslims. In the socialist states of today as in the parliamentary democracies of yesterday, official ideologists are not lacking to prove that what the government does is right—*i.e.,* conforms to the inherited tradition. That too, after all, is part of the tradition.

This raises the question of authority and freedom, with which that of tradition is closely linked. It is often said that Islam is an authoritarian religion, which inculcates an attitude of fatalism in man's relations with God and the world, and of quietism in his relations with the state and society. This judgment of Islam might be difficult to maintain in abstract theological terms; it would, however, derive much support from the historic practice of Muslim states and communities, as recorded for the greater part of Muslim history.

Even here, some traces of another attitude remain. Not long ago it was fashionable for both Turks and Arabs to complain of the loss of their pristine freedom, and to accuse one another of responsibility for that loss. Both complaints are true; both accusations are false. The Arabs among whom Islam was born were a people just emerging from nomadism, and retained much of the anarchic freedom of the nomad. This freedom, it may be noted in passing, has nothing to do with democracy—a term relating to the manner in which authority is acquired, organized, and exercised in the state, and therefore irrelevant to a society in which there is neither authority nor state. Like other peoples at the same stage of development, they had a simple, rudimentary political system, with a chieftain ruling—or rather leading—by consent according to custom. The advent of the Islamic theocracy transferred the ultimate source of authority from the people to God, thus removing the consensual and revocable element in sovereignty, and immensely strengthening the prestige and authority of the sovereign. Within a few generations of the death of the Prophet the Islamic state was transformed under the influence of the absolutist traditions of the old oriental Empires. The Arabs from Arabia—as later the Turks from Central Asia—forgot the nomadic freedom of the desert and the steppe, and became part of the immemorial city and peasant civilization of the Middle East. The memories of ancient freedom are enshrined in the classical formulations of constitutional principles by the early Muslim jurists, with their insistence on the subordination of the sovereign to the law, and the duty—duty, not right—of the subject to disobey an unlawful command.

These principles, however, were theoretical rather than practical, and soon lost all real meaning. As restrictions on the sovereign's absolutism they were not very serious. For one thing, the law itself concedes him virtually absolute power, in all but religious matters. For another, the law—and the lawyers—never answered, or even asked, the question of how one would test the lawfulness of a command, or deal with a sovereign who gave unlawful commands. Before very long, even the jurists accepted the view that the subject owed the sovereign a duty of absolute and unquestioning obedience—a religious duty, failure in which was a sin as well as a crime.

At first, this duty of obedience was claimed only for the legitimate or rightful sovereign ruling according to Holy Law. Later, the logic of events and the deductions of jurists from them extended it to any ruler irrespective of how he obtained power, and of how he exercised it. "*Man ishtaddat waṭ'atuhu wajabat ṭā'atuhu,*" "whose power prevails must be obeyed" say the jurists—meaning that the religious duty of obedience relates to any holder of effective power. The same point is made in such oft repeated dicta as that "tyranny is better than anarchy" or "sixty years of tyranny are better than an hour of civil strife". Islamic political literature is full of exhortations to the sovereign to be generous and to be just, both in his own interest and as a religious obligation. But—and here is the fundamental point—this is a duty of the sovereign, not a right of the subject. The subject may have needs and hopes; he has no rights. The very idea of such rights is alien, appearing for the first time in the 19th century, when writers in Turkey and Egypt begin to use such expressions as the "rights of freedom" and the "rights of the citizen". The source of these new ideas is obvious. The traditional attitude is well expressed in the old Arabic dictum: "If the Caliph is just he will be rewarded and you must be thankful. If he is unjust he will be punished and you must be patient."

Such a system gives great privileges to the holders of power; it also imposes great duties on them, which in the main they have discharged conscientiously and diligently, if not always effectively. However great these burdens, the ruling groups have rarely been willing to share them with others. The 19th century, on the whole, strengthened rather than weakened the power of the state, as social changes enfeebled or removed the classes and interests which had formerly limited it, and technical changes reinforced its means of surveillance and coercion. There was even some ideological reinforcement, as the ideas of the central European Enlightenment were brought to the notice of Turkish and other statesmen. For authoritarian reformers, such ideas were welcome and familiar; they too knew what was best for the people, and did not wish to be distracted by so-called popular government from the business of applying it. This view still commands some support at the present time in various countries, and is frequently expressed in terms of socialism. As the bourgeois liberal revolution was introduced in the 19th century, without a bourgeoisie and without liberalism, by decision and action of the governing élite, so the socialist revolution is to be introduced in the 20th century, without a proletariat or a working class movement, by the military and political élite of the nation. One wonders whether it will be more successful.

There was, however, another view, drawing its inspiration from the political and, to a lesser extent, the economic liberalism of Western Europe. For Namik Kemal (1840–1888) and the

Young Ottoman liberal patriots, the people had rights, and these must be secured, together with the progress of the country, by representative and constitutional government. And that is not all:

> If there is anything we want [Namık Kemal complained in 1872] we first wait for the government to provide it, and then for God. There must be no doubt that the government is neither the father nor the teacher, neither the tutor nor the nursemaid of the people. . . . What right have we to compel the government to act as our nursemaid? And for that matter, it is not God's duty to improve the world, nor are the prosperity of a country or the education of a nation necessary to Him.[3]

The battle was joined—between those on the one hand who believed in self-help, self-government, and the effective sovereignty of the people, and those on the other who believed that the inert masses, accustomed by age-old tradition to follow and to obey, cannot yet be entrusted with their own fate but must be taught and commanded by those whose historic function it is to teach and to command—the intellectuals and the soldiers. So far the second school of thought has prevailed in most developing countries. It will probably continue to prevail until such qualities as initiative, enterprise, and self-reliance are accorded the same honors in the popular scale of values as are at present given to discipline, endurance, and obedience.

These military virtues are necessary in the armed forces and public services, and more widely in times of war or national emergency. But for economic growth, intellectual progress and political liberalization, other and somewhat different values and qualities must be added.

One of the more important methods of achieving this is education, and much effort is expended in developing countries on educational reform and expansion. But there are difficulties. Social change and political reform brought great changes in education; the new-style officials and officers of the post-reform period, and still more so the followers of such new professions as journalism and secular law, required a new type of education, different from the traditional religious and literary learning of the old schools and colleges. There was need, too, for new conceptions of knowledge and learning. For the old-style teachers and scholars, knowledge consisted of a finite number of pieces of information; learning consisted of acquiring them. Neither the scientists and philosophers of Islam on the one hand, nor the mystics on the other, would have accepted this view of knowledge and education. The schoolmasters and professors and their pupils did, however, and they applied it in the schools. The new intelligentsia required new pabulum—Western languages and literatures, history, geography and law, to which were later added the economic, social and political sciences. Most of these subjects were at first new and strange but they were familiar in that they were all literary in form. They could be learnt in words, from books or lectures, and then memorized. That is to say, they could be assimilated to traditional methods of education, relying chiefly on the authority of the teacher and the memory of the pupil. There were not a few teachers who saw that this was not enough, and told their pupils that they must use their own judgment, exercise their critical faculties, and decide things for themselves. The pupils accepted this because their teachers said so, and they learnt this lesson also by heart. It is not easy to impose freedom by authority.

The literary and authoritarian character of traditional pedagogy, as well as the attitudes of traditional society, made it very difficult to assimilate either the physical and natural sciences, or the practical and technical skills associated with them. Society despised manual skills, and rejected as inferior those who taught, acquired or exercised them. A good illustration of this is the low rating and limited attention given to artists in traditional Islamic society, as contrasted with the high respect accorded to poets and scholars—artists of the word, not the hand. The only exception to this rule was the architect who, as an officer concerned with bridges and fortifications, and as a director of building operations rather than a mere builder, qualified as a gentleman.

The position of the scientist was somewhat higher than that of the artist, but, in post-classical times, with little justification. The once great Muslim tradition of scientific research and experiment had long since withered and died, leaving a society strongly resistant to the scientific spirit. In the words of the late

Dr. Adnan Adivar: "The scientific current that arose in the time of Mehmet the Conqueror broke against the dykes of literature and jurisprudence."[4] The new literary, legal, and even social sciences could be assimilated without great difficulty by societies with rich and varied experience of all three; the natural and physical sciences could not. In many countries the scientific schools remained alien and exotic growths, in constant need of renewed transplants from the West. In a few non-Western countries there has been a real development of original scientific work, making important contributions to the common stock of modern knowledge; in most there has been little or none, and each generation of students must draw again from the sources in the West, which has meanwhile itself been making immense progress.

A century and a half ago, when the movement of Westernization began in Turkey and Egypt, its main purpose was to achieve military parity with the advancing West. There is bitter irony in the fact that the disparity in scientific knowledge, technological capacity, and, therefore, of military power between the Middle East and the advanced countries of the West is greater now than it was then, before the whole process of Westernization began. The result is certainly disappointing; the disappointment can be only slightly diminished by the realization that the disparity would have been infinitely greater—and the consequences far more deadly—had the attempt never been made.

The authority of the word, and of those who wield it professionally, has not infrequently been a major obstacle to progress —not a medium but a barrier in education, not a guide to reality but a shield against it. This danger is especially great where the written language of the learned is a complex and artificial idiom, divorced from the living speech of the common people. In Turkey and Persia this gap has substantially been closed, and the divergence between the written and spoken forms of the national language is hardly greater than in the countries of Europe. In the Arab world, the gap remains very wide, and the written and spoken forms of Arabic are in effect different languages.

In education and afterwards in life, the word, written or even spoken, has a magic and potency of its own, independent of, even transcending, both meaning and reality. There is a sense in which assent is more important than compliance, promise than fulfilment, law than observance, project than execution. The Turks, long accustomed to the exercise of power and responsibility, are relatively—though not wholly—free from this tendency. Among other peoples, long deprived of any power of determining or even influencing the course of events, there is a vast hiatus between expression and reality which must be closed before either serious discussion or effective action becomes possible. The difference between the practical, factual view of the West and the eastern concern with words and status is illustrated in the contrast between two proverbs, one English and one Turkish. "Sticks and stones may break my bones but words can never harm me" says the one. "The hurt of a blow passes but the hurt of a word endures" says the other.

But perhaps the most important single obstacle to progress, in the world of values and attitudes, remains the deep-rooted feeling that what is old is good, that change is bad, and that progress, or, to be more precise, improvement, consists in restoring what existed before the change. This feeling manifests itself in a variety of ways. A good example from Turkey may be found in the analyses and recommendations of the long series of writers and observers who examined the causes of the decline of Ottoman power and propounded remedies.[5] They were men of both vision and courage, who, within the limitations of their time and place, saw in detail what was wrong, and wrote in detail of what they saw. It is the more striking that for centuries all of them, without exception, saw the basic fault as a falling-away from the high standards and good practices of the Islamic and Ottoman past, and the basic remedy as a restoration of those standards and practices. By the 18th century it was becoming clear to some at least that the return to the past was a mirage, and that the path of progress lay in another direction. But even they, with greater or lesser sincerity, disguised their recommendations as a return to a past which they reinterpreted to suit their own ideas.

A similar tendency has already been noted in the writings of the liberals and reformers of the 19th century and after, who, despite their subjection to Western influences and adoption of Western views, still seek to relate these, even to identify them, with tradition—not in the existing form, but in one allegedly more ancient. They revolt against today and yesterday—not in the name of tomorrow, but of the day before yesterday. Thus, Namîk Kemal identifies constitutional government with old Islamic principles of jurisprudence, sees a chamber of deputies in the assembly of mutinous janissaries and equates the "natural law" of Montesquieu with the Holy Law of Islam—since the "natural law" comes from the "nature of things", the Holy Law comes from God, and God, after all, *is* the nature of things. It is not surprising that neither the radicals nor the conservatives were wholly convinced. But the same kind of argument continued to be advanced, with national and ethnic, instead of or as well as religious loyalties behind them.

It has been claimed that such reinterpretation of the past does no harm—that indeed it does good, since it prepares deeply conservative peoples to accept novel and foreign ideas which they would otherwise reject, by concealing their novelty and foreignness—the sugar-coating on the pill, so to speak.

There is some truth in this. Tradition should not lightly be cast aside or abandoned, and progress will be surer and healthier if it can be related to the deeper sentiments, loyalties, and aspirations which a people has inherited from its past. Particularly in a tradition as rich and diversified as that of Islam, there is enough to support, by changes of selection, emphasis, and interpretation, most of the desired variation in attitudes and values. But the changes must be of interpretation and presentation, not of content—a reappraisal, not a perversion of the past. We live in a time when great energies are devoted to the falsification of history—to flatter, to deceive, or to serve a variety of sectional purposes. No good can come of such distortions, even when they are inspired by the best of motives. Men who are unwilling to confront the past will be unable to understand the present, and unfit to face the future.

NOTES

Chapter 1. The Study of Islam

[1] See for example the prayer recited in Egyptian mosques and published on the front pages of the Egyptian papers on 17 March 1959:

"God is great! God is great! There is no might and no power save in God! May He strengthen the martyrs with His grace and ordain them everlasting life in His mercy and abase their enemies in shame and ignominy! God is great! God is great! There is no victory save in God! Whoever offends, God will crush him; whoever exalts himself by wrongdoing, God will humble him! Consider not those who are killed in the cause of God as dead, but as living, with their Lord who sustains them.

"O God Almighty, All-powerful! Conquer Thine enemy with Thine omnipotence so that he returns to Thee! O God, Almighty, All-powerful, strengthen the community of Thy Prophet with Thy favor, and ordain defeat for their enemy. O God, O Lord of the Qur'ān, give victory to Thy Qur'ān as Thou gavest victory to 'Abd al-Muṭṭalib on the Day of the Elephant, when Thou didst send against them flights of birds who pelted them with clay stones, so that they became like consumed chaff [Qur'ān 105]! In faith we worship Thee, in sincerity we call upon Thee, the blood of our martyrs we entrust to Thee, O merciful and compassionate One, Who answers the prayers of him who prays—our innocent martyrs and pure victims for the sake of Thy religion. For the glory of Thy religion they shed their blood and died as martyrs; believing in Thee, they greeted the day of sacrifice blissfully. Therefore place them, O God, as companions with the upright and the martyrs and the righteous—how good these are as companions! [Qur'ān, iv, 69]."

[2] W. Cantwell Smith, *Islam in Modern History* (Princeton, N.J., 1957), p. 151.

[3] In *Religion in the Middle East*, ed. A. J. Arberry, i (Cambridge, 1969), p. 415.

[4] Letter to Isaac da Costa, 11 February 1823, in *Brieven van Mr. Willem Bilderdijk*, iv (Rotterdam, 1837), pp. 75–6; cited by C. F. Pijper, *Islam and the Netherlands* (Leiden, 1957), p. 16.

[5] Charles Forster, *Mahometanism Unveiled*, ii (London, 1829), pp. 365, 378. *Cf.* N. Daniel, *Islam, Europe and Empire*, (1966), p. 33; Albert Hourani, "Islam and the Philosophers of History", in *Middle Eastern Studies*, iii (1967), pp. 223–5.

[6] See below, p. 127 ff.

[7] François Bernier, *Histoire de la dernière révolution des états du Grand Mogol* (4 vols., Paris, 1670–71). There are numerous later editions and translations of Bernier's travels, correspondence, and other writings. A revised English translation of the travels was edited by V. A. Smith (Oxford, 1914).

8 Volney, *Voyage en Egypte et en Syrie* (1787, English tr. 1787); ed. Jean Gaulmier (Paris & The Hague, 1959); *Les Ruines, ou Méditations sur les révolutions des Empires* (Paris, 1791).

9 A. Slade, *Turkey and the Crimean War* (London, 1867), pp. 31–2. See further below, p. 140 ff.

10 The effect of this Western mood on the dialogue between Islamicists and Muslims is discussed by G. E. von Grunebaum, "Approaching Islam: a Digression", in *Middle Eastern Studies*, vi (1970), pp. 127–49.

11 On these controversies, see the excellent study by Gianni Sofri, *Il modo di produzione asiatico; storia di una controversia marxista* (Turin, 1969). For Turkish views, see Muzaffer Sencer, *Osmanlı toplum yapısı* (Istanbul, n.d.) and Sencer Divitçioğlu, *Asya üretim tarzı ve Osmanlı toplumu* (Istanbul, 1967).

12 E. A. Belyaev, *Arabs, Islam and the Arab Caliphate in the Early Middle Ages* (tr. from the Russian by Adolphe Gourevitch; New York, London, Jerusalem, 1969).

13 Clifford Geertz, *Islam Observed: Religious Development in Morocco and Indonesia* (New Haven, 1968).

Chapter 2. Some English Travelers in the East

1 To cite a few examples: J. M. Carré, *Voyageurs et écrivains français en Égypte*, 2 vols. (Cairo, 1932); M. H. Braaksma, *Travel and Literature* (Groningen, 1938) (on English travel-books about Persia); N. Jorga, *Les Voyageurs français dans l'Orient européen* (Paris, 1928); W. Barthold, *Die geographische und historische Erforschung des Orients, mit besonderer Berücksichtigung der russischen Arbeiten* (Leipzig, 1913, translated from Russian; also available in French translation, Paris, 1947); M. Sommerfeld, "Die Reisebeschreibungen der deutschen Jerusalempilger", in *Deutsche Vierteljahrschrift für Literaturwissenschaft und Geistesgeschichte*, ii (1924), pp. 816–51; M. Leo, *La Bulgarie et son peuple sous la domination ottomane, tels que les ont vus les voyageurs Anglo-Saxons (1586–1878)* (Sofia, 1949); Mohammad Ali Hachicho, "English Travel Books about the Arab Near East in the 18th Century", in *Die Welt des Islams*, new series ix/1–4 (1964), pp. 1–206; M. Anis, "British Travellers' Impressions of Egypt in the late 18th Century", in *Bulletin of the Faculty of Arts, Cairo*, xiii/2 (1951), pp. 8–37; F. Dirimtekin, *Ecnebi seyyahlara nazaran xvi yüzyılda Istanbul* (Istanbul, 1964); M. Ish-Shalom, *Mas'ê Noṣerim be-Ereṣ Israel (Christian Travels in the Holy Land)*, (Jerusalem, 1965). Besides the general bibliographical guide to travel by E. G. Cox (*A Reference Guide to the Literature of Travel...*, 2 vols., Seattle, 1935–38), there are invaluable specialized bibliographies by Shirley Howard Weber (*Voyages and Travels in the Near East Made During the XIX Century*, Princeton, 1952, and *Voyages and Travels in Greece, the Near East and adjacent regions made previous to the year 1801*, Princeton, 1953); Berna Moran (*Türklerle ilgili Ingilizce yayınlar bibliografyası: xv yüzyıldan xviii yüzyıla kadar*, Istanbul, 1964); P. Thomsen, *Die Palästina-Literatur...*, 6 vols. (Leipzig–Berlin 1911–56), article "Reisen".

2 "A Prefatory Discourse to an Essay on the History of the Turks", in *The Works of Sir William Jones*, ii (London, 1807), pp. 456–7.

[3] Of these, it may be noted that Burkhardt, Lane and Burton were Arabic scholars, and both Niebuhr and Doughty had some competence in the language.

[4] Or rather pseudo-letters, copied by the authoress in two albums and possibly based on real letters sent to her friends. First published in 1763, without permission and from an imperfect manuscript, the Turkish letters were reprinted many times, the first critical edition appearing in 1861. These letters have now been published as part of a definitive scholarly edition, *The Complete Letters of Lady Mary Wortley Montagu, i, 1708–1720*, edited by Robert Halsband (Clarendon Press, Oxford, 1965).

[5] *Letters*, pp. 315–6.

[6] *Letters*, p. 368.

[7] *Letters*, pp. 396–7.

[8] *Letters*, p. 415.

[9] Translated into Turkish by the well-known historian Ahmed Refik (Istanbul, 1933). Other travel books translated into Turkish include those of Chateaubriand, Moltke, Vambéry, and the *Letters from Turkey* of the 18th-century Hungarian author Kelemen Mikes. Translations into Arabic and Persian are also rare. Burckhardt was translated into both languages, Vambéry into Persian; Lawrence's *Seven Pillars* was published in Arabic in 1947.

[10] *Records of Travels in Turkey, Greece, &c and of a Cruize in the Black Sea with the Capitan Pasha, in the years 1829, 1830, and 1831*, 2 vols. (London, 1832), second edition 1854; *Turkey, Greece, and Malta*, 2 vols. (London, 1837).

[11] *Turkey and the Crimean War* (London, 1867). The facts of Slade's career (he was born in 1804 and died in 1877) are briefly given in the *Dictionary of National Biography*, in O'Byrne's *Naval Biographical Dictionary*, and in an obituary notice in the *Times* of 15 November 1877.

[12] Nassau W. Senior, *Journal Kept in Turkey and Greece in the Autumn of 1857 and the Beginning of 1858* (London, 1859), p. 36.

[13] Slade, *Records*, i, p. 276; developed at some length in *Turkey, Greece....* See further Bernard Lewis, *The Emergence of Modern Turkey* (revised edition, London, 1968), pp. 125, 144.

[14] *Crimean War*, p. 20.

[15] *Crimean War*, pp. 31–2.

[16] *Records*, ii, p. 239.

[17] *Records*, ii, p. 242.

[18] *Crimean War*, pp. 30–1.

[19] *Crimean War*, p. 25.

[20] *Records*, i, p. 215.

[21] *Records*, i, p. 216.

[22] *Records*, i, p. 220.

[23] *Records*, i, p. 214.

[24] *Records*, i, pp. 214–5.

[25] *Records*, i, p. 218.

[26] *Records*, i, p. 230.

[27] *Records*, i, p. 234.

[28] *Records*, i, pp. 270–6.

29 Sir Charles Eliot, *Turkey in Europe* (London, 1965). A biographical memoir on Sir Charles Eliot, by Sir Harold Parlett, is prefixed to the posthumous edition of one of Eliot's major works of scholarship, his *Japanese Buddhism* (London, 1935).
30 *Turkey in Europe*, p. 56.
31 *Turkey in Europe*, p. 290.
32 *Turkey in Europe*, p. 90.
33 *Turkey in Europe*, p. 151.
34 *Turkey in Europe*, pp. 130–1.

Chapter 6. Sources for the Economic History of the Middle East

1 For discussions of archival and documentary sources for Islamic history, see *Jean Sauvaget's Introduction to the History of the Muslim East: A Bibliographical Guide, based on the second edition as recast by Claude Cahen* (Berkeley and Los Angeles, 1965), pp. 16–21; C. Cahen, "L'histoire économique et sociale de l'Orient musulman", *Studia Islamica*, iii (1965), pp. 93–115, especially 98 ff.; H. H. Roemer, "Über Urkunden zur Geschichte Ägyptens und Persiens in islamischer Zeit", *Zeitschrift der Deutschen Morgenländischen Gesellschaft*, cvii (1957), pp. 519–38; S. M. Stern, *Fāṭimid Decrees* (London, 1964), p. 1 ff.; H. Ernst, *Die mamlukischen Sultansurkunden des Sinai-klosters* (Wiesbaden, 1960, with detailed bibliography); Muḥammad Aḥmad Ḥusayn, *Al-Wathā'iq al-ta'rīkhiyya* (Cairo, 1954), p. 58 ff.; *Encyclopaedia of Islam*, 2nd edition, under "Diplomatic".
2 Brief accounts of the Ottoman archives, with bibliographical guidance, will be found in *Encyclopaedia of Islam*, 2nd edition, under "Başvekâlet Arşivi" (by B. Lewis) and "Daftar-i khāḳānī" (by Ö. L. Barkan); S. J. Shaw, "Archival Sources for Ottoman History: the Archives of Turkey", *Journal of the American Oriental Society*, lxxx (1960), pp. 1–12. Ottoman materials relating to Egypt and the Fertile Crescent are discussed in B. Lewis, "The Ottoman Archives as a Source for the History of the Arab Lands", *Journal of the Royal Asiatic Society*, 1951, pp. 139–55; S. J. Shaw, "Cairo's Archives and the History of Ottoman Egypt", *Report on Current Research, Spring 1956*, Middle East Institute (Washington, 1956), pp. 59–72; S. J. Shaw, "The Ottoman Archives as a Source for Egyptian History", *Journal of the American Oriental Society*, lxxxiii (1963), pp. 447–52.
3 B. Lewis, "Registers on Iran and Âdharbâyjân in the Ottoman *Defter-i Khâqânî*", in *Mélanges Henri Massé* (Tehran, 1963), pp. 259–63.
4 For a brief account in English see M. Yuldashev, "The State Archives of XIX Century Feudal Khiva", in *Papers Presented by the Soviet Delegation at the XXIII International Congress of Orientalists: Iranian, Armenian, and Central-Asian Studies* (Moscow, 1954), pp. 221–30, where other Russian publications are cited. See further H. H. Roemer, "Vorschläge für die Sammlung von Urkunden zur islamischen Geschichte Persiens", *Zeitschrift der Deutschen Morgenländischen Gesellschaft*, civ (1954), p. 364 ff. The archives of the Shaykhs of Jūybār, edited by P. P. Ivanov, *Iz arkhiva Šeykhov Džuybary* (Moscow–Leningrad, 1954), date from the sixteenth century.
5 The literature is reviewed by Roemer, "Über Urkunden . . .", Stern, and Ernst. More recent publications include a group of articles, in Arabic, on

documents in the St Catherine's Monastery in the *Bulletin of the Faculty of Arts*, University of Alexandria, xviii (1964).

6 For an example, see Ḥasanayn Muḥammad Rabī', "Ḥujjat tamlīk wa-waqf," in *Al-Majalla al-ta'rīkhiyya al-Miṣriyya*, xii (1964–5), pp. 191–202. See further Muḥammad Aḥmad Ḥusayn, *Al-Wathā'iq*, p. 97 ff.

7 On the Arabic papyri, see A. Grohmann, *Einführung und Chrestomathie zur arabischen Papyruskunde*, i (Prague, 1954); A. Grohmann, *Arabische Chronologie, Arabische Papyruskunde* (Leiden–Cologne, 1966), (*cf.* the review by Claude Cahen in *Arabica*, xv (1968), pp. 104–6), and, more briefly, Cahen–Sauvaget, pp. 16–18.

8 Cahen–Sauvaget, p. 17.

9 On the *Geniza*, see S. D. Goitein, "Geniza", in *Encyclopaedia of Islam*, 2nd edition, where further references are given, and his *A Mediterranean Society: the Jewish Communities of the Arab World as Portrayed in the Documents of the Cairo Geniza*, i: *Economic Foundations* (Berkeley and Los Angeles, 1967). A bibliography has been published by S. Shaked, *A Tentative Bibliography of Geniza Documents* (Paris–The Hague, 1964).

10 At 'Awjā' al-Ḥafīr, and in the neighbourhood of Damascus and Sāmarrā. See Grohmann, *Einführung*, pp. 28–30.

11 See S. D. Goitein, *Studies in Islamic History and Institutions* (Leiden, 1966), Part 3.

12 Grohmann, *Einführung*, p. 56.

13 Janine Sourdel-Thomine and D. Sourdel, "Nouveaux documents sur l'histoire religieuse et sociale de Damas au Moyen Age", *Revue des Etudes Islamiques*, xxxii (1964), pp. 1–25; Janine Sourdel-Thomine and D. Sourdel, "Trois actes de vente damascains du début du IVe/Xe siècle", *Journal of Economic and Social History of the Orient*, viii (1965), pp. 164–85.

14 V. Minorsky, "Some Early Documents in Persian", *Journal of the Royal Asiatic Society*, 1942, pp. 181–94.

15 See *Encyclopaedia of Islam*, 2nd edition, "Diplomatic iii" (by H. Busse), and the two articles by H. H. Roemer, cited in notes 1 and 4 above.

16 For a brief account, see Cahen–Sauvaget, pp. 52–7, and, on recent work, G. C. Miles, "Islamic Numismatics: A Progress Report", in *Congresso Internazionale di Numismatica: Roma 1961, Relazioni*, i, pp. 181–92.

17 See for example T. Lewicki, "Il commercio arabo con la Russia e con i paesi slavi d'Occidente nei secoli ix–xi", *Annali, Instituto Universitario Orientale di Napoli*, new series, viii (1959), pp. 47–61, and J. Duplessy, "La circulation des monnaies arabes en Europe occidentale du VIIIe au XIIIe siècle", in *Revue Numismatique*, 5th series, xviii (1956), pp. 101–63.

18 Lewicki, p. 48.

19 Cited in Cahen–Sauvaget, p. 52.

20 For examples of both kinds see M. Sharon, "A Waqf Inscription from Ramlah", *Arabica*, xiii (1966), pp. 77–84; J. Sauvaget, "Décrets mamelouks de Syrie, 3", *Bulletin d'Etudes Orientales*, xii (1947–8), pp. 1–56.

21 See, for example, G. C. Miles, "Early Islamic Glass Weights and Measures in Muntaza Palace, Alexandria", *Journal of the American Research Center in Egypt*, iii (1964), pp. 105–13; G. C. Miles, "Egyptian Glass Pharmaceutical Measures of the 8th Century A.D.", *Journal of the History of Medicine and Allied Sciences*, xv (1960), pp. 384–9; G. C. Miles, "Islamic Numismatics . . ." (cited in note 16 above), pp. 188–9.

22 Cahen–Sauvaget, p. 22.

23 Qur'ān, ii, 275 ff. *Cf.* iii, 125; iv, 159.

24 Qur'ān, ii, 194, 276 ff., 282 ff.; iv, 33; vi, 153; lxii, 9–11.

25 Abū 'Amr Muḥammad al-Kashshī, *Ma'rifat akhbār al-rijāl*, Bombay A.H. 1317, p. 249. For other similar stories see Goitein, *Studies*, pp. 224–5; *cf.* Max Weber, *The Sociology of Religion*, trans. E. Fischoff (London, 1965), p. 263.

26 The original text is lost, but the work survives in an abridgment, with refutation, by the author's pupil Ibn Samā'a (*d.* 847), entitled *Al-Iktisāb fī'l-rizq al-mustaṭāb* (Cairo, 1938). It is examined in Goitein, *Studies*, p. 220 ff.

27 An incomplete and somewhat garbled edition in *Iḥdā 'ashrata rasā'il* (Cairo, 1324/1906), pp. 155–61; partial translation of the edition in O. Rescher, *Excerpte und Übersetzungen aus den Schriften des . . . Ǵaḥiẓ* (Stuttgart, 1931), pp. 186–8. *Cf.* C. Pellat in *Arabica*, iii (1956), p. 177.

28 On this literature, see W. Björkman, "Kapitalentstehung und -anlage im Islam", *Mitteilungen des Seminars für orientalische Sprachen*, xxxii (1929), p. 81 ff.; Sir T. W. Arnold, "Arab Travellers and Merchants", in A. P. Newton, *Travel and Travellers of the Middle Ages* (London, 1926), p. 92 ff.; "Tidjāra" in *Encyclopaedia of Islam*, 1st edition (by W. Heffening); Goitein, *Studies*, p. 220 ff.; Ann K. S. Lambton, "The Merchant in Medieval Islam", in *A Locust's Leg: Studies in Honour of S. H. Taqizadeh* (London, 1962), pp. 121–30.

29 *Rasā'il Ikhwān al-Ṣafā*, i (Cairo, 1928), pp. 210–26; *cf.* B. Lewis, "An Epistle on Manual Crafts", *Islamic Culture*, xvii (1943), pp. 142–51. For an earlier consideration of the crafts see Jāḥiẓ, *Rasā'il*, ed. Ḥasan al-Sandūbī (Cairo, 1352/1933), pp. 126–7.

30 On Ghazzālī, see Arnold, pp. 93–4: Ann K. S. Lambton, "The Merchant . . .", p. 123 ff.

31 On al-Dimashqī see H. Ritter, "Ein arabisches Handbuch der Handelswissenschaft", *Der Islam*, vii (1917), pp. 1–91; C. Cahen, "A propos et autour d'ein arabisches Handbuch der Handelswissenschaft", *Oriens*, xv (1962), pp. 160–71. The text was published in Cairo in 1318 A.H.

32 Jāḥiẓ (attrib.), "*Al-Tabaṣṣur bi'l-tijāra*," ed. Ḥasan Ḥusnī 'Abd al-Wahhāb, *Revue de l'Académie Arabe de Damas*, xii (1932), reprinted Cairo 1354/1935; French translation by C. Pellat, "Gāḥiẓiana, I: le *Kitāb al-Tabaṣṣur bi'l-tigāra* attribué à Gāḥiẓ", *Arabica*, i (1954), pp. 153–65. The attribution to Jāḥiẓ is dubious.

33 Ibn Buṭlān, *Risāla fī shirā al-raqīq wa-taqlīb al-'abīd*, ed. 'Abd al-Salām Hārūn, in *Nawādir al-Makhṭūṭāt*, iv, no. 15 (Cairo, 1373/1954), pp. 333–89. An English translation was prepared by the late Professor D. S. Rice, but not published.

34 Al-Jawbarī, *Al-Mukhtār fī kashf al-asrār* (Cairo, A.H. 1353).

35 On this literature see "Filāḥa", in *Encyclopaedia of Islam*, 2nd edition (by various authors), where further references are given.

36 D. M. Dunlop, "Sources of Gold and Silver in Islam According to al-Hamdānī", *Studia Islamica*, viii (1957), pp. 29–49. See further the materials collected by Ḥamd al-Jāsir in the review *Al-'Arab* of Riyād, ii (1399/1968), p. 798 ff.

[37] A. S. Ehrenkreutz, "Extracts from the Technical Manual on the Ayyubid Mint in Cairo", *Bulletin of the School of Oriental and African Studies*, xv (1953), pp. 423–47. The Arabic text of Ibn Ba'ra's manual was published in Cairo in 1966.

[38] C. Cahen, "Le service de l'irrigation en Iraq au début du XIe siècle", *Bulletin d'Etudes Orientales*, xiii (1949–50), pp. 117–43; C. Cahen, "Documents relatifs à quelques techniques iraqiennes au début du onzième siècle", in *Ars Islamica*, xv–xvi (1951), pp. 23–8; C. Cahen, "Quelques problèmes économiques et fiscaux de l'Irâq Buyide d'après un traité de mathématiques", *Annales de l'Institut des Etudes Orientales*, x (1952), pp. 326–63.

[39] A notable example is Professor Schacht's studies on the use of *Ḥiyal*, legal devices to extend the sanction and protection of the law to transactions, such as lending on interest, which are strictly speaking outside it. See J. Schacht, *Introduction to Islamic Law* (Oxford, 1964), especially p. 76 ff.; Schacht, "Ḥiyal" in *Encyclopaedia of Islam*, 2nd edition. On the special brand of legal writing concerned with the supervision of the markets, see "Ḥisba" in *Encyclopaedia of Islam*, 2nd edition.

[40] For an introduction to Jewish Responsa, see S. B. Freehof, *The Responsa Literature* (Philadelphia, 1959); bibliography by Boaz Cohen, *Quntres ha-Teshubot* (Budapest, 1930).

[41] For an example, see C. Cahen, "Fiscalité, propriété, antagonismes sociaux en Haute-Mésopotamie au temps des premiers 'Abbasides, d'après Denys de Tell-Mahré", in *Arabica*, i (1954), pp. 136–52.

[42] On the biographical literature, see Sir Hamilton Gibb, "Islamic Biographical Literature", and Ann K. S. Lambton, "Persian Biographical Literature", in B. Lewis and P. M. Holt, eds., *Historians of the Middle East* (London, 1962), pp. 54–8 and 141–51.

[43] Al-Iṣfahānī, *Kitāb al-Aghānī*, Būlāq, xix, p. 18; third edition, iii, p. 45. *Cf.* Ibn 'Abd Rabbihi, *Al-'Iqd al-farīd* (Cairo, 1305 A.H.); iii, p. 181 (Cairo, 1372/1953), vii, pp. 13–14; English translation by H. G. Farmer, *Music, the Priceless Jewel* (Bearsden, 1942), p. 24.

Chapter 7. The Muslim Discovery of Europe

[1] This paper contains the modified text of a communication read to the International Congress of Historical Sciences in Rome, September 1955.

[2] Ṣā'id al-Andalusī, *Kitāb Ṭabaqāt al-Umam*, Part I. The Arabic text was edited by Father L. Cheikho in *Mashriq* in 1911. A French translation by R. Blachère appeared in Paris in 1935.

[3] This adaptation formed the subject of an important study by C. A. Nallino, "Al-Khuwārizmi e il suo rifacimento della Geografia di Tolomeo", *Memorie della Reggia Accademia dei Lincei, Classe di Scienze morali, storiche e filologiche*, series v, vol. ii, part 1a. Reprinted in C. A. Nallino, *Raccolta di scritti editi e inediti*, v (Rome, 1944), pp. 458–532.

[4] M. J. de Goeje (ed.), *Bibliotheca Geographorum Arabicorum*, Leiden, vi (1889), p. 155.

[5] *Ibid.*, vii (1892), p. 85.

[6] *Murūj al-dhahab, Les prairies d'or*, iii (Paris, 1861 ff.), pp. 66–7, 69–72.

[7] G. Levi Della Vida, "La traduzione araba delle storie di Orosio", *Al-Andalus*, xix (1954), pp. 257–93.

[8] E. Lévi-Provençal, "Un échange d'ambassades entre Cordoue et Byzance au IXe siècle", *Byzantion*, xii (1937), pp. 15–16 =*Islam d'Occident* (Paris, 1948), pp. 95–8.

[9] *Cf.* Majīd Khaddūrī, *Al-ṣilāt al-diblūmātīqīya bayna Hārūn al-Rashīd wa Shārlamān* (Baghdad, 1939).

[10] M. Hamidullah, "Embassy of Queen Bertha to Caliph al-Muktafi billah in Baghdad 293/906", *Journal of the Pakistan Historical Society*, i (1953), pp. 272–300; G. Levi Della Vida, "La corrispondenza di Berta di Toscana col Califfo Muktafi", *Rivista Storica Italiana*, lxvi (1954), pp. 21–38.

[11] *Bibliotheca Geographorum Arabicorum*, vii (1892), pp. 127–30. This passage was discussed and translated by J. Marquart, *Osteuropäische und ostasiatische Streifzüge* (Leipzig, 1903), p. 260 ff.

[12] Yāqūt, *Mu'jam al-buldān*, article *Rūmiya*. Yāqūt's text was studied and translated by Ignazio Guidi, "La descrizione di Roma nei geografi arabi", *Archivio della Società romana di Storia patria*, i (1877), pp. 173–218.

[13] T. Kowalski, *Relacja Ibrahima b. Ja'ḳuba z podróży do krajow slowiańskich w prekazie al-Bekriego* (Cracow, 1946). My thanks are due to my colleague Mr. B. W. Andrzejewski, who very generously translated several chapters of this book for me.

[14] *Cf.* R. W. Southern, *The Making of the Middle Ages* (London, 1953), p. 36 ff.

[15] For an example of Idrīsī's geography see A. F. L. Beeston, "Idrisi's Account of the British Isles", *Bulletin of the School of Oriental and African Studies*, vol. xiii, no. 2 (1950), pp. 265–80.

[16] K. Jahn, "Les légendes de l'Occident chez Raşīd al-Din", *Mélanges Fuad Köprülü* (Istanbul, 1953), pp. 255–7; K. Jahn, *Histoire universelle de Raşīd al-Din. . . . I. Histoire des Francs* (Leiden, 1951).

[17] *Muqaddima* (ed. Quatremère), iii, p. 93 (translation, De Slane, iii, p. 129).

[18] G. S. Colin, "Un petit glossaire hispanique arabo-allemand du début du XVIe siècle", *Al-Andalus*, xi (1946), pp. 275–81.

Chapter 8. The Use by Muslim Historians of Non-Muslim Sources

[1] "*Accessit praeterea domini Almarici regis (cujus anima sancta requie perfruatur) illustris memoriae, et inclyptae in Domino recordationis jussio, non facile negligenda, et instantia multiplex, quae ad id ipsum nos maxime impulit, cujus etiam rogatu, ipso Arabica exemplaria ministrante, aliam Historiam a tempore seductoris Mahumeth, usque in hunc annum, qui est nobis ab Incarnatione Domini 1184, per annos quingentos septuaginta decurrentem conscripsimus: auctorem maxime secutivirum venerabilem Seith, filium Patricii, Alexandrinum patriarcham.*" William of Tyre, Prologue.

[2] *Cf.* A. Momigliano, "The Place of Herodotus in the History of Historiography", *History*, xliii (1958), pp. 1–13, for an illuminating discussion of these questions.

[3] It is noteworthy that the first efforts to develop Sanskrit and Chinese studies in the Middle East were made in Ankara and Jerusalem.

[4] "The Arabic Historiography of the Crusades", in Bernard Lewis and P. M. Holt (eds.), *Historians of the Middle East* (London, 1962), p. 98 ff.

[5] A possible exception is the account *(sīra)* "of the European Christians who in those years had come to the Muslim countries", mentioned by Ibn Muyassar (p. 70) and cited by F. Rosenthal, *A History of Muslim Historiography*, 2nd ed. (Leiden, 1968), p. 62. It is however symptomatic of the general lack of interest that this work has not survived even in quotation. See further above, p. 92 ff.

[6] "The Influence of Biblical Tradition on Muslim Historiography", in Lewis and Holt, *Historians*, pp. 35–45.

[7] The Persian sagas of the mythical emperors of ancient Iran, and the Egyptian legends woven around the broken, massive remnants of the Pharaohs, throw into relief the lack of real historical knowledge about the pre-Islamic past.

[8] *Murūj*, iii, pp. 66–7, 69–72. *Cf.* the new French translation by C. Pellat, *Les Prairies d'or*, ii (Paris, 1965), pp. 344–5. See also B. Lewis, "Mas'ūdī on the Kings of the 'Franks'," *Al-Mas'ūdī Millenary Commemoration Volume* (Aligarh, 1960), pp. 7–10.

[9] Ibn Khaldūn does indeed discuss the Mongols at some length, but this is preliminary to an account of their invasion of the lands of Islam. *Cf.* W. J. Fischel, "Ibn Khaldūn's Sources for the History of Jenghiz Khān and the Tatars", *Journal of the American Oriental Society*, lxxvi (1956), pp. 91–9.

[10] *Cf.* G. Levi Della Vida, "La Traduzione araba delle storie di Orosio" *Al-Andalus*, xix (1954), pp. 257–93; W. J. Fischel, "Ibn Khaldūn and Josippon", *Homenaje a Millas-Vallicrosa*, i (Barcelona, 1954), pp. 587–98; W. J. Fischel, "Ibn Khaldūn: on the Bible, Judaism and the Jews", *Ignace Goldziher Memorial Volume II* (Jerusalem, 1956), pp. 147–71.

[11] K. Jahn, "Les légendes de l'Occident chez Raşīd al-Din", *Mélanges Fuad Köprülü* (Istanbul, 1953), pp. 255–7; K. Jahn, *Histoire universelle de Raşid al-Din. . . . I. Histoire des Francs* (Leiden, 1951).

[12] *Cf.* F. Babinger, *Geschichtsschreiber der Osmanen. . . .* (Leipzig, 1927), p. 107.

[13] The *Tā'rīkh al-Hind al-Gharbī*, written *c.* 1580 for Murād III, and printed at the Müteferriqa press in 1142/1729. The same interest is reflected in other Turkish writings, notably in the geographical section of 'Ālī's *Künh al-akhbār*.

[14] Babinger, p. 170.

[15] *Encyclopaedia of Islam*, 1st edition, under Ḥādjdjī Khalīfa, followed by Babinger, p. 200. There is some confusion here with another work by Ḥājjī Khalīfa—a history of Constantinople, based on the *Historia rerum in Oriente gestarum. . . .* (Frankfort, 1587), which included translations from Chalcocondyles and other Byzantine historians. See V. L. Ménage, "Kātib Čelebiana", *Bulletin of the School of Oriental and African Studies*, xxvi (1963), pp. 173–4.

[16] Adnan Adivar, *La Science chez les Turcs Ottomans* (Paris, 1939), p. 118, repeated with some modification in Adivar, *Osmanlı Türklerinde ilim* (Istanbul, 1943), p. 129; Orhan Şaik Gökyay, in *Kâtib Çelebi, hayati ve eserleri hakkında incelemeler* (Ankara, 1957), pp. 54–6; V. L. Ménage, "Three Ottoman Treatises on Europe", in C. E. Bosworth, ed., *Iran*

and Islam, in memory of the late Vladimir Minorsky (Edinburgh, 1971), p. 430, n. 13.

17 Ménage, pp. 421–3.

18 *Tārīkh-i Pechevī*, i, p. 106.

19 "Okuttuk ve ničesin türkīye terjüme ettik." The implication would seem to be that Pechevi had the chronicles read to him and then himself turned some of these into written Turkish prose—a procedure reminiscent of the Toledo school of translators. I owe this observation to Professor P. Wittek.

20 F. v. Kraelitz, "Der Osmanische Historiker Ibrâhîm Pečewi", *Der Islam*, viii (1918), pp. 252–60.

21 The MSS. are listed in Babinger, *Geschichtsschreiber*, pp. 229–30. I was able to consult one belonging to the Hunterian Museum in Glasgow (*cf. Journal of the Royal Asiatic Society*, 1906, pp. 602 ff.). It was made at the French Embassy in Constantinople, according to the colophon by "Frānsīs al-Shahīr bi'l-Ṣalībī", presumably an Arabicized form of François Pétis de la Croix, the French dragoman to whom the manuscript originally belonged. On Hezārfen's dealings with Europeans, see Heidrun Wurm, *Der osmanische Historiker Ḥüseyn b. Ġaʻfer, genannt Hezarfenn, und die Istanbuler Gesellschaft in der zweiten Hälfte der 17 Jahrhunderts* (Freiburg in Breisgau, 1971), especially pp. 122–49.

22 On Münejjimbashi see Babinger, pp. 234–5, Brockelmann, *Geschichte der arabischen Litteratur*, ii, p. 443, and Supplement ii, 637; A. Dietrich, "A propos d'un précis d'histoire gréco-romaine dans la chronique universelle arabe de Müneccimbaşī," in *Correspondance d'Orient*, xi, *Ve Congrès international d'arabisants et d'islamisants . . . Actes* (Brussels, 1971), pp. 172–88. The Turkish version, entitled *Ṣaḥā'if al-akhbār*, was published in 3 volumes, in Istanbul in 1285/1868–9. References are to the Turkish edition.

23 Faik Reşit Unat, "Ahmet III devrinde bir Islahat Takriri", *Tarih vesikaları*, i (1941), p. 107.

24 Cited by Selim Nüzhet Gerçek, *Türk Matbaacılığı*, i (Istanbul, 1939), p. 44.

25 Ménage, "Three Ottoman Treatises. . . .", pp. 423–9.

26 For descriptions of these works see *Istanbul Kütüphaneleri tarih-coğrafya yazmaları katalogları. 1. Türkçe tarih yazmaları*, fascicule 1, *Umumi tarihler* (Istanbul, 1943), and fascicule 3, *Arab tarihi, Iran tarihi, Diğer milletler tarihleri* (Istanbul, 1945). On 'Os̱mān b. Aḥmed see R. F. Kreutel and Otto Spies, *Leben und Abenteuer des Dolmetschers Osman Aga* (Bonn, 1954) especially p. xxv. A topographic description of Istanbul, in Italian, by "Cosimo Comidas di Carbognano, Constantinopolitano", was published in Bassano, Italy, in 1794. My thanks are due to Professor Adnan Erzi for drawing my attention to this. Cosmo di Carbognano, who served as interpreter to the Spanish Embassy in Istanbul, was the grandson of a famous Armenian Catholic martyr; see A. Ubicini, *Lettres*, ii (Paris, 1854), p. 257.

27 On the productions of the Būlāq press see A. Perron, "Lettre à M. Mohl sur les écoles et l'imprimerie du pacha d'Egypte", *Journal Asiatique*, 4th series, ii (1843), p. 5–23; J. H. Dunne, "Printing and Translation under Muḥammad 'Ali", *Journal of the Royal Asiatic Society* (1940), pp. 325–49. The most recent and most detailed study is that of the late Professor

Jamāl al-Dīn al-Shayyāl, *Ta'rīkh al-tarjama wa'l-ḥaraka al-thaqāfiyya fī 'aṣr Muḥammad 'Alī* (Cairo, 1951), with full lists of publications.

[28] E. Kuran, "Ottoman Historiography of the Tanzimat Period", in Lewis and Holt, *Historians*, p. 422 ff.

Chapter 9. The Cult of Spain and the Turkish Romantics

[1] Henri Pérès, *L'Espagne vue par les voyageurs musulmans de 1610 à 1930* (Paris, 1937), p. 52 ff.

[2] Pérès, p. 55 ff.

[3] Pérès, p. 53.

[4] On Munīf Pasha see Ahmet Hamdi Tanpinar, *XIX Asir Türk Edebiyati Tarihi*, 2nd edition, i (Istanbul, 1956), p. 150 ff. For a contemporary impression [A. D. Mordtmann], *Stambul und das moderne Türkenthum*, i (Leipzig, 1877), p. 173 ff.

[5] Osman Ergin, *Türkiye Marrif Tarihi*, iii (Istanbul, 1941), p. 802 (*cf.* p. 778). According to Ergin, despite his contributions to educational development he left a bad impression in Istanbul.

[6] On Ziya Pasha see E. J. W. Gibb, *A History of Ottoman Poetry*, v (London, 1907), pp. 41–111; Tanpinar, *op. cit.*, pp. 279–321; Alessio Bombaci, *Storia della letteratura turca*, 2nd edition (Milan, 1969), pp. 420–3; Bernard Lewis, *The Emergence of Modern Turkey*, 2nd edition (London, 1968), p. 138 ff.

[7] Gibb, p. 58.

[8] *Encyclopaedia of Islam* (2nd edition), under "'Abd al-Ḥaḳḳ Ḥāmid" (by A. Hamdi Tanpinar); Bombaci, pp. 430–6.

[9] These derive in the main from the writings of the Young Ottomans.

[10] For appreciations of *Ṭāriq* see Tanpinar, pp. 576–7; *cf. Islam Ansiklopedisi*, i, p. 70 (by Sabri Esat Siyavuşgil).

[11] *Ibn-i Mūsā* was not published until 1917.

[12] *Encyclopaedia of Islam*, 1st edition, article by Theodor Menzel.

[13] Siyavuşgil, *loc. cit.*

Chapter 10. The Pro-Islamic Jews

[1] T. P. O'Connor, *Lord Beaconsfield, A Biography* (1879), 8th ed. (London, 1905), pp. 607–10, 654.

[2] E. A. Freeman, *Ottoman Power in Europe: Its Nature, Its Growth, and Its Decline* (London, 1877), pp. xviii–xx.

[3] W. F. Monypenny and G. E. Buckle, *The Life of Benjamin Disraeli, Earl of Beaconsfield*, 1st ed. (London, 1910–1920), revised ed. (London, 1929), ii, p. 930.

[4] Sir James Headlam-Morley, *Studies in Diplomatic History* (London, 1930), p. 206. *Cf.* R. W. Seton-Watson, *Disraeli, Gladstone and the Eastern Question* (London, 1935), p. 3; E. Kedourie, *England and the Middle East: The Destruction of the Ottoman Empire 1914–1921* (London, 1956), pp. 82–4; R. Blake, *Disraeli* (London, 1966), pp. 60, 204, 600 ff. An amusing variant occurs in a letter written by Wilfrid Scawen Blunt to Wilfred Meynell in 1903: "His Semitic politics of course were genuine enough. For his fearlessness in avowing these I hold him in esteem—for a Jew ought to be a

Jew—and I enjoy, as a tour de force, his smashing of those solemn rogues the Whigs, and his bamboozling of the Tories. Our dull English nation deserved what it got, and there is nothing funnier in history than the way in which he cajoled our square-toed aristocratic Party to put off its respectable broad-cloth, and robe itself in his suit of Imperial spangles, and our fine ladies after his death to worship their old world-weary Hebrew beguiler under the innocent form of a primrose." W. S. Blunt, *My Diaries, Being a Personal Narrative of Events, 1888–1914*, ii, *1900–1914* (London, 1920), pp. 74–5.

5 Blake, *Disraeli*, p. 59.

6 *Tancred*, book iv, ch. vii; *cf.* ch. iii.

7 Monypenny and Buckle, ii, pp. 930–1.

8 *Contarini Fleming*, part iv, ch. xix; Monypenny and Buckle, i, pp. 170–1.

9 On the place of these scholars in the development of Arabic studies in Europe, see Johann Fück, *Die arabischen Studien in Europa bis den Anfang des 20. Jahrhunderts* (Leipzig, 1955), and, for Russia, Ignatii Yulyanovič Kračkovsky, *Izbranniye Sočineniya*, v (Moscow-Leningrad, 1958). On Gustav Weil, see Gustave Dugat, *Histoire des orientalistes de l'Europe du XIIe siècle au XIXe siècle*, i (Paris, 1868), pp. 42–8, and D. M. Dunlop, "Some Remarks on Weil's History of the Caliphs," in Bernard Lewis and P. M. Holt, eds., *Historians of the Middle East* (London, 1962), pp. 315–29. Biographies and appreciations of the work of individual scholars will be found in the obituary notices published in specialist journals. These are listed, together with articles on the history of Islamic studies, in J. D. Pearson, *Index Islamicus 1906–1955* (Cambridge, 1958), p. 1 ff., and supplements. Some are the subjects of articles in the *Jewish Encyclopaedia* and other works of reference. For critical assessments of the treatment of Islam by Western Orientalists, see Jean-Jacques Waardenburg, *L'Islam dans le miroir de l'occident* (Paris–The Hague, 1963), including a detailed consideration of Goldziher; Albert Hourani, "Islam and the Philosophers of History," in *Middle Eastern Studies*, iii (1967), pp. 206–67; Khurshid Ahmed, *Islam and the West* (Karachi, no date, ? 1958); A. L. Tibawi, "English-Speaking Orientalists," in *The Muslim World* (1963), pp. 185–204 and 298–313. For Western attitudes to Islam in general see Norman Daniel, *Islam, Europe and Empire* (Edinburgh, 1966).

10 On Davids see James Picciotto, *Sketches of Anglo-Jewish History* (London, 1875), pp. 316–8; Harold Bowen, *British Contributions to Turkish Studies* (London, 1945), pp. 43–4; A. Galante, *Recueil de nouveaux documents inédits concernant l'histoire des juifs de Turquie* (Istanbul, 1949), pp. 71–3; Şerif Mardin, *The Genesis of Young Ottoman Thought: A Study in the Modernization of Turkish Political Ideas* (Princeton, N.J., 1962), p. 250; and, in Turkish, Akçuraoğlu Yusuf, "Türkçülük," in *Türk Yîlî*, i (1928), pp. 310–1, and Ahmet Hamdi Tanpınar, *XIX asır Türk edebiyatı tarihi* (Istanbul, 1949), revised ed. (Istanbul, 1956), pp. 220–2.

11 On Cahun see *Jewish Encyclopaedia*, article by Zadoc Kahn; Mardin, p. 61; Akçura, p. 359; C. W. Hostler, *Turkism and the Soviets* (London, 1957), p. 141.

12 The best sources of information on Vambéry are his own autobiographical writings: *Arminius Vambéry, His Life and Adventures Written by Himself* (London, 1884), and *The Story of My Struggles* (London, n.d.). There are

short articles on him in the *Encyclopaedia of the Social Sciences* and in a number of general encyclopedias. For a Turkish appreciation, see Akçuraoğlu Yusuf, *loc. cit.*, pp. 313–5. On the influence of Davids, Cahun and Vambéry on the growth of Turkish nationalism see Bernard Lewis, "History-Writing and National Revival in Turkey," in *Middle Eastern Affairs*, iv (1953), pp. 221–2; Lewis, *The Emergence of Modern Turkey*, 2nd ed. (London, 1968), pp. 346–8; Niyazi Berkes, *The Development of Secularism in Turkey* (Montreal, 1964), pp. 314–5.

13 Arthur Lumley Davids, *Grammaire turke* (London, 1836), p. ix; L. Cahun, *Scènes de la vie juive en Alsace* (Paris, 1885).

14 For a rather interesting exception, see *The Memoirs of Ismail Kemal Bey*, edited by Sommerville Story (London, 1920), pp. 71–2. In general, however, even the contribution made by Jewish subjects of Muslim states attracted very little attention. Thus, the Jewish participation in the Young Turk movement, which aroused so much hostile comment in the West, is barely mentioned in Turkish sources. See Lewis, *Emergence*, pp. 212–3.

15 *Coningsby*, book iv, ch. x.

16 On the parallel cult of Spanish Islam among 19th-century Muslims see Aziz Ahmad, "Islam d'Espagne et Inde musulmane moderne", in *Etudes d'orientalisme dédiées à la mémoire de Lévi-Provençal*, i (Paris, 1962), ii, pp. 461–70, and above, p. 115 ff.

17 A. Vambéry, *The Story of My Struggles*, p. 395.

18 During the last twenty years a vast anti-Jewish—not merely anti-Zionist or anti-Israeli—literature has appeared in the Arab countries, in which racial, theological and demonological themes, as well as political arguments, are used. It is significant that the ideas, the documentation, and often even the actual texts are overwhelmingly of Christian European origin. In the bookshops of the Arab Socialist states, Marx on the Jewish question is flanked by Hitler's *Mein Kampf*, the *Protocols of the Elders of Zion*, Henry Ford's *International Jew*, and a variety of local adaptations and imitations. Even the anti-Jewish cartoons that are common in the Arabic press reflect European anti-Semitic stereotypes, mostly German and Russian, and do not derive from any local tradition.

19 There are important direct Islamic influences on Jewish worship. See N. Wieder, "*Hashpa'ot Islamiyyot 'al ha-pulhan ha-yehudi*" (Hebrew), in *Melīla*, ii (1946), pp. 37–120. The self-conscious "Orientalism" of emancipated European Jews can also be seen in the pseudo-Moorish motifs that sometimes occur in modern synagogue architecture.

20 Cited by L. Massignon in B. Heller, *Bibliographie des oeuvres de Ignace Goldziher* (Paris, 1927), p. xvi, note i (*cf.* p. viii, note i).

Chapter 11. Semites and Anti-Semites

1 This article is based on a paper which was delivered to the Institute of Race Relations on 3 February 1971.

2 See S. W. Baron, *A Social and Religious History of the Jews*, 2nd ed., xiii (New York, 1969), p. 84 ff.; L. Poliakov, *Histoire de l'antisémitisme* (Paris, 1955–). The anti-semitism of the right is well known; that of the left is often overlooked. See A. Hertzberg, *The French Enlightenment and the Jews* (New York, 1968); E. Silberner, "The Anti-Semitic Tradition in Modern

Socialism", in *Scripta Hierosolymitana*, iii (1956), pp. 378–96; Silberner, *Sozialisten zur Judenfrage* (Berlin, 1962).

3 For a comprehensive study, see L. Hirszowicz, *The Third Reich and the Arab East* (London, 1966; original Polish edition, Warsaw, 1963). See further E. Rossi, *Documenti sull'origine e gli sviluppi della questione araba (1875–1944)* (Rome, 1944); E. Be'eri, *Army Officers in Arab Politics and Society* (Jerusalem, 1969; original Hebrew edition, Tel Aviv, 1966), p. 28 ff., 41–9. For personal testimony see Anwar el Sadat, *Revolt on the Nile* (London, 1957), p. 34 ff.; J. W. Eppler, *Rommel ruft Kairo* (Bielefeld, 1959); A. W. Sansom, *I Spied Spies* (London, 1965); F. Grobba, *Männer und Mächte im Orient* (Göttingen, 1967).

4 On blood-libels see J. Landau, *Jews in Nineteenth Century Egypt* (New York, 1969), index; M. Franco, *Essai sur l'histoire des Israélites de l'Empire ottoman depuis les origines jusqu'à nos jours* (Paris, 1897), pp. 220–33; A. Galante, *Histoire des Juifs d'Anatolie, Les Juifs d'Izmir (Smyrne)* (Istanbul, 1937), pp. 183–99; Galante, *Documents officiels turcs concernant les Juifs de Turquie* (Istanbul, 1931), pp. 157–61, 214–40; Galante, *Encore un nouveau recueil de documents concernant l'histoire des Juifs de Turquie: Etudes scientifiques* (Istanbul, 1953), pp. 43–5.

5 On the position of the non-Muslim in the Muslim state, see *Encyclopaedia of Islam*, 2nd ed., article "Dhimma", where further literature is cited. For a recent study of Islamic attitudes see Rudi Paret, "Toleranz und Intoleranz im Islam", in *Saeculum*, xxi (1970), pp. 344–65.

6 The most detailed examination of Arabic anti-Semitic literature is contained in Y. Harkabi, *Arab Attitudes to Israel* (Jerusalem, 1971; original Hebrew edition, Tel Aviv, 1968). See also Sylvia G. Haim, "Arabic Anti-Semitic Literature", in *Jewish Social Studies*, vol. xvii no. 4 (1955), pp. 307–12; Dafna Alon, *Arab Racialism* (Jerusalem, 1969). A good specimen of this literature is 'Abdallah al-Tell's 400-page book *The Menace of World Jewry to Islam and Christendom*, published in Cairo in 1964. A very laudatory review, by Muḥammad 'Abdallah al-Sammān, appeared in the distinguished Egyptian literary magazine, *Al-Risāla*, 7 January 1965, pp. 54–6. Connoisseurs of anti-Jewish invective will also appreciate a poem by Ṣāliḥ Jawdat, which appeared in the special commemoration issue of the Egyptian magazine *al-Hilāl*, published in November 1970, after Nasser's death. Little is available in Western languages, though some idea of the flavor of this literature may be obtained from a collection of papers presented to a conference at al-Azhar by an impressive group of Egyptian and other professors, politicians, and divines—Al-Azhar Academy of Islamic Research, *The Fourth Conference of the Academy of Islamic Research, Rajab 1388/September 1968* (Cairo, Government Printing Offices, 1970). Such publications are not limited to the Arab countries, but may also be found in other Islamic lands. See for example a Pakistani publication in English—*Jewish Conspiracy and the Muslim World*, ed. Misbahul Islam Faruqi (Karachi, February 1967). The subject is treated from time to time in *Patterns of Prejudice* and in *The Wiener Library Bulletin*, both published in London.

7 For a brief account of these events, see S. Landshut, *Jewish Communities in the Muslim Countries of the Middle East* (London, 1950). On the Baghdad massacre, see H. J. Cohen, "The Anti-Jewish *Farhud* in Baghdad, 1941",

in *Middle Eastern Studies*, iii (1966), pp. 2–17, and E. Kedourie, *The Chatham House Version* (London, 1970), p. 306 ff. These events are glossed over or omitted in most histories of modern Iraq and of the other countries concerned.

8 In June 1940 and again in February 1941 a high-level inter-Arab committee sent emissaries to make approaches to the Axis. The declaration for which they asked included the following clause: "Germany and Italy recognize the right of the Arab countries to solve the question of the Jewish elements which exist in Palestine and in the other Arab countries, as required by the national and ethnic *(völkisch)* interests of the Arabs, and as the Jewish question was solved in Germany and Italy." Fritz Grobba, *Männer und Mächte im Orient* (Göttingen, 1967), pp. 194–7, 207–8. It will be noted that this draft was an Arab request to the Germans, not a German offer to the Arabs.

9 The point was vividly made by President Sadat in his speech on the Prophet's birthday, delivered in Cairo on 25 April 1972: "We shall not only liberate our country but also crush this Israeli overweeningness and this disorderly outbreak *('arbada)*, so that they go back to be once again as our Book told us: 'Humiliation is destined for them, and poverty'." The reference is presumably to Qur'ān, iii, 108, though the quotation is not quite accurate. For discussions of this aspect of the problem, see G. C. Alroy, "Two Decades of Arab-Jewish war", in *Jewish Social Studies*, xxxii (1970), pp. 52–3; Bernard Lewis, *The Middle East and the West* (London and Bloomington, Ind., 1964), pp. 125–6. There are many descriptions of the traditional relationship, of which one, from a recently published document, may suffice. It comes from a report by H. E. Wilkie Young, the British Vice-Consul in Mosul, written in January 1909: "The attitude of the Moslems towards the Christians and Jews, to whom as stated above, they are in a majority of ten to one, is that of a master towards slaves whom he treats with a certain lordly tolerance so long as they keep their place. Any sign of pretension to equality is promptly repressed. It is often noticed in the street that almost any Christian submissively makes way even for a Moslem child. Only a few days ago the writer saw two respectable-looking, middle-aged Jews walking in a garden. A small Moslem boy, who could not have been more than eight years old, passed by and, as he did so, picked up a large stone and threw it at them—and then another—with the utmost nonchalance, just as a small boy elsewhere might aim at a dog or bird. The Jews stopped and avoided the aim, which was a good one, but made no further protest." *Middle Eastern Studies*, vii (1971), p. 232.

10 The whole question is discussed in E. Rosenberg, *From Shylock to Svengali: Jewish Stereotypes in English Fiction* (London, 1961). The curious reader may note that some of the more striking phrases found in the English editions of Miss Christie's detective stories have for some reason been omitted from the American editions.

11 See for example reports of proceedings at the Central Criminal Court against Colin Jordan and John Tyndall, then respectively leader and deputy leader of the British National Socialist movement, in early October 1962; *cf.* an interview with Tyndall in the *Sunday Telegraph* of 10 March 1963. For a more recent example see the report in the *Daily*

Telegraph of 13 January 1970 on the trial of T. O. Williams.

A recent writer, very sympathetic to the Palestine guerrilla movement, describes a visit to a Fatah training camp, and notes the literature in use: "There are political books available: Castro, Guevara, Mao Tse-tung, Giap, Rodinson; General de Gaulle's memoirs; and also *Mein Kampf*. When I expressed surprise at the presence of this last volume, the political commissar replied that it was necessary to have read everything, and that since the Israelis behaved like Nazis it was useful to know precisely what Nazism was." Gérard Chaliand, *The Palestine Resistance* (London, 1972), p. 10. M. Chaliand does not comment on this reply; neither shall I.

12 See for example the article by R. Massigli, published in *Le Monde*, 27 February 1970, and the comments of Romain Gary (1 and 2 March), I. Lacouture (23 March), and I. Kaplan (25 March). See further Raymond Aron, *De Gaulle, Israel and the Jews* (London, 1969; French original, Paris, 1968), and Renee Weingarten, "Jews in the Mind of France", in *Commentary*, November 1970, pp. 64–8.

13 For a striking example see Elie Kedourie, "Sir Mark Sykes and Palestine 1915–16", in *Middle Eastern Studies*, vi (1970), pp. 340–5.

14 On Jewish self-hate, see Isaiah Berlin, "Benjamin Disraeli, Karl Marx, and the Search for Identity", in *Transactions of the Jewish Historical Society of England*, xxii (1970), pp. 1–20, especially p. 17 ff.; and earlier studies by T. Lessing, *Jüdischer Selbsthass* (Berlin, 1930), and D. Abrahamsen, *The Mind and Death of a Genius* (New York, 1946).

15 For an example of how such concerns influenced British policy towards Turkey on the eve of the First World War, see E. Kedourie, "Young Turks, Freemasons and Jews", in *Middle Eastern Studies*, vii (1971), pp. 89–104.

Chapter 12. An Ode Against the Jews

1 R. Dozy, *Recherches sur l'histoire et la littérature de l'Espagne pendant le moyen âge*, 3rd ed., i (Paris-Leiden, 1881), pp. 282–94 and lxi–lxviii; E. García Gómez, *Un alfaquí español: Abū Isḥāq de Elvira* (Madrid-Granada, 1944); García Gómez, "Abū Isḥāḳ al-Ilbīrī" in *Encyclopaedia of Islam*, 2nd ed.

2 Dozy, pp. 286 and lxii; García Gómez, xix, p. 125.

3 Dozy, *Recherches*. The French translation is reproduced in Dozy's *Histoire des musulmans d'Espagne*, revised ed., iii (Leiden, 1932), pp. 71–2.

4 *Geschichte der Juden*, vi, pp. 48–53. The poem and episode are discussed in S. W. Baron, *A Social and Religious History of the Jews*, iii, p. 158; v, p. 93; E. Ashtor, *Qōrōt ha-Yehūdīm bi-Sĕfarad ha-Moslemīt*, ii (Jerusalem, 1966), pp. 115–7, and also by H. Pérès, *La poésie andalouse en arabe classique au XIe siècle*, 2nd ed. (Paris, 1953), pp. 272–3.

5 Ed. E. Lévi-Provençal (Rabat, 1934), pp. 265–7.

6 García Gómez, *Un alfaquí español*, see note 1 above. The *qaṣīda* is no. xxv, pp. 149–53. The introduction is reproduced in E. García Gómez, *Cinco poetas musulmanes* (Madrid, 1944), pp. 95–138.

7 Nykl, *Selections from Hispano-Arabic Poetry* (Beirut, 1949), pp. 141–3; Nykl, *Hispano-Arabic Poetry* (Baltimore, 1946), pp. 197–200.

8 M. Perlmann, "Eleventh-century Andalusian Authors on the Jews of Granada", in *Proceedings of the American Academy for Jewish Research*, xviii (1949), pp. 284–90.

[9] The poet is appealing to the Ṣanhāja, the dominant Berber tribe in the Zirid monarchy.

[10] From Dozy's text; this line is missing in the *Dīwān.*

[11] From Dozy's text. The *Dīwān* has a slightly different text for this line, meaning "And destruction approaches, and they do not know".

[12] Thus *Dīwān:—fāḍil qānit.* Dozy reads *rāghib rāhib*, which might be translated: "[How many a Muslim] torn between fear and desire."

[13] A standard insult. In the vocabulary of abuse, Jews are apes and Christians are pigs—though sometimes the latter term is also extended to Jews. The association with apes may be based on the Qur'ān (ii, 61; v, 65; vii, 166). See Pérès, *La poésie andalouse*, pp. 240–1; Perlmann, "Eleventh-century Andalusian Authors. . . .", pp. 287–8. The conventional association of certain animals with certain beliefs, in formalized abuse, still survives in part of Europe.

[14] The poet may here be alluding to the ruler, Bādīs, or, more probably, to some Muslim ally of the Jewish minister—possibly the colleague condemned in the poem cited above.

[15] *Dīwān*: *akhrāj.* Perlmann translates "tatters"; Dozy reads *afwāj* and translates "*par troupes*".

[16] *Mulawwana.* Perlmann suggests amending this to *mulawwatha,* filthy (pp. 286, n. 52). This line is missing in both Dozy's text and the *A'māl.*

[17] *Dīwān*: *wākabūhum,* in preference to Dozy's *rākabūhum,* "made them ride".

[18] *Cf.* Qur'ān, v, 25–6, where the reference is specifically to Jews.

[19] An allusion to an Arabic proverb which implies that one may begin by nibbling or gnawing with the front teeth, and end by crunching with the whole mouth. *Cf.* G. W. Freytag, *Arabum Proverbia*, ii (Bonn, 1839), pp. 245–6. The meaning seems to be approximately that of the English phrase "Give him an inch and he takes an ell".

[20] Dozy reads *bi-asḥārikum,* and explains *asḥār* as meaning "*les paroles que prononce le muézin au lever de l'aurore*"; *cf.* his *Supplément aux dictionnaires arabes*, i, pp. 635–6. It seems likely that Abū Isḥāq is alluding to the Hebrew word *Shaḥarīt*, the morning prayer; this would parallel the use of another Hebrew word in the next line. The *Dīwān* reads *bi-asmārikum*—presumably a copyist's attempt to cope with an unfamiliar term.

[21] Thus Dozy; *Dīwān* reads *bi-aswāqihā.*

[22] Not kosher—food which is ritually unclean for Jews. Dozy: *li-aṭrīfihim; Dīwān: li-aṭrāfihā.* In other words, the Muslims eat what the Jews reject.

[23] A common Islamic formula. See for example Qur'ān, xxiii, 60.

[24] Here the poet is addressing the king, with obvious intentions.

[25] Thus *Dīwān: wa-kayfa takūnu lahum dhimma.* Dozy reads *lanā himma* and translates: "*Comment pourrions-nous aspirer à nous distinguer.*"

[26] Tha'lab, *Qawā'id al-shi'r*, ed. C. Schiaparelli, in *Actes du VIIIe Congrès international des orientalists*, vol. ii, part 1 (Leiden, 1893), pp. 183–4; cited by G. E. von Grunebaum, *Medieval Islam: A Study in Cultural Orientation*, 2nd edition (Chicago, 1953), p. 262.

[27] *Cf.* H. A. R. Gibb, *Modern Trends in Islam* (Chicago, 1947), p. 5; Jacques Berque, *Les arabes d'hier à demain* (Paris, 1960), p. 173 ff.; M. Berger, *The Arab World Today* (London, 1962), pp. 158–9; Hisham Sharabi, *Nationalism and Revolution in the Arab World* (Princeton, 1966), pp. 93–103.

[28] See M. Canard, "L'Impérialisme des Fatimides et leur propagande", in

Annales de l'Institut des Études Orientales, vi (1942–1947), pp. 156–93; E. García Gómez, "La poésie politique sous le califat de Cordoue", in *Revue des Études Islamiques*, 1949, pp. 5–11; S. D. Goitein, *Jews and Arabs: Their Contacts Through the Ages* (New York, 1955), pp. 161–3. On some economic uses of poetry, see above pp. 90–1. For examples of the poet as blackmailer, see *Encyclopaedia of Islam*, 2nd edition, articles "Al-Ḥakam b. 'Abdal", "Hidjā' ", and "Hutay'a".

29 See for example F. Gabrieli, "La poesia hariǵita nel secolo degli Omayyadi", in *Rivista degli Studi Orientali*, xx (1943), pp. 331–72.

30 S. Moscati, "Le massacre des Umayyades dans l'histoire et dans les fragments poétiques", in *Archiv Orientální*, xviii (1951), pp. 88–115.

31 For a literary analysis of the poem see García Gómez, pp. 38–40; *cf.* Pérès, pp. 273–4.

32 Dozy, p. lxii (translation, p. 285).

33 Dozy, p. lxviii (translation, p. 289).

34 The sources differ on the number of Jews killed. For a brief discussion see Ashtor, *Qōrōt ha-Yehūdīm*, p. 363, n. 281.

35 Abraham ben David, *Sefer ha-Qabbālā*, in A. Neubauer, ed., *Mediaeval Jewish Chronicles* (Oxford, 1887), p. 73. Shělomo ibn Verga, *Sheveṭ Yěhūdā*, ed. A. Shohat (Jerusalem, 5707), p. 22, with notes by I. Baer, p. 169; *Cf.* Samuel Usque, *Consolaçam ás tribulaçoens de Israel*, ed. Mendes dos Remedios (Coimbra, 1906), 3rd dialogue, ch. 24; English translation by Martin A. Cohen, *Consolation for the Tribulations of Israel* (Philadelphia, 1965), pp. 197–8 (*cf.* p. 279 ff.).

36 García Gómez, pp. 28–30; Perlmann, pp. 284–5; H. R. Idris, "Les Zīrīdes d'Espagne", in *Al-Andalus*, xxix (1964), p. 74 ff.; p. 88 ff. The most important Arabic source, the memoirs of the Zirid ruler 'Abdallāh, who reigned in Granada from 1077 to 1090, describes the crisis in Granada in detail, without saying a word about Abū Isḥāq or his poem. See E. Lévi-Provençal, "Les 'mémoires' de 'Abd Allah, dernier roi Ziride de Grenade", in *Al-Andalus*, iii (1935), p. 295 ff.; ed. Cairo, *Kitāb al-Tibyān 'an al-ḥāditha al-kā'ina bi-dawlat Banī Zīrī fī Gharnāṭa* (Cairo, 1955), p. 55 ff.

37 Dozy, *Recherches*, i, p. 293; García Gómez, pp. 50–1.

38 There is an extensive literature on the position of the non-Muslim in Muslim law and under Muslim rule. For a brief account, see the two articles "Dhimma" in the *Encyclopaedia of Islam*, 2nd edition, by Claude Cahen (history) and Chafik Chehata (law), where further references are given. On the Jews in particular see S. D. Goitein, *Jews and Arabs*, *passim*, especially p. 62 ff., and H. Z. (J. W.) Hirschberg, "The Oriental Jewish Communities", in A. J. Arberry, general editor, *Religion in the Middle East*, i (Cambridge, 1969), pp. 119–225.

39 On anti-*dhimmī* propaganda see M. Steinschneider, *Polemische und apologetische Literatur in arabischer Sprache* (Leipzig, 1877); R. Gottheil, "An Answer to the Dhimmis", in *Journal of the American Oriental Society*, xli (1921), pp. 383–457; M. Perlmann, "Notes on Anti-Christian Propaganda in the Mamluk Empire", in *Bulletin of the School of Oriental and African Studies*, x (1942), pp. 843–61; Perlmann, "Eleventh-century Andalusian Authors . . ."; S. W. Baron, *A Social and Religious History of the Jews*, v, p. 95 ff. Ibn Hazm's tract against Ibn Nagrella, cited by

Perlmann, has now been published: *Al-Radd ʿalā Ibn al-Naghrīla al-Yahūdī wa-rasā'il ukhrā*, ed. Iḥsān ʿAbbās (Cairo, 1380/1960). For other anti-Jewish poems, see W. J. Fischel, *Jews in the Economic and Political Life of Medieval Islam* (London, 1937), pp. 88–9 and 111; Pérès, pp. 268–73 (including some other contemporary attacks on Ibn Nagrella).

40 This theme, already discernible in the Qur'ān (ii, 61 and iii, 112), is common in later writings. *Cf.* the remarks of M. Perlmann, in his "Eleventh-century Andalusian Authors. . . .", pp. 289–90. For a modern example see chapter 11, note 9, p. 139 above.

Chapter 13. The Sultan, the King and the Jewish Doctor

1 See, for example, D. Yellin and I. Abrahams, *Maimonides* (London, 1903), pp. 113–4. "It may have been from el-Adil (the brother of Saladin and ruler of Egypt) that Richard heard of the fame of Maimonides as a medical practitioner. The 'King of the Franks in Ascalon' sought his services as his physician, but Maimonides declined the honour. He was well content with his position under the Vizir Alfadhel, and if he was acquainted with the events which had occurred at Richard's coronation, he must have felt safer in Cairo than in London."

2 Al-Qifṭī: *Ta'rīkh al-Ḥukamā'*, ed. Lippert (Leipzig, 1903).

3 *Bibliotheca Arabico-Hispana Escurialensis* . . ., i (Madrid, 1760), pp. 293–4.

4 Al-Qifṭī, p. 319. In Lippert's edition the word *Ghuzz*—a common term for the Turks—is misread as *Muʿizz*, thus adding to the confusion. Casiri gives the word correctly.

5 Casiri, *Bibliotheca Arabico-Hispana, loc. cit.*

6 H. Graetz, *Geschichte der Juden*, vi, p. 331.

7 M. Meyerhof, "L'Oeuvre médicale de Maimonide", *Archeion*, xi (1929), p. 138.

8 C. Cahen, "Indigènes et Croisés—un Médecin d'Amaury, *Syria* (1934), p. 353.

9 See the two important articles of Y. Prawer on Ascalon in the period of the Crusades: *Eretz Israel*, iv (1956), pp. 231–48, and v (1958), pp. 224–37; also, more briefly, *Encyclopaedia of Islam* (2nd ed.), "'Asḳalān".

10 Bahā' al-Dīn, *Sīrat Ṣalāḥ al-Dīn* (Cairo, 1903), p. 189; *cf.* Abū Shāma, *Al-Rawḍatayn*, ii (Cairo, 1872), p. 203; Ibn Wāṣil, *Mufarrij al-Kurūb*, ii (Cairo, 1957), p. 402; Richard of Devizes, *De Rebus gestis Ricardi Primi*, Rolls series (London, 1886), p. 445.

11 *Historia Rerum in Partibus Transmarinis Gestarum*, xx, ch. 31.

12 Ibn Abī Uṣaybiʿa, *Ṭabaqāt al-Aṭibbā'* (ed. Müller), ii, pp. 121–3.

13 This often-cited letter has been printed a number of times. *Cf.* Yellin and Abrahams, *Maimonides*, p. 148.

14 Ibn Abī Uṣaybiʿa, *op. cit.*, ii, p. 117.

15 *Relation de l'Egypte par Abd al-Latif* (Paris, 1810), p. 466.

16 *Geschichte der Arabischen Aerzte* (Göttingen, 1840), no. 198.

17 *Geschichte der Juden*, vi, p. 399.

18 S. Munk, "Notice sur Joseph ben-Jehouda", *Journal Asiatique* (1842), pp. 24, 29–30. *Cf.* B. Dünaburg, *Rambam* (Tel Aviv, 1935), pp. 13–4.

19 Munk, *Notice*, pp. 21–2. On this whole question see E. Ashtor-Strauss, "Saladin and the Jews", *Hebrew Union College Annual*, xxvii (1956), p. 312 and n. 25.

Chapter 14. The Mongols, the Turks and the Muslim Polity

[1] Arnold Hottinger, "Patriotismus und Nationalismus bei den Arabern", *Neue Zürcher Zeitung*, 12 May 1957. On modern Muslim views of the Mongol invasions see further W. Cantwell Smith, *Islam in Modern History* (Princeton, N.J., 1957), pp. 32 ff., 164 ff.; G. E. von Grunebaum, *Modern Islam: the Search for Cultural Identity* (Berkeley and Los Angeles, 1962), pp. 44 ff., 185, 213, 255–6.

[2] E. G. Browne, *A Literary History of Persia from Firdawsi to Saʿdi* (London, 1906), pp. 426–7; *cf.* Browne, *A History of Persian Literature under Tartar Domination* (Cambridge, 1920), pp. 14–5. Like most other Western writers, Browne bases his account of the Mongols largely on Baron C. d'Ohsson's *Histoire des Mongols*, 1st ed., 1824 (2nd considerably amplified ed., The Hague and Amsterdam, 1834–5).

[3] V. V. Bartold, *Mussulman Culture*, translated from the Russian by Shahid Suhrawardy (Calcutta, 1934), pp. 110–2; *cf.* the very much better Turkish translation edited by M. Fuad Köprülü, *Islam medeniyeti tarihi*, 2nd ed. (Ankara, 1963), p. 62. The Russian original was reprinted in Bartold's collected works, *Sochineniya*, vi (Moscow, 1966). Bartold's views on the Mongol invasions and their effects are developed in many of his writings. In attempting a more positive assessment of the Mongols, he was to some extent anticipated by Sir Henry Howorth *(History of the Mongols*, London, 1876–88) and, still more, by Léon Cahun *(Introduction à l'histoire de l'Asie*, 1896). These works were, however, written without reference to oriental sources, and are of no scholarly significance. Cahun's book, written with some skill and much enthusiasm, became a source of inspiration for Turkish and pan-Turkish nationalist theories.

[4] I. P. Petrushevsky, *Zemledelie i agrarniye otnosheniya v Irane xiii-xiv vekov* (Moscow-Leningrad, 1960), p. 36; Persian translation by Karīm Kishāvarz, *Kishāvarzī va munāsabāt-i arzī dar Irān ʿahd-i Moghūl*, i (Tehran, 1344 Persian solar era), p. 48. *Cf.* Professor Petrushevsky's introduction to the new edition of Bartold's collected works, *Sochineniya*, i (Moscow, 1963), especially pp. 32–3.

[5] Ibn Wāṣil, *Mufarrij al-kurūb*, MS. Paris, Arabe 1703, folio 126 b, cited by D. Ayalon, "Studies on the Transfer of the ʿAbbāsid Caliphate from Baghdād to Cairo", *Arabica*, vii (1960), p. 59.

[6] Constantine K. Zurayk, *The Meaning of the Disaster*, trans. R. B. Winder (Beirut, 1956), p. 48; cited by G. E. von Grunebaum, *Modern Islam*, p. 255.

[7] See Ann K. S. Lambton, *Landlord and Peasant in Persia* (London, 1953), p. 77 ff., Petrushevsky, *Zemledelie*, and, on the Mongol Empire in general, J. J. Saunders, "Le nomade comme bâtisseur d'empire: conquête arabe et conquête mongole", *Diogène*, no. 52 (1965), pp. 85–109, where other recent literature is cited.

[8] Even in Iraq, however, the extent of the economic damage done by the Mongols has been exaggerated. See the important study by Dr. Jaʿfar H. Khesbak, "Aḥwāl al-ʿIrāq al-iqtiṣādiyya fī ʿahd al-Ilkhānīyīn al-Mughūl", *Majallat Kulliyyat al-Ādāb* (Baghdad, 1961), pp. 1–56.

[9] Wladyslaw Kotwicz, "Les Mongols, promoteurs de l'idée de paix universelle au début du xiiie siècle", *Rocznik Orientalistyczny*, xvi (Cracow, 1950), p. 429.

[10] Abu Shāma, *Tarājim rijāl al-qarnayn al-sādis wa'l-sābi'*, ed. Muḥammad al-Kawtharī (Cairo, 1947), p. 208.

[11] A. T. Hatto, "Ḥamāsa iv", in *Encyclopaedia of Islam*, 2nd ed., iii, p. 116. The whole problem of Turkish-Mongol relationships is discussed in an important article by Professor Ibrahim Kafesoğlu, "Türk tarihinde Moğollar ve Cengiz meselesi", *Tarih Dergisi*, v (1953), pp. 105–36.

[12] W. Barthold, *Turkestan Down to the Mongol Invasion* (London, 1928), p. 305.

[13] Ibn Khaldūn, *Kitāb al-'Ibar*, v (Cairo, 1867), p. 371. Professor Ayalon was the first to draw attention to this very important passage: "The Wafidiyya in the Mamluk Kingdom", *Islamic Culture* (1951), p. 90; *cf.* Ayalon, *Jewish Observer*, 23 November 1956, p. 19.

[14] Osman Turan, "The Idea of World Domination among the Medieval Turks", *Studia Islamica*, iv (1955), pp. 80–1; Ann K. S. Lambton, "Quis Custodiet Custodes: Some Reflections on the Persian Theory of Government", *Studia Islamica*, vi (1956), p. 130. *Cf.* Fuad Köprülü, "Les institutions juridique turques au moyen-age", *Belleten*, ii, nos. 5–6 (1938), pp. 41–76; Köprülü, "Bizans müesseselerinin Osmanlı müesseselerine te'siri hakkında bâzı mülâhazalar", in *Türk Hukuk ve Iktisat Tarihi Mecmuası*, i (1931), pp. 165–313; Italian translation, *Alcune osservazioni intorno all' influenza delle istituzioni bizantine sulle istituzioni ottomane* (Rome, 1953).

Chapter 15. Ottoman Observers of Ottoman Decline

[1] The Turkish original was edited and published together with a German translation by Rudolf Tschudi, *Das Āṣafnâme des Lutfi Pacha* (Berlin, 1910). Another edition, giving a somewhat better text, was published by Shukrī in Istanbul, 1326. On Lûtfi Pasha see *Encyclopaedia of Islam*, article by Th. Menzel: *Islâm Ansiklopedisi*, article by Tayyib Gökbilgin: and F. Babinger, *Die Geschichtsschreiber der Osmanen und ihre Werke* (Leipzig, 1927), pp. 80–1.

[2] *Āṣafnāme*, p. 6; tr., p. 7.

[3] *Āṣafnāme*, pp. 6–7; tr., p. 8.

[4] *Āṣafnāme* pp. 10–1; tr., p. 11. Lûtfi Pasha was much concerned by the oppressive working of the courier system, and discusses it at some length in his history *Ta'rīkh āl-i 'Oṣmān* (Istanbul, 1341), p. 371 ff. For a brief but very well documented account of the Ottoman courier system, see J. H. Mordtmann, in *Mitteilungen des Seminars für Orientalische Sprachen*, xxxii, section 2 (1929), pp. 23–5.

[5] *Āṣafnāme*, p. 12; tr., p. 12.

[6] *Āṣafnāme*, pp. 12–3; tr., p. 13.

[7] *Ibid.*

[8] *Āṣafnāme*, pp. 14–5; tr., p. 14. The asper was an Ottoman silver coin. On its value see below, note 19.

[9] *Āṣafnāme*, p. 23; tr., p. 20. On the Ottoman system of price-control *(narkh)* see R. Mantran, "Règlements fiscaux ottomans. La police des marchés de Stamboul au début du XVIe siècle", in *Cahiers de Tunisie*, no. 14 (1956), pp. 213–41; R. Mantran, "Un document sur *l'iḥtisab* de Stamboul à la fin du XVIIe siècle", in *Mélanges Louis Massignon*, iii (Damascus, 1957), pp. 127–49; W. Hahn, *Die Verpflegung Konstantinopels durch staatliche Zwangswirtschaft. . . .* (Stuttgart, 1926). Many documents from Turkish archives, relating to *narkh* and *iḥtisāb*, have been edited by Osman Nuri

(in *Mejelle-i Umūr-i Belediye*, i, 1922), by Omer Lûtfi Barkan (in *Tarih Vesikaları*, ii, 1942), and by Ahmed Refik (in his four volumes of documents on life in Istanbul, *Istanbul ḥayatı*, Istanbul 1929–1935).

10 *Āṣafnāme*, p. 22; tr., pp. 19–20.

11 *Āṣafnāme*, pp. 32–3; tr., pp. 26–7. *Cf.* Bernard Lewis, *The Emergence of Modern Turkey*, 2nd edition (London, 1968), p. 24 ff.

12 *Āṣafnāme*, p. 35; tr., p. 29.

13 A well-known Turkish proverb. On Veysī, and the problems of his identity, see E. J. W. Gibb, *A History of Ottoman Poetry*, iii (London, 1904), pp. 208–18; Babinger, *Die Geschichtsschreiber*, pp. 152–4.

14 The first *risāle* of Kochu Bey was published in Istanbul in 1277; in London in 1862; in Istanbul again in 1303 and in a new edition, in the new Turkish script, by Ali Kemalî Aksüt (Istanbul, 1939), cited here. All these editions were preceded by the German translation of W. F. A. Behrnauer, "Kog'abey's Abhandlung über den Verfall des osmanischen Staatsgebäudes seit Sultan Suleiman des Grossen", *Zeitschrift der Deutschen Morgenländischen Gesellschaft*, xv (1861), pp. 272–332. A Russian translation, with an edition of the text, was published in St Petersburg by V. D. Smirnov in 1873. Unpublished translations into French and Arabic exist in manuscript in Paris and Cairo. A second *risāle*, presented to Sultan Ibrāhīm in 1640, was at first not recognized as the work of Kochu Bey. A German translation was published by Behrnauer in *Zeitschrift der Deutschen Morgenländischen Gesellschaft*, xviii (1864), pp. 699–740, but the text was not published until 1939, when it was included by Ali Kemalî Aksüt in his edition. It was translated into Russian by A. S. Tveritinova, in the Proceedings *(Zapiski)* of the Institute of Orientalism (Moscow-Leningrad, 1953), pp. 212–68. An important study on the memoranda of Kochu Bey was published by M. Çağatay Uluçay in *Zeki Velidi Togan'a Armağan* (Istanbul, 1955), pp. 177–99. See further the articles in *Encyclopaedia of Islam* and *Islam Ansiklopedisi*, and Babinger, *Die Geschichtsschreiber*, pp. 184–5.

15 *Risāle*, p. 18; tr. Behrnauer, p. 274.

16 *Risāle*, pp. 32 and 45; tr., pp. 288 and 301. The term "Turk" in these passages refers to the Anatolian Turkish peasants and Turcoman nomads, hitherto excluded from the imperial household and Janissary corps. A similar observation was made some decades earlier by the historian Selānikī Muṣṭafā, who says: "In the reign of the late Sultan Murād Khān [1574–95], a vile rabble of contemptible interlopers entered the respected household and, through bribery, the regiments of Janissaries, armorers and gunners were opened to peasants, to farmers who have abandoned their farms, to Tat, Chepni, Gypsies, Jews, Laz, Russians and townspeople. When these joined the ranks, tradition and respect disappeared entirely; the curtain of reverence of government was riven, and, in this way, men with neither aptitude nor experience of affairs came and sat in the seats of power. . . ." (quoted from manuscript by I. H. Uzunçarşılı, *Osmanlı Devleti teşkilâtından Kapıkulu Ocakları*, ii [Ankara, 1944], p. 201).

17 In Turkish *bashmaklîk* or *pashmaklîk*—a term applied in Kochu Bey's time to appanages granted to certain ladies of the Imperial harem, for their personal needs in clothing, etc.

[18] *Risāle*, p. 47; tr., p. 306.

[19] The *jizye* was, in accordance with Islamic law, assessed in gold, though it could be paid in silver currency. The sharp rise in the rate of payment in silver aspers, mentioned by Kochu Bey, is attested by many documents of the period, and was due to the devaluation of the Ottoman silver currency during the late 16th and early 17th centuries. Ottoman fiscal records of the early 16th century give the rate of the asper as 40 to the gold piece. By the time of Süleyman the Magnificent it had fallen to 60 and then 80, and under his successors dropped very steeply in value, at times to above 200. Kochu Bey, not unnaturally, fails to take account of these financial fluctuations. On Ottoman currency changes see J. von Hammer, *Histoire de l'Empire ottoman*, vii (Paris, 1837), pp. 410–5; I. S. Emmanuel, *Histoire des Israélites de Salonique*, i (Paris, 1936), pp. 233–4, 263 n. 51; R. Anhegger, *Beiträge zur Geschichte des Bergbaus im osmanischen Reich*, ii (Istanbul, 1944), pp. 432–3; Halil Inalcık, "Remarks on an essay on the economical [*sic*] situation of Turkey during the foundation and rise of the Ottoman Empire" (in Turkish with English summary), in *Belleten*, xv (1951), pp. 629–90.

[20] *Risāle*, p. 48; tr., p. 306. *Cf.* the remark of Lûtfi Pasha quoted above, n. 10. The 16th-century writer 'Ālī (on whom see the article in *Encyclopaedia of Islam*, 2nd edition) says: "The treasure of sovereigns is their subjects *(ra'iyyet)*; the need of the subjects is for care *(ri'āyet)* and safeguarding from injustice", *Künh al-Akhbār*, v (Istanbul, 1285), p. 5. This phrase is repeated in a simpler and more direct form in the second *risāle* of Kochu Bey (ed. Aksüt, p. 105). The idea is already familiar to the 9th-century Arabic author Ibn Qutayba, who cites an unnamed Persian source: "The hearts of the subjects are the treasure-houses of their kings; what they deposit in them, they know is there". Ibn Qutayba, *'Uyūn al-Akhbār* (Cairo, n.d.), i, p. 10; *cf.* English version by J. Horovitz, in *Islamic Culture*, 1930, p. 194.

[21] *Risāle*, p. 66; tr., p. 325.

[22] The *Destūr al-'Amel li-Iṣlāḥ al-Khalel* was published in Istanbul in 1280 A.H. as an appendix to the *Qavānīn-i Āl-i 'Oṣmān* of 'Ayn-i 'Alī. A German translation by Behrnauer had already appeared in *Zeitschrift der Deutschen Morgenländischen Gesellschaft*, xi (1857), pp. 110–32. Some account of the circumstances in which the memorandum was drafted is given by the Ottoman historian Na'īmā, under the events of the year 1063 A.H. *(Ta'rīkh*, 4th edition, v, pp. 281–3). On Kâtib Çelebi see *Encyclopaedia of Islam*, article on Ḥādjdjī Khalīfa; Babinger, pp. 195–203; and the collection of essays and studies published by the Turkish Historical Society, *Kâtip Çelebi, Hayatı ve Eserleri hakkında incelemeler* (Ankara, 1957). Another of his works, the *Mīzān al-ḥaḳḳ*, has appeared in English translation: Katib Chelebi, *The Balance of Truth*, trans. G. L. Lewis (London, 1957).

[23] *Cf.* Ibn Khaldūn, *The Muqaddimah*, trans. F. Rosenthal (New York, 1958), i, p. 339 ff.; ii, p. 117 ff., etc. On Ibn Khaldūn's influence in Turkey, see Fındıkoğlu Ziyaeddin Fahri, "Türkiyede Ibn Haldunizm", in *Fuad Köprülü Armağanı* (Istanbul, 1953), pp. 153–63. especially 156–7. Already in antiquity, the Roman historian Florus divided the life of Rome into the four periods of infancy, youth, manhood, and old age. It may be noted that Florus's history was widely read in medieval Europe. For another version of the three phases, see Francis Bacon's *Advancement of Learning*, book II, x, p. 13.

24 *Destūr*, pp. 119–23; tr., pp. 115–91.
25 *Destūr*, pp. 124–9; tr., pp. 119–24.
26 *Destūr*, pp. 129–32; tr., pp. 124–6.
27 *Destūr*, pp. 132–5; tr., pp. 126–8.
28 *Destūr*, pp. 136–9; tr., pp. 129–32.
29 *Feżleke* (Istanbul, 1287), pp. 384–5; *cf.* Behrnauer, p. 115.
30 On Ḥüseyn Hezārfen see Babinger, pp. 228–31. The full Turkish text of his *Telkhīs al-Bayān fī qavānīn-i āl-i ʿOṣmān* has still not been edited, but some extracts were published, together with a study, by R. Anhegger, "Hezarfen Hüseyin Efendi'nin Osmanlı devlet teşkilâtına dair mülâhazalar", *Türkiyat Mecmuası*, x (1951–3), pp. 365–98. A French translation, reputedly by Pétis de la Croix, was published in Paris in 1695.
31 The *Naṣāʾiḥ al-Vüzerā va ʾl-Umerā* of Sarı Meḥmed Pasha was edited with an English translation and notes by W. L. Wright (Princeton, 1935). *Cf. Sosyoloji Dergisi*, iii (Istanbul, 1946), pp. 141–5.
32 F. Babinger, "Die türkischen Quellen Dimitrie Kantemir's", in *Zeki Velidi Togan'a Armağan* (Istanbul, 1955), p. 56 ff.
33 Hezārfen, ed. Anhegger, p. 376; *cf.* Ibn Qutayba, *ʿUyūn al-Akhbār*, i, pp. 8–9 (=Horovitz' version in *Islamic Culture* [1930], p. 192), and A. K. S. Lambton, "Quis custodiet custodes", *Studia Islamica*, v. (1956), pp. 144, 147. In Ottoman usage the term *siyāset* frequently denotes capital or other bodily punishment inflicted under the discretionary authority of the ruler, as distinct from the penalties specified in the *Sharīʿa*. On *siyāsa* in the sense of administrative, non-canonical justice, see the observations of al-Maqrīzī in *Khiṭaṭ*, ii, pp. 219–22. Al-Maqrīzī connects this meaning of *siyāsa* with the Mongol *yasa*.
34 For discussions of the larger historical problem, see B. Lewis, "Some Reflections on the Decline of the Ottoman Empire", *Studia Islamica*, ix (1957), pp. 111–27, reproduced with some modifications in his *The Emergence of Modern Turkey*, pp. 21–39; and H. A. R. Gibb and Harold Bowen, *Islamic Society and the West*, vol. i, part 1, *Islamic Society in the Eighteenth Century* (London, 1950), p. 173 ff.
35 Some of these texts, with others, have been discussed, from different points of view, by Babinger, *Geschichtsschreiber*, p. 152, n. 1; I. H. Uzunçarşılı, *Osmanlı Tarihi*, iii, 2 (Ankara, 1954), pp. 501–2; Anhegger, pp. 365–9; E. I. J. Rosenthal, *Political Thought in Medieval Islam* (Cambridge, 1958), pp. 224–33 (from Behrnauer's translations only); A. S. Tveritinova, *Social Ideas in Turkish Didactic Politico-Economic Treatises of the XVI–XVII Centuries*. Papers presented by the USSR delegation to the XXV International Congress of Orientalists, Moscow 1960; and M. Tayyib Gökbilgin, "XVII. asırda, Osmanlı devletinde islahat ihtiyac ve temayülleri ve Kâtip Celebi", in *Kâtip Celebi* . . . (Ankara, 1957), pp. 197–218.
36 Bernard Lewis, *The Emergence of Modern Turkey*, p. 56 ff.

Chapter 16. The Significance of Heresy in the History of Islam

1 Cevdet (Jevdet), *Tarih*, 2nd edition, viii (Istanbul, 1309 A.H.), pp. 147–8.
2 I. Goldziher, *Vorlesungen über den Islam*, 2nd ed. (Heidelberg, 1925), pp. 183–4.
3 Al-Ghazālī, *Fayṣal al-tafriqa bayn al-Islam wa'l-zandaqa* (Cairo, 1901), pp. 10–18.

[4] *Ibid*, pp. 18–19; *cf.* al-Ghazālī, *Al-Iqtiṣād fī'l-i'tiqād* (Cairo, n.d.), p. 111 ff.
[5] *Ḥayawān*, 1st ed. (Cairo, 1325), 1, p. 80: 2nd ed. (Cairo, 1938), 1, p. 174; *cf.* Goldziher, *Vorlesungen*, p. 186.
[6] *Fayṣal al-tafriqa*, p. 68.
[7] Goldziher, *Vorlesungen*, pp. 185–6.
[8] E. Strauss, "L'inquisition dans l'état mamlouk", in *Rivista degli Studi Orientali*, xxv (1950), pp. 11–26.

Chapter 17. The Revolutions in Early Islam

[1] Al-Mas'ūdī, *Murūj al-dhahab*, ed. C. Barbier de Meynard and Pavet de Courteille, iv (Paris, 1861–77), pp. 253–5.
[2] Bernard Lewis, "The Regnal Titles of the First Abbasid Caliphs", in *Dr. Zakir Husain Presentation Volume* (New Delhi, 1968), pp. 13–22.
[3] Abu'l-'Aṭā' al-Sindī, cited in Abu'l-Faraj al-Iṣfahānī, *Kitāb al-Aghānī*, xvi (Bulaq, 1285), p. 84; *cf.* H. Lammens, *Études sur le règne du calife omeiyade Mo'âwiya Ie* (Beirut, 1906), p. 188.

Chapter 18. Islamic Concepts of Revolution

[1] Attributed to Ibn al-Muqaffa', *Al-Adab al ṣaghīr*, in *Rasā'il al-bulaghā*, ed. Muḥammad Kurd 'Alī, 4th ed. (Cairo, 1954), pp. 17, *cf.* p. 18.
[2] *Al-Adab al-kabīr*, *ibid*, p. 50.
[3] *Ibid*, p. 125; Ṭabarī, *Ta'rīkh*, ed. M. J. de Goeje and others, iii (Leiden, 1879–1901), p. 30.
[4] Ṭabarī, p. 86.
[5] O. Loth, "Al-Kindi als Astrolog", in *Morgenländische Forschungen, Festschrift . . . H. L. Fleischer* (Leipzig, 1875), pp. 263–309; *Rasā'il Ikhwān al-Ṣafā* (Cairo, 1928), i, pp. 106, 130–1; iii, p. 258; iv, pp. 234 ff., 237; *cf.* A. L. Tibawi, "Ikhwān as-Safā and their Rasā'il", in *Islamic Quarterly*, ii (1955), p. 37, n. 4. See further "Dawla" in *Encyclopaedia of Islam*, 2nd edition, by F. Rosenthal.
[6] *Rasā'il al-Jāḥiẓ*, ed. Ḥasan al-Sandūbī (Cairo, 1933), pp. 295–6; French translation by Ch. Pellat, "La 'Nabita' de Djâhiz", in *Annales de l'Institut d'Etudes orientales*, x (Algiers, 1952), pp. 317–8.
[7] Al-Muttaqī, *Kanz al-'ummāl*, iii (Hyderabad, 1312), pp. 201–3.
[8] Al-Muttaqī, iii, pp. 197–8.
[9] Al-Ījī, *Mawāqif*, viii (Cairo, 1907), p. 375; *cf.* p. 348 ff.
[10] *Risāla fi'l-Ṣaḥāba*, in *Rasā'il al-bulaghā'*, pp. 120–1. On the duty of disobedience see further H. Laoust, *Essai sur les doctrines sociales et politiques de . . . Ahmad b. Taimīya* (Cairo, 1939), pp. 310–5.
[11] 'Āṭif Efendi, "Memorandum of 1798", in Cevdet, *Tarih*, vi (Istanbul, 1309 A.H.), p. 394; *Bonapart tarihi* (Turkish translation of Botta's *Storia d'Italia*) (Cairo, 1249 A.H.); reprinted Istanbul, 1293, p. 8; *cf.* Shaykh Rifā'a Rāfi' al-Ṭahṭāwī, *Talkhīs al-ibrīz* (Bulaq, 1834), new edition Cairo 1958, pp. 252, on the revolution of 1830, and 259, on 1789—*al-fitna al-ūlā li'l-ḥurriyya*, the first *fitna* for freedom. On classical usage, see "Fitna" in *Encyclopaedia of Islam*, 2nd edition, by L. Gardet, and E. L. Petersen, *'Alī and Mu'āwiya in Early Arabic Tradition* (Copenhagen, 1964), pp. 9 ff. On *Bid'a* see above, p. 226.

12 The name of the sect called the Khārijīs—those who go out—probably derives from an episode in their early history, the secret departure of the sectaries from Kufa, rather than from the general sense of seceders or rebels.
13 See "Ibn Faradj al-Djayyāni" in *Encyclopaedia of Islam*, 2nd edition, by H. Monés.
14 See for example M. Hamidullah, *Muslim Conduct of State*, revised edition (Lahore, 1945), p. 168 ff.
15 See for example 'Izzī, *Tarih* (Istanbul, 1199 A.H.), pp. 128, 136, and *Tarih Vesikaları*, vol. ii, no. 7 (1942), p. 65 ff.
16 'Āṭif, *ibid*, p. 395; Aḥmed Efendi, in *Tarih Vesikaları*, vol. iii, no. 15 (1949), p. 184; *cf. Bonapart tarihi*, pp. 8, 70, etc.
17 Cevdet, ii (Istanbul, 1309), p. 265 ff.
18 Ṭabarī, iii, p. 30; G. C. Miles, "Al-Mahdi al-haqq, Amīr al-Mu'minīn" in *Revue Numismatique*, 6e série, vii (1965), p. 335; Abū Shāma, *Kitāb al-Rawḍatayn*, 2nd edition, ed. M. Ḥilmy M. Aḥmad, i/ii (Cairo, 1962), p. 563.
19 Examples in Ra'īf al-Khūrī, *Al-Fikr al-'Arabī al-ḥadīth* (Beirut, 1943), pp. 118 f., 168, 220 ff., etc.
20 From the verb *raj'a*, to return. The Arabic term *raj'ī* was probably inspired by the slightly earlier Ottoman Turkish neologisms *irtijā'*, reaction, and *mürteji'*, reactionary, both from the same root.
21 Loth, *loc. cit.*, p. 303; *cf.* pp. 274, 277.

Chapter 19. The Idea of Freedom in Modern Islamic Political Thought

1 See F. Rosenthal, *The Muslim Concept of Freedom* (Leiden, 1960).
2 Turkish text in Cevdet (Jevdet), *Tarih*, 2nd ed., i (Istanbul, 1309 A.H.), pp. 358–9; *Mecmu'a-i mu'ahedat*, iii, p. 254; Italian text in G. F. de Martens, *Recueil des traités . . .*, iv (Göttingen, 1795), pp. 610–2.
3 E.g. *Tarih-i Osmanî Encümeni mecmuasî* (Journal of the Ottoman Historical Society), xxiii (1329 A.H.), pp. 1458, 1460. On the display of the "symbols" of freedom by Frenchmen in Turkey, see Cevdet, *Tarih*, vi, pp. 182–3.
4 Cevdet, *Tarih*, vi, pp. 395, 400; *cf.* Bernard Lewis, "The Impact of the French Revolution on Turkey", in *Journal of World History*, i (1953), p. 120 ff. (revised version in G. S. Métraux and F. Croizet, eds., *The New Asia* (New York–London, 1965), p. 47 ff., and *Slavonic Review*, xxxiv (1955), pp. 234–5). On the development of modern political thought in Turkey see Niyazi Berkes, *The Development of Secularism in Turkey* (Montreal, 1964), and B. Lewis, *The Emergence of Modern Turkey*, 2nd edition (London, 1968).
5 *'ala asās al-ḥurriyya wa'l-taswiya*; versions in al-Jabartī, *Muẓhir al-taḳdīs* (Cairo, n.d.), i, p. 37; Niqūlā al-Turk, *Mudhakkirāt*, ed. G. Wiet (Cairo, 1950), p. 8; the text also appears in al-Jabartī, *'Ajā'ib*, iii (Cairo, 1879), p. 4; Ḥaydar al-Shihābi's *Lubnān*, etc. The pioneer work on modern Arab political thought is the much-used and insufficiently acknowledged anthology of Ra'īf al-Khūrī, *Al-Fikr al-'Arabī al-ḥadīth (Modern Arab Thought)*, (Beirut, 1943), a collection of excerpts, with an introduction, illustrating the influence on Arab thought of the French Revolution. This was followed by numerous other studies and books, the most notable of

which is A. H. Hourani, *Arabic Thought in the Liberal Age 1798–1939* (London, 1962).

[6] J. F. Ruphy, *Dictionnaire abrégé français-arabe* (Paris, An X [1802]), p. 120. As late as 1841 the Phanariot Handjeri renders "*liberté civile*" and "*liberté politique*" by *rukhṣat-i sherʻiye* and *rukhṣat-i mülkiye* respectively (*Dictionnaire français-arabe-persan et turc*, ii (Moscow, 1840–1), p. 397, with explanations and examples). The connotation of *rukhsat* in Ottoman usage was permission, licence or, in the religious sense, dispensation.

[7] Shanizade, *Tarih*, iv (Istanbul, 1291), pp. 2–3; *cf.* B. Lewis, *Emergence*, pp. 72–3.

[8] Cairo, 1249/1834, reprinted Istanbul 1293/1876.

[9] *Takhlīṣ al-ibrīz fī talkhīṣ Bāriz*, ed. Mahdī ʻAllām, Aḥmad Badawī and Anwar Lūkā (Cairo, n.d. [1958?]).

[10] Cairo, 1862, p. 127 ff. An unpublished Arabic translation of Machiavelli's *Prince*, prepared for Muḥammad ʻAlī Pasha c. 1825, renders the phrase in Chapter I "dominions . . . which have been free states" as "*amīriyyāt iʻtādat an takūn muḥarrara*".

[11] See L. Zolondek, "Al-Ṭahṭāwī and Political Freedom", in *Muslim World*, liv (1964), pp. 90–7.

[12] Text in Sadîk Rîfat Pasha, *Müntehabat-i asar* (Istanbul), *Avrupanîn ahvaline dair . . . risale*, p. 4; *cf. ibid*, *Idare-i hukumetin bazî kavaid-i esasiyesini mutazammin . . . risale*, *passim*; another version in Abdurrahman Şeref, *Tarih musahabeleri* (Istanbul, 1340), p. 125 f.

[13] Text in *Düstūr*, first series, i, pp. 4–7; in modern script, in A. Şeref Gözübüyük and S. Kili, *Türk anayasa metinleri* (Ankara, 1957), pp. 3–5; English trans. in J. C. Hurewitz, *Diplomacy in the Near and Middle East*, i (Princeton, N.J., 1956), pp. 113–6.

[14] Philippe and Farīd Khāzin, *Majmūʻat al-muḥarrarāt al-siyāsiyya wa'l-mufāwaḍāt al-duwaliyya ʻan Sūriyya wa-Lubnan*, i (Jūniya, 1910), p. 1 ff. *Cf.* Hourani, *Arabic Thought*, pp. 61–2.

[15] Anṭūn al-ʻAqīqī, ed. Yūsuf Ibrāhīm Yazbak, *Thawra wa-fitna fī Lubnān* (Damascus, 1938), p. 87; English translation by M. H. Kerr, *Lebanon in the Last Years of Feudalism* . . . , (Beirut, 1959), p. 53. See further P. K. Hitti, "The Impact of the West on Syria and Lebanon in the Nineteenth Century", in *Journal of World History*, ii (1955), pp. 629–30.

[16] Ahmed Lûtfi, *Tarih*, iii (Istanbul, 1292 A.H.), p. 100; *cf.* Ahmed Emin, *The Development of Modern Turkey Measured by Its Press* (New York, 1914), p. 28.

[17] *Ghābat al-ḥaqq* (Beirut, 1866, reprinted Cairo 1298/1880–1).

[18] *Aqwām al-masālik fī maʻrifat aḥwāl al-mamālik* (Tunis, 1284–5/1867–8); French trans. *Réformes nécessaires aux états musulmans* (Paris, 1868); Turkish version (Istanbul, 1296/1879); English translation by L. Carl Brown, *The Surest Path: the Political Treatise of a 19th Century Muslim Statesman* (Cambridge, Mass., 1969).

[19] Cited in B. Lewis, *The Emergence of Modern Turkey*, p. 137.

[20] See for example the article from *Hürriyyet* published by M. Colombe in French translation in *Orient*, xiii (1960), pp. 123–33. On the Young Ottomans see Şerif Mardin, *The Genesis of the Young Ottomans* (Princeton, N.J., 1962).

21 Namik Kemal, "Hukuk-i umumiye", in *Ibret*, no. 18 (1872); reprinted in Ebüzziya Tevfik, *Nümune-i edebiyat-i Osmaniye*, 3rd edition (Istanbul, 1306), pp. 357–8, and, in the new Turkish script, in Mustafa N. Özön, *Namik Kemal ve Ibret gazetesi* (Istanbul, 1939), pp. 96–7; English trans. in Lewis, *Emergence*, p. 140.
22 See *Encyclopaedia of Islam*, 2nd ed., under "Bay'a".
23 Namik Kemal, *Hukuk-i umumiye, loc. cit.*
24 *Ibret*, no. 46 (1872), cited by Ihsan Sungu, *Tanzimat ve Yeni Osmanlılar*, in *Tanzimat*, i (Istanbul, 1940), p. 845; English translation in Lewis, *Emergence*, p. 167.
25 Sadullah Pasha, *1878 Paris Ekspozisyonu*, in Ebuzziya Tevfik, *Nümune . . .*, p. 288; English translation in B. Lewis, *The Middle East and the West* (London–Bloomington, 1964), p. 47.
26 Preface to *Shipsevdi* (Istanbul, 1912), English translation in Niyazi Berkes, *Secularism*, p. 292.
27 Cairo 1316/1898 and 1905; Turkish versions: Cairo 1326/1908, Istanbul 1329/1911, and, in Northern Turkish, Kazan 1909.
28 Reprinted in *Orient*, v (1958), pp. 29–38.
29 Cairo, n.d. See Sylvia G. Haim, "Alfieri and al-Kawākibī", in *Oriente Moderno*, xxxiv (1954), pp. 321–34; E. Rossi, "Una traduzione turca dell'opera 'Della Tirannide' di V. Alfieri", *ibid*, pp. 335–7.
30 *Risālat al-kalim al-thamān* (Cairo, 1298/1881).
31 *Risālat al-kalim al-thamān*, p. 2.
32 *Risālat al-kalim al-thamān*, pp. 36–7.
33 The writings and ideas of Luṭfī al-Sayyid have been examined by (among others) J. M. Ahmed, *The Intellectual Origins of Egyptian Nationalism* (London, 1960), and N. Safran, *Egypt in Search of Political Community* (Cambridge, Mass., 1961).
34 There is now an extensive, if uneven literature devoted to the more recent ideological trends and expressions in Islamic lands. A useful selection of Arabic, Turkish and Persian writings, in translation, will be found in Kemal H. Karpat (editor), *Political and Social Thought in the Contemporary Middle East* (New York, 1968). The authors cited are concerned mainly with nationalism, socialism, and various combinations of the two, and with few exceptions, mostly Turkish, show little interest in classical liberal values.

Chapter 20. On Modern Arabic Political Terms

1 On loan-words, see further Charles Issawi, "European Loan-Words in Contemporary Arabic Writing: A Case Study in Modernization", in *Middle Eastern Studies*, iii (1967), pp. 110–33.
2 See *Encyclopaedia of Islam*, 2nd edition, under "Djumhūriyya". The term *mashyakha* is still used for republic in an Arabic translation of Machiavelli's *Prince*, made for Muḥammad 'Alī Pasha in about 1825. This text, a manuscript of which exists in the Egyptian National Library, is of considerable interest for the history of modern Arabic political terminology, and deserves a critical edition.
3 Midhat Cemal Kuntay, *Sarıklı ihtilâlcı Ali Suavi* (Istanbul, 1946), pp. 58–9; Şerif Mardin, *The Genesis of Young Ottoman Thought* (Princeton, N.J., 1962), p. 372.

[4] Mehmet Akif Ersoy, "Hakkın sesleri", in *Safahat*, 6th ed. (Istanbul, 1963), pp. 205–6; Bernard Lewis, *The Middle East and the West* (London and Bloomington, Ind., 1964), p. 89.

[5] Ahmed Naim, *Islâmda dava-yi kavmiyet* (Istanbul, 1913), cited by Niyazi Berkes in *The Development of Secularism in Turkey* (Montreal, 1964), pp. 374–5.

[6] U. Heyd, *Foundations of Turkish Nationalism* (London, 1950), p. 60; *cf.* Ziya Gökalp, *Turkish Nationalism and Western Civilization*, translated and edited by Niyazi Berkes (London, 1959), pp. 79 ff., 97 ff., 113 ff., 126 ff.

[7] C. Ernest Dawn, "Ideological Influences in the Arab Revolt", in *The World of Islam: Studies in Honour of Philip K. Hitti*, ed. James Kritzeck and R. Bayly Winder (London, 1959), p. 240, citing *Revue du Monde musulman*, xlvii (1921), pp. 24–7 of Arabic text, 15–20 of translation.

[8] See *Encyclopaedia of Islam*, 2nd edition.

[9] See Ḥasan al-Bāshā. *Al-Alqāb al-Islāmiyya fi'l-ta'rīkh wa'l-wathā'iq wa'l-āthār* (Cairo, 1957), pp. 310–11; R. Dozy, *Supplément aux dictionnaires arabes*, 2nd ed. (Leiden–Paris, 1927), i, p. 593; additional examples in Abū Shāma, *Tarājim rijāl al-qarnayn al-sādis wa'l-sābi'*, ed. Muḥ. Zāhid al-Kawtharī (Cairo, 1947), p. 81; Ibn al-Fuwaṭī, *Al-Ḥawādith al-jāmi'a*, ed. Muṣṭafā Jawād (Baghdad, 1351 A.H.), p. 218; Ibn al-'Adīm, ed. Bernard Lewis, in *Arabica*, xiii (1966), p. 266.

[10] See above, p. 263; also Bernard Lewis, *The Emergence of Modern Turkey*, 2nd edition (London, 1968), p. 156; Ş. Mardin, *The Genesis of Young Ottoman Thought*, pp. 23, 215.

[11] In classical usage this was a legal, occasionally a social, but never a political term. On its modern development see above, p. 267 ff.

Chapter 21. Islam and Development: The Revaluation of Values

[1] C. H. Becker, "Islam und Wirtschaft", in his *Islamstudien*, i (Leipzig, 1924) pp. 54–65.

[2] See above, p. 226.

[3] Mustafa Nihat Özön, *Namık Kemal ve Ibret Gazetesi* (Istanbul, 1938), pp. 42–3.

[4] Abdülhak Adnan, *La Science chez les Turcs Ottomans* (Paris, 1939), p. 57.

[5] See above, p. 199 ff.

Note on transcription

Arabic and Persian have been transcribed in accordance with a system of transcription commonly used by British and American orientalists. Turkish is written in some articles according to the same system, in others according to the official new Turkish orthography, with the following modifications (except in bibliographical references):

for c – j for ç – ch for ş – sh

BIBLIOGRAPHY

1. *Encounter* (London), January 1972.
2. *Middle Eastern Studies* (London), 1968.
3. *Times Literary Supplement* (London), 8 August 1968.
4. *Middle East Forum* (Beirut), 1958, and partly from *Middle Eastern Studies*, Vol. I, April 1965.
5. *The Spectator* (London), 26 June 1971.
6. M. A. Cook (editor), *Studies in the economic history of the Middle East*, (London), 1970.
7. *Bulletin of the School of Oriental and African Studies* (London), 1957.
8. B. Lewis and P. M. Holt (editors), *Historians of the Middle East* (London), 1962.
9. *Études d'orientalisme dédiées à la mémoire de Lévi-Provençal* (Paris), 1962.
10. *Judaism* (New York), 1968.
11. *Survey* (London), 1971.
12. *Salo W. Baron Jubilee Volume* (in the press).
13. *Eretz-Israel* (Jerusalem), 1963.
14. *Transactions of the Royal Historical Society* (London), 1968.
15. *Islamic Studies* (Karachi), 1962.
16. *Studia Islamica* (Paris), 1953.
17. *Studia Islamica*, 1970.
18. P. J. Vatikiotis (editor), *Revolution in the Middle East* (London), 1972.
19. *Encyclopaedia of Islam*, 2nd edition.
20. *Homenaje Felix Pareja* (in the press).
21. *Social Aspects of economic development* (Istanbul), 1964.

Chapter 9 is published here in English for the first time, Chapters 4, 19 and 21 have been extensively rewritten. Most of the other chapters have been revised to a greater or lesser extent.

INDEX